Religion and Emotion

Religion and Emotion

Approaches and Interpretations

EDITED BY JOHN CORRIGAN

UNIVERSITY PRESS

2004

OXFORD

UNIVERSITY PRESS

Oxford   New York
Auckland   Bangkok   Buenos Aires   Cape Town   Chennai
Dar es Salaam   Delhi   Hong Kong   Istanbul   Karachi   Kolkata
Kuala Lumpur   Madrid   Melbourne   Mexico City   Mumbai   Nairobi
São Paulo   Shanghai   Taipei   Tokyo   Toronto

Published by Oxford University Press, Inc.
198 Madison Avenue, New York, New York 10016

www.oup.com

Oxford is a registered trademark of Oxford University Press

Library of Congress Cataloging-in-Publication Data
Religion and emotion: approaches and interpretations / edited by John Corrigan.
p. cm.
Includes bibliographical references and index.
ISBN 0-19-516624-8; 0-19-516625-6 (pbk.)
1. Emotions—Religious aspects. I. Corrigan, John, 1952–
BL65.E46R45 2004
200'1'9—dc22   2003056467

9 8 7 6 5 4 3 2 1

Printed in the United States of America
on acid-free paper

Contents

Religion and Emotion

Introduction: Emotions Research and the Academic Study of Religion

Defining Religion

From its beginnings in Enlightenment philosophical debate and its consequent development in nineteenth-century *Religionsgeschichte* and in the ascendant social sciences, the academic study of religion has been fraught with problems of definition. Most eighteenth-century Christian observers of the religious landscape meant "Christianity" when they wrote "religion" and accorded other faiths to various categories of superstition, heresy, political regimes, and cultural infantilism. Judaism was viewed as legitimate religion inasmuch as it shared canonical writings with Christianity, but it, too, most of the time failed to measure up to the definitional standards concocted by the philosophes. In the nineteenth century, the problem of definition became more complex, as researchers studied religions of the ancient Mediterranean and Near East, India, and Africa. Such research eventuated in shared understandings about major structural features of religions, including myth, ritual, symbol, patterns of authority, ethics, and material culture, at the same time that it complicated the engagement of science to theology. As that research advanced, it cut deeply into the element of Christian triumphalism that had so largely determined interpretation in the previous century, and in so doing cleared the way for even more vigorous cultivation of knowledge about non-Christian, and non-Western, religions. Writers in due course reported confidently on "aboriginal religion" in Australia, African "spiritism," and Hinduism, an ancient and magnificent religion among "Hindoos." This trajectory, one of broadmindedness and accommodation but one that also embodied the sticky residue of colonialist denigration, took shape as the "science of religion." In the process, the way religion was defined was greatly enlarged, particularly during the mid-twentieth century, when the influential Protestant theologian Paul Tillich began to refer to religion as a person's "ultimate concern," and semiosis—a concern for signs and symbols—became a standard part of the study of religion, a project increasingly undertaken as a form of cryptanalysis, or code breaking. The reconceptualization of religion that ensued was played out in the second half of the twentieth century as theory-driven academic propensity for outing covert or cryptoreligious phenomena, so that researchers discovered in persons' exercise routines and patriotism structural features coincident with those found in world religions. Some accordingly anointed jogging, flag waving, and esoteric philosophizing as religion alongside Buddhism, Islam, and Christianity. Such pronouncements, rich in cultural baggage, complicated and enhanced discourse about religion at the same time that they deflated hopes for consensus about definition. Discussion remains lively, so that at the beginning of the twenty-first century, academic attention to the business of "defining religion" is deeply embedded in university curricula. However, it frequently takes the form there of opportunities to rehearse established (and difficult) theoretical terrain rather than critical experimentation with new visions.[1]

The impressive growth of the academic study of religion since the 1960s has been propelled by the lively debate about what religion is and how it ought to be studied. A central component of the debate historically has been concern about what is sometimes called "reductionism," a term that has a range of meanings in the academic disciplines. In its relation to religious studies, it is best understood as a reference to meaning that is lost and gained in the process of explanation. How does one explain the game of professional basketball to a person unfamiliar with it? Is it true, as comedian Woody Allen observed, that it is largely an exercise involving hyperthyroidic persons running around in their undershorts? Does such a definition miss the point? Does it "reduce" basketball to a precious few components that only marginally, or even inaccurately, represent the game? Is there an "essence" to the game of basketball that an observer cannot understand? Would a longer, more elaborate explanation of the game manage to avoid reductionism? Could any definition ever include everything? Is all explanation of basketball necessarily reductive? Similarly, are all attempts to explain religion undermined by reductionism? Does the translative process of interpretation guarantee that explanations of religion will always come up short? And, most interesting, does interpretation inevitably render ordinary what some believe to be a mysterious and transcendent essence of religion? Does the study of religion, as students (and anxious parents) occasionally remark to me, kill religion? Or, on the other hand, to borrow from the philosopher Owen Flannagan, are those who question reductivist reasoning the "new mysterians"?[2]

Persons whose livelihood is the academic study of religion are in a particularly complicated position vis-à-vis the issue of reductionism because of the relative newness of religious studies as a formal academic enterprise and because the field as yet has no method that clearly distinguishes it from other academic disciplines. These problems are represented in ongoing debates about how religion should be defined. In the world of competing program budgets in institutions of higher education, these lingering issues continue to inform at least one possible vision of the field's future: if the academic study of religion existed to explain religion ("reductionistically") as brain chemistry, or social structure, or family dynamics, religious studies professors would risk losing their jobs to neuroscientists, sociologists, and psychologists. Accordingly, the field of religious studies, like some other academic fields, has generated over time a number of strategies that protect against the realization of such a scenario. One of those strategies has been to posit an essential, irreducible component of religion, one that cannot be analyzed into its parts, parsed, as it were, into nonreligious artifacts. For many, that component is emotion.

It might seem odd to claim, in light of a recent twelve-hundred-item inventory of writings on religion and emotion,[3] that the academic study of religion has avoided engaging that theme. There is, unmistakably, a tradition of inquiry into the place of emotion in religion that is represented, in the West, in a wide range of figures, from mystics to psychologists, theologians to artists, scriptural exegetes to literary and social structuralists and poststructuralists. But it is also clear that much of that inquiry has been conducted in the service of religious traditions, as apology for religion, or as constructive theologizing, or through the adoption of some species of the descriptive/typological approach as pioneered by the American psychologist William James (i.e., inventories of "kinds" of religious experiences) and other methods that can slip some of the hard questions we might ask about emotion, especially those that inquire of cultural differences. The analytical method modeled by French sociologist Emile Durkheim and others (i.e., investigation of sources and "causes" of religion; "explanation" of religion) until recently has proven less attractive to scholars writing about religion and emotion. Perhaps it is the centuries-long intertwining of language about religion and emotion in theological writing that has framed the current state of religious studies scholarship in which emotion is not explored as vigorously as in related disciplines. Scholars who might seek to disembed the discussion of religion and emotion from that theologically flavored discourse accordingly must confront the long, imposing, and seemingly overwhelming history of Western theological investigation. Such a prospect is daunting. And the fact is that until recently most scholars, influenced by theological discourses about emotion, have taken emotion for granted as a category of analysis. Scholarly expositions of religions have tended to appeal to emotion as if it were a universal, rich in explanatory power, a common denominator of experience bridging the widely varying contexts of lived traditions. From such a starting point, historical researchers have distinguished among religious groups by remarking that one was "more emotional" than the other. Philosophers and theologians have arranged analyses of religious ideas around poles of "emotion" and "reason." And psychologists have fashioned reports about the extent to which persons were "emotionally fulfilled" or challenged through their practice of the religious life. But what is meant by "emotion"? And how to account for most writers' inattention to the nature of emotion itself?

In many cases where researchers have chosen not to press the analysis of emotion, that choice has been framed by academic concern about possible reductionism in the analysis of religious ideas and practices. Emotion was— and for some scholars still is—inexplainable. That is, it has been viewed as irreducible and, as such, a legitimate foundation for interpretations of religion that wish to leave room for the mysterious, inexplicable, and transcendent. Interestingly, this has been true as well in cases where scholars actually have challenged some of the truth claims of religion, whether they involve literal meanings of scripture, theological doctrine, the efficacy of ritual, or the structuring of authority. In such cases, a defense against the charge of reductionism can be sustained because the interpretation itself has left room for the indefinable by granting emotion an unqualified, primary, and ultimately undefined role. Accordingly, neglect of analytical study of emotion in the literature of religious studies has not been merely an accident or oversight. In many cases it has been a part of the self-sustaining nature of religious scholarship itself, which consistently has deployed claims for the uniqueness of its subject even as it went through the steps of critically dissecting it, demonstrating the rational structures of its working, and, most important, constructing a discourse of its sympathy with other aspects of culture.

The field of religious studies in recent years has been challenged by research in other disciplines to work harder at understanding emotion in religion. That challenge arises from the fact that the study of emotion currently is undergoing a renaissance in most of the humanities, sciences, and social sciences. Indeed, the development of emotions research recently has been called a "revolution" in scholarship.[4] Leading university presses have launched projects to capture the cutting-edge research on this theme: the Oxford University Press Series in Affective Science, the Cambridge University Press Studies in Emotion and Social Interaction, the New York University Press Series in the History of Emotion, and an assortment of other publishing projects, such as the *Dictionnaire des sentiments* (1993–   ). Journals recently founded to publish emotions research include *Social Perspectives on Emotion* (1992), *Stress and Emotion* (1991), *Cognition and Emotion* (1987), and *Consciousness and Emotion* (2000). The *International Review of Studies on Emotion* was founded in 1991, and international conferences such as the NATO Advanced Workshop on Everyday Conceptions of Emotion (Spain, 1994), the International Conference on Emotion and Culture (Oregon, 1992), and the meeting at the Royal Netherlands Academy (1993) are only several of the major gatherings of scholars in the past decade. New organizations such as the International Society for Research on Emotion, the Geneva Emotion Research Group (Switzerland), and Emonet (Australia) coordinate and promote emotions research through meetings, collaborations, and publication projects, and research laboratories, such as Stanford University's Culture and Emotion Lab, increasingly focus on emotion. Doctoral dissertations exploring religion and emotion have dramatically increased in number.

Universalism and Cultural Relativism in the Study of Emotion

The study of emotion, like the study of religion, is steeped in issues of definition, questions about reductivity, and debate about the role of emotion in cultures. From Plato's theory of affect and Aristotle's classification of the emotions, to Enlightenment theories that generated language about "faculties," "vibrations," and "associations" and recent research in neuroscience, investigation into emotion has been characterized by debate about its nature, especially about what constitutes its "essence." As behavioral and social scientists, literary critics, and historians have become more active in their investigation of emotion, the question of essence increasingly has been framed with regard to historicity, cultural difference, and the diverse circumstances of various individual lives. At the same time, the work of neuroscientists and research centered on physiological aspects of emotion has put a new face on the search for essence. Accordingly, cutting-edge debate currently is characterized by, on the one hand, claims for the universality of emotion across cultures and historical settings, and, on the other, arguments supporting the cultural construction of emotion, the distinctiveness of local and even personal emotional experiences and styles. Some writers have attempted to stake out a middle ground, and the search for that middle ground is becoming more vigorous as each side compounds the evidence for its claims. Is emotion universal or culturally constructed? The investigation of physiological aspects of emotion is providing concrete substantiation for universalistic interpretations at the same time that increasing awareness of cultural differences translates into deeper support for theories recognizing the cultural derivation of emotion.

There are several pathways into the universalist view. A seminal work in the debate about emotion is Charles Darwin's *The Expression of the Emotions in Man and Animals* (1872), which set the terms for much subsequent materialist theorizing of emotion and, consequently, for certain kinds of claims of universalism in emotion. For Darwin, adaptation included the acquisition of skillfulness in emotional expression, because such expression signaled others about how one would behave. The process was observable throughout the species and across national borders, regions, languages, climates, and cultures, and research conducted by followers of Darwin was advanced on the assumption that emotions were universal. Darwin's influence is visible especially in the work of Paul Ekman, who has productively complicated Darwin's ideas and whose research on the expression of emotion in the exercise of facial muscles led him to conclude that a number of emotions, including happiness, anger, and fear, are common across cultural lines and that emotional essence is located in biology, where it is elicited by culture.[5]

Another way the universalist interpretation has been argued is with reference to language about emotion. With roots deep in the emotional inventories and taxonomies of the Renaissance and Enlightenment (the models for which were derived from Aristotle), this approach centers on the production of emotional lexicons—lists of words bearing on emotion in various cultures—and the demonstration of comparisons among them. Linguists and anthropologists understandably have been at the forefront of this aspect of emotions research, which Anna Wierzbicka has described as follows: "The basic idea is that language is a key issue in 'emotion research' and that progress in understanding of 'emotions' requires that this issue be addressed. 'Human emotions' vary a great deal across languages and cultures, but they also share a great deal," which can be discovered "by anchoring the analysis in universal human concepts [e.g., good and bad, know and want] and their 'universal grammar.'" Wierzbicka accordingly deploys a method of linguistic semantics to conclude that all languages have a word for *feel*, have words comparable with *cry* and *smile*, and describe some feelings as good and others as bad, among other similarities. Research on Native American and Indonesian communities has contributed important data to this approach.[6]

The structuralist approach to emotion associated with Durkheim and developed by Victor Turner and others has yielded another kind of argument for universality, one that stresses performance as a human activity across cultures and, as Pnina Werbner and Helene Basu point out, "recognizes the emotional underpinnings of the normative."[7] The performer, as Claude Levi-Strauss remarked in observing the work of a shaman, does not merely walk through a scripted ritual, but experiences it profoundly: "But we must not be deceived by the word *performance*. The shaman does not limit himself to reproducing or miming certain events. He actually relives them in all their vividness, originality, and violence."[8] For some theorists, the performance of emotion is similarly conditioned in different cultures through universally realized structures of social life. So, for example, similarities in rituals of grief and mourning predict similarities in emotional experience.

A fourth way of engaging the universalist standpoint is with reference to theological/philosophical perspectives that are deeply ingrained in Euro-American cultures and have profoundly influenced thinking about emotion. Simply put—and this leads us back to the previous discussion—Western intellectual traditions, especially those associated with Christianity, frequently have posited emotion as an abstract and universal essence. This claim, which has structured understanding of the relationship between humanity and God, transcendence and immanence, body and soul, has been made foundational to an assortment of Christian theologies. In one of its most important and influential forms, for example, it is the "feeling of absolute dependence"—an emotional state qualitatively different from other feelings—that German theologian Friedrich Schleiermacher proposed as the essence of religion two hundred years ago. Such a notion was developed by Rudolf Otto, who fostered thinking about emotion as a mysterious human experience in claiming a priori status for religious emotion that he described as "mysterium tremendum":

> We are dealing with something for which there is only one appropriate expression, *mysterium tremendum*. . . . The feeling of it may at times come sweeping like a gentle tide pervading the mind with a tranquil mood of deepest worship. It may pass over into a more set and lasting attitude of the soul, continuing, as it were, thrilling vibrant and resonant, until at last it dies away and the soul resumes its "profane," non-religious mood of everyday experience. . . . It has its wild and demonic forms and can sink to an almost grisly horror and shuddering. . . . It may become the hushed, trembling, and speechless humility of the creature in the presence of—whom or what? In the presence of that which is a *Mystery* inexpressible and above all creatures.[9]

Theological foundationalisms of various sorts have been closely linked historically with the preference for viewing emotion as mysterious, and that linkage predates by many centuries Otto's argument in *The Idea of the Holy* (*Das Heilige*, 1917). The influence of Otto's theorizing about the "numinous" as a mysterious presence that inspires awe and dread, however, has been felt in broader circles and is apparent in approaches to religion that reject religious experience as a cultural artifact, as the result of social and psychological conditioning. Such an approach results in a conceptualization of emotion that has been widely criticized, for example, by philosopher Rom Harré, who characterizes such a notion of emotion as "ontological illusion."[10]

A final way universalist arguments about emotion are made is through the invocation of biology, neuroscience in particular (this research overlaps in some ways with research agendas growing out of Darwin's legacy). Scientists currently are exploring the manner in which chemical cascades in neural function, electrical activity in the various lobes of the brain, and other physiological features of emotion can be correlated with assorted aspects of religion.[11] Some research on emotion and culture has argued for universality in emotional life on the basis of psychobiology.[12] The cutting edge of this approach to emotional life, on the whole, has avoided doctrinaire assertions of universalism, and some investigators, while predicating research on assumptions about similarity in physiological functioning across cultures, have suggested the complicity of biology with culture to bring forth emotional states in culturally variable ways. It may be the case that scientific research of this sort on religion will manage to avoid reductionism of a universalist sort. A recent observation of research in this area remarks that "the poststructuralist dogmas of the social construction of reality . . . are coming under criticism by careful scholarship and science. It is becoming clear how much of our basic mental and experiential equipment is genetically given and neurologically based," while warning of the dangers of a new kind of reductionism:

> But the picture is not a simple one of biological enlightenment
> dawning after a dark night of social-constructionist obscurantism.
> We must not go back to the old doctrines of biological determinism
> and the human as genetic robot, or forget the reasons—good ones
> at the time—why social constructionism itself first arose as a correc-
> tive to Social "Darwinism." Religion is seen in biological-
> reductionist terms as a disease of subjectivity. . . . We must beware
> lest we replace social reductionism with biological reductionism.[13]

Some theorizing about universalism in emotional life leaves room for the role of local cultures in shaping the way people feel. Other research focuses *primarily* on the authority of local culture, on the constructedness of emotionality, the ways emotional life is fashioned historically and culturally by "feeling rules."[14] This sort of relativism in studying emotion has emerged prominently in the social sciences and in historical scholarship, where research has tended to explore emotion less as an aspect of human "inferiority" and more as the representation of persons' compliance with social codes of meaning and conduct. Such an understanding framed the pioneering work of Weston LaBarre, who, in "The Cultural Basis of Emotions and Gestures" (1947), argued in a discussion of laughter that "even if the physiological behavior be present, its cultural and emotional functions may differ. Indeed, even within the same culture, the laughter of adolescent girls and the laughter of corporate presidents can be functionally different things," so that there is "no natural language of emotional gesture."[15]

An abundance of ethnographic studies of emotion over the past twenty years or so has contributed substantially to the interpretation of emotional life as culturally relative. At one end of the spectrum of this ethnopsychological research are studies that take the self as a social construct and argue accordingly that emotions are largely cultural creations. Such an approach is based on the observation, here articulated by Michelle Rosaldo, that "cultural idioms provide the images in terms of which our subjectivities are formed, and furthermore, these idioms themselves are socially ordered and constrained"; or, as Benedicte Grima has written, "emotion is culture."[16] In this view, the emotional lives of people—thought by some to be part of an inaccessible interior of self—are in fact socially dictated performances, social scripts, as it were, grounded in shared understandings about the meanings of social events and actions. For this reason, what one culture understands as "emotional" can differ from what another understands, as in the case of Tahitians whose indigenous conceptualization of emotion does not include some states that Westerners would consider emotional. Emotions that are viewed in certain kinds of situations in one culture as "natural" are absent from seemingly similar situations in others, as in Utku Eskimo society, whose members, according to one study, do not experience anger. Distinctions among emotions, and even differences of degree of feeling, vary from culture to culture as well. The seemingly contradictory compound of feelings (compassion/love/sadness) in the Ifaluk emotion of *fago* is understandable only when one appreciates that the context for such an understanding is an Ifaluk culture that associates the suffering of one person with the compassionate nurturing of another. The emotion of shame for the Australian Pintupi is closely associated with an understanding of sexuality as a potential disrupter of controlled social relations. Such is not the case at all for the Illongot in the Philippines, whose sense of the person does not include a belief that lusts or drives exist within the bounded self and that these must be repressed, and who construct shame as part of social performances involving anger and the show of force. The concept of anger might be fundamental to one culture's system of meanings, whereas another hides or denies it.[17] As notions of self vary from one culture to another, so too does the practice of emotional life.[18]

Claims for culturally variant emotional life—for relativistic as opposed to universalistic views of emotion—have been grounded in an assortment of methodological preferences and disciplinary approaches. On the whole, however, such claims draw on a conception of emotion as an aspect of cultural life formed by the navigation of persons through various matrices of social relations. Emotion is not theorized as an unconditioned, essential phenomenon, but as an aspect of human experience that is constituted in the ongoing, everyday performance of social life. Emotions are the result of a person's engagement of highly complex social codes governing such things as status, authority, relationality, life passages (e.g., birth, marriage, death), and contact with outsiders. An emotion in this sense is given by culture, that is, made normative through "feeling rules" that dictate the proper linkages between social experiences and emotional states. Among one group of persons, culturally derived commandments for emotional life, therefore, might require the feeling of joy on one occasion and of anger on another, whereas among another population, fear rather than joy is prescribed for seemingly similar events, and envy rather than anger. Will a person experience jealousy on finding an intimate with another lover? Will a person be angry if made the butt of jokes in public? Will a person feel sad in confronting tragedy or explain the experiences as "illness"? For relativists, local culture will tell. Nevertheless, we must bear in mind that the theorizing of emotion is an ongoing project shaped and reshaped by criticism, and that some recent ethnography that admits the influence of culture in emotional life has challenged the strongly constructivist stance: Charlotte Hardman, after a term of cohabitation with the Lohorung in Nepal, concluded that emotion was only partly constructed in culture, and William Reddy, working from the standpoint of a historical ethnographer, has likewise criticized accounts of emotional life that rely on highly constructivist interpretations.[19]

Some historians have argued that the emotional lives of people vary in relation to their historical predicament, that is, with regard to the age in which they live and the circumstances, the "imprisoning structures," that set the terms for their lives.[20] Historians' research in this regard is not appreciably different from the work of some social scientists when one considers that studying the past is in many ways like studying a "foreign country."[21] The history of emotions, a field that has developed rapidly since the 1980s, has been concerned, like all historiography, with narrating historical change. Accordingly, this area of historical research has contributed largely in terms of its insight into the historically variable ways persons conceive of emotion and the ways emotional life has changed over time because of altered contexts for social life, shifting ideological grounds, revolutions in family, gender, and class experience, and other such structural features of historical settings. Historians accordingly differentiate the emotional life of persons in the past from that of persons in the present. So, for example, what might appear to twentieth-century observers to be the free and enthusiastic venting of anger in the curses of medieval monks in fact was an exercise in patience and calmness. And where the twentieth-century American was likely to conceive a show of anger as an objectionable social display worthy of recrimination, a citizen of ancient Greece could regard such a display, especially in its manifestation as a frenzied rage, as a heroic, even divine-like performance. By the same token, jealousy has not always been thought the "green-eyed monster," at least not in early modern France, where it had a positive connotation. Did colonial New Englanders have the same feelings about their children as New Englanders do today? Has emotional pain always been a part of courtship? Does the experience of joy change from one historical period to another? The history of emotions intends to answer such questions by comparing people's lives in different historical periods, with an eye especially to the ways different modes of social organization, the production of commodities, political administration, gender roles, disease, and even climate, among other factors, may have conditioned emotionality.[22]

The development of more precise discourses about the determinative roles of sociocultural structures in the construction of self and emotion has taken place alongside a broad philosophical reconsideration of the relation of emotion to the body and to cognition. Such reconsideration has shaped and supported the work of historians and social scientists, as well as those whose research focus is primarily literature. A line of inquiry that has been especially important began as criticism of the James-Lange theory of emotion. The American psychologist William James and the Danish physician Carl George Lange, working independently, concluded at the end of the nineteenth century that emotion was the experience of physiological alterations, the perception of various kinds of disturbances within the body: changes in respiration, heart rate, perspiration, and so forth. Fear accordingly was the perception of the body's response to a bear running toward one, and sorrow an emotion that followed on the body's tearful response to another kind of stimulus. Such a view of emotion as a physiological stimulus-response mechanism took emotionality as a matter of hydraulics: emotions were forces that developed a critical level of pressure internally through intense physiological change and then burst forth in urgency to be recognized by the individual. Criticism of this theory has centered on the reconceptualization of emotion in its linkages to ideas, or, as the philosopher Robert Solomon has proposed, the adoption of "a cognitive theory of emotions" where by concepts and beliefs are fundamental to the creation of emotionality. Emotion, steeped in ideas, attitudes, and desires, accordingly is an interpretation of the world and a judgment about it. If it is supposed that ideas are culturally specific and context-bound, we are then led to the conclusion, as stated by Clifford Geertz, that "not only ideas, but emotions too, are cultural artifacts."[23]

Some cognitivist theories of emotion leave room for biological aspects of emotionality in the same way that some approaches that are primarily universalist still allow a formative role for culture in emotion. One of the most difficult challenges currently facing emotions researchers is how actually to establish a ground on which insights drawn from scholarship in each paradigm can be joined. Part of the problem has to do with the usual roadblocks to interdisciplinary research, and in this case, especially the bridging of discourses operative in neuroscience and biological research to the research models of scholars working primarily in the humanities and social sciences. Theoretical synthesis in emotions research, though highly anticipated, has not yet arrived.

Religion and Emotion: Some Themes

Recent research on religion and emotion has addressed a wide range of concerns and has done so from an equally wide range of disciplinary perspectives.

Several themes recur in this research, in a few cases across its entire spectrum; other themes are primarily located in investigations of religion and emotion within disciplinary clusters (e.g., social sciences). The most promising explorations of these themes are those that fashion interpretations responsive to the current debates about the nature of emotion, its relationship to culture, its physiological and cognitive aspects, and its variability across time and space.

For Catherine Lutz and Geoffrey M. White, "emotions are a primary idiom for defining and negotiating social relations of the self in a moral order."[24] That is, emotionality plays a key role in shaping a person's action in social settings where choices must be made, where the agent must negotiate a pathway through various situations by distinguishing right from wrong, good from evil, the useful from the useless, pain from pleasure. As Steven M. Parish has argued in his study of the Newar inhabitants of Nepal, the emotions that a person feels in the process of choosing a course of action in effect guide that action, so that "moral emotions are moral judgments." A feeling of shame or embarrassment indicates a level of engagement of moral norms that exceeds a purely cognitive judgment. Among the Newar, "hot, flushed, red-faced feelings of embarrassment, and cold, metaphorically deathlike, empty feelings of shame, *embody* moral evaluations: to *feel* judgments of self in this way alters the way people know moral values and know themselves."[25] Anger also can be viewed in social context in such a way as to understand it as "moral anger," as the "perception of moral transgression." On a Micronesian atoll, it represents among the Ifaluk "the violation of those aspects of the moral code seen as most crucial"; for twelfth-century French aristocrats, it could take the form of "zealous anger" when directed against vice, including one's personal failings.[26] Pintupi in Australia link feelings of happiness to a complex conceptualization of the sociomoral order, so that the "central themes of the Pintupi moral order revolve around the ideal of closely cooperating kin, and it is in terms of this understanding that Pintupi attempt to define when and how one should be happy (*pukurlpa*)."[27] Social morality in nineteenth-century Manchester was built around the promotion of the experience of joy in submitting to higher powers, and Sikhs in North America organize social life around a "moral affect," a complex of emotions that represents and informs moral behavior.[28] Research increasingly has shown that the association of emotion with morality, while perceptible in virtually all societies, varies widely from culture to culture, and in so doing it has challenged views rooted in theological doctrine that link certain emotions with certain moral actions without regard to cultural context.

In the West, the nature of the relationship of emotion to cognition has been the subject of inquiry for centuries; in recent philosophical literature it has emerged as an especially important area of investigation, particularly in discussions of moral reasoning. Debate has been sharp, given that many philosophers reject a role for emotion in moral reasoning. But among those who have argued most forcefully for emotion in moral psychology is Michael

Stocker, who, in *Valuing Emotions* (1996), rejects philosophical positions that leave no room for emotion, claiming that emotionality is a constituent of social relations, so that although "the relations can exist without the emotions, when they do they are defective." Emotions accordingly "are important for ethical knowledge" and "values are constituted by emotions." Emotions are "emotionally held thoughts."[29] Such a view, reaching back to Aristotle and Hume, is grounded in a twentieth-century discourse built on footings provided by both psychological and philosophical research, and in its developed state is represented by Robert M. Gordon's claim that certain emotions are "epistemic emotions," that is, emotions that bear strong functional resemblance to belief.[30]

Recent theological investigation of emotion, informed by philosophical studies, has led to an assortment of theories about the relationship of emotion to cognition. For theologians, a central issue has been the role of emotion in faith, and theories about "religious affections" have stressed their connection to intellectual and volitional aspects of religion.[31] Variously referred to as "emotional knowledge," perception, and the "emotional relation to otherness" (an experience prior in meaningfulness to the intellectual relation), cognitive aspects of emotional experience, as theorized by a growing number of theologians, have come to play an important part in Christian theological debate.[32] With roots in Schleiermacher and Otto, these approaches range from sweeping universalistic statements to context-specific understandings of emotion in religion. That range is recognizable in attempts to ground actual doctrine in certain understandings of the role of emotion as well as in efforts to address the manner in which local narratives shape emotion for its roles in moral evaluation and appraisal.[33] The latter project has come to be most visibly represented in work that allows for a certain amount of social constructivism through claims for "narrative emotion." Intellectually kin to "narrative theology," which shifts the focus of theologizing from abstract argument to concrete centeredness on people living and acting within distinct cultural contexts, theories about narrative emotion in religion, inasmuch as they take seriously the local contexts of narrative, represent an attempt to discover a middle ground between relativism and universalism in a theological context.[34]

The search for clarity in the theological study of emotion has been oriented toward understanding the place of emotion in religious belief. As such, it has been largely concerned with propositions about the nature of faith, religious knowing, moral reasoning, revelation, and doctrinal integrity, and unfolds with a keen eye to explicitly stated religious doctrines. Less observant of theological doctrines are explorations of emotion and religion that are focused on how persons and groups *behave* emotionally in religious settings. Through observation of ritual performances, researchers working this vein attempt to gather data that will enable them to understand how societies construct canopies of order and meaning out of the experiences of many persons. This venture, which views religious emotion as a performance of feeling according to culturally derived guidelines, strives to identify linkages between emotional styles and a society's most deeply held values, on the assumption that emotions, as Werbner and Basu write, "are imbedded in implicit local ontologies."[35] Accordingly, research of this type frequently invokes status, gender, collective identity, authority, and power as overlapping and conditioning frameworks for the performance of emotion in religion. That performance is to a large extent scripted, but it does not directly articulate the specific conceptual foundations of social and cultural life. It is, rather, more subtle and ambiguous. Emotional performance in religious ritual *symbolically* manifests intersections of morality, aesthetics, cognition, and memory in ways that disclose lived social orders and cultural presuppositions.

Rituals involving spirit possession, group prayer, dance, and healings are typical subjects for research on the performance of emotion in religion. Often intensely emotional, rituals such as these can appear to an observer as occasions marked by spontaneity and open-ended improvisation, involving the expression of emotion across a wide range of states: joy, fear, anger, despair, and so forth. But the expression of joy among a community of Pentecostal women, for example, is shown to be social and cultural code for the group's self-understanding in the face of public skepticism. Zulu Zion gatherings that might be seen as the enthusiastic abandonment of self-control in fact are carefully organized proceedings grounded in a sense of authority and social order ingrained in the performers. A ride on a Malay hobbyhorse that leads to union of the rider with divine spirits in heaven is undertaken against the background of culturally grounded expectations for the experience of ecstasy in certain situations. The enactment of violent emotions among dancers at some shrines in India serves a practical social function of renewal and remembrance of deeply held values. In short, emotion is performed in such instances according to rules, as part of a script, the end point of which is the disclosure of patterns of order and cultural meanings fundamental to the life of the community.[36]

As already noted, the study of emotion undertaken as an investigation of language is an important part of emotions research.[37] Among studies of religion, emotion, and language, there are several approaches. Some investigators have focused on the construction of lexicons of religious emotions, a project represented variously in studies of "heart" in the Hebrew Bible and in the proposal of a scholar of Sri Lankan religion, Gannath Obeyesekere, who, in engaging Christian theology bearing on emotion, prospected a cross-cultural "vocabulary of emotions."[38] Another avenue has been the development of the ideas of Schleiermacher and Otto, an enterprise given life by Richard R. Niebuhr, who drew directly on the former to argue for an intimate relation between language and feeling in Christian experience.[39] This trajectory has taken the form not only of lexical studies but of investigations of "religious grammar," such as in a study that claims that the "language of prayer" elicits and shapes "Christian affections."[40] Other research focused on language deploys more theoretically sophisticated perspectives in exploring "sacred rhetoric." Wendy Olmstead's study of emotion in Augustine's *Confessions* concludes that the language of that account has "an emotional as well as an intellectual purpose" and that Augustine's "theory of signs emphasizes the cognitive and emotional effect of language."[41] Defining language itself more broadly, a study of Bengal religion claims that the language of gesture can be linked with religious emotions in Hindu *bhakti*.[42] Less numerous but also significant are attempts to link the narrative/dramatic structure of emotion to language and morality.[43] All of these kinds of research are devised as ways of uncovering what is thought to be a correlation between language/grammar and emotion in religious contexts. In those cases where strong confessional undertones are present, it has offered only a glimpse of what language/emotion studies in religion might eventually contribute to the emergent discourses about language and emotion in other parts of the humanities and social and behavioral sciences, and it has limited its potential by failing to draw on insights derived from that other scholarship. But in some lexical, rhetorical, and grammatical studies the investigation of religion and emotion is taking shape in ways that demonstrate a productive intersection with philosophical and psychological research about cognition.

Research on emotion that has developed with emphases on these themes—morality, cognition, performance, and language—represents just a part of the interest among scholars in the role of emotion in religion. The new study of emotion, like innovations or revivals of research in any field, is developing in many different directions at once, and work on religion and emotion reflects that in the range of topics invented by scholars in their various projects. It is likely the case that inquiry into religion and emotion will continue to emphasize themes such as morality and cognition because they effectively represent research across an assortment of fronts: in philosophy, history, literary studies, anthropology, sociology, and psychology. Inasmuch as religious studies researchers broaden their familiarity with research in multiple fields— and the study of religion and emotion can advance only in that way—these themes will grow more prominent.

Studying Religion and Emotion

To study religion and emotion, researchers must gather data. There are some academics who would reject the notion that such data are obtainable, others still who question the relevance of the term "data" to any study of religion.[44] But, taking leads from the emergent history of emotions and work in the social and behavioral sciences, those who wish to explore emotion in religion can organize the business of data gathering in several different ways. It is essential for investigators to remain aware, however, that all emotion to some extent is

governed by culture, by culturally derived expectations for emotional performances. These performances are enacted with regard to what the historian Peter
Stearns has called the "emotionology" of a society, that is, the rules for emotional expression and concealment that are coded in the social frameworks for
everyday life.[45] And so a part of research must always be the discovery of the
emotionology that conditions the emotional lives of actors. At the same time,
researchers must glean from various sources the recoverable traces of the emotional life of individuals inasmuch as it differs, in large part or small, from the
social code: emotionologies, like all cultural artifacts, can be rendered out-
moded or inadequate by changes in the emotional experience of groups or
individuals. Studying emotion in religion, then, is complicated from the outset
by the necessity of making distinctions between emotional life as commanded
by culture and rebellion against that authority by individuals and groups for
whom the canopy of emotionology no longer provides order and meaning.

The feeling rules of a culture are everywhere represented: in art, literature,
sports, bureaucracy, family, dress, courtship, language, and music, among
other ways. Persons encounter in novels, advertising images, parental influence, self-help books, sermons, legal codes, organizations, and recreational
settings a continuous stream of cues about how to be emotional. Sometimes
the cues are transparent: parents encourage displays of joy, stadium sports
announcers urge shows of zeal, government officials criticize expression of
fear, counselors warn against jealousy, police arrest persons with "road rage,"
and newspaper columnists call on their readers to feel shame. At other times,
the message is less direct, wrapped in a more complex grammar but no less
forcibly interjected into consciousness: the atmosphere of the Lincoln Monu-
ment, the demeanor of a boss, the tone of an academic committee meeting,
and displays made during a protest march all influence the ways persons feel,
offering examples of normative emotionality in those contexts.

Religions offer both direct and indirect cues about emotionality to their
adherents. Ministers preach for the cultivation of certain emotions, devotional
reading models desirable emotionality, scriptures are interpreted to support
certain emotional styles and discourage others, ritual performs emotion in
ways sanctioned by religious authorities, and material culture—a cathedral
window, for example—inspires awe and in so doing legitimates it for religion.
Exploring the language of sermons, the details of ritual, or the ways a religion
has materially represented itself accordingly can yield much information about
what a religion expects emotionally of its members.

Individuals, guided by the standards imposed on them by religious adherence, construct their emotionality with regard to religion in ways that place
them somewhere along a spectrum of greater or lesser orthodoxy. With this in
mind, it is especially important to attempt to gain understanding of the ways
individuals, in their practice of religion, confirm or challenge the authority of
religious emotionology. Religious leadership might stress the importance of

hope over despair, but persons' diaries might reveal that despair above all else drives their religious life. Scriptural interpretation might stress shame, but in the personal correspondence of a person might be found a boldness, self-confidence, and joy in religion. Liturgical gatherings might include the recitation of words signifying intense emotion, but an autobiography might reveal that a person felt little or nothing in such circumstances. Indeed, it is commonly the case that clergy accuse congregants of failing to feel properly, intensely enough, or the right emotion. And, as the records of religious organizations evidence, dissatisfied members of a religious group often criticize their leaders for exactly the same. Great divides sometimes open between seemingly official church endorsements of a certain kind of emotionality in religion and the religious experiences of the lay membership. In short, the study of emotion in religion has to be conducted simultaneously on two fronts. Researchers must gather data on officially sanctioned religious emotionality at the same time that they pursue, through examination of the lives of individual participants or discrete subgroups, understanding of the nature of the correlation (including negative correlation) with rank-and-file experiences. Then, with great sensitivity, the two sets of data must be organized in such a way as to illuminate the complex relationship between what individuals feel and what religions expect them to feel. The best of this work will be undertaken with a strong regard for the cultural context as a whole, for politics, social change, gender, sexuality, family structures, organizational life, reading, art, and all of the other parts of persons' social lives that contribute to the making of a culture of emotion.

Taking stock of a wide array of cultural artifacts, then, requires that those who research religion and emotion develop a familiarity with the ways emotion is studied in various branches of the arts and sciences. This is necessary, first and foremost, as an exercise in separation from ideologies of emotion grounded in religious tradition, from Buddhist assumptions about the unwelcomeness of desire, to Christian hypervaluation of love, Sufist absolutization of mystical feeling, Pascal's claim that "the heart has its reasons" that are hidden from cognition, and Otto's dictum that emotion is ultimately mysterious. The study of religion and emotion means taking emotion as a datum that can be subjected to examination from an assortment of disciplinary perspectives. (The full potential of the study of emotion in any area will be realized through interdisciplinary analysis.) Just as certain notions of race and gender— as they were coded in religious, political, and social traditions—inhibited the development of research, for example, on women's history or African American literature until the 1960s, so, too, unexamined assumptions about emotion can impede its investigation today, especially in its connection to religion. The academic area of religious studies must subject ideologies of emotion that are embedded in the field to the same far-reaching criticism that historians and sociologists and literary scholars brought to the study of race and gender thirty-five years ago. The foundation for such criticism can be fashioned from active conversation with emotions researchers in other branches of the humanities and social sciences, and with neuroscientists as well.

The essays collected in this book all remark on the interweaving of emotional life with morality, especially on the manner in which emotionality expresses, reinforces, is shaped by, and challenges social and moral orders. In this volume the settings for religious emotion vary widely, from medieval Europe and Japan to nineteenth-century Korea and twentieth-century Melanesia and India. An assortment of religious traditions is represented: Judaism, Christianity, Islam, Hinduism, Buddhism, Confucianism, and indigenous religions. Much of the analysis in these various studies would comport with the observation of William A. Christian Jr. in Chapter 1 that "People in society produce their own stimuli—entertainment in the form of theater, games, celebrations, religious rituals—that provoke necessary emotions, whether laughter and fun, tension and release, or weeping and sorrow." Christian explores the "economy of sentiment" underlying religious weeping in Spain in the fifteenth and sixteenth centuries. For Christian, Spanish weeping was a learned behavior, and expression of emotion in the religious context accordingly was a matter of individual discernment of cultural expectations for feeling and of the effectiveness of theological ideas and social mores in organizing the timing and expression of emotion in tears. Religious weeping expressed feeling, but at the same time it served as a means to produce a desired emotional state. The public performance of weeping at various times in the annual Catholic calendar was a collective testimony of religiously licit feeling toward God, and the expectation of the performers was that God would respond benevolently.

The investigation of culturally shaped emotional performances in religion has borne fruit with regard to a number of religious traditions. Another body of research illustrates the manner in which the display of emotion in ritual settings, or the depiction of emotion in religious literature, challenges, rather than cooperates with, dominant social mores. In a study of Sufi emotionality, Helene Basu details, in Chapter 2, the way the emotional element in the religious life of Indian Sufis is fundamental to the construction of resistance to traditional social hierarchies. Basu shows how groups of low status manipulate culturally derived understandings of emotion in such a way as to lay claim, through their emotionality, to the pinnacle of social status, and how religious ritual facilitates the performance of such status reversal. Her exposition of the complex nature of local Sufi ritual, where numerous ideological threads—good and evil, male and female, hot and cold, and so forth—are interwoven, reveals both the clarity and ambiguity of a culture of religion and emotion. Her study also exemplifies how a focus on emotion can lead to the discovery of previously unsuspected linkages among the various elements of religious ritual. For Basu, the subversive aspect of religion consists of emotional experiences and cognitions interwoven in the liminal contexts of ritual, where status reversal takes place.

Another challenge to the social order framed by religiously grounded conceptualization and performance of emotion is represented in a study of religious literature and family structure in Korea. In Chapter 3, JaHyun Kim Haboush demonstrates how the depiction of emotion in Buddhist-based popular literature provided a framework for challenging Confucianist insistence on primogeniture and resistance to female filiality. Engaged by Koreans as myth, that literature was embraced as counter-hegemonic discourse and served to delegitimate a dominant Confucian worldview. Its effectiveness in so doing rested on the fact that although it shared with the Confucian worldview a valuation of filial emotion, it depicted love of one's parents in such a way as to critically confront the social logic of Confucianism, to advance a view of the social consequences of filial emotion that Confucianist policy disallowed. Haboush, in focusing on characterizations of emotion in religious literature, is able to identify key contradictions in Korean social life and to demonstrate how ideals and imagery drawn from one religious tradition can be marshaled both to reinforce and to undermine another.

The place of emotion in religious literature is likewise the subject of Debora K. Shuger's study of Renaissance literature in Chapter 4. Shuger aims squarely at the view of the history of Western thought as a struggle between philosophy as the pursuit of truth, and rhetoric as sophistic discourse characterized by emotional play. Offering the example of Renaissance sacred rhetorics—religious writings published between 1500 and 1700—Shuger argues that emotion, taken to be a key element of religious experience, was linked with knowledge in premodern epistemology. Sacred rhetorics were important because they were conceived as the means by which knowledge that was hidden from the mind was made visible. Rhetorical writings, through their appeal to the emotions, allowed persons to fully apprehend truth that was otherwise only vaguely sensed. Religious writings opened pathways to truth by sparking the imagination with images that "make what is unseen accessible to both feeling *and* thought." Emotion accordingly was fused with argument. In the sacred rhetorics, emotion and knowledge were "mutually dependent," joined in the perception of truth and the judgment of propositions, and thereby equally represented in the construction of moral visions.

The association of emotions with cognition likewise is the subject of Harvey Whitehouse's analysis of Melanesian initiation rites in Chapter 5. The "rites of terror," that is, the ordeals undertaken by initiates, are for Whitehouse more than simple cognitive processes in which the transmission of religious knowledge takes place through a transaction between teacher and pupils. Drawing on psychological research supporting the claim that events are better remembered if they are emotionally rich, and emphasizing the collective aspect of initiation rites—initiates together with their supervisors—Whitehouse argues that "extreme emotions and cognitive shocks become intertwined" in the rites of terror, leaving a "flashbulb memory" of the events. In this way the proceedings form an occasion of collective revelation for all involved, leaving a powerful and living residuum of images (of persons and particular events) that continuously shape religious and political community.[46]

For Shuger, images that appealed to the emotions were the portal to philosophical truth for Renaissance religious writers, and for Whitehouse, the formation of commanding images in initiation rites came about through the combination of emotional and cognitive elements in those events. In Chapter 6, Steven M. Parish, in a study of the Newars of the Kathmandu Valley, proposes, like Shuger, that emotions are judgments and, like Whitehouse, that emotions engage people more powerfully with their world and "prepare people to be agents. The experience of emotion mediates engagement with life, priming social actors to find meaning in events and experiences . . . readying them to act." Like Whitehouse, he views emotion as more than cognitive judgment, as more than moral discourse. In proposing a middle ground between theories that decontextualize emotion (i.e., in favor of universal psychological/physiological processes) and those that disembody it (i.e., those that focus exclusively on its cultural embeddedness), he argues that the Newar feel moral evaluations as well as experience them cognitively. For Parish, moral emotions are moral judgments in the sense that feelings embody moral evaluations. Persons do not form judgments based solely on their understanding of social norms, but actually feel the pain of shame or remorse in their moral orientations. The heart, *nuga*: as the center of emotional life, actually hurts, flutters, and sinks. Through this embodiment of emotion and moral judgment, Newars frame a worldview, they "ethicize and sacralize mind, emotion, and self and come to know themselves as moral beings."

Like Parish, Gary L. Ebersole, in Chapter 7, complicates our understanding of the relationship between emotional expression and moral discourse. In a study of ritual weeping, he observes the tendency of some researchers to view the tears of other peoples and times through a lens ground by the ideas and cultural assumptions of their own situations. This inclination to universalize the meaning of tears, especially with regard to the moral dimensions of weeping, sometimes includes a view of ritual weeping as faked behavior. Ebersole criticizes such projects as shortsighted, first of all, for their inability to recognize how actors exploit ritual weeping for their own purposes—how they turn cultural expectations into legitimations for personal rather than collective ends—and second, for how they depersonalize those who participate in ritual weeping, rendering them passive players, emotionally disconnected as they go through the motions of a collective drama. He proposes that ritual weeping be viewed as "symbolic activity that marks out the existence or the breach of social and/or moral relationships" so that some weeping might be understood as resistance to social norms, rather than performance of them. Or, as in the case of filial emotion in Korea, weeping may have contested meanings. For Ebersole, the moral discourses represented in incidences of ritual weeping are complex, at times even contradictory, and consist of meanings framed by personal interests as well as social expectations.

The fact of variant meanings of an emotional performance is directly addressed in Chapter 8 by Paul M. Toomey in observing three bhakti traditions at Mount Govardhan. Arguing that bhakti devotionalists objectify emotion as food, Toomey takes a forthrightly constructivist position, and as such his approach shares much with Basu's. But where Basu focuses on evidence of conceptual correspondences across an extended sample of contexts—cosmic, gender, social status, and so forth—to strengthen her claim for coherency among seemingly diverse aspects of religious life, Toomey takes a more explicitly comparative tack. He organizes his study in such a way as to account for variations in the construction of the emotional component of religious pilgrimage. He analyzes how emotion is objectively represented in the ritual of eating, which includes all aspects of setting, menu, preparation (including the identity of the preparer), calendar, duration, and consumption. Material aspects of religious culture, especially icons and food, are associated with emotion as repositories for it, in fact serving as a reservoir for emotion that is transmitted to devotees in the course of the food ritual. In consuming food, persons take into themselves holy emotion supplied to them by the deity. Toomey then shows how variations in the experience of emotion—as motherly love, erotic passion, and so forth—rest on differences in the background of the performers, determined by their membership in one or another of a particular sect of pilgrims.

The association of emotion with material substance is present in many religious traditions. The identification of emotion with food, as in certain cases of bhakti devotionalism, and the association of shame with the pain of the heart among the Newars are two examples of the ways certain aspects of emotionality and morality are materialistically coded. In her analysis of emotion in Bengali religious thought in Chapter 9, June McDaniel writes about the way emotion is "substantial rather than conceptual" in Indian traditions, one part of the Indian universe that is experienced as networks of continually flowing substance. Emotion is not a passive response to the world, but an active engagement in it, a matter of aesthetic and spiritual self-making, in which persons arrange emotions (*rāga*, colors) as paints on a canvas as they construct the "subtle body," or ideal self. McDaniel's interpretation is grounded in analysis of language, especially with regard to the complexes of metaphors that are deployed by Indians in addressing various aspects of emotional life. And, like several of the other authors whose work is represented here, she stresses the difference between Western and Indian approaches to emotion, in particular the Indian focus on intense emotion as opposed to the everyday.

Elliot R. Wolfson in Chapter 10 also focuses on extreme emotion in writing about sixteenth-century Jewish mysticism. In his exploration of the emotional dynamics underlying the Kabbalists' ecstatic journey to the heavenly realms, Wolfson proposes that weeping served as the focal point for a complex of religious ideas and behavior. Sixteenth-century Jews linked ecstasy with esoteric knowledge and cultivated weeping as an "ecstatic technique" that would gain them that knowledge. Wolfson invokes testimony from the diary of a Jew from that period, Hayyim Vital, arguing that Vital viewed weeping as both the avenue to ecstatic experience and a means to knowledge. Weeping opened the gates of the higher realms, and as such was associated with the ascent of the soul. In this study, Wolfson also demonstrates the manner in which ideas about gender, the phallus, seminal emissions, the symbolism of the eye, sleep, and death were interwoven in Kabbalists' views of the meanings of ecstatic weeping. The picture of Jewish mysticism that emerges is one in which emotional experience itself is the goal of the mystical ritual of weeping, as well as the means by which the soul makes its ascent and obtains gnosis. The performative aspects of mystical emotionality accordingly stand side by side with the acquisition of religious knowledge in this form of Jewish mysticism.

The focus on a single individual, such as Hayyim Vital, can reveal something of the complexities and subtleties of emotional life that the investigation of collective emotional experience cannot. Moreover, in certain cases it is possible to situate an actor within a historical context in such a way as to illustrate that person's creativity in negotiating overlapping individual and collective frameworks for emotional life. In Chapter 11, Catherine Peyroux sets out to describe the "affective world of Frankish nobility" through an analysis of St. Gertrude's *furor*. Gertrude's anger is linked to her rejection of a suitor proposed to her by her parents. By demonstrating the location of Gertrude's emotionality within the world of feeling of the seventh-century nobles, with particular attention to Gertrude's self-understanding of her betrothal to Christ, Peyroux is able to explain the intensity of Gertrude's response, its religious meaning, and the appeal of the story to her subsequent hagiographers. Gertrude's rage at her parents' presentation to her of a prospective husband reveals both her devotion to God, whom she takes as her only true husband, and her realization that she will open herself to the charge of adultery should she agree to the marriage her parents have arranged. Working from a hagiographic text, Peyroux examines the various possible meanings of the *furor* therein described on the way to concluding that the saint's rage was in fact taken by her community as a sign of her status as the beloved spouse of Christ. For those who knew her as abbess and for those who engaged *The Life of St. Gertrude,* her anger represented her religious identity as the bride of Christ, her authority as a spiritual leader, and her keen grasp of the socioemotional codes of the Frankish aristocracy.

Just as cultural codes govern the emotional lives of persons as they interact in various social settings, certain cultural assumptions about emotional aspects of self can frame a group's understanding of the relationship between humans and superhuman beings. Charlotte E. Hardman, in observing Lohorung Rai in Nepal, notes how emotion saturates the relationships of Lohorung with the powerful spirits of ancestors (*sammang*). In the relatively seamless world of people, nature, sammang, society, mind, body, past, and present, emotion experienced by the sammang is also experienced by the Lohorung. Because of the interconnectedness of all phenomena, the anger of sammang, which can be the result of persons' transgression of social codes for behavior, is also experienced by Lohorung, usually as physical pain or misfortune, such as a landslide. Just as the social expression of anger is accepted and even encouraged by Lohorung in certain situations, so, too, are maladies engendered by the angering of sammang understandable as part of the dynamics of emotion on a grand scale. The "emotion rules," as it were, are not merely social, they are cosmic. By focusing on emotion as a key to understanding Lohorung conceptualizations of morality, self, and the superhuman, Hardman is able to demonstrate the profundity of the linkages among those aspects of Lohorung culture, and contribute as well to discussions about the embodiedness of emotion alongside its construction in culture.

By linking various aspects of religion—ritual, authority, community, ideas, and other features—to a new center, the study of religion and emotion promises to disclose meanings previously hidden. Thus far, research has taken shape as an assortment of approaches and themes. Like most new academic ventures, it enjoys the luxury of relative freedom from confining academic discourses and, in the absence of a tradition of investigation that maps and authorizes specific terrain, it can explore where it wishes.

The study of religion and emotion is in an early stage, well-begun but still finding its feet, and not yet invested in a secret language, an exclusivistic discourse that identifies it as a field of study and reduces its view to a handful of official themes. To realize its ample possibilities, however, it eventually will have to generate classifications of its subject matter and develop linkages among its various foci. But in the course of that enterprise, it must avoid doctrinaire taxonomies. It must look beyond disciplinary boundaries in theory and method. It must remain sensitive to the differences and similarities between culturally constructed standards for emotion and the actual emotional experiences of people. The research represented in this volume exemplifies some of the most promising approaches to religion and emotion, but it by no means exhausts them. Other studies framed by theological and philosophical concerns, and especially the work of neuroscientists, will make their own contributions to the development of this area of study. The consequences of all of this research may be far-reaching. As investigation of religion and emotion from all of these perspectives progresses, it is likely to challenge current paradigms for the study of religion, and it may lead to the reconsideration of the study of religion as a whole.

NOTES

1. Discussion of some relevant issues is in Donald Wiebe, *The Politics of Religious Studies: The Continuing Conflict with Theology in the Academy* (New York: St. Martin's Press, 1999).

2. Owen Flannagan, *Consciousness Reconsidered* (Cambridge, MA: MIT Press, 1992), 8–11.

3. John Corrigan, Eric Crump, and John Kloos, *Emotion and Religion: A Critical Assessment and Annotated Bibliography* (Westport, CT: Greenwood Press, 2000).

4. Kurt W. Fischer and June Price Tangney, "Introduction: Self-conscious Emotions and the Affect Revolution: Framework and Overview," in *Self-conscious Emotions: The Psychology of Shame, Guilt, Embarrassment, and Pride,* ed. June Price Tangney and Kurt W. Fischer (New York: Guilford Press, 1995), 3–24.

5. Charles Darwin, *The Expression of the Emotions in Man and Animals,* ed. Paul Ekman New York: Oxford University Press, 1998); Paul Ekman, "Biological and Cultural Contributions to Body and Facial Movement in the expression of Emotion," in *Explaining Emotions,* ed. Amelie Rorty (Berkeley: University of California Press, 1980), 73–101. Ekman claims the existence of six common emotions, but is not clear about whether elicitors of emotion are identical across cultures. Discussion of several key questions about emotions and universals by James Averill, Paul Ekman, Phoebe C. Ellsworth, Nico H. Frijda, and others is "How Is Evidence of Universals in Antecedents of Emotions Explained?" in *The Nature of Emotion: Fundamental Questions,* ed. Paul Ekman and Richard J. Davidson (New York: Oxford University Press, 1994), 144–178.

6. Anna Wierzbicka, *Emotions across Languages and Cultures: Diversity and Universals* (Cambridge: Cambridge University Press, 1999), 34–35. While emphasizing the importance of cultural diversity in forming emotional life, Wierzbecka proposes eleven "emotional universals" based on language analyses (275–307). Much research in language universals is indebted to Noam Chomsky, who has written, "We may take UG (Universal grammar) to be a theory of the language faculty, a common human attribute, genetically determined, one component of the human mind." *Essays on Form and Interpretation* (New York: North-Holland, 1997), 164. Karl G. Heider, *Landscapes of Emotion: Mapping Three Cultures of Emotion in Indonesia* (Cambridge, UK: Cambridge University Press, 1991); Spero M. Manson, James H. Shore, and Joseph D. Bloom, "The Depressive Experience in American Indian Communities: A Challenge for Psychiatric Theory and Diagnosis," in *Culture and Depression: Studies in the Anthropology and Cross-cultural Psychiatry of Affect and Disorder,* ed. A. Kleinman and B. Good (Berkeley: University of California Press, 1985), 331–368.

7. Emile Durkheim, *The Elementary Forms of the Religious Life,* trans. Joseph Ward Swain (London: G. Allen & Unwin 1954); *Suicide: A Study in Sociology,* trans. George Simpson (Glencoe, IL: Free Press, 1951); Victor W. Turner, *The Forest of Symbols* (Ithaca, NY: Cornell University Press, 1967); *The Ritual Process; Structure and Anti-*

structure (London: Aldine Publishing, 1969); Helene Basu and Pnina Werbner, "The Embodiment of Charisma," in *Embodying Charisma: Modernity, Locality and the Performance of Emotion in Sufi Cults,* ed. Helene Basu and Pnina Werbner (London: Routledge, 1998), 7.

8. Claude Lévi-Strauss, *Structural Anthropology,* trans. C. Jacobsen and S. G. Schoeff (New York: Basic Books, 1963), 180–81.

9. Rudolf Otto, *The Idea of the Holy: An Inquiry into the Non-rational Factor in the Idea of the Divine and Its Relation to the Rational,* trans. John W. Harvey (London: Oxford University Press, 1936), 12–13.

10. "This ontological illusion, that there is an abstract and detachable 'it' upon which research can be directed, probably lies behind the defectiveness of much emotion research." Rom Harré, "An Outline of the Social Constructionist Viewpoint," in *The Social Construction of Emotions,* ed. Rom Harré (Oxford: Basil Blackwell, 1986), 4.

11. Nancy Eisenberg, "Emotion, Regulation, and Moral Development," *Annual Review of Psychology* 51 (2000): 665–697. On religious experience and brain scans, see the provocative but flawed study by Andrew Newberg and Eugene G. d'Aquili, *Why God Won't Go Away* (New York: Ballantine Books, 2001).

12. E. L. Schiffelin, "Performance and the Cultural Construction of Reality," *American Ethnologist* 12 (1985): 707–724; Arthur Kleinman, *Patients and Healers in the Context of Culture* (Berkeley: University of California Press, 1980).

13. Frederick Turner, "Transcending Biological and Social Reductionism," *Substance* 30 (2001): 220.

14. On "feeling rules," see Arlie R. Hochschild, *The Managed Heart: Commercialization of Human Feeling* (Berkeley: University of California Press, 1983).

15. Weston LaBarre, "The Cultural Basis of Emotion and Gestures," *Journal of Personality* 16 (1947): 52, 55.

16. Michelle Z. Rosaldo, "Toward an Anthropology of Self and Feeling," in *Culture Theory: Essays on Mind, Self, and Emotion,* ed. Richard A. Schweder and Robert A. LeVine (Cambridge, UK: Cambridge University Press, 1984), 150; Benedicte Grima, *The Performance of Emotion among Paxtun Women* (Austin: University of Texas Press, 1992). An overview of themes and methods in the social scientific study of emotion as it was emerging in the 1980s is in Catherine Lutz and Geoffrey M. White, "The Anthropology of Emotions," *Annual Review of Anthropology* 15 (1986): 405–436. See also Lila Abu-Lughod, *Veiled Sentiments: Honor and Poetry in a Bedouin Society* (Berkeley: University of California Press, 1986).

17. Michelle Z. Rosaldo, *Knowledge and Passion: Illongot Notions of Self and Social Life* (Cambridge, UK: Cambridge University Press, 1980); Signe Howell, "Rules Not Words," in *Indigenous Psychologies: The Anthropology of the Self,* ed. Paul Heelas and Andrew Lock (London: Academic Press, 1981), 133–144; Karen Ann Watson-Gegeo and David W. Gegeo, "Shaping the Mind and Straightening Out Conflicts: The Discourse of Kwara'ae Family Counseling," in *Disentangling: Conflict Discourse in Pacific Societies,* ed. Karen Ann Watson-Gegeo and Geoffrey M. White (Stanford: Stanford University Press, 1990), 161–213.

18. Robert I. Levy, *Tahitians: Mind and Experience in the Society Islands* (Chicago: University of Chicago Press, 1973); Jean Briggs, *Never in Anger: Portrait of an Eskimo Family* (Cambridge, MA: Harvard University Press, 1970); Catherine A. Lutz, *Unnatu-*

ral Emotions; Everyday Sentiments on a Micronesian Atoll and Their Challenge to Western Theory (Chicago: University of Chicago Press, 1988); Fred R. Myers, *Pintupi Country, Pintupi Self: Sentiment, place, and politics among the Western Desert Aborigines* (Washington DC: Smithsonian Institution Press, 1986); Rosaldo, *Knowledge and Passion.*

19. Charlotte E. Hardman, *Other Worlds: Notions of Self and Emotion among the Lohorung Rai* (Oxford: Berg, 2000). William M. Reddy has challenged what he characterizes as extreme constructionism in the work of Rosaldo, Abu-Lughod, and Grima, and offers an alternative approach that focuses on strategies for the concentration of attention. See "Against Constructionism: The Historical Ethnography of Emotions," *Current Anthropology* 38 (1997): 327–351.

20. The historical study of emotion began in the rich ferment of ideas among historians in France in the 1920s. Lucien Febvre outlined the direction of that project in an essay published in 1938 entitled "Histoire et Psychologie": "The task is, for a given period, to establish a detailed inventory of the mental equipment of the men of the time, then by dint of great learning, but also of imagination, to reconstitute the whole physical, intellectual and moral universe of each preceeding generation." "History and Psychology," in *A New Kind of History and Other Essays,* ed. Peter Burke, trans. K. Folca (New York: Harper & Row, 1973), 9. For Febvre, this task translated to a test of the historian's ingenuity in developing investigative techniques that would make it possible "to reconstitute the emotional life of the past." "Sensibility and History: How to Reconstitute the Emotional Life of the Past," in *A New Kind of History,* 12–26. The groundwork to Febvre's new kind of history had already been laid by Marc Bloch, whose study of popular belief in the cure of scrofula by the king's touch in medieval and early modern times was predicated on the notion that "the miracle of scrofula is incontestably bound up with a whole psychological system," Marc Bloch, *The Royal Touch,* trans. J. E. Andersen (1923; New York: Dorset Press, 1961), 29. Bloch later detailed his thinking in the posthumous *The Historian's Craft,* wherein he argued that "historical facts are, in essence, psychological facts. Normally, therefore, they find their antecedents in other psychological facts." *The Historian's Craft,* trans. Peter Putnam (New York: Knopf, 1953), 194. Taken together, these "psychological facts" and the circumstances of their existence made up for Bloch social reality understood "as a whole." The historian's task accordingly was to reconceive the whole to uncover the implicit meanings of collective behavior. Fundamental to the project of the history of emotion as represented in the work of Febvre and Bloch was a design of imaginative interrogation of historical artifacts that would, as Febvre wrote, "make mute things talk." Johan Huizinga's classic characterization of medieval emotionality, *The Waning of the Middle Ages* (London: E. Arnold & Co., 1924) had broken fresh ground for such an undertaking a few years earlier. But the new endeavor made its most dramatic appearance in Fernand Braudel's study of the Mediterranean world in the age of Philip II, and eventually took shape as a species of social history characterized by its attention to everyday life, or what once was called "total history." Braudel also articulated one of the cardinal verities of the Annales school: events, or actions (*histoire événementielle*) not only were to be distinguished from the historical structures that limited and controlled events (*histoire de la longue durée*), but actors themselves were considered to be imprisoned within those structures and thus determined in their possibilities. So, for example, in his study of capitalism and material life Braudel

argued that "the hazards of harvest, the slowness or lack of transport, incomprehensible and contradictory demographic movements . . . and the chronic deficiency of power resources" made people "unconscious prisoners," "locked in an economic condition" that determined their possibilities for action. In line with Febvre's call for an inventory of the "mental equipment" of people, annalistes surmised that not only political, economic, and social activity, but mental activity as well was constrained and compelled by historical structures. Thus *mentalités collectives,* or cast of mind, was ratified as an object of historical study, and the historical study of emotion was placed on firm ground, Fernand Braudel, *Capitalism and Material Life* (New York: Harper, 1983), xiv, ix. Braudel proposed to explore "the foundations of the house" before he analyzed the activity of agents within it (445). He wrote that "little or nothing existed before 1949 in the immense domain of 'structural history.' " *The Mediterranean and the Mediterranean World in the Age of Philip II,* (New York: Harper & Row, 1972), 1274. He traced his brand of (histoire événementielle) to the influence of French economic historian and Durkheimian François Simiand: "My definition of 'event' is closer to that of Paul Lacombe and François Simiand: the pieces of flotsam I have combed from the historical ocean and chosen to call 'events' are those essentially *ephemeral* yet moving occurrences, the 'headlines' of the past" (1243). For a brief survey of the development of the history of emotions and some reference to the historical study of religion and emotion, see John Corrigan, *Business of the Heart: Religion and Emotion in the Nineteenth Century* (Berkeley: University of California Press, 2002), 269–280.

21. See David Lowenthal, *The Past Is a Foreign Country* (New York: Cambridge University Press, 1985).

22. Lester K. Little, "Anger in Monastic Curses," in *Anger's Past: The Social Uses of an Emotion in the Middle Ages,* ed. Barbara H. Rosenwein (Ithaca, NY: Cornell University Press, 1998), 9–35; Carole Z. Stearns and Peter N. Stearns, *Anger: The Struggle for Emotional Control in America's History* (Chicago: University of Chicago Press, 1986); Peter N. Stearns, *Jealousy: The Evolution of an Emotion in American History* (New York: New York University Press, 1989); John Corrigan, *Business of the Heart: Religion and Emotion in the Nineteenth Century* (Berkeley: University of California Press, 2002).

23. Robert C. Solomon, *Passions* (New York: Anchor Press Doubleday, 1976); Clifford Geertz, "The Growth of Culture and the Evolution of Mind," in *The Interpretation of Cultures* (New York: Basic Books, 1973).

24. Catherine Lutz and Geoffrey M. White, "The Anthropology of Emotions," *Annual Review of Anthropology* 15 (1986): 417.

25. Steven M. Parish, *Moral Knowing in a Hindu Sacred City: An Exploration of Mind, Emotion, and Self* (New York: Columbia University Press, 1994), 216.

26. Lutz, *Unnatural Emotions,* 159–160; Richard E. Barton, " 'Zealous Anger' and the Renegotiation of Aristocratic Relationships in Eleventh- and Twelfth-Century France," in *Anger's Past: The Social Uses of an Emotion in the Middle Ages,* ed. Barbara H. Rosenwein (Ithaca, NY: Cornell University Press, 1998), 153–170.

27. Myers, *Pintupi Country,* III.

28. Howard M. Wach. "A 'Still, Small Voice' from the Pulpit: Religion and the Creation of Social Morality in Manchester, 1820–1850," *Journal of Modern History* 59 (1991): 317–330; Verne A. Dusenbery, "On the Moral Sensitivities of the Sikhs in

North America," in *Divine Passions: The Social Construction of Emotion in India*, ed. Owen M. Lynch (Berkeley: University of California Press, 1990), 239–261.

29. Michael Stocker, with Elizabeth Hegeman, *Valuing Emotions* (Cambridge, UK: Cambridge University Press, 1996), 177, xiv; Michael Stocker, "Emotional Thoughts," *American Philosophical Quarterly* 24 (1987): 59.

30. David Hume, *A Treatise of Human Nature: Being an Attempt to Introduce the Experimental Method of Reasoning into Moral Subjects*, ed. David Fate Norton and Mary J. Norton (Oxford: Oxford University Press, 2000); Stanley Schachter and John Singer, "Cognitive, Social and Physiological Determinants of Emotional State," *Psychological Review* 99 (1962): 554–560; Magda B. Arnold, *Emotion and Personality*, vol.1, *Psychological Aspects* (New York: Columbia University Press, 1960); Robert Solomon, "On Emotions as Judgments," *American Philosophical Quarterly* 25 (1988): 183–191; Nico H. Frijda, *The Emotions* (New York: Cambridge University Press, 1986); Justin Oakley, *Morality and the Emotions* (New York: Routledge, 1992); Robert M. Gordon, *The Structure of Emotions: Investigations in Cognitive Philosophy* (Cambridge, UK: Cambridge University Press, 1987), especially 65–85.

31. The classic statement is William Ralph Inge, *Faith and Its Psychology* (New York: C. Scribner's Sons, 1910). Andrew Tallon, "The Experience of Grace in Relation to Rahner's Philosophy of the Heart," *Philosophy & Theology* 7 (1992): 193–210.

32. Michael P. Morissey, "Reason and Emotions: Modern and Classical Views on Religious Knowing," *Horizons: The Journal of the College Theology Society* 16 (1989): 275–291; Robert C. Roberts, "Emotions as Access to Religious Truths," *Faith and Philosophy* 9 (1992): 83–94; H. Richard Niebuhr, "Toward the Recovery of Feeling," in *Theology, History, and Culture: Major Unpublished Writing*, ed. William Stacy Johnson, foreword by Richard R. Niebuhr (New Haven: Yale University Press, 1996), 34–49.

33. Richard R. Niebuhr, "The Widened Heart," *Harvard Theological Review* 62 (1969): 127–154.

34. Martha Craven Nussbaum, "Narrative Emotions: Beckett's Genealogy of Love," *Ethics* 98 (1988): 225–254; Richard B. Steele, "Narrative Theology and the Religious Affections," in *Theology without Foundations: Religious Practice and the Future of Theological Truth*, eds. Stanley Hauerwas, Nancy C. Murphy, and Mark Nation (Nashville: Abingdon Press, 1994), 163–179, 327–332; James E. Gilman, "Reenfranchising the Heart: Narrative Emotions and Contemporary Theology," *Journal of Religion* 74 (1994): 218–239; Stephen Mulhall, "Can There Be an Epistemology of Moods?" In *Verstehen and Humane Understanding*, ed. Anthony O'Hear (Royal Institute of Philosophy Supplement 41, Cambridge, UK: Cambridge University Press, 1996), 191–210.

35. Basu and Werbner, "The Embodiment of Charisma," 9.

36. R. Marie Griffith, " 'Joy Unspeakable and Full of Glory': The Vocabulary of Pious Emotion in the Narratives of American Pentecostal Women, 1910–1945," in *An Emotional History of the United States*, ed. Peter N. Stearns and Jan Lewis (New York: New York University Press, 1998), 218–240; Jim Kiernan, "Authority and Enthusiasm: The Organization of Religious Experience in Zulu Zionist Churches," in *Religious Organization and Religious Experience*, ed. J. Davis (London: Academic Press, 1982), 169–179; Mohammed Ghouse Nasuruddin, "Dancing to Ecstasy on the Hobby Horse," in *Emotions of Culture: A Malay Perspective*, ed. Wazir Jahan Karim (Singapore: Oxford University Press, 1990), 142–158; Gervin Flood, "Ritual Dance in *Kerala*: Perfor-

mance, Possession and the Formation of Culture," in *Indian Insights: Buddhism, Brahmanism, and Bhakti. Papers from the Annual Spalding Symposium on Indian Religions*, ed. Peter Connolly and Sue Hamilton (London: Luzac Oriental, 1997), 169–183.

37. E. R. Gerber, "Rage and Obligation: Samoan Emotions in Conflict," in *Person, Self, and Experience: Exploring Pacific Ethnopsychologies*, ed. Geoffrey M. White and John Kirkpatrick (Berkeley: University of California Press, 1985), 121–167; Catherine Lutz, "The Domain of Emotion Words on Ifaluk," *American Ethnologist* 9 (1982): 113–28; J. A. Russell, "Pancultural Aspects of the Human Conceptual Organization of Emotions," *Journal of Personality and Social Psychology* 45 (1983): 1281–1288; Charles E. Osgood, William H. May, and Murray S. Miron, *Cross-Cultural Universals of Affective Meaning* (Urbana: University of Illinois Press, 1975); J. D. Boucher and M. E. Brandt, "Judgment of Emotion Form American and Malay Antecedents," *Journal of Cross-Cultural Psychology* 12 (1981): 272–283.

38. Heinz-Josef Fabry, "*leb; lebab* [heart]," in *Theological Dictionary of the Old Testament*, ed. G. Johannes Botterweck, Helmer Ringgren, and Heinz-Josef Fabry (Grand Rapids: Eerdmans, 1978), 399–437; Gannath Obeyesekere, "Language and Symbolic Form in Psychoanalysis and Anthropology," in *The Work of Culture: Symbolic Transformation in Psychoanalysis and Anthropology* (Chicago: University of Chicago Press, 1990). See the fourth part of his fourth Morgan Lecture.

39. Richard R. Niebuhr, "Schleiermacher on Language and Feeling," *Theology Today* 17 (1960): 150–167.

40. Don E. Saliers, "Religious Affections and the Grammar of the Prayer," in *The Grammar of the Heart: New Essays in Moral Philosophy and Theology*, ed. Richard E. Bell (San Francisco: HarperCollins, 1988), 188–205.

41. Wendy Olmstead, "Invention, Emotion, and Conversion in Augustine's *Confessions*," in *Rhetorical Invention and Religious Inquiry: New Perspectives*, ed. Walter Jost and Wendy Olmstead (New Haven: Yale University Press, 2000), 82. Debora K. Shuger has observed that Renaissance rhetoric through its excavation of Augustinian psychology linked emotion with rhetoric in such a way that "emotional persuasion" aimed "at the transformation of the moral and spiritual life." "The Philosophical Foundations of Sacred Rhetoric," in *Rhetorical Invention and Religious Inquiry*, 54.

42. Federico Squarcini, "Gesture Language as a Vehicle in the Expression of Emotion: A Phenomenological Investigation of the Use of Non-Verbal Expression in Monotheistic Gaudiya Vaisnava Tradition," *Social Compass* 42 (1995): 451–460.

43. George W. Turski, "Experience and Expression: The Moral Linguistic Constitution of Emotions," *Journal for the Theory of Social Behavior* 21 (1991): 373–392.

44. Jonathan Z. Smith, in remarking on the construction of religion as an object of academic study, has written that "there is no data for religion" except what the researcher imagines. In the same sense, there is no data for emotion but what the investigator can create through typology, comparison, reduction, and generalization. *Imagining Religion* (Chicago: University of Chicago Press, 1982), xi.

45. Peter N. Stearns and Carol Z. Stearns, "Emotionology: Clarifying the History of Emotions and Emotional Standards," *American Historical Review* 90 (1985): 813–836.

46. On the ways such images, through their distinctive constitution, shape community, see Harvey Whitehouse, *Inside the Cult: Religious Innovation and Transmission in Papua, New Guinea* (Oxford: Clarendon Press, 1995).

I

Provoked Religious Weeping in Early Modern Spain

William A. Christian Jr.

This study of Spanish Catholic piety in the fifteenth and sixteenth centuries proposes that emotional experiences were measures of the health of the soul, and religious weeping was evidence of the disposition of the heart toward God. Tears were especially important as signs of contrition. They washed away sins at the same time that they revealed guilt. Collective weeping was both a dramatic admission by townspeople that they had transgressed God's law and an appeal to God for mercy and forgiveness. The Holy Week processions (with their representation of the pain and suffering of Jesus), the various Lenten performances, and public dramas enacted on occasions of revival served as stimuli to provoke religious weeping. Weeping was learned behavior, both a sign of feeling and a means to excite it. And the spectacle of public weeping was grounded in a set of assumptions about the necessity for emotional display to God, to one's neighbors, and to oneself. As William A. Christian Jr. writes, "People went to certain places and did certain things in order to weep." This approach, then, focuses on the manner in which emotion is elicited and structured in ritual fashion through participation in public dramas and explores linkages between seemingly private emotional experience and collective, public religiosity.

How did people learn to weep? By what means did they decide to participate in rituals of public weeping, to link their private devotions with the public spectacle enacted in the streets? Was the character of religious piety changed in relocating its performance from one sphere to the

William A. Christian Jr., "Provoked Religious Weeping in Early Modern Spain," in *Religious Organization and Religious Experience*, ed. J. Davis (London: Academic Press, 1982), 97–114. Used by permission of the author.

other? Did the collective admission of guilt in weeping serve social functions? By what historical process might certain dramas have come to be associated with public weeping? Could the association have been coincidental, or organized by church authorities? How much of a role for institutional control was there in such displays? Is this popular religion?

The relative frequency and intensity of emotions and their public expression varies from culture to culture and within cultures over time. This variation has a certain logic that we ought to be able to study and understand. Johannes Huizinga pointed to the ease with which people of the Netherlands and France wept in the late Middle Ages as evidence for a special emotional intensity. Although his explanation of such a special intensity is not convincing (he attributed it to life's violent contrasts and impressive forms; "all experience had yet . . . the directness and absoluteness of the pleasure and pain of child-life"), his examples of weeping, especially public religious weeping, should be addressed. They include the mother of St. Colette weeping and lamenting the Passion, preachers like Vincent Ferrer and Bernardino of Siena making congregations weep, and the people of Paris weeping during processions in 1412.[1] People in sixteenth-century Spain wept in similar circumstances, and their diaries, autobiographies, letters, inquisition testimony, and devotional literature point to compelling, systematic reasons why.

Weeping is not necessarily a spontaneous manifestation of emotion; it may be a formal, ritual act, as with the Andaman Islanders, the Tapirapa Indians of Central Brazil, and ritual mourners of southern Italy.[2] In these societies, some weeping has been described as voluntary, something people can decide to do, which in the very act provokes emotion in those weeping and those watching.

Similarly, in early modern Spain, weeping was considered something that people could learn how to do, in the course of exciting their emotions. People went to certain places and did certain things in order to weep. For the pain, pious tenderness, or sorrow that accompanied weeping was part of an economy of sentiment that could influence God. Conversely, God, angels, and devils could cause emotions. The principles for discerning the supernatural meaning of strong, unexpected sensations were known to literate and illiterate alike, women and men, clergy and laity. The various potential religious significance of emotions meant that attentiveness to feelings, the engendering of certain feelings, and the public display of certain feelings were all encouraged. Tears were considered significant visible evidence for some feelings. Because they were visible and their presence was recorded, they permit us in retrospect to observe some of the occasions on which private and public sentiment was provoked for religious purposes.

Public Weeping in Early Modern Iberia

Huizinga gave an example of one kind of collective, provoked weeping: the processions of Paris in 1412, centering on relics, for the royal campaign against the Armagnacs. According to the journal of a bourgeois of Paris, people wept piteously while they watched or followed "the most touching processions in the memory of man."[3] Such processions in times of crisis were intended to obtain a specific end. In 1507 in Barcelona during a great plague, a procession was held to lay the cornerstone of a chapel to St. Sebastian, the plague saint. Periodically the procession would pause, and a group of children who were flagellating themselves would fall on their knees and cry out for mercy to a man dressed as Sebastian, complete with arrows. "And those who said this wept with tears and lamentations so piercing that it almost broke the hearts of those who cried and those who heard them."[4]

In these processions the public was a knowing, willing participant. Other tear-provoking scenarios were sprung on the public by surprise, and some of them, at least, no less effectively. On the week before the feasts of Saint James and Saint Anne in 1552 the people of Gandia could receive a jubilee indulgence if they received communion; almost all of them did. The Jesuits, however, were upset that on the feasts of Saint James and Saint Anne, as was usual, a bullfight and jousting were to be held, in indecorous contrast, they thought, to the climate of piety. Four priests and four brothers decided to disrupt the festivities by provoking penitential tears. One father carried a crucifix, and others went with a skull, barefoot and bareheaded and with ropes around their necks; with them went two flagellants whipping themselves. When they reached the plaza where people were gathered for the festivities, the people began to cry out "Misericordia," as in a crisis procession. One of the Jesuits went to the town gibbet and preached to the crowd, and the others continued through the streets. When they returned to the plaza, "everyone began to weep once more and cry out for mercy," and the Jesuits went to the opposite side where the duke, duchess, gentlemen, ladies, and clergy were seated, and one of the Jesuits preached there. "From time to time great cries of misericordia spread through the plaza, the Duchess weeping along with everyone else, the people coming down from the stands and following after the Jesuits with copious tears and cries for mercy." There was no bullfighting or jousting, "although it had been prepared at great expense"[5]

Barefoot and hatless, with ropes around their necks and whipping themselves, the Jesuits were acting out the humiliation of the Christ they carried on the crucifix, were living images like the Barcelona St. Sebastian with arrows. In the same year of 1552 the rector of the Jesuits of Coimbra did a self-imposed public penance, whipping himself and weeping copiously.

I think I went to twelve different places and knelt down asking for
pardon and saying in a loud voice, "Nobles and commoners of
Coimbra, for the wounds, death and passion of Christ our redeemer
I ask that you forgive me all the scandals and disedifications that
you have received from the Jesuit school, for before God I confess
that it was my fault and that my sins were the cause of it all," and
almost every time I said this Our Lord gave me so many tears that I
could not finish.[6]

Part of the power of this Jesuit's act came from the fact that it was unusual
for priests to whip themselves in public. However, lay flagellants and other
public imitators of Christ, mass participants in this same kind of emotional
public drama, periodically paraded in the streets and highways of sixteenth-
century Iberia.[7] The Jesuit's tears were as important an element of his public
penance as the whipping and were a feature of the most serious public processions. The town of Ajofrín (Toledo) made one annual procession (and others
in times of drought) 50 kilometers to the shrine of Mary in the town of San
Pablo de los Montes. An elderly priest of Ajofrín wrote in 1596, "In the last
forty years I have taken part in many processions worthy of memory, which
truly can be called processions, for they were made with much devotion and
shedding of tears and even blood and many bare feet." He remembered in
particular a procession in the drought of 1567: "They walked as true penitents
without saying a word to each other, carrying rosaries in their hands, their feet
bare, and tears on their cheeks." In the region it was considered that the procession of Ajofrín was particularly efficacious for rain. Some villages fed the
pilgrims "and received them very well with many tears and much self-
flagellation," so that at times, both the people in the procession and delegations
from towns they passed were weeping.[8]

There was also the calendrical collective weeping of Holy Week. In a brief
aside in his widely read devotional guide, *Audi Filia* (1556), Juan de Avila referred to the dressing of images, probably in Holy Week, to provoke tears:
"When they want to take out an image, to *make people weep,* they dress it in
mourning and arrange it so it provokes sadness."[9] In the following decades,
newly carved specialized Holy Week images began to be used in which mourning (of Mary) or scenes from the Passion (of Christ) were incorporated as part
of the imagery. In 1580 the Brotherhood of the Sepulcher of Jaén had a flexible
image of Christ that, on the appropriate day, they took down from the cross,
wrapped with a shroud, and placed in a tomb, "provoking many people to shed
tears." As in several Holy Week processions today, in seventeenth-century Jaén
an image of Mary was carried to meet an image of Christ in the streets. The
Marian image was articulated so that on meeting Christ her head nodded and
her arms stretched out to embrace her son, "which deeply moved those who,
in dramatic silence, observed it."[10] The weeping images of Mary were a way of

incorporating the profound Marian devotion of Iberia, evident in the vast majority of powerful shrines, in the heightened attention to the Passion of Christ.[11] Mary weeping was thus as much a model to imitate as Christ being whipped.[12]

This kind of Holy Week weeping survives today, the only collective religious weeping that I know of in present-day Spain. A Sevillano (with tears in his eyes) describes the weeping at the departure of La Macarena (a weeping Madonna) from her shrine on the night of Holy Thursday as "aesthetic tears." He does not consider himself a Catholic, and so refers to his attitude as "idolatry," but says it stems from an identification with La Macarena on a human level as a suffering person who is intensely loved. He says it probably also has to do with staying up all night, the end of winter, the scent of orange blossoms on the air, the full moon on Holy Thursday night, and the effect of a very realistic and artistic image. This kind of public weeping, then, like that of the crisis processions, was provoked by a religious dramaturgy in which relics, images, or people representing saints played an important part.

The weeping that stopped the bullfight at Gandia was provoked by a combination of penitential drama and preaching—symbolically from the *picota*, the place of punishment and symbol of secular justice. The Jesuits were effective practitioners of a long tradition of medieval preachers and celebrants who provoked tears, including, as Huizinga mentions, Vincent Ferrer and Bernardino. The quarterly letters of Jesuits houses to Loyola in Rome commonly refer to priests whose effectiveness is measured by their ability to make their audiences weep. The rector of Gandía, Juan Bautista la Barma, regularly made people weep who heard him say mass ("They cannot keep from weeping"). The sermons in Seville, wrote Gonsalvo González in January 1556,

> continue with much concourse of people and emotion and especial devotion, which the Lord gives them, of compunction and tears that they cannot stop; especially after some sermons about death and the judgment they went weeping and moaning in the streets, straightening out their lives and preparing to do penance.[13]

Like the weeping in penitential processions and that provoked by dramaturgy involving saints, weeping provoked by preachers also has its modern survivals, particularly in the sermons of missionaries, in Lent or at other times of the year. It was especially characteristic of famous charismatic preachers like Diego de Cádiz and Antonio Maria Claret, who, like Vincent Ferrer and Francisco Borja, were itinerant revivalists. In Lent 1919, the first time people saw the eyes of the famous Christ of Limpias (Santander) move and shed tears was immediately after the climactic mass, in which most people wept, of a week-long mission given by two Capuchin friars.[14] Spanish newspaper accounts show that weeping was common in the final days of missions conducted by Jesuits, Claretians, Redemptorists, Passionists, and Capuchins during the religious revival of 1947–54, particularly those associated with traveling statues

of the Virgin of Fatima. The more modern weeping, however, seem more limited to the services, more isolated in rural areas, and less vehement and spontaneous than that described in the Jesuit letters. In some American evangelical
churches, especially in Appalachia, weeping is still a common feature in ordinary Sunday services as well as revivals.[15]

Other incidents described in the Jesuits letters indicate that there was a
general easiness of tears, not only in ritual settings. When, on Palm Sunday
1553, Juan Bautista la Barma went from Gandía to another village to preach,
he was accompanied by many people he met along the way, in the manner of
Christ's entry into Jerusalem. As they proceeded together, he invited them to
tell how they had been blessed in their lives, and many of them wept. I cite
this incident at length because it provides a good example of the ambiance of
devotion in which so much of the public weeping took place:

> They went with him slowly, reciting a litany and invoking the angels
> and saints of the town they were going to. And then the Father said
> that since on that day Jerusalem had received the Lord with praises,
> they too should praise the Lord, each inviting the others to praise
> the Lord because of a personal blessing. The Father began, saying
> they should praise the Lord because He had made him a priest. An-
> other said because he had been a great sinner, had realized it, and
> now he wanted to serve God. Another, because he had been a *Moror*,
> but had been brought to his true understanding. Another, because
> he had been a great swearer and blasphemer and never tired in sin-
> ning, and then became very sick, at which time he realized what he
> was, and now he was well and wanted to serve God. In this way they
> walked on, each saying in turn so many things, and with so many
> tears, that it was heartbreaking.[16]

The tears were shed in public by single persons as well as person in groups.
After Lent in 1553 six brothers from the Jesuit house in Medina del Campo
received permission to *peregrinar*. Their chief purpose seems to have been to
edify. At one town they came across people dancing and enjoying themselves.
One of the brothers began to preach to them about heaven and the life of
Christ, and those who were dancing fell on their knees "to hear the word of
God with great attention and reverence." The village parish priest was there
and "went up to the pilgrims, prostrated himself, and weeping with great sorrow, with his white hair worthy of respect, said he was a great sinner, and that
for the love of God that they commend him to Our Lord." Another day they
came to a village where they heard there was a woman who had not spoken to
her relatives for seven years. "Then our brothers in their poor garments went
to the woman, and Our Lord gave them such words that not only did they
soften the woman's hard heart, they even broke it, and with tears and ardent
love she went to embrace her enemies."[17]

While the creativity and fervor of the early Jesuits (like that of Loyola himself) may have been especially strong stimulants to religious sensibilities, evidence from other sources (including extensive testimony in investigations of divine sings) supports the notion that at least in public, people in early modern Spain wept more easily than they do now.

Self-observation: Emotions as Signs

In early modern Spain, some emotions were considered a form of obscure communication; like dreams they were messages to be deciphered. For this purpose "emotion" must be considered equivalent to "feeling." People did not make such an arbitrary distinction as now between emotion and sensory perception, physical pain and sorrow, happiness and healthiness. People's emotions were a kind of test for their spiritual condition. One of the tasks of the spiritual directors of persons actively seeking holiness was to discern the meaning of their confessants' feelings. Because there was an important religious significance to unexplained emotional shifts and movements of the heart, lay people as well as religious were attentive to them.

In 1523 Francisca la Brava, the wife of a wool carder in the agricultural town of La Mota del Cuervo (Toledo), described to town authorities the emotional events leading up to her first vision of Mary. She was very attentive to her feelings: "She could not sleep the whole night because a sorrow [or pain] came to her heart, although in her face and body she did not feel bad, but rather healthy [or happy]." Sleepless, "she prayed to Our Lady the Virgin Mary to guide her in what was best for the salvation of her soul to a completely sound mind, and shortly after this she fell asleep." The next night the same thing happened. "She asked Our Lady, since she was so sad without knowing why, to guide her and tell her what was the cause of the great sorrow [or pain] she felt in her heart."[18]

Note how, in describing the pain and sorrow, Francisca located it in the heart, checking to make sure it was not in her face or body, and the important fact that it was a sadness she could not account for. This kind of attention to the heart's feelings as possible spiritual signs, I submit, has by and large disappeared. A modern equivalent might be the notion of a bad or guilty conscience, but one generally knows the cause of that, and in Francisca la Brava's case, the cause is unknown (and could even be unrelated to her actions).

Two years earlier, in 1521, a soldier named Ignatius Loyola was reading the lives of saints and the life of Christ while convalescing in the Basque country. He was struck by a correspondence between the emotions he felt and the thoughts he had been thinking. Later in life he described how he came to this perception:

When he thought about the profane world he had great pleasure,
but when he was tired of it he found himself dry and discontented;
and when he thought about going to Jerusalem barefoot, and eating
only herbs, and doing all the other privations that he saw the saints
had done, he was not only consoled while he was having these
thoughts, but he remained contented and happy afterward. At first
he did not notice this, or stop to think about the difference, until
one time when his eyes were opened a little, and he began to marvel
at this contrast and reflect upon it, learning by experience that from
some thoughts he remained sad and others, happy; and little by little
he came to know the difference in the spirits that were at work—
one of the devil, and the other of God.[19]

This perception, at the root of Loyola's conversion, was made an integral part
of his *Spiritual Exercises*. The tens of thousands of persons who followed the
exercises in early modern Europe were instructed to notice how they felt as
they said each word of their prayers, "noting and pausing at those points in
which I have felt more consolation or desolation or more spiritual feeling."
The range of possible feelings were described in detail in the commentary
accompanying the exercises, and rules were given "to feel and know the various
motions caused in the soul: the good ones so they will be received, and the
bad ones so they will be ejected." In this way those taking the exercises were
sensitized to the "reality" of the divine and the demonic at work within them.[20]

In 1527, when Loyola was a student at Alcalá, he was already giving rudi-
mentary exercises to a group of young women and having them pay attention
to their emotional states. María de la Flor, a young weaver who characterized
herself as someone who had been "a bad woman, who went with many students," told inquisitors investigating Loyola that after following him in prayer
for some weeks

four times there came to this witness very great sadness, and nothing seemed good to her, and she could not raise her eyes to look at
Ynigo; and that when she was sad and spoke with Ynigo or Calixto,
the sadness left her. And the wife of Benavente and her daughter
said they too experienced the same sadness, or even stronger. And
[María] asked Ynigo what that sadness was and where it came from.
And he said that when one enters the service of God the devil introduces it; and that she should remain strong in the service of God,
and that they were undergoing this for the love of God.[21]

Like Francisca la Brava, María de la Flor identified her sadness as spiritual.
Both sought guidance from religious sources—Francisca from the Virgin
Mary, and María from her spiritual guide. Even before consulting Loyola, how-

ever, María had noted when it came, how many times it came, and when it went away.

Loyola was hardly the inventor of the discernment of spirits by emotions, although his use of it as a tool of spiritual pedagogy was innovative. This kind of discernment dated from pre-Christian times, was approved by Church Fathers, and was commonly practiced by religious to know if they were being inspired by God or misled by the devil. In fifteenth-century Spain it was a criterion commonly used to test lay visionaries.[22] The printing of spiritual handbooks in romance in the first decades of the sixteenth century by Catherine of Siena, Angela of Foligno, Vincent Ferrer, and Francisco de Osuna gave to all who could read instructions for the evaluation of emotions. But when the Protestant heresies arose, autoevaluation of religious sentiment and inspiration was seen as a dangerous business.

For in practice it was very difficult to distinguish "true" from "false" happiness or consolation. Visionaries like Francisca la Brava and Jeanne d'Arc would insist that their visions made them happy and thereby acquire in their own minds a kind of immunity from the arguments put forth by their spiritual superiors. The Franciscan preacher Francisco Ortiz was sure, in the jail of the Inquisition of Toledo in 1529, that his friend the *beata* Francisca Hernández was doctrinally correct, he said, "because of the continued increase of holy joy and happiness that every day God gives in my soul for preaching against the culpable malfeasance of the representatives of the Inquisition." (Ortiz had been hauled out of the pulpit for denouncing the Inquisition after the beata's arrest.) The inquisitor asked him how he knew his feelings were not illusions of the devil. Ortiz replied, "For the devil never places truth in the heart nor a true despising of the world and of life in favor of God." Ortiz said he knew, "as the saints have said," that the devil can give "some sweetness and false happiness, but all the saints say that very soon the old serpent shows his tail and leaves the heart unquiet and sad: that this is the condition of miserable sin."

The inquisitor, however, had some counterexamples. "Sometimes there has been someone who despised the things of this world and received death willingly, affirming that he or she serves God and has the spirit of God, and the Church has held that person to be a heretic and in error." Fray Francisco allowed that the inquisitor had a point, but said that in those cases appearances were deceiving. "Many appear to despise the world who really do not, for they were really seeking their own glory, which they loved more than God. In that way many Romans died for honor, and many true heretics received death with outward signs of joy . . . [but inwardly] with proud and rebellious hearts, full of true sadness, confusion, and protest from the soul." His own feeling, however, he well knew. It was far from pride, and consisted only in love of God and humble subjection to the Church.

The inquisitor moved on to another matter; he was not convinced, and the formal charges eventually read that Ortiz had been tricked by the devil, but there was no way the inquisitor could prove how Ortiz felt, that only Ortiz could know. Ortiz eventually gave in when he learned that his friend Francisca, though still a virgin, was not as chaste as he had thought.[23] But his interrogation shows the problematic nature of the use of emotions to determine truth for a Church that considered itself beleaguered.[24]

One strategy to counter this situation was to limit information on the evaluation of spirits available to the lay public and to encourage individuals with spiritual questions to consult ordained directors. In 1559 much devotional literature in the vernacular was banned and burned. In one section left out of Juan de Avila's *Audi Filia* when it was reissued in 1574 were some signs for distinguishing true from false revelations; people were instead instructed to consult their spiritual director.[25]

This in fact controlled the problem only in part. For in practice the spiritual-minded who trusted their own reading of their emotions could look around until they found a spiritual director who agreed with them.[26] Teresa of Avila through much of her life was in doubt whether the consolations and graces she received were of God or the devil. Different confessors had different opinions. At one point six theologians were consulted; they agreed that it was the devil and instructed her to give it *higas*. Only gradually did a consensus emerge that her spirits and feelings were good ones, and even after her death there were efforts to ban her books. A chapter in her autobiography on the evaluation of the causes of emotions is as nuanced and subtle as that of Catherine of Siena. Reading emotions for their spiritual meaning, perhaps in part because it was so difficult, was a highly developed art.[27]

Tears as Evidence for Changes of Heart

The special arena of spiritual emotions was thought to be the heart.[28] That is where Francisca la Brava located her sorrow and what Francisco Ortiz referred to as the locus of emotional truth and demonic inquietude; it was the heart of the obdurate woman that was softened by the Jesuit brothers until it broke and she wept, and the hearts of onlookers and listeners that were broken by the Barcelona processional drama and the life histories that people told to each other on the way out of Gandía on Palm Sunday. *Hard-hearted, a change of heart, tenderhearted, heartrending,* and *brokenhearted* are terms that we still use in a secular sense. In sixteenth-century Spain they also had rather precise religious meanings derived from the Bible, referring to a person's relative openness to the love of God.

The eyes were thought to have a special connection to the heart, to express it to the outside. "I want you to know," said Catherine of Siena, "that every tear comes from the heart, for there is no part of the body that wants to satisfy the heart as much as the eye."[29] The Lord could hear hearts, but people could not. Because it was difficult for people to know the nature of the motions of their own hearts, much less anyone else's, outward signs like tears were especially important.

Weeping was one of the ways one could know one's own heart. According to Teresa of Avila, writing in 1562, seeing oneself weep was itself a consolation given by the Lord in return for devotion: "If [in contemplating the Passion] there is some love, the soul is rewarded, the heart is softened, and tears come; sometimes it seems we draw them out by force, other times the Lord seems to make it so we cannot resist them. It appears that His Majesty repays our small attention with a very great gift, which is the consolation that he gives a soul when *it sees itself weep* for such a great lord."[30] Perhaps some inkling of this kind of consolation is the kind of peace and calm one experiences after sympathetic weeping in films or at funerals.[31] Most devotional weeping (like Huizinga's example of St. Colette's mother, who wept daily for the Passion) was solitary and could be a visible sign of a softened heart only for the weeper.

Spiritual treatises in use in sixteenth-century Spain refer to a number of kinds of devotional tears, generally ranked in order of preferability. On the first level or levels were tears that purged sins; this was the kind most emphasized in most handbooks for lay people.

Though not obligatory, tears were considered a favorable sign of contrition.[32] "Our tears have great force before God," wrote El Tostado. He instructed sinners "to have sorrow for their sins, moving themselves to sorrow and tears the most that they can, for because of this sorrow their sins will be forgiven."[33] "Tears wash sins away" begins a chapter on tears of a fifteenth-century book of exempla.[34] Juan de Avila recounted the story of Hezekiah from Isaiah (38: 4) to show the power of tears: "Hezekiah turned his head to the wall and wept with many tears, asking the Lord for mercy. . . . he asked the judge himself to be his lawyer, appealing from the just to the merciful. His defense is self-accusation; his rhetoric is sobs and tears." The Lord answered, "I heard your heart and I saw your tears," and granted him fifteen more years of life. Avila apostrophized on this sudden suspension of the Lord's punishment as a result "of a few tears, shed not in the temple, but in a corner of a bed, and not by eyes looking to the sky, but rather at a wall, and not by a just man, but by a sinner." He told the sinner to take heart "and humble yourself weeping to him whom you ignored while sinning, and receive forgiveness from he who wants so much to give it to you."[35]

Like tears of contrition, tears wept externally in the contemplation of the Passion were thought to have a purgative effect on sins, and in Spain this remained the great spiritual exercise of the sixteenth century.[36] The *Vita Christi* of Ludolphus of Saxony, first published in Catalan in 1495–1500 and Castilian in 1502–3, was one of the books Ignatius Loyola was reading when he reached his understanding of spiritual emotions. "El Cartujano," as the author was known, invited the reader to "understand, contemplate, weep over, and feel the course of this most holy death." In reading the Passion, one was encouraged to experience an ordered series of emotions, one of which, compassion, would call forth tears.[37]

Wept under these circumstances, tears would have great value.

> The extent of the efficacy of tears shed in prayer, and particularly in memory of the passion of Christ is very clear from a certain person's revelation. The Lord appeared to the person in spirit and said: "If anyone in memory of my passion weeps tears with devotion, I wish to take them into my kingdom as if they had suffered for me." So that when a man remembers this *paso* [Christ sweating blood in Gethsemane] he should fall to the ground on his face, praying with the heart . . . and try as hard as he can to have tears, having compassion and sorrow for Jesus Christ. And if the eyes, tired from love, will not shed them, shed them at least with the will.[38]

Similarly, Loyola instructed the participants in the first week of his spiritual exercises to try to weep: "And here begin with much effort to force [yourself] to sorrow, mourn, and weep, and continue doing so while considering the following points."[39]

In her *Life*, Teresa of Avila recounts episodes of purgative weeping. "I felt so bad for not having thanked [Christ] for those wounds that my heart was rending, and I threw myself next to Him [a crucifix] with copious weeping, asking Him to fortify me once and for all so I would not offend Him." Earlier, her failure to weep when reading the Passion at age sixteen (in 1531) she attributed to a hardness of heart: "And if I saw a [nun] have tears when she prayed, or other graces, I was very envious of her, for my heart was so tough (*recio*) that if I read the entire Passion I would not shed a single tear; this caused me sorrow."

For Teresa the contemplation of the Passion was the beginning stage in a spiritual progress. "In thinking about and dwelling on what the Lord underwent for us we are moved to compassion, and this pain and the tears that result from it are savory."[40] Similarly, Tomás of Villanueva, the Augustinian saint who was archbishop of Valencia, wrote in his *Brief Way of Serving Our Lord*, "Our soul considers our Redeemer bound to the column or nailed on the cross and understands that the innocent Lamb suffers for our sins. From this consideration one becomes sad, moans, and weeps for having offended God and caused his death. This way is called purgative, for by it one purges one's sins." Following earlier treatises, he presented the purgative as the first step in a spiritual progression.[41]

Spiritual writers agreed there were other, "higher" kinds of weeping. Frequent tears were a feature of early Cistercian spirituality. The *Liber Miraculorum* of Caesarius of Heisterbach has many cases of copiously weeping monks and nuns. Tears were some monks' greatest desire, the source of vainglory for others ("How I wish there was someone here to see this grace of mine!"), and their absence was considered a spiritual trial.[42] For Catherine of Siena the highest form of tears, higher than those of contrition, are those wept when one is not concerned with self at all, but only in the love of others and of God.[43]

Spiritual weeping was an important element in recollection (*recogimiento*), a form of Franciscan spirituality popularized by Francisco de Osuna and considered by him an alternative to contemplation of the Passion. Its practitioners tried to clear their minds for God's grace and consolations, and tears were both a technique and a result of the method. For beginners they were wept with effort and were weapons to use in obtaining grace, like those of contrition. For the more advanced they were like a fountain ("issuing without moan or sigh hot from the heart and flowing easily from the eyes without interior or exterior noise, for these people are not thinking of things to provoke their crying, but only attempting to recollect their hearts"). And for the perfect they were a fountain that was ever-running, effortless tears of joy. Osuna was proud to say that "weeping comes more easily to the followers of recollection than to other people."[44]

Teresa of Avila, who learned the method from Osuna's book, experienced this "gift of tears," as did Ignatius Loyola, whose spiritual diary (1544–45) is in large part a record of the occasions on which tears came to him in prayer, the diary itself being a prime example of the observation of one's own emotions. For Loyola also, the most preferable tears were those "in consideration of or love for Divine Persons." Laínez, who succeeded Loyola as the head of the order, observed Loyola in prayer on a terrace in Rome. First Loyola took off his hat and looked at the sky, then he knelt and made a reverence to God, then he sat on a small bench, too old and weak to kneel for long. "There he remained, his head uncovered, weeping two trails of tears with such softness and silence that one heard no sob or moan, nor any movement of the body."[45]

I doubt that this kind of mystical weeping was widespread in early modern Spain. But saints weeping this way were painted in pictures and described in books, and it would have been clear to the faithful that in addition to purgative weeping there were other kinds performed by the spiritually advanced.

Public Tears as Evidence of Collective Contrition

In most of the instances given at the beginning of this paper, the collective public weeping was purgative in nature. In the crisis processions it would be an acknowledgment of collective sin in the hope of receiving the kind of forgiveness Hezekiah received for his tears on a collective basis, a collective appeal to the merciful God from the just God to avert plague, drought, locusts, military defeat, and other collective afflictions. The Holy Week processions and the Lenten and revival sermons provoked on a collective level the kind of purgative weeping encouraged in the private contemplation of the Passion. Processions in Holy Week, in which the home town became Jerusalem, were efficient ways to provoke compassion and tears that served the purgation not only of the individuals in question, but also of towns as collectivities. They thereby averted, hopefully, future collective punishments from God. There was thus a collective, as well as individual, economy of sentiment.

Such weeping had to be public. In these collective situations it was as important to see your neighbor's tears as your own, for only if tears were shed generally could it be known that the hearts of the entire community had been moved. Hence drama that provoked collective weeping did not merely serve an individual's spiritual promotion; it was also a way to know by tears, the outward signs of the heart, that collective repentence was in progress.

Small wonder, then, given theological notions of the times, that people were easily moved to tears. A certain kind of tenderheartedness and consequent weeping was of vital practical importance to communities, as well as of spiritual importance to individuals. Without it God would not be moved. Weeping was not, as Huizinga would have it, the expression of a childlike sensibility that we have largely outgrown. Emotions were serious business; provoked, collective, weeping could be effective. One is tempted to say it was rational to weep. A science for provoking public tears and compassion existed, with specialized artists, sculptors, choreographers, and actors.

Note that this was a tenderness of heart in relation to Christ above all, not necessarily to other people. The ruthlessness of the Spanish reaction to the iconoclasts of the Netherlands was doubtless due at least in part to the particular nature of this tenderness, which was above all cultivated through the contemplation of images of the Passion and the imitation of the Passion in penitential behavior. From a Spanish Catholic's perspective, the destroyers of images were willfully repeating the Passion that the Spaniard had been taught to contemplate and weep over. Teresa of Avila could not understand those who did away with images, for she could not do without them:

> I had so little ability to represent things in my mind, except for what
> I could see. I could profit nothing from my imagination, [unlike]
> other persons who can see things in their minds wherever they pray.
> ... for this reason I was such a friend of images. Unhappy those
> who by their fault lose this good! It surely seems that they do not
> love the Lord, for if they loved him, they would delight in seeing his
> portrait, just as here one is still happy to see someone one loves
> dearly.[46]

Afterthoughts

Obvious factors in the relative incidence and intensity of emotions in a given society are external conditions such as nutrition, climate, and the level of security. Less obvious but perhaps equally important are the societal solutions to the universal problem of maintaining a relative psychological balance or homeostasis in individuals.[47] People in society produce their own stimuli—entertainment in the form of theater, games, celebrations, religious rituals—that provoke necessary emotions, whether laughter and fun, tension and release, or weeping and sorrow.

Weeping appears to be involved in the reduction of stress, the relief of suffering, and the release of tension.[48] Surely these must be some of the psychological byproducts of (or equivalents for) grace, atonement, and consolation. In early modern Spain they were obtained on an individual and communal basis by the cultivation at a high pitch of sympathetic sorrow. So that while people might consciously manipulate their emotions for religious purposes, the strictly emotional consequences were real and no doubt effective in and of themselves. In some churches in the mountains of West Virginia, according to K. Stewart (unpublished data), a similar process appears to serve people as well now as it did in Spain four hundred years ago.

In *The Civilizing Process*, Norbert Elias has addressed some of the ways body functions have been privatized over the intervening centuries through the spread of notions of decorum from centers of power. The privatization of weeping also corresponds to a de-emphasis in theology on punishment and contrition and the virtual disappearance of the notion of collective community responsibility to God. I am unsure whether the tension, stress, and suffering that public weeping addressed has been reduced or merely transferred to issues that are considered personal and not soluble by collective ritual.

NOTES

Many people contributed to this essay with suggestions and references. I am particularly grateful to F. Márquez Villanueva, K. Stewart, T. Tentler, R. Trexler, T. Yager, and L. W. Bonbrake. I wrote this essay while on a fellowship from the American Council of Learned Societies with funds provided by the National Endowment for the Humanities.

    1. J. Huizinga, *The Waning of the Middle Ages* (London: Edwin Arnold, 1963), 1–3, 173–175, 182.
    2. A. Radcliffe-Brown, *The Andaman Islanders* (Cambridge, UK: Cambridge University Press, 1922), 116–117, 238–243; C. Wagley, *Welcome of Tears: The Tapirapa Indians of Central Brazil* (Oxford: Oxford University Press, 1978); E. De Martino, *Morte e pianto rituale nel mondo antico dal lamento pagano al pianto di Maria* (Torino: Edizioni Scientifiche Einaudi, 1958).

3. Huizinga, 3.

4. *Dietari* of Barcelona, *Manual de Novells Ardits* (Barcelona: Henrich, 1894), 3: 201.

5. *Litterae Quadrimestres* (Madrid: Augusintus Avrial, 1894–1897), 1: 724–744; 8: 31–1552. Hereafter cited as *LQ*.

6. Ibid., 2: 58, 11: 14–1552.

7. W.A. Christian Jr., *Local Religion in Sixteenth Century Spain* (Princeton: Princeton University Press, 1981), 182–190; G. Llompart, *Desfile iconográfico de penitents españoles* (siglos xvi al xx). *Revista de Dialectología y Tradiciones Populares* (1969), 25: 32–51; G. Llompart, *Penitencias y penitents en la pintura y en la piedad catalanas bajomedievales. Revisata de Dialectogía y Tradiciones Populares* (1972), 28: 299–249.

8. Biblioteca de la Real Academia de la Real Academia de Historia, Madrid, Collección Salazar N-7, folios 294–301, an untitled manuscript memoir dated June 10, 1596 by Pedro Gómez Molino about the devotion of the town of Ajofrín to the shrine of Mary in San Pablo de los Montes. 295v: "Vo de xl años a esta pte me e hallado en muchas digas de memoria y q verdaderamente se pueden dezir proçesiones por ser hechas con mucha deuocion y derramami° de lagrimas y avn de sangre y muchos pies descalços . . . 297r: yban como verdaderos penitentes sin hablarse vna palabra uno a otro sino los rosarios en sus manos los pies descalços las lagrimas por sus mexillas . . . 297v: y en el camino los regalaron mucho y fueron muy bien recebidos con muschas lagrimas y disciplinas." For the complete Spanish text of the Ajofrín account, see Christian, *Religiosidad local en la España de Felipe II* (Madrid: Nerea, 1991), 227–298. For processions and weeping, see also Richard C. Trexler, *Public Life in Renaissance Florence* (New York: Academic Press, 1980).

9. Juan de Avila, *Avisos y reglas cristianas sobre aquel verso de David: Audi, Filia (1555)* (Barcelona: Flors, 1969), 2642, my italics: "Cuando quieren sacar una imagen, para hecer llorar, vistenla de luto y pónenle todo lo que incita a tristeza."

10. R. Ortega Sagrista, "Historia de las cofradías de la Pasíoon de Semana Santa," *Boletín del Instituto de Estudios Giennesis* 3, no. 10 (1956): 32, 39.

11. See table of shrines to Mary compared with those to other saints and Christ in Christian, *Local Religion*, 74.

12. Shiite Moslem weeping of a more violent nature, accompanied by flagellation, occurs in a commemoration similar to Holy Week, the ten days of mourning for Husayn, the prophet Muhammed's martyred grandson; M.M.J. Fischer, *Ivan, from Religious Dispute to Revolution* (Cambridge: Harvard University Press, 1980).

13. *LQ,* 2: 212, 4:6–1553, 84.

14. *Diario Montañés* 4: 8–1919.

15. Kathleen Stewart, unpublished field notes on the region of Beckley, West Virginia, 1981.

16. *LQ* 2: 212–213, 4: 6–1553: "Que era para quebrantar los coraçones."

17. Ibid., 2: 269–270, 5: 4–1553: "No solamente ablandaron el corazon duro de la mujer, mas aún lo quebrantaron."

18. Cited in Christian, *Local Religion*, 164–165, 315–317.

19. I. Loyola, *Obras completas* (Madrid: Biblioteca de Autores Cristianos, 1947), 1: 133–134.

20. I. Loyola, *Exercitia Spiritualia* (*MHSI* 100, Rome: Institutum Historicum Societatis Iesu, 1969), 198, 374–394.

21. I. Loyola, *Scripta* (*MHSI 25*, Madrid: López del Horno, 1904), 1: 612–613; María de la Flor, testifying on May 10, 1527 in the third Alcalá investigation of Loyola by the Inquisition of Toledo.

22. Christian, *Local Religion*, 193, 199–201.

23. A. Selke, *El Santo Oficio de la Inquisición: Proceso de Fr. Francisco Ortiz (1529–1532)* (Madrid: Ediciones Guadarrama, 1968), 131–133, 204, 209.

24. A. Huerga, *Historia de los alumbrados* (Madrid: Fundación Universitaria Española, 1978), 1: 407–411, 430–431.

25. *Avisos y reglas*, 48–49. See introduction by Luis Sala Balust. Juan de Avila, following Gerson, had played down the use of emotions of joy or sorrow for discernment, instead emphasizing the seers' pride or humility and the veracity and orthodoxy of the vision messages (203–20).

26. This was commonly the case with urban beatas investigated by the Inquisition of Toledo in the late sixteenth and early seventeenth centuries.

27. Teresa de Jesús, *Obras Completas* (Madrid: Bibliotheca de Autores Cristianos, 1967), chapter 25; Caterina de Siena, *Il Libro* [*The Dialogues*] (n.p.: Edizione Paoline, 1969), 284–287; Tomás de Villanueva (1488–1555), *Sermón sobre la Anunciación de la Virgen María* in *Obras* (Madrid: Bibliotheca de Autores Cristianos, 1952), 236–239.

28. On the symbolism of the heart see bibliography in G. Brauer, *Claustrum Animae* I (Munich: Wilhelm Fink Verlag, 1973).

29. Caterina de Siena, *Il Libro* [*The Dialogues*], 235: "Io voglio che tu sappi che ogni lagrima procede dal cuore, perché neuno membro e nel corpo che voglia tanto satisfare al cuore quanto l'occhio."

30. Teresa de Jesús, *Libro de la vida*, 10:2, my italics: "Parece nos paga Su Magestad aquel cuidadito con un don tan grande, combo es el consuelo que da a un alma ver que llora por tan gran Señor."

31. It has been suggested that such weeping may be a way of eliminating toxic substances from the body and redressing a chemically based emotional imbalance. W.H. Frey II, "Not-So-Idle Tears," *Psychology Today* (January 1980).

32. T. N. Tentler, *Sin and Confession on the Eve of the Reformation* (Princeton: Princeton University Press, 1977), 237–248.

33. A. Tostado, *Tratado de confession llamado tostado.* (Alcala de Henares: Arnao guillen de brocar, 1517), a ii v°, a v r°, E. Hernández Garcia, *Guiones para un cursillo práctico de dirección espiritual* (Comillas, Santander: Pont. Univ. Comillensis, 1960), 322. This publication is evidence that the discernment of spirits and the cultivation of private devotional tears continue in modern Spain.

34. *El Especulo de los legos* (Madrid: Consejo Superior de Investigaciones Cientificas, 1951), 246.

35. Juan de Avila, *Avisos y reglas*, 217–219.

36. M. Bataillon, *Erasmo y España* (Mexico City: Fondo de Culture, 1966); *Corrientes Espirituales en la España del siglo XVI* (Barcelona: Flors, 1963).

37. Ludolphus de Saxonia, *Vita cristi romãçado por fray ambrosio* (Alcalá, 1502–1503), ch. 58, 48rv. 55r.

38. Ibid., vol. 4, ch. 59, 65v: "Pues quando el hombre se acordare deste paso: derribese en tierra sobre su cara orando con el coraçon . . . r esfuerçe quanto pudiere por tener lagrimas aviendo conpasion r dolor de jesu christo. E fatigados por amor/ r

si por los ojos aviendo conpasion r dolor de jesu christo. E fatigados por amor/ r si por los ojos no las pudiere derramar: derramar: a lo menos con la voluntad."

39. Loyola, *Exercitia Spiritualia*, 282, 214, 374.

40. Teresa de Jesús, *Libro de la vida*, 9: 1, 12:1, 3:1.

41. Thomás de Villanueva, *Obras* (Madrid: Biblioteca de Autores Cristianos, 1952), 511.

42. Caesarious of Heisterbach, *Dialogue on Miracles* (London: Routledge, 1929), bk. 1, ch. 35; bk. 2: 19–22; bk. 4: 30; bk. 8: 11–13.

43. Caterina da Siena, *Il Libro*, 233–361.

44. Francisco de Osuna, *Tercer abecedario espirtual (1527)* (Madrid: Biblioteca de Autores Cristianos, 1972), 334–353. On the practice of the method, see the introduction by Melquiades Anderés. Also see M. Andres, *Los recogidos* (Madrid: Fundación Universitaria Española, 1976), and A. Selke, *El Santo Oficio de la Inquisición; proceso de Fr. Francisco ortiz (1529–1532)* (Madrid: Ediciones Guadarrama, 1968), 239–243.

45. Loyola, *Obras completas*, 1: 644–645; Ignatius Loyola, letter to Francisco Borja, IX-20-1548, and Pedro de Ribadeneira, *Vida de San Ignacio* I 325; both cited by V. Larrañaga in his introduction to the *Diario Espiritual* (Loyola, *obras completas*, 644–645).

46. Teresa de Jesús, *Libro de la vida*, 9:6.

47. H. M. Rosenthal, "On the Function of Religion in Culture," *Review of Religion* 5 nos. 2, 3 (January, March, 1941).

48. C. Darwin, *The Expression of the Emotions in Man and Animals* (London: John Murray, 1872); Frey, "Not-So-Idle Tears."

2

Hierarchy and Emotion: Love, Joy, and Sorrow in a Cult of Black Saints in Gujarat, India

Helene Basu

In investigating the worship of Sufi saints in India, Helene Basu has focused on the emotional coding that lies at the center of those devotions. She demonstrates that within the cult certain emotional states are associated with masculinity and femininity and that they are connected as well to cultural notions of hot and cold, good and evil, pure and impure, virility, fertility, and nurture. Her interpretation of the rituals of three Sufi groups takes as a primary context the caste system, which ranks participants socially. But she then explains how the emotional component of ritual (linked as it is to many other aspects of religious belief and practice) is crucial to the construction of a counterdiscourse that reverses the status order. Black beggars, normally consigned to the lowest ranks, are elevated to superior position in the overlapping cosmic and social orders through ritual that exploits weaknesses in cultural definitions of emotion. In this study, then, we find an approach that draws new conclusions about the meanings of religious ritual by approaching it through analysis of its emotional components.

How does the focus on emotion disclose networks of meaning in the religious life of these Sufis? In what ways are overlapping contexts for religious and social life focused on emotion? How is emotion conceived and how is it performed in these rituals? What is the nature of evil for participants in the cult? In what ways is cosmic disorder addressed through the cultivation of certain emotional states? How is personal and social trans-

Helene Basu, "Hierarchy and Emotion: Love, Joy, and Sorrow in a Cult of Black Saints in Gujarat, India," in *Embodying Charisma: Modernity, Loyalty, and the Performance of Emotion in Sufi Cults*, ed. Pnina Werbner and Helene Basu (New York: Routledge, 1998), 117–139. Used by permission of the publisher.

formation accomplished through the cultivation of emotion, and how is a discourse of emotion deployed to challenge established social orders of purity and pollution? To what extent are emotions ambivalent for these Sufis?

Introduction: The Hierarchy of Saints' Cults

Sufism is often presented as a realm of Islamic emotional discourse opposed to the cold and "technical" constructions put forward by theologians and judicial scholars.[1] The core of Sufi mysticism consists of divine love conceptualized as inner experiences of growth and realization in the relationship between individual worshippers and a saint.[2] Such concepts, historically developed by Sufi literati, also shape contemporary cults of saints. Emotional experiences, especially love (*'isha, muhabbat*), are crucial to Sufi practices.[3] It would be misleading, however, to assume that the meanings of these terms always accord with those established by the textual tradition. Nor do they refer exclusively to inner experiences of the self characteristic of Western individualism. Rather, they are constituted situationally in social discourses by eliciting and evaluating social relationships.[4] In some cults, as in the one I deal with below, emotional constructs are used to enact hierarchical relationships *against* dominant social and moral evaluations. It is this connection between constructions of emotions and the creation of a counterhegemonic worldview, one that seeks to give asymmetrical ritual exchanges a different meaning, that is the subject of the present essay.

In Gujarat, Muslim conceptions of social hierarchy are often merged with ideas about the embodied charisma of saints.[5] Shrine cults revolve around exchanges of ritual services and gifts between unequals, and the rank of different regional cults, coexisting within a single area, may be inferred from the direction of the gifts between cults. The most important cult centers are managed by *Sayyid pirs*, who deny taking gifts altogether but assert their supreme status by displaying generosity and giving. God is perceived as the ultimate source of wealth, and Sayyid pirs act as mediators through whom the grace of Allah flows downwards.[6] The poor, on the other hand, appear as paradigmatic recipients of the grace of superiors. In the moral vision animating ritual worship at saints' cults, the poor are elevated as the subjects of specific saintly love because of the purity of their faith. According to Pinto, divine love is a mystery that should be received in the same way a poor person reciprocates, with "gratefulness, faith and a pure heart."[7]

Besides those shrine cults that are dominated by high-status Sayyids, credited with inherited charisma originating in the family of the Prophet, there are cults venerating non-Sayyid saints who derive their charisma from other sources. The cult I am concerned with here is managed by *faqirs* of black

African saints said to be descended from Bilal, an Ethiopian who was the companion of the Prophet Muhammad. In Islamic history, Bilal is famous for his loyalty to the Prophet and recognized as the first to call the faithful to prayer at the mosque. In Gujarat, the cult of black saints, an assembly referred to as *kulpir* (clan saints), is a cult of the poor, managed by a small African diaspora who identify themselves as *Sidi faqirs*. For them, the idea of the "pure love" that saints in general are said to harbor for the poor is of great importance in constructing a self-image that reconciles ideas of moral and ritual superiority with the acceptance of alms.

When the Sidi in Gujarat talk about the cult of Bava Gor, emotional concepts such as love (*muhabbat*), joy (*maja*), and sorrow (*dukh*) are often evoked in association with social relations between supplicants and Sidi saints, and between Sidi and Sayyid saints, both of which are governed by hierarchical exchanges of gifts and services.

Dumont defines the notion of hierarchy in terms of a logic of encompassment by higher of lower levels and their situational reversal of qualities such as purity and pollution.[8] A similar hierarchical logic is operative in the realm of Muslim shrines, in which the pure saint encompasses the impure temporal order. Against this logic, the Sidi operate through a complementary and encompassing logic of heating and cooling. Hot and cold qualities are understood as embodiments of ethically grounded emotions,[9] and their use by the Sidi inverts the hierarchy of purity and pollution by posing an alternative moral order which is also connected to fertility and social reproduction. This is of critical importance when looking at the regional cult hierarchy in Gujarat from the point of view of those who represent the lower pole, in this case the Sidi. It highlights the fact that shrine hierarchies are not merely imposed givens but are constantly created and recreated through asymmetrical social interactions. Cosmologically, the hierarchies are articulated by the Sidi through the complex of relations said to exist among saints, demons, and humans.

In Gujarat, Muslims represent a heterogeneous social ensemble comprising about 10 percent of the population. Organized in different castes and sects (Sunni and Shi'a), the higher categories correspond principally to the pattern prevalent in north India (where they are called *ashraf*, the "noble ones"), whereas the middle and lower rungs display regional particularity. As elsewhere, the Sayyid are accorded the highest prestige due to their claim of descent from the family of the Holy Prophet through his daughter Fatimah. On the basis of notions of genealogical closeness to the Prophet, the Sayyid claim an inherited charisma, in the form of *baraka* (blessings, spiritual power) and *karāmāt* (capacity to perform miracles), that is manifested and routinized in shrines managed by their families. Inheritable charisma ("blood") distinguishes Sayyid from all other Muslim castes.[10] A large section of Muslims in Gujarat belongs to one of the many regional trading castes such as *Bohra* (or *Vohra*), *Memmon*, *Khoja*, and *Khatri*, settled mostly in town.

The Sidi constitute one of several other Muslim servant castes who are also predominantly urban based. They, however, differ from other servant castes due to their African origin. They are descendants of slaves from the shores of East Africa who were sold in western India until the late nineteenth century, often by Muslim traders.[11] The Sidi in Gujarat number around six thousand to seven thousand, and some live in town working as domestics. Yet, while acknowledging the ritual superiority of the Sayyid, the Sidi claim a similar though lower-order charisma transmitted by birth from their African saintly ancestors. Most Sidi are convinced that a special *bakshish* (gift) has been bestowed on them by their apical ancestor, Bilal.

Despite systematic attacks by Muslim reformers, ritual worship at saints' shrines remains for many Muslims an expression of true faith. In Gujarat, the hierarchical network connecting shrines is controlled by men. Status differences between shrines and their spiritual representatives are emphasized by a terminology distinguishing Sayyid from non-Sayyid saints. The Sidi address only Sayyid saints with the title *pir*, whereas the term *murshid* or *faqir* denotes a holy person from their own *jama'at* (caste) or any other non-Sayyid social category.[12]

The Sidi maintain many small shrines all over Gujarat. In each of their settlements there is at least one shrine housing ancestor saints, but the highest place is accorded the shrine of Bava Gor in South Gujarat (another large shrine, Nagarchi Pir, is situated at Saurashtra). The three saints enshrined at Bava Gor—the elder brother, Bava Gor, his sister, Mai Mishra, and his younger brother, Bava Habash—are regarded as the founding ancestors of the Sidi *jama'at*. Bava Gor is the largest shrine maintained by the Sidi and the only one that provides a basic livelihood to a few families. Those Sidi who perform ritual services on behalf of the ancestor saints are distinguished as faqirs, a term that in this context includes women as well, unlike the Malang described by Ewing.[13] The role of a faqir is explained in two ways: as a spontaneous charismatic calling based on a *hukm* (order) received from one of the ancestor saints, or as privileged access to shrine service inherited from a kinsman or kinswoman.

Whereas in the past the shrine seems to have been mainly a centre for Sidi faqirs, their families, and peasants from the area, during the past thirty years the cult following has expanded considerably. In addition to "Tribals" (Bhil) and Hindus from surrounding towns and villages, the *dargah* (court or shrine) of Bava Gor is visited by an ever increasing number of Muslims. In the large industrial centers such as Surat, Bharuch, Baroda, and Ahmadabad, the *dargah* has, since the mid-1980s, been discovered as a major destination of weekly pilgrimages. Followers originate from an urban, lower-middle-class milieu, many from the Sunni Bohra caste. The clientele includes shopkeepers, small traders, manufacturers, artisans, and workers from the industrial cities of mainland Gujarat, all of whom visit the shrine on a regular basis. This trend is also noticeable in the shift in the day of the week attracting the most visitors.

Whereas formerly it was Thursdays, the day reserved for the memory of the dead, which drew the largest crowds (around 150–200), nowadays Sundays tend to be even busier. Such expansion and shifts in the cult clientele are accompanied, moreover, by changes in its organizational structure.

Legally, the shrine falls under the laws of the religious endowment act, which places it under state control vested in the charity commissioner. Formally managed by a trust consisting of three male members—two Bohras, one Sidi—control over the shrine and access to its ritual positions have long since been contested among different Sidi factions. Conflicts over traditional rights at the shrine originated in the 1970s, when the charity commissioner's officers charged the customarily installed *mujavirs* (officiating faqirs) with misuse of religious donations and subsequently dismissed them from their offices. Many Sidi emphasize that until this time the shrine was managed on behalf of the jama'at as a whole. Shrine services were carried out by three faqir families taking weekly turns. In addition, Sidi faqirs fulfilled several distinct roles related to the performance of specific shrine rituals. Authority over shrine rituals was held by the elders, several of whom happened to be women. At the occasions of large shrine festivals, gifts of money and natural products given to the saints were redistributed among the other members of the Sidi jama'at. Whereas the traditional system focused on the collectivity as a whole, the intervention by state agencies into the formal organization of the cult resulted in the centralization of authority in the family of the Sidi trustee and an increasing dependence or marginalization of other Sidi.

Gender and the Cosmic Order

The Sidi cult differs importantly from other saint cults practiced in the area in the emphasis it places on complementary male and female ritual domains. Although most dargahs of Muslim saints contain tombs of female relatives within their precincts, these are usually not treated as the object of special ritual attention. Such tombs are declared sacred and accorded respect by virtue of the dead saint's relation to deceased kinswomen buried there. By contrast, the sister of Bava Gor, Mai Mishra, occupies a central, designated symbolic space associated with values of femininity. To worship Mai Mishra requires the performance of rituals by women. Moreover, complementing the exclusion of women from the inner sanctum of a Sayyid shrine[14] no men may enter or touch the interior of the shrine of the female saint. Close contact with Mai Mishra is restricted to women, who also keep the tomb and receive the offerings of visiting devotees.

In this and other ways Sidi women are actively involved in the routine of the shrine. Those who organize rituals and other services mostly belong to the households of men employed by the trust as mujavir. The shrine of the female saint Mai Mishra is looked after by the female members (wife, daughters, and daughters-in-law) of the household of the Sidi trustee. On Thursdays and Sundays, when pilgrims visit the shrine in greater numbers, other Sidi women sit at one of the many tombs scattered over the landscape—which do not fall under the direct management of the trust—ready to receive alms (jakat).

The ideology of the cult of Bava Gor is embedded in a cosmology that places God (Allah) over and above a hierarchy of saints, humans, and (Satanic) demons. The cosmic order is structured by Sufi principles of closeness and distance to God that define high (uncha) and low (niche) status. Saints are closer to God and higher than human beings, to whom they mediate his grace. Among themselves, saints are divided according to the same principles. Situated beneath the level of humans, the lowest category of beings, comprising demons and evil spirits, is not only distant from but opposed to God.

The distinctions among saints, humans, and demons may be conceptualized in terms of the relation between "type" and "token" suggested by Valerio Valeri, according to which the deity is "a paragon for empirical actions and subjects . . . and endows their actions with significance."[15] Applying this to our context, saints and demons represent opposed types of positively and negatively evaluated exemplary moral person. At the same time, both work on each other through human embodiment and mediation, as human actions and conditions may instantiate either saintly or demonic attributes. In Sidi discourse, qualities of hot and cold are critical characterizations of saints and demons. But when attempting to ascertain their respective values, what becomes evident is the fundamental ambivalence inherent in these qualities: they refer metonymically to both physical and mental processes, to fertility, death, gender, power, ecstasy, possession, emotion, purity, and impurity. They are thus manifestations of a scale of evaluation that depends on relationships and transformation.

The hierarchy produced by the categories of heat and coolness is in continuous oscillation, displaying reversals and combinatorial juxtapositions. The Sidi hierarchy appears itself as a reversal: the assembly of Sidi saints is divided by gender according to a male-female duality as represented by the brothers (Bava Gor and Bava Habash) and the sister (Mai Mishra). At the same time, they refer to ancillary forms of dual hierarchies of male and female saints. Bava Gor encompasses a group of subordinate, locally enshrined brother saints, Mai Mishra a group of seven sisters. But whereas the category of male saints is internally divided according to senior and junior status, the category of female saints remains undifferentiated. Mai Mishra represents female to male as a sister-brother relationship, as well as female relationships between sisters unaffected by seniority.

The spatial pattern of the tombs provides another clue to the relationship between brothers and sister. The tombs of the three saints are situated on top of a series of hills rising abruptly from the plains below. That of the elder brother, Bava Gor, is sheltered by the largest shrine, indicating by its architecture its position at the apex of the shrine hierarchy. Attached to it is a small mosque. At the left, somewhat behind the sanctuary of Bava Gor but on the same hill, lies the shrine of the sister, smaller in size and placed at the back. The female saint's subordinate position in relation to the male saints is implied by the spatial order. Further away, on a second hill, rests the tomb of the younger brother, Bava Habash. It is slightly bigger than Mai Mishra's but smaller than the shrine of Bava Gor. This spatial constellation maps the asymmetry between brothers, defined by order of seniority, and the closeness between brothers and sisters.

The male-female bisection of the saintly order is matched by a similar division between demons or spirits (*bhut*) and saints. While the latter reside in higher spheres ("up" on a hill), demons inhabit the lower realms, an underworld beneath the earth. The category of bhut includes the restless spirits of men or women who died an unnatural death or the sexually lustful and amoral male and female *jinn* (spirits). All of them are classified as hot. The bhut prefer impure, filthy surroundings such as cremation places, graveyards, and public latrines. Jealous of the power of the saints, spirits make use of human bodies to destroy the moral order and to satisfy their own greedy desires. According to a psychoanalytic interpretation put forward by Sudhir Kakar, spirits "are the reification of certain unconscious fantasies of men and women which provoke strong anxiety in the Indian cultural setting."[16] However, as Kapferer has convincingly shown, demonic illness cannot be reduced to the individual that is the focus of Western therapeutical models.[17] It involves not only the social context of a patient but also, more generally, the society as a whole. Seen at this level, demons and malign spirits are reifications of social disorder. When low and impure spirits take control over human beings, the hierarchical social order is threatened.

Healing Cosmic Disorder

In the context of the cult of Bava Gor, the healing of possession is seen more as a means of countering a cosmic threat to the hierarchical order than as a cure centered on the individual patient. Attacking their victims from below, through the genitals and excretory organs, male spirits may demand sexual intercourse with female victims of possession, whereas female spirits crave the blood (semen) of men.

Both saints and demons are distinguished by their thermodynamic qualities of heat and coolness. According to dominant taxonomies, being cool carries superior value. In relation to humans, saints pirs are said to be cold because they have overcome the hot *nafs* (desiring soul), that is, the instinctual, "animal" nature of humans.[18] Whereas nafs are classified as hot and low—like demons that leave humans with unfulfilled desires and strivings—the blessings (baraka) transmitted by saints have positive, cooling effects on humans troubled by the heat of the nafs.[19]

Yet, when confronted with the Sidi hierarchy, the ambiguous qualities of heat and cold become evident. For one thing, hot and cold reflect gender distinctions: Bava Gor, the senior saint, is reputed to be cool-minded (thanda magaj); Bava Habash, the young saint, is hot-minded (garam magaj); and the female saint is "hot-cold" (garam-thanda). In terms of seniority, then, heat is encompassed by the superior quality of coolness, and male encompasses female. Yet the female encompassing of heat, mediating between male coolness and hot youth, is grasped as generative, embodying fertility and reproduction. The connection between gender distinctions and thermodynamic qualities is thus most evident in relation to sexual reproduction.

According to fundamental assumptions of femininity in South Asia, shared by both Hindus and Muslims, menstruation, pregnancy, and parturition are hot (and impure) bodily states. Because heat is a necessary precondition of female fertility, it must be successively transformed into a cold state of nurturing motherhood to control its dangerous potential. As is well-known, the control of feminine (and male) heat is a major theme of life cycle rituals, especially marriage.[20] Mai Mishra, the hot-cold female saint, therefore embodies a basic cultural paradigm of femininity.

Male virility (semen), on the other hand, is equally perceived as hot and potentially dangerous, though for different reasons. Male heat may turn dangerous if controlled too much, especially through the asceticism of renouncers, as a powerful cultural stereotype personified by the Hindu god Shiva exemplifies.[21] As is hinted in the myth I examine below, Bava Gor shares with the renouncer a rejection of sexuality. His cold attributes seem to be derived not only from sexual control but from a complete victory over sexual desire (in accordance with ideas regarding the nafs). Such a transformation is, moreover, hinted at by a fire kept continuously burning near his tomb, at a site where Bava Gor is reputed to have meditated for twelve years. Bava Gor is cold because he burned his own desire as the fire consumes wood and turns it into cold ash. Bava Habash, by contrast, represents the male virility necessary for human reproduction. This aspect is particularly elaborated in the ritual context to which I shall return soon.

Overcoming Evil: The Myth of the Powerful Demoness

While the categories of hot and cold construe asymmetrical relationships among saints, they are differently evaluated in relation to the demonic, marked by a reversal of levels. The relationship between saints and demons is established in a myth that is often told by the Sidi. In this narrative, Bava Gor is represented as a fighting holy man who came to Gujarat in obedience to the commands of the Prophet to spread Islam in this part of the world. The saint met his opponent in the form of Makhan Devi, a powerful, evil demoness typifying hot, uncontrolled, and dangerous spirits. Characterized by a series of inversions of female heat, Makhan Devi is associated with blood and unrestrained sexuality. Her rule, the narrative continues, was based on the workings of evil spirits, who brought sorrow and destruction to the population. Instead of harvesting fertile crops, people were famished and died of starvation; in place of truth, Makhan Devi used trickery and illusion to uphold her power. Most dramatically, Makhan Devi did not give birth but "consumed" embryos and small children out of a perverse desire for blood. The rule of Makhan Devi meant chaos, destruction, and death. This was the situation when Bava Gor arrived. However, the saint refused to enter into battle, because, as narrators emphatically stress, the demoness was a woman, and a man cannot fight a woman. Given the implication of physical contact in battle, Bava Gor appears to have rejected a situation of sexual seduction. When his hot-headed younger brother came on the stage and threatened to kill the demoness in great rage, he was restrained by the saint and sent to another hill. Finally, the female saint arrived on the scene. Enraged like her brother Bava Habash, Mal Mishra overwhelmed the demoness by pushing her into the interior of the earth.

This narrative reveals a striking reversal of hierarchy in the relation between male and female saints, according superior value to female actions. Whereas the spatial order of the shrine manifests the superiority of male over female, the myth establishes an inversion of female and male positions. This is achieved by the transformative logic of hierarchy that creates a continuous process of balancing ambiguous hot and cold forces. Its logic requires that heat should be cooled and cold be heated. The cold saint is simultaneously superior to heat and juxtaposed to (positive) fire, while the hot saint encompasses (negative) coolness through his impotent followers. In successive stages of the ritual process, one of the poles gains prominence over the other and vice versa. The battle between the demoness and the female saint represents, symbolically, the transformation of female ambivalence. Negatively evaluated, uncontrolled female heat is projected upon the demoness, who embodies the terrifying aspects of femininity. The female saint, by contrast, represents in this constellation the positive or cold aspect of femininity; that is, controlled, dangerous heat is transformed into potentially nurturing motherhood. Thus, the male-female hierarchy is reversed when cold or superior femininity is marked. Its relationship to the male domain is, moreover, indicated by the battle scene. While the battlefield is normally the domain of men, in contrast with the domestic as the female realm, at a cosmic level, male actions of power and war are attributed to women. This temporary female superiority is expressed by evoking a male idiom.

However, although Makhan Devi's power has been subdued it cannot be completely extinguished. From below, spirits continue to harass people, who seek the power of the Sidi saints in order to get rid of them. Thus the struggle of Mai Mishra against evil forces is continuously recreated through ritual exorcism. In the relationships between saints, humans, and demons, the complementary categories of hot and cold serve to distinguish several parallel hierarchies. One is the hierarchy established between saints, humans, and demons; the second is a discourse of gendered substances and conditions; the third is that of emotions and emotionality.

Emotional States

In Sidi ideology, the hot and cold qualities of saints are related to special emotional dispositions. These are crucial for defining them as archetypal representations of morally grounded human action. Emotions are thus localized in a configuration that resembles English notions of temperament, and is called *magaj* by the Sidi *Magaj* is a key term used to refer to experiences of the self embedded in a mind-body-emotion ensemble. Thus the cold saint Bava Gor represents an exemplary thanda magaj (cold temperament) that includes patience, personal restraint, leniency, empathy (understanding), *muhabbat*, and general benevolence. Such a cold saint or person inspires trust, love, loyalty, and a sense of protection and shelter in others. In contrast, Bava Habash represents the distinct emotional pattern of an exemplary garam magaj (hot temperament). Bava Habash is also referred to as the saint with an "angry mind" (*gusso magaj*). This includes wilfullness, anger, rage, and passion. The hot saint is perceived as both powerful and fierce. He may inspire raging passion or deadly fears in his followers. Easily angered by minor offences, Bava Habash is said to pursue his enemies in his anger and bring misfortune on their homes and families. Moreover, the hot saint is said to react especially fiercely against those who take a favor but neglect to fulfil their promises. On the other hand, people stress that once the hot saint has accepted a devotee, his love and support knows no limits.

Compared to the male saints, the female saint is less elaborately identified with a specific emotional pattern. More importantly, she represents ideals of Muslim womanhood. Chaste (*in parda*) and in control of the dangerous aspects of femininity, Mai Mishra manifests cold motherly love and nurturing aspects. The demoness, by contrast, represents a negatively evaluated hot emotional pattern consisting of selfishness, jealousy, hatred, greed, and dishonesty.

Saints and demons, thus defined by hot and cold qualities that are associated with specific emotional patterns, represent types of morally approved or disapproved actions. Interaction between saints and demons is embodied in human struggles. Sidi faqirs become tokens of the saints, whereas those of demons and spirits are embodied in the possessed supplicants who seek a cure at the shrine of Bava Gor. The interactive process involving shrine followers, Faqirs, and saints is again conceptualized in an emotional idiom constituted by the categories of *dukh* (sorrow, suffering, pain) and *maja* (joy, fun). The ritual routine of the shrine is designed to transform dukh into maja. The category of sorrow encompasses hunger, unemployment, illnesses, marital problems (divorce), imprisonment of family members, and material and physical injuries inflicted by communal riots. In addition to such experiences of suffering characteristic of the life of the poor, the evil doings of the demoness stop human fertility, creating female barrenness and male impotence, and affect people's mental well-being through possession. People coming to the shrine seek a change in their own personal conditions experienced as suffering. Whereas dukh is located close to the demonic, maja is associated with the relationship to the saints. Ritually enacted by their tokens, the Sidi faqirs, maja is principally mediated through music and dance (*goma/dammal*).

In Sidi discourse, the musical repertoire of goma (possibly derived from Swahili *ngoma*, dance, and also known as *dammal* in Hindi, from *dam*, healing breath) is specific to the Sidi caste. Goma refers to rhythms and movements not practiced otherwise by Gujaratis. Vaguely associated with their African origins, the performance of percussion and dance is restricted to Sidi as agents of joy. These ideas are, moreover, embedded in a cluster of concepts arising from the transformative qualities of hot and cold, an emotional idiom that articulates the self-perception of the Sidi as a caste descended from saintly ancestors.

To begin with, the collective image of the Sidi caste is modeled on Bava Habash, the hot saint. The Sidi are hot. Their "hotness" manifests itself on several levels, starting with food. A Sidi, it is maintained, needs two types of food: hot (meat and chillies) and "sweet" food. Second, the Sidi get easily angered by insolence (*abhiman*) and hypocrisy. Such behavior is attributed to the faculty of *ʿaql* (reason) that governs desire for social prestige, material wealth, and worldly power. According to the Sidi, such strivings are built on deceit, cheating, and cunning. ʿAql is devalued by Sidi ideals, which emphasize their identity as "people without reason" (*ʿaql vagar loko*). Thus, the Sidi often refer to the members of their caste as "mad people" (*ganda loko*). Whereas madness is normally seen as a negative state closely connected with spirit possession, this value inversion is related to privileging the faculty of emotion located in the heart (*dil*) over ʿaql.

By defining themselves as mad the Sidi also claim a superior status as *dilvale* or "people of the heart." Thus, another name the Sidi call themselves is "Badshah *loko*" or kingly people. They see themselves as superior in terms of emotional experiences especially, expressed through royal metaphors. Sidi are "kings of the heart." Abundant emotional experiences of joy are summarized in the concept of *mast*, which refers to ecstasy, spiritual intoxication, fun, joy, pleasure, and trance induced by the saints.[22] The concept of mast is also related to ideas of the *majzub* (intoxicated or mad with divine love). Consonant with maja, mast appears as another key concept of the Sidi cult.

As I mentioned before, the Sidi jama'at is divided into ritual specialists and lay persons. Among the faqirs those who are called *mastans* stand out as tokens of particular saints. Whereas mast as an emotional state may be experienced temporarily by any Sidi mastans are permanently absorbed in this blissful state. They are believed to have been selected by one of the saints to act as mediums, which intoxicates them with *muhabbat*. Therefore, mastans experience reality in other ways than ordinary people. Their behavior might seem bizarre when considered from the perspective of norms that ordinarily govern social interactions. At times, a mastan talks in a seemingly silly manner, uses abusive language, mocks expressions of respectability, and refuses to use gestures of respect toward superiors. Such actions are seen not as offensive but as confirmations of his or her closeness to the saints. Through these unexpected utterances and gestures he or she exposes the hypocrisy and falseness of the world, contrasting it with the truth of the saints.

An outstanding place among mastans is accorded the *gaddivaras*, the ritual head of the cult and representative of the senior saint Bava Gor. As the gaddwaras also emblematically represents the Sidi caste, the relationship between saint and gaddivaras introduces a hierarchical distinction between saints and humans that is consituted through the relative encompassment of cold and hot: the superior, cold saint is represented by an inferior, hot man. The hotness of the gaddiwaras, however, is induced by the saint, whose "throne" (*gaddi*, pillow) is extremely hot and affects successors instantly. Thus, the ambiguity of the position of the gaddivaras, who mediates in two directions—upward and downward—is matched by the shifting value of heat as a negative or positive quality. While being hot marks him as inferior in relation to the superior, cold saint, his powerful heat distinguishes him as superior in relation to ordinary devotees because of the supreme intensity of his devotional emotionality.

The transformative power of heat and coolness, and the emotional qualities they substantialize symbolically, are embodied in the powers of healing, exorcism, and divine judgment that Sidi faqirs possess.

The Transformative Power of Saintly Rituals

Devotees come to the shrine to "work" (*kam*) with the saints, who are seen as powerful agents capable of controlling both worldly and otherworldly conditions. Using the general word for work, people indicate that they need the services of Sidi faqirs to mediate their request for saintly intervention or protection against personal misfortune. Such services (*seva*) are carried out not by the gaddivaras or by mastans but by the shrine servants called *mujavir*. Whereas the ritual transactions I am considering here are aimed at a concrete change in the personal condition of supplicants, the gaddwaras and mastans assume prominent roles, as we shall see, in another type of ritual, the *'urs* (commemoration of a saint's death), performed on behalf of the black saints.

Most cases brought to the shrines are concerned with one of three distinct spheres of power vested in them: divination through ordeal, human fertility, and exorcism. Each of these requires a different type of ritual, specifically related to one of the saints. Thus, truth ordeals are performed in the name of the senior saint, Bava Gor, who represents the highest authority and absolute truth; the female saint Mai Mishra is addressed in female fertility rituals; and exorcised spirits are banished to the trunk of a tree overlooking her shrine. The hot saint, Bava Habash, is invoked to restore virility or male fertility. The supplications and rituals thus reinforce the saintly images constructed in the myth and their reality as symbolic types. Accordingly, some rituals must be performed exclusively by male or female faqirs, others by men and women together. I begin with the ordeal.

Bava Gor: Divination through Ordeal

The coolness of Bava Gor is associated with the power of truth, knowledge, and divinely inspired judgment. Hence, divination ordeals transform his shrine into a court of law. Called *bedi,* the term literally denotes the iron rings put around the ankles of a criminal suspect. Most common ordeals relate to accusations of witchcraft, adultery, or theft. Whereas only male faqirs may perform the bedi divination ritual, accused subjects are frequently women, especially when the accusation concerns witchcraft or adultery.

In the cultural context of the cult, witchcraft is related to ideas of inverted motherhood, personified by the demoness Makhan Devi. Women accused of being witches (*dakan*) are taken to the shrine to disclose their "true nature." Most come from the Tribal (Bhil) population of the area. Whereas neither Sidi nor other Muslims level such accusations, few among them seriously doubt the reality of witches, who are said to crave the blood of embryos and newborn babies. That they are found mainly among the *jungli* (uncivilized) Bhil seems only natural.

More common, however, are accusations of adultery or theft. To find out whether a suspicion is justified, the accusing party takes the suspect to the shrine. Refusal to undergo this ordeal is almost impossible, being tantamount to an admission of guilt. At the time of my fieldwork, every week between ten and thirty bedi cases were brought before the saint. The majority came from towns and big industrial centers. Among the accusers were *kharkhana* (factory) and shop owners who suspected their employees of stealing money from their businesses, middle-class women suspicious of their maidservants, and several husbands, accompanied by their mothers, who suspected their wives of sexual infidelity.

The procedure of the ordeal is a serious affair. The saint is believed to see through the person, right into his heart. The necessary acts are usually carried out by the Sidi trustee himself. At first, the suspect is given a purificatory bath behind the shrine by another Sidi mujavir. Only a person rendered *pak* (pure) is allowed to receive the judgment of Bava Gor. Performed in public under the eyes of many uninvolved spectators, this phase of the ordeal is itself a humiliating affair. Clad only in a wet loincloth in the case of a man, or in a wet sari in the case of a woman, the accused must stand at a place outside the shrine where bedi (iron rings) are put around his or her ankles by the mujavir performing the ordeal. He purifies the person and the area with burning *loban* (incense) and utters an oath promising to accept the judgment of Bava Gor, which the accused must repeat. While a large drum is beaten inside the shrine, the mujavir takes the lead and runs toward the tomb of the saint at great speed, followed by the accused. If the iron rings spring open during the run, the innocence of the suspect is established. But if the rings do not open, he or she is plainly proved guilty. The iron rings are seen as signs through which the saint directly communicates the truth to the people. If they do not open, there is no way to deny the accusation. The punishment of a culprit, however, is beyond the jurisdiction of the shrine. It is left to the accusers to mete out appropriate retribution.

In the context of the ordeal, the leading saint's supernatural powers are constructed in relation to worldly hierarchies and economic powers: Bava Gor supports the more powerful against the less powerful; the dominant (patrons, employers) against the dominated (laborers, clients, and women). Seen in this context, the dargah is a place where class-based social control is publicly exercised. It is an attempt to check transgressions against the morally sanctioned cultural order that are seen to arise from selfishness and greed (theft) or from a lack of control over negative femininity (witchcraft, adultery).

Mai Mishra: Rituals of Motherhood

Mai Mishra, it will be recalled, is the hot-cold saint able to transform infertile heat into cooling nurture. Hence, the second domain of saintly power is the restoration of fertility and the rituals confirming a vow (*mannat*), made either by a woman or by a man, to secure the birth of a child. In the cultural context of South Asia female barrenness is dreaded by married women as the cause of great *dukh*. Men, on the other hand, often suffer from fear of or actual impotence.[23] Procreation and sexuality seem to be under a perpetual threat of malfunction, caused by a physical imbalance of hot and cold forces. A barren woman is said to be too hot, because the heat necessary for procreation is not transformed into cool motherhood after having given birth.

The desire for offspring and the belief that fulfillment is dependent on the beneficial powers of saints are visibly manifested by numerous small, wooden, brightly painted cradles that are decoratively placed on the frames protecting the tombs of the three saints. In more severe cases of childlessness, suspected of being caused by female infertility, a ritual called *Mai Mishra ni khichadi*, performed by Sidi women, is sponsored by the barren woman herself or by a close relative (usually her mother). This ritual requires that seven Sidi women, who represent the seven sisters of the female saint, consume a dish made from rice and lentils mixed with sugar and ghee. Seven is, of course, an auspicious number, and it is used by Hindus as well to refer to seven goddesses. Here, sweetness is associated with special food prepared for the female saint. One of the women, usually a wife of one of the mujavir, is responsible for the organization of the ritual, including the purchase of the necessary food items. She receives a lump sum from the sponsor which covers the food expenses and a small money gift for each of the participating Sidi women.

After the dish has been cooked by the seven "sisters" themselves, they gather in a room adjacent to the shrine of Bava Gor. The first stage of the ritual requires that the women eat "in *pardd*," that is, hidden from the gaze of men and strangers not involved in its performance. As is the custom in this Muslim social milieu, the women share the food from one common dish. Their leftovers are afterward distributed as *niaz* (blessed food), first to the afflicted woman herself, then to other women devotees. Mai Mishra's *khichadi* is not shared with men.

The second part of this ritual consists of goma, the dance that is performed in different ritual contexts. The Sidi women gather next to the shrine of the female saint and sing songs (*jikkar*) dedicated to Mai Mishra and her saintly sisters. This performance is intended to give them maja and to invite them to show their benevolence. For a short time, one or two of the women actually begin to move and dance, swinging their hips while spectators wave rupee notes over the heads of the musicians as a sign of auspiciousness. Throughout the ritual the afflicted woman presides over the whole event.

Bava Habash: Restoring Virility

A man who doubts his virility will sponsor a ritual, performed by Sidi men, that addresses the hot saint Bava Habash and is therefore called *Bava Habash ni dudh*. Impotence is regarded as arising from a lack of the bodily heat considered necessary to transform blood into semen. The ritual of Bava Habash ni dudh is structured very similarly to the one performed for Mai Mishra, but involves exclusively male actors. A man concerned about his virility will select one of the Sidi mujavir to organize the rite, which requires that at least seven Sidi men (it might be more) gather in front of Bava Habash's shrine and consume a hot liquid mixture made from milk, ginger, and spices. Again, the leftover is given as niaz, first to the sponsor and then to other men present. Afterward, a short drumming and dancing session is performed by Sidi men.

The main medium employed in both these gendered rituals is food given to the Sidi as the recipients of a conditional sacrifice. The rituals mimetically enact what they want to achieve: female fertility and male virility. The blockage in the female body—hot procreative powers that are not cooled through motherhood—is metonymically overcome through the consumption of solid, sweet, and cool food. The male body, by contrast, is metonymically worked on through milk. Milk, a cool substance, is turned hot through the addition of hot spices. The weak male body is reempowered through the consumption of a hot liquid carrying the heat of the powerful saint. Both substances, the solid and the liquid, are consecrated through their conversion into a sacrifice mediated by Sidi men and women as representatives of their respective saints. Such thermodynamic "tempering" and "framing" of heat in coolness for the sake of fertility is widely found throughout South Asia and even beyond it.[24] It embodies synergetically, emotional, physiological, and social transformations in the condition of the afflicted, simultaneously setting limits to heat, casting out anger or pollution, and bringing a personal support circle concerned about the person's suffering.

Bava Gor: Rites of Exorcism

Bava Gor, the cool saint, is also the saint with the power to overcome and exorcise hot demons. At the time of my fieldwork, between thirty and fifty people suffering from symptoms of spirit possession came to the shrine on Thursdays. They are called *hajrivale*, that is, people experiencing a trance. *Hajri* literally means "presence" and refers here to the presence of a possessing spirit that manifests itself and speaks when the patient is entranced. The majority being women, hajrivale settle close to the tomb of Bava Gor, where the drama of possession trance unfolds. At the shrine of Bava Gor, hajrivale are completely left to themselves until the behavior of the patients indicates that the bhut is ready to leave their body.

Dyadic relationships between Sidi healers and patients suffering from demonic illness, comparable to those reported from other Muslim contexts; are operative only at the local levels of the cult.[25] Faqirs performing healing functions are usually based at a small Sidi shrine in an urban neighborhood. They provide the first remedies for people in distress and, most important, decide whether a person showing symptoms not yet clearly identified is possessed by a bhut or suffering from some other affliction. When such a healer diagnoses a demonic illness the faqir usually prescribes at least five visits to the shrine of Bava Gor. The place is considered more important than the individual healer because the sacred area represented by the tombs is imbued with those saintly powers (*karāmāt*) that ultimately provide the most effective means of exorcising spirits. Seen from this angle, the shrine appears as a healing space.

At the same time, the shrine is a battlefield where the saints fight directly with the spirits. Proximity to a tomb provokes the spirit to reveal itself, which it often does by shows of resistance. Some hajrivali scream their protest as their relatives drag them close to the tomb and refuse to drink the water of Bava Gor or eat the ash from his fire, both of which carry powerful healing substances. Some of them spit at the tomb, heap insults on the saints, or boast that they will never succumb. If the initial resistance is broken, patients often remain in a trance induced by hyperventilation for hours. The saint may chase the spirit by making the patient move between the different tombs of the three saints. While the bhut speaks through the mouth of the patient, relatives try to find out its identity and demands.[26] In successful cases, a bhut finally accepts the superior power of the saints and agrees to leave the body of his victim. Only then is a Sidi mujavir called. In accordance with the pattern established in the myths, departing spirits are banished to a large tree overshadowing the dargah of Mai Mishra, the female saint. Strands of the patient's hair are nailed to its trunk by a mujavir while he again confirms the final identity of the bhut.

Sorrow and Suffering: Saintly Rituals and Worldly Hierarchies

The rituals described so far are classified as seva, service performed for the sake of supplicants. Through such rituals, I propose, worldly and cosmic hierarchies of superior Sidi and inferior cult followers are constructed. The lowest position at the shrine is accorded to Hindu and Tribal women afflicted by spirit possession. Embodying evil spirits, they are identified with this category of beings. In accordance with the hot identities of the gadivaras and Sidi caste, most rituals, as we have seen—although, significantly, not all—emphasize thermal transformations. The superior qualities of coolness are most clearly revealed in the truth ordeals that affirm the spiritual authority of Bava Gor, the cool saint. In this ritual, people who normally wield greater worldly power and influence than the Sidi (for example, small-scale manufacturers) accept the Sidi's superior authority when submitting to the revelatory powers of the saint. The ritual addressing Mai Mishra, the female saint, frames heat in positive coolness, that is, motherhood. The reverse is true for the ritual involving Bava Habash, the hot saint: here negative cold is transformed into positive heat. Again, exorcism involves cooling a dangerously hot state. Thus, seva rituals display a series of movements between cooling and heating and the implicit positive and negative emotional conditions underpinning these qualities.

In contrast to seva rituals, which emphasize hierarchy and its transformations, at the large annual shrine rituals ('urs) hierarchy is temporarily collapsed. The context, however, is provided not by the relationship between cult followers and the Sidi but by that between saints and humans. The radical break of context is signified by a different style of goma stressing experiences of trance. It is here that the concept of mast is most prominently invoked.

Joy and Fun: Embodying Community

'Urs celebrations stress the relationship between the saints as ancestors and their Sidi descendants. They involve the Sidi collectivity, whose members travel from all over Gujarat to the shrine of Bava Gor—far in the south, by local standards—to celebrate the death anniversary of their *kulpir* (clan saints). This also means that large groups of Sidi dance together, which is seen by many as a major attraction promising a lot of maja. Such dancing sessions differ considerably in scope from those performed in the context of seva rituals. Most important, they involve a positively evaluated trance (*hal*) that is opposed to the trance of spirit possession (*hajri*). During trance dances many Sidi experience temporarily a state of ecstatic love for the saints, which is the permanent condition of mastans.

In 'urs rituals, the Sidi seem to express literally the metaphorical Sufi idea that for a saint, death means spiritual marriage to God. The last day of the 'urs is not only referred to as the *sagai* (engagement) of Mai Mishra, but throughout the festive period maja is produced. This joy is related to an inversion of the mystical notion of "union with the divine." Instead of merging with God, Sidi saints unite with their living descendants. They step down to earth for a few moments. Such moments are extremely hot. However, while the hierarchy of saints and humans is collapsed in trance, the gender hierarchy is maintained and emphasized. Consequently, men are possessed exclusively by male saints, women by Mai Mishra or another female saint. A woman seized by the female saint is easily recognizable by the veil put over her face. Men in trance tie a green cloth around the lower parts of their bodies. Sidi trance implies a complete abandonment of control over physical movements, with the entranced possessed by a saint who speaks through his or her body. While in trance, men and women are looked after by other Sidi not presently possessed. They see to it that the clothes of the dancers are modestly arranged, they give them water to drink when exhausted, and they keep a lemon over the head of a person entranced too violently. A cool lemon is said to balance an overdose of saintly heat.

Thus, different styles of goma correspond to different types of relationship implicit in the performances. In its "small version," carried out by a few Sidi singing songs in praise of the saints in the context of a conditional sacrifice, the relationship between Sidi faqirs and cult followers is distinguished. When goma involves large numbers of Sidi and practices of trance, the relationship between Sidi and ancestor saints is saliently marked. A third type of dance is performed in the context of the wider shrine regional network hierarchy, to which I turn below. In advance, it can be stated that each type of goma involves an inversion of hierarchy at a different level. By way of a conclusion, I examine the discourses of the cult of Bava Gor in the context of the regional shrine hierarchy.

Saintly Regional Hierarchies

So far we have seen that the shrine of Bava Gor constitutes hierarchical space in which Sidi faqirs are constructed as superior to cult followers. At the same time, it is encompassed by a wider hierarchical system of regional shrines. In this context, the shrine of Bava Gor and Sidi faqirs are accorded a lower place vis-à-vis high-ranking Sayyid shrines and pirs. That shrines, faqirs, and pirs do not constitute separate and atomistic local universes but are systematically related to each other becomes manifest in several ways.

Shrines of reputedly high status are usually not confined to narrow functions but are instead taken to transmit general and powerful baraka to human beings as a necessary life-giving force.[27] The power of small saints and lower-order shrines is conceived as more limited and specific, as in the case of the dargah of Bava Gor, the reputation of which derives from its specific healing and divinatory powers. Such shrines do not exist in isolation but are connected by spiritual master-disciple bonds (*pir-khalifa, pir-murid*). Higher and lower saints are linked through a spiritual genealogy (*silsila*) and, most important, by the master-disciple relations of pir (spiritual guide, teacher) and *murid* (spiritual disciple). An intermediate position between pir and murid is accorded to *khalifas*, that is, delegates or vicegerents of the pir, often carrying the message of his spiritual authority to geographically or socially distant places and contexts.

In the present case, Sidi faqirs are linked to a hierarchically structured universe of saints through the pir-khalifa bond that existed between Bava Gor and Sayyid Ahmad Kabir Rifa'i, the founder of a Middle Eastern Sufi order that has branches in Gujarat.[28] As is told in more elaborate versions of the myth, on his journey to India Bava Gor passed through Baghdad, where he met Sayyid Ahmad Kabir Rifa'i and became his murid. It was Rifa'i who changed his name from Sidi Mubarak Nobi to Bava Gor. The pir made him a khalifa for the area where he ultimately settled. The symbolic logic of the myth constitutes a pardigmatic template of the asymmetrical relationship between Rifa'i Sayyid pirs and Sidi faqir.[29] This relationship is revealed particularly at 'urs celebrations at Rifa'i shrines when Sidi men and women perform ritual services for the pir. Thus the Sidi, although low and marginal, are not beyond the fold of a regional Muslim hierarchical system represented by shrines.

Most important, the hierarchy of shrines is continuously recreated through asymmetrical exchanges of gifts to God. Analyzing different categories of gifts through which hierarchical relationships are established between donor and recipient, Pnina Werbner writes: "Gifts to God, including animal sacrifices and offerings of food and money, while always unilateral, are directed either 'downward,' to the poor, in the form of *sadaqa*, or 'upwards' as religious tribute to saints and holy men, whether alive or dead." In accordance with values of generosity associated with high status, the pir is the ultimate giver, who accepts gifts only from God.[30] The goods and donations he receives from his followers are classified as *nazrana*, that is, tributary gifts such as those given by a client to a patron. Nazrana, formally the possession of the saint, are usually redistributed at the shrine and used for the benefit of all, as are other offerings to the *langar*, blessed food handed out to all pilgrims and supplicants at the shrine.[31] The distribution of langar to devotees is a common practice at higher-status shrines, especially during the festive days of the ʿurs celebration.[32]

At the shrine of Bava Gor, by contrast, Sidi faqirs receive gifts to God in a downward direction. They embody the category of the poor whose gifting increases the religious merits of the donor. In addition to *jakat* (alms), the Sidi accept sadaqa and *qurbáni* (animal sacrifices). At the Islamic festival of *eid* celebrated at the end of Ramadan, the month of fasting, for example, other Muslims visit Sidi hamlets and distribute parts of a sacrificial ram. Moreover, no langar is provided at the shrine of Bava Gor. Instead, niaz is given by individual cult followers in fulfillment of a vow. The term niaz refers generally to food consecrated by sacrifice. Although such a meal is shared by all those who happen to be at the shrine at the moment of its distribution, it is explicitly prepared for and directed to the Sidi as recipients.

As is well-known, however, gifts are not neutral objects but imbued with the "spirit of the donor."[33] According to Parry, gifts (*dan*) given to the brahmin funeral priests at Benaras are negatively charged with the sins of devotees.[34] These sins, transmitted to the priests, render them inauspicious and impure. Gifts given to Sidi faqirs are similarly charged with ambivalence. In this context, instead of sins, they are perceived to be loaded with negatively evaluated emotions of hot dukh. But unlike Hindu funeral priests in Benares, the Sidi do not absorb dukh but transform it into positive emotions of maja. This, again, is achieved through a situational inversion of hierarchy.

The ambiguity of gifts given in a downward direction corresponds to the ambivalence contained in the image of a poor faqir. Although routinely invoked by high-status pirs for themselves, mendicant faqirs are in practice often despised and feared for their powers to bless *and* curse.[35] Opposed to the superior pir, the category of inferior faqir is at the same time encompassed by the former. For the present context, this encompassing relationship can be detected in the use of the concept of mastan by the Rifa'i. As noted by van der Veer, in each generation one member of the family that inherits the *sajjada nishin* (the spiritual succession of Sayyid Ahmad Kabir Rifa'i) becomes a mastan. "Stories abound about these men who combine strong spiritual powers with anti-social, unpredictable behaviour. . . . A *mastan* is clearly beyond the Law but . . . he can never be head of the family, *sajjada nishir.*"[36] Hence, we are confronted with the same type of hierarchical relationship in the category of superior pirs that marks the asymmetrical alliance between Sayyid (Rifa'i) pirs and Sidi faqirs.

Conclusion: The Emotional Reversal of the Status Hierarchy

Sidi constructions of hierarchy are built on a productive ambivalence, implying a constant shift between positive and negative evaluations of hot and cold. While coolness and the complex of ethical imperatives and emotional temperaments associated with these qualities marks the unequivocal superiority embodied by the Sayyid, the subordinate and encompassed quality of the "hot" is ambiguously defined: powerfully good or dangerously bad. The positively hot mastan over comes negatively hot spirits. By adopting a discourse of emotions, the Sidi create an alternative taxonomy of values that undermines the fixed, frozen truths of the status hierarchy, based on the absolute opposition between purity and pollution. Thus, the dukh of cult followers is confronted with the maja associated with saints and their tokens. The ambivalence connected to receiving gifts and alms is rejected by the evocation of maja, which inverses its negative value and symbolically devalues the donors. This is most prominently displayed in yet another style of goma performed at the shrines of high-status saints.

NOTES

1. Annemarie Schimmel, *Mystical Dimensions of Islam* (Chapel Hill: University of North Carolina Press, 1975); Fazlur Rahman, *Islam,* 2nd ed. (Chicago: University of Chicago Press, 1979).

2. Desiderio Pinto, "The Mystery of the Nizamuddin Dargah: The Accounts of Pilgrims," in Christian W. Troll (ed.), *Muslim Shrines in India: Their Character, History and Significance* (Delhi: Oxford University Press, 1989), 112–124.

3. N. Bikman Nanda and Mohammad Talib, "Soul of the Soulless: An Analysis of Pir-Murid Relationships in Sufi Discourse," in Christian W. Troll (ed.), *Muslim Shrines in India: Their Character, History, and Significance* (Delhi: Oxford University Press, 1989), 125–144; Pinto, "The Mystery of the Nizamuddin Dargah: The Accounts of Pilgrims."

4. Catherine A. Lutz and Lila Abu-Lughod (eds.), *Language and the Politics of Emotion* (Cambridge, UK: Cambridge University Press, 1990).

5. Marc Gaborieau, "Les orders mystiques dancs le sous-coninent indien," in A. Popovic and G. Vensten (eds.), *Les orders mystiques dans l'Islam* (Paris: Editions de L'Ecole des Hautes Etudes en Sciences Sociales, 1986), 105–134.

6. Pnina Werbner, "Economic Rationality and Hierarchical Gift Economies: Value and Ranking among British Pakistanis," *Man* n.s. 25 (1990): 266–285.

7. Pinto, "The Mystery of the Nizamuddin Dargah: The Accounts of Pilgrims," 124.

8. Louis Dumont, *Homo Hierarchicus: The Caste System and Its Implication* (Chicago: University of Chicago Press, 1980); Louis Dumont, *Essays on Individualism: Modern Ideology in Anthropological Perspective* (Chicago: University of Chicago Press, 1986).

9. Richard Kurin, "'Hot' and 'Cold': Towards an Indigenous Model of Group Identity and Strategy in Pakistani Society," in S. Pastner and L. Flam (eds.), *Anthropology in Pakistan: Recent Sociocultural and Archaeological Perspectives*, South Asia Program Occasional Papers and Theses, 8 (Ithaca, NY: Cornell University Press, 1982), 89–102; Richard Kurin, "Modernization and Traditionalism: 'Hot' and 'Cold' Agriculture in Punjab, Pakistan," *South Asian Anthropologist* 4, no. 2 (1983): 65–75; Richard Kurin, "Indigenous Agronomics and Agricultural Development in the Indus Basin," *Human Organization* 42, no. 4 (1983): 283–294.

10. S. C. Misra, *Muslim Communities in Gujarat* (New Delhi: Munshiram Monoharlal, 1985).

11. Helene Basu, *Habshi-Sklaven, Sidi Fakire: Muslimische Heiligenverehrung im westlichen Indien* (Berlin: Das Arabische Buch, 1995).

12. For a variation, see A. C. Mayer, "Pir and Murshid: An Aspect of Religious Leadership in West Pakistan," *Middle Eastern Studies* 3, no. 2 (1967): 160–169.

13. Katherine Ewing, "Malangs of the Punjab: Intoxication of *Adab* as the Path to God?" in Barbara Daly Metcalf (ed.), *Moral Conduct and Authority: The Place of Adab in South Asian Islam* (Berkeley: University of California Press, 1984), 357–371.

14. Beatrix Pfleiderer, "Mira Datar Dargah: The Psychiatry of a Muslim Shrine," in Imtiaz Ahmad (ed.), *Ritual and Religion among Muslims in India* (New Delhi: Manohar, 1981), 226.

15. Valerio Valeri, *Kingship and Sacrifice: Ritual and Society in Ancient Hawaii* (Chicago: University of Chicago Press, 1985), 54.

16. Sudhir Kakar, *Mystics, Shamans and Doctors: A Psychological Inquiry into India and Its Healing Traditions* (Delhi: Oxford University Press, 1982), 29.

17. Bruce Kapferer, *A Celebration of Demons: Exorcism and the Aesthetics of Healing in Sri Lanka* (Bloomington: Indiana University Press, 1983).

18. Richard Kurin, "Morality, Personhood and the Exemplary Life: Popular Conceptions of Muslims in Paradise," in Barbara Daly Metcalf (ed.), *Moral Conduct and Authority: The Place of Adab in South Asian Islam* (Berkeley: University of California Press, 1984), 196–220.

19. Kurin, "Indigenous Agronomics and Agricultural Development in the Indus Basin."

20. Pnina Werbner, "The Virgin and the Clown: Ritual Elaboration in Pakistani Migrants' Weddings," *Man* n.s. 21 (1986): 227–250.

21. Wendy Doniger O'Flaherty, *Siva the Erotic Ascetic* (Oxford: Oxford University Press, 1973).

22. For another context for mast see Owen M. Lynch, "The Mastram: Emotion and Person among Mathura's Chaubes," in Owen M. Lynch (ed.), *Divine Passions: The Social Construction of Emotion in India* (Berkeley: University of California Press, 1990), 91–115.

23. Sudhir Kakar, *Intimate Relations: Exploring Indian Sexuality* (New Delhi: Viking, 1989).

24. See Brenda Beck, "Colour and Heat in South Asian Ritual," *Man* n.s. 4 (1969): 553–572; Werbner, "The Virgin and The Clown: Ritual Elaboration in Pakistani Migrants' Weddings"; Pnina Werbner, *The Migration Process: Capital, Gifts and Offerings among British Pakistanis* (Oxford: Berg, 1990); C. J. Fuller and Penny Logan, "The Navratri Festival in Madurai," *Bulletin of the School of Oriental and African Studies, University of London* 48, no. 1 (1985): 79–105, Wendy Doniger O'Flaherty, *Women Androgynes and Other Mythical Beasts* (Chicago: University of Chicago Press, 1980); Richard Werbner, *Ritual Passage, Sacred Journey: The Process and Organization of Religious Movement* (Washington, DC: Smithsonian Institution Press, 1989).

25. Kakar, *Mystics, Shamans and Doctors: A Psychological Inquiry into India and Its Healing Traditions,* 15ff; Pfleiderer, "Mira Datar Dargah: The Psychiatry of a Muslim Shrine."

26. For an elaborate account of this, see Phleiderer, "Mira Datar Dargah: The Psychiatry of a Muslim Shrine."

27. P. M. Currie, *The Shrine and Cult of Mu'in al-din Chishti of Ajmer* (Delhi: Oxford University Press, 1989).

28. J. Spencer Trimingham, *The Sufi Orders of Islam* (Oxford: Oxford University Press, 1971); Peter van der Veer, "Playing or Praying: A Sufi Saint's Day in Surat," *Journal of Asian Studies* 51, no. 3 (1992): 545–564.

29. Helene Basu, "Muslimische Lachkultur in Gujarat/Indien," in Georg Elwert, Jürgen Jensen, and Ivan R. Kortt (eds.), *Kulturen und Innovationen: Festschrift für Wolfgang Rudolph* (Berlin: Duncker and Humblot, 1996).

30. Werbner, "Economics Rationality and Hierarchical Gift Economies: Value and Ranking among British Pakistanis," 27, 272 see also chapter 5 in Prina Werbner and Helene Basu (eds.), *Embodying Charisma: Modernity, Loyalty, and the Performance of Emotion is Sufi Cults* (New York: Routledge, 1998).

31. See Werbner, in Prina Werbner and Helene Basu (eds.), *Embodying Charisma: Modernity, Loyalty, and the Performance of Emotion in Sufi Cults* (New York and London: Routledge, 1998).

32. Currie, *The Shrine and Cult of Mu'in al-din Chishti of Ajmer*; van der Veer, "Playing or Praying: A Sufi Saint's Day in Surat."

33. Marcel Mauss, *The Gift* (London: Cohen and West, 1966).

34. Parry, "Ghosts, Greed and Sin: The Occupational Identity of the Benares Funeral Priests."

35. Ewing, "Malangs of the Punjab: Intoxication or *Adab* as the Path to God?"

36. van der Veer, 560.

3

Filial Emotions and Filial Values: Changing Patterns in the Discourse of Filiality in Late Chosŏn Korea

JaHyun Kim Haboush

Filiality was understood to be the foundation of the social order in Confucian society. Taken by Confucian society to be "the most natural and universal of human emotions," the love of one's parents, experienced according to certain conventions in early modern and modern Korea, linked private activity and public life and served as the axis on which turned both Korean society and the moral order of the Confucian universe. A competing discourse about filiality, which emerged in literature strongly tinctured with Buddhist ideas, grew in popularity as it challenged primogeniture and framed a case for filial daughters. JaHyun Kim Haboush explores the dynamics of the encounter between the Confucian view of filiality—and its associated moral ordering of the universe—and the counterhegemonic discourse redolent in the popular literature. Although both views upheld the central importance of filial emotion in the social and cosmic order, the Buddhist-influenced view of filiality shaped a new set of social values that were embraced by both elite and nonelite populations in Korean society. Haboush's analysis demonstrates the manner in which a key emotion—conceived by a society as foundational to social and universal order—was shaped over time by religious ideas and appropriated as the basis for a new social logic governing family relations, personal agency, and public life. Haboush concludes, "By presenting

JaHyun Kim Haboush, "Filial Emotions and Filial Values: Changing Patterns in the Discourse of Filiality in Late Chosŏn Korea," *Harvard Journal of Asiatic Studies* 55, no. 1 (June 1995): 129–177. Used by permission.

alternative views of the role of emotion, these popular works posed a counterpoint
to the vision of a perfect moral order presented in the prescriptive literature."

    What exactly was the role of filial emotion in Confucianism? To what extent
did the popular Buddhist literature embrace that conception of emotion and in
what ways did it turn it in new directions? How is the social order linked to cos-
mic order in each of these two worldviews? What is meant here by a "discourse of
emotion"? Are either of the discourses—popular or prescriptive—consistent in
their view of filial emotion and its consequences for the structuring of society? Are
there contradictions in those discourses, and, if so, what does this say about the
effectiveness of emotional discourses for linking a conception of social order to a
perceived moral order of the universe? To what extent are emotional discourses cen-
tral to social life and to moral order broadly considered?

It is generally acknowledged that filiality was accorded a central place in a
Confucian society. Filiality was viewed not only as the essence of one's personhood but also as the kernel of familial harmony and social order. Thus, it is
not surprising that, although stories of filial devotion were prominently represented in histories as early as the twelfth century,[1] the advent of the Chosŏn
dynasty (1392–1910), with its avowed aim of transforming Korea into a normative Confucian society, gave rise to an active discourse on filiality. In the
early Chosŏn, however, this discourse took the form of prescription within the
confines of the hegemonic ideology. Hegemonic ideology, as Habermas argues,
regularly legitimates normative ideals with metaphysical interpretations of reality.[2] Thus, at the inception of the Chosŏn dynasty, the social order based on
Confucian patriarchy and patrilineality was made to correspond with what was
understood to be the moral order immanent in the universe. The state sought
to implement this order with an impressive deployment of means, including
legal sanctions, moral suasion, and social pressure.

    The adoption of the Confucian model of patriarchy and patrilineality was
a complex and evolving affair. Recent scholarly works discuss this process as
a dialectical and dynamic interaction between the normative ideal and the indigenous family structure and between ideology and social practice.[3] This adoption was accompanied by a redefinition of family. What was altered was not
just the structure of authority or the pattern of socialization within existing
family units but the concept and actual composition of family. Lineage came
to be constructed in a patrilineal unit defined by the five mourning degrees.
Within this, a smaller family unit practiced primogeniture. Accordingly, the
concept of filiality was reconstructed with respect to differentiation of gender,
birth order, maternal status, and so on.

    The list of changes in practice is by now familiar. During the Koryŏ (918–
1392), sons and daughters, both before and after marriage, were equal members of a family. Uxorilocal marriage was common, and even when married

daughters left their natal homes for a separate household, they remained active family members. Sons and daughters received an equal share of the inheritance in property and daughters' children often succeeded to the family line. In the early years of the Chosŏn, when ancestral rites were introduced, daughters shared ritual duties with their brothers, often on a rotating basis. Gradually, and rather conspicuously by the mid–seventeenth century, daughters of *yangban* families began to lose their ritual heirship and their fair share of inheritance in property. Upon marriage, they left their natal homes. Such practices as the adoption of ancestral rites and the accompanying notions of ancestral spirits as well as legal sanctions against the remarriage of widows all conspired to make women into members of their husband's family while they were alive and, once dead, ancestors in that family. Upon marriage, daughters left home for the inner quarters of another patrilineal family. They were now supposed to offer their primary allegiance and loyalty to their husband's family.

If daughters bore the brunt of the redefinition of family, sons' roles were also realigned to meet the demands of the patrilineal system. Clear demarcations were drawn, in terms of both privileges and responsibilities, between the primary heir and younger sons and between legitimate sons born of the legal wife and secondary sons born of concubines.[4]

The reconstruction profoundly transformed the fabric of family life and the way parents and children related to each other. The emotional and psychological impact this reconstruction had on people must have been considerable. One is curious about a number of issues. What was the role of consciousness in this complex process of change? How was this change perceived and what kind of discourse did it produce? What was the range of discourse on filiality? How was it related to the processes of restructuring, particularly in the area of evolving ideology?

It seems that the range of ideological discourse on family and filiality widened as the popular consciousness was more directly affected by changes in family life. Naturally, when the restructuring began to touch on aspects of personal life with deep emotional resonances, responses grew sharper and more varied. The discourse on filiality diversified within the hegemonic discourse. As the Confucian sphere of influence expanded, what began as prescription became the dominant ideology in the sense that it acquired wide currency among the elite population.[5] Instructional manuals and moral tracts promoting Confucian family norms and mores had been, in the main, sponsored by the state in the early years of the Chosŏn. Gradually, private individuals grew very active in this and, in the seventeenth, eighteenth, and nineteenth centuries, private efforts became the mainstay of this endeavor. The representation of filiality in this type of writing began to vary. *Sasojŏl* (Small manners for scholars), one of the best-known manuals on manners for the yangban class written in the late eighteenth century, for instance, contains stinging criticism of discriminating against daughters which it considered to be a widespread contemporary practice.[6] In addition, writings in new genres both in classical Chinese and vernacular Korean, such as memoirs and letters, expressed a diversity of views.

It was in popular vernacular literature, however, that alternative, or counterhegemonic, discourse emerged. This paper concerns the changing patterns in the discourse of filiality as it moved from hegemonci to alternative discourse. After analyzing the representation of filiality in the prescriptive literature, I discuss its representation in several famous vernacular works. Like the hegemonic discourse, popular discourse accepted the primacy of filiality, but it did not necessarily endorse the vision of harmony between filial emotion and filial value. Even when it affirmed such a unity, it was premised on a different vision of the roles filial emotion and value should play in relation to social norms. In fact, both prescriptive and popular works contained contradictions arising from the dissonance between the idealized vision in which emotion and value are seen to be in harmony and social norms that put them at odds. This contradiction is handled in distinctive ways in these two categories of works. In the prescriptive literature, social norms are reenforced by values. Filial emotion is presented as a variable that should rise to the challenges of social norms. The unity between emotion and value is thus achieved at the expense of emotion. In contrast, popular works are constructed on the premise of the invariability of filial emotion. Either social norms are reaffirmed in emotion or, when this proves impossible, the unity between filial emotion and filial values is challenged. In this way, the prescriptive literature endorses social norms, whereas popular works display a vibrant resistance to them.

Filial Emotions and Filial Values

Of the three bonds and the five relations that constitute basic Confucian social ethics, filiality is a precept built on the rhetoric of the most natural and universal of human emotions: What could be more natural than to love one's parents? *Hsiao-hsüeh/Sohak* (Elementary learning) says: "One's parents give one birth, thus one continues the line. Parents and the king instruct, thus one is supremely indebted to them. If one does not love one's parents and loves someone else, it is a perversion of virtue. If one does not revere one's parents and reveres someone else, it is a perversion of propriety."[7] This signified a view that filiality was rooted in emotions exclusively directed toward the parents who gave birth and provided nurture and that filial emotions resulted in filial values. Filiality, the most basic and personal of relations, was also viewed as the basis of order in a Confucian society. *Hsiao-ching/Hyogyŏng* (Book of filial piety) says: "Filiality is the basis of virtue and the source of instruction," and, just afterward, "Filiality begins with serving one's parents, advances with serving one's lord, and ends with establishing oneself."[8] Here, personal virtue extends to the public good seamlessly and naturally. In this idealized vision of filiality, emotions and values are seen as being in harmony, both reenforcing social norms and supported by them.

One immediately notices that this Confucian vision differs from the prevailing Western view. To begin with, there is the *Oresteia* of Aeschylus, in which filial emotion and values are in fundamental conflict and order is restored only when filial emotion is suppressed in support of filial values. Orestes has to kill his mother, Clytaemnestra, to avenge her murder of his father, Agamemnon, to restore order. In the modern era, we are pervasively influenced by the Freudian notion of the Oedipus complex as a constituent element of filial emotion. Some anthropologists seem to have subscribed to this view. Melford Spiro, for instance, hypothesized that the Oedipus complex could well be universal.[9] In a recent article, he applies this model to East Asia and concludes that filial emotions are in conflict with filial values and that filial emotions should be repressed to maintain social order.[10]

The Confucian vision, of course, expresses an ideology of harmony and a preferred method of resolving the tension between filial emotions and filial values born of this ideology, rather than a denial of the existence of tension. Many stories of ideal filiality, in a subtle and implicit manner, acknowledge the tension. The story of the sage king Shun, the paragon of filiality whose story appears as the first among the famous twenty-four stories of model filial children, illustrates this. He served his father and his mother with utmost devotion despite the fact that they, being stupid and perverse, treated him cruelly. His younger brother Hsiang, who was very conceited, was insolent to him. The story emphasizes the fact that despite the numerous difficulties that Shun had to endure, he resolutely adhered to his filial affections. His conformance to social norms was not achieved by repressing his emotion, but through his willfully persevering in his filial love. In this story, tension failed to emerge only because of the single-mindedness of Shun's filial affection. In fact, the purity of his affection was so great that it had transformative power. Moved by his sincerity, his parents repented and became pleasant to him. His younger brother turned virtuous.[11] Thus, it was the persistence of filial emotion that upheld social norms, which, in turn, validated filial values.

A more fundamental contradiction was posed by parental figures who were not natural parents, namely, stepparents and, for women, parents-in-law. Filiality was in essence posited on the special and spontaneous nature of filial love for one's own parents. Then how can one reconcile filiality based on exclusively toward one's natural parents with social norms that did not recognize this exclusivity? The question was not merely whether one could love nonnatural parents or whether one could render them requisite service. Rather, it was how filial values and filial emotions could still be seen as being in harmony when social norms ran counter to the exclusivity of filiality. This question arose because the ideal of filiality toward stepparents and parents-in-law was based on the same standards of filiality as those governing relations to one's own parents.

The most common way to resolve this conflict was to portray devotion to a stepparent as having been motivated by devotion to one's natural parent and siblings. Min Sun, who appears in the fourth of the twenty-four stories of filial children and also the first in the *Oryun haengsil to* (Illustrated exemplary conduct of the five bonds),[12] is a good example. Sun's mother died when he was young. His father remarried and the new wife gave birth to two sons. During the cold months, she clothed Sun in thin garments padded with reed while she clothed her own children in warm garments padded with thick cotton. When his father discovered this, he wished to send her away, but Sun pleaded against it, saying that if that were to happen, three brothers, instead of one, would suffer. The stepmother was moved by his devotion and became loving to him.[13] Hsieh Pao was another whose unswerving devotion to a stepmother who had ejected him from his home moved and transformed her in the end. These stories imply that Sun's and Pao's steadfastness stemmed from their devotion to their father and brothers.[14]

Another explanation for devotion to a stepmother was that, having been brought up by this stepmother, one was indebted to her for parental care. Wang Hsiang, whose great devotion to his stepmother moved Heaven, enabling him to procure carp from a frozen river, is said to have been brought up by her.[15] Still, ambiguities remain. The admirableness of the filial son sometimes rested purely on the fact that he remained devoted to a cruel nonnatural parent, who was diametrically opposite the loving image of a parent on which the ideal of filiality was premised. These stories unmistakably undermined the exclusivity of filiality.

This ambiguity was even more pronounced in women's relationships to their parents-in-law. Praiseworthy though Shun's steadfast affection was, the objects of his devotion were his immediate family: his parents and his younger brother. When this ideal of unity between filial emotions and filial values was imposed on the social norms of the patrilineal family, the contradictions became obvious. The construction of an ideology supporting the patrilineal family in Korea calls to mind a well-known Marxian notion—that the function of ideology is to conceal contradictions in the status quo, for instance, by recasting them into a diachronic narrative of nostalgia. In other words, an appeal to the archaic sensibilities of an earlier system may be used to defend a later system which in practice undermines the material basis of those sensibilities.[16] The new ideology of filiality evokes the warmth and affection of the pre-Confucian Korean family of parents and siblings to support the patriarchal and patrilineal family. Affection and loyalty were constantly appealed to, but the objects of devotion now were defined by the family structure of the patrilineal five mourning grades. The contradiction was most acute in the case of married women, who were supposed to render their primary filial devotion to their parents-in-law.

How did the hegemonic ideology confront this contradiction for women? Narratives of a more public nature seem to have been constructed in the belief that a daughter's filial affections toward her natal parents should be transferable to her husband's parents. Instructional literature promoted by the state set forth this point, as in *Nei-hsün* (Instructions for the inner quarters), the fourteenth-century Chinese book that was translated and published as one of the *Nü ssu-shu/Yŏsasŏ* (Four books for women)[17] in the eighteenth century under royal auspices: "If you transfer the way you serve your parents to serving your husband's parents, you will not be remiss."[18] This view had already been promoted in the prescriptive literature published in the earlier part of the Chosŏn dynasty. In fact, the successful transfer of filial emotion became the hallmark of filiality for women. The filial women who graced the pages devoted to biographies of persons of exemplary behavior are mostly those who successfully made this transfer.[19] Madame Ch'en in the *Oryun haengsil to* illustrates this. When her husband left for battle, he asked her that, in the event of his death, she care for his mother. She promised that she would. When her husband died, she firmly refused her parents' solicitous urgings that she remarry, and she remained devoted to her mother-in-law for twenty-eight years. When her mother-in-law died, she sold everything in her possession to have a proper funeral for her. Madame Ch'en is portrayed as exemplary because she understood that a woman's foremost loyalty lay with her husband and his family.[20]

But what of women's special affections for their own parents? How was this transfer related to the view of women as moral beings? Were women seen as more virtuous than men because they had to transcend their exclusive filial affections to their own parents to render devotion to their parents-in-law? Or were they regarded as inconstant creatures who, unlike men who remained constant to their parents, could transfer their affection? In other words, were women viewed as possessing essentially the same nature as men or one quite different? The prescriptive literature is generally silent on this issue, but it is discussed elsewhere.

The writings of private individuals, even those of an admonitory nature, show a little more sensitivity to this question. *Naehun* (Instructions for the inner quarters) by Queen Sohye (1437–1504), the Korean manual of the selfsame title and of the same period as the Chinese *Nei-hsün*, treats a woman's filiality to her natal parents and her filiality to her parents-in-law in similar fashion.[21] The implication seems to be that, although upon marriage a woman acquires another set of parents to whom she owes filiality, she naturally remains devoted to her own parents. Writings of the later period stress filial affection to parents-in-law, but this is phrased as an extension of filial love to one's own parents. *Kyenyŏsŏ* (Admonitions to a daughter), a manual Song Siyŏl

(1607–89), a renowned scholar of the Chu Hsi school, wrote upon his daughter's marriage, begins with a preface stating that his daughter owes filial piety to her parents and that the way to fulfill this obligation is to faultlessly discharge her duties in her own marriage. These include service to her parents-in-law: "You should serve your parents-in-law with more devotion than you would your own. If you fail to serve them as parents, then they will not treat you as a daughter."[22] Madame Yi, the mother of Lady Hyegyŏng who married Crown Prince Sado in 1744, is even more determined on this point. After the wedding of her daughter, Madame Yi is preparing to leave. To her young daughter, weeping at the impending separation, she says: "Your Ladyship's duty requires that you ever more exert yourself in filial devotion [to the elders of your new family]. That is the best way to serve your natal family. If Your Ladyship were to think of your parents, rather than to cry, please apply yourself in filial devotion."[23]

In these instances, although filial emotion (affection for one's own parents) is being evoked, it is a filial value (duty to one's parents-in-law) that is being served. Whether this was done through transfer or extension of filial emotion, the ideology was predicated on an assumption that filial emotions can be *willed* to serve the social norms of the patrilineal family system. In this way, emotion and value are made to remain in harmony. This is the premise that popular vernacular works challenge. They deny that filial emotions can be willed to serve social norms. In fact, while these stories celebrate the supremacy of filial emotions, their very power is predicated on the autonomy of those emotions. Filial emotions are reciprocal and directed to the parent who nurtures and loves the child.

The works I discuss are *Chŏk Sŏngŭi chŏn* (The tale of Chŏk Sŏngŭi) and *Sim Ch'ŏng ka* (The song of Sim Ch'ŏng), both of which deal with the theme of filiality. To trace changes in the popular consciousness that concerned filiality and its relationship to ideology, I discuss them in relation to either presumed antecedents or to stories with related themes which are rooted in alternative value systems. *Chŏk Sŏngŭi chŏn*, a vernacular novel, will be compared to *Sŏnu t'aeja chŏn* (The tale of Prince Sŏnu), a Buddhist *jātaka* story, and *Sim Ch'ŏng ka*, a tale narrated in songs, to *Pari kongju* (The cast-out princess), a shaman song.

Popular Literature

In the seventeenth century, a great deal of vernacular writing in Korean appeared. Despite the invention of the Korean alphabet, *han'gŭl*, in the fifteenth century, the written discourse had been dominated by writings in classical Chinese. Classical Chinese continued to be used for writings of a public and scholarly nature, but the increasing popularity of vernacular Korean added a wholly new dimension to the written culture of Korea.[24] Vernacular writings encompassed many different genres but "popular" literature, such as I am considering in this essay, consists mainly of works of fiction, often anonymous.[25] These works circulated in different editions, both woodblock and manuscript, but most are extant only in manuscript editions.[26] The existence of a woodblock edition attests to the wide circulation of a given work. There were three centers of woodblock printing: Seoul; Anšong, a town about forty miles from Seoul; and Wanju, the present day Chŏnju, the capital city of Chŏlla Province in the southwestern region.

The number of works extant in woodblock editions is not large. Skillend puts the number found in Seoul of woodblock prints at about fifty, those in Ansŏng at a dozen, and those in Wanju, known as Wanp'an editions, at about fifteen. Frequently, the same work appears under a number of different titles, and each title has numerous editions. The examination of extant prints reveals that two copies of the same story rarely come from the same engraving[27] and that they often differ from one another. This indicates that the printing was done on a small scale and that changes were continually made to cater to the sensibilities or at least the perceived sensibilities of the reading public. One can say that these works evolved through multiple authorship and that they represent voices of different regions and classes of the period of their composition. Not surprisingly, editions from different centers of woodblock printing conform to distinct traditions. The Seoul editions are seen as representing the metropolitan elite taste, and Wanp'an editions the provincial taste.[28]

The profusion of editions seems to have been most extreme when the story was of a purely Korean origin and when it evolved into several genres, including a performing genre. A survey of the extant editions of Chŏk Sŏngŭi and Sim Ch'ŏng narratives seems to make this point. They both circulated in woodblock prints from the three centers, which indicates that they were quite popular.[29] Skillend lists about eight different editions for Chŏk Sŏngŭi and close to forty for Sim Ch'ŏng.[30] Chŏk Sŏngŭi is based on a tale of foreign origin and remained exclusively in the form of prose fiction. Sim Ch'ŏng, on the other hand, is of Korean origin and evolved into a novel, p'ansori, and a shaman song.[31] Each genre developed along the lines of its own distinct traditions. The Seoul editions are linked to the written tradition, represented in the novel Sim Ch'ŏng chŏn (The tale of Sim Ch'ŏng), and the Wanp'an editions are linked to the oral tradition which spawned the p'ansori, Sim Ch'ŏng ka.[32] It appears that p'ansori texts outnumber the novel texts. Pihl, who found many more Sim Ch'ŏng texts than Skillend, discovered some sixty manuscript and a dozen woodblock editions of p'ansori dating between 1893 and 1920 alone.[33] It is not surprising that there are many p'ansori texts. In each performance, the narrative was recreated through interaction between the singer and the audience. Texts were produced in a close, almost participatory interaction between those who wrote or performed them and the audience. Texts are fixed points in this process, but different versions reveal the evolving nature of the performing texts. The fact that there are many more manuscript[34] than woodblock editions of p'ansori seems to suggest the fluidity of the process. Public influence, however, was not limited to performing texts. The large number of different Seoul editions of the *Sim Ch'ŏng chŏn*, which are believed to have been reading texts, suggests that the reading public also had an impact on them.

These works of Korean popular literature seem interesting from the point of view of recent critical theories. Popular literature occupies a curious position between collective *langue* and individuated *parole,* and between myth and literary works of individual authorship. At the same time, the fluid nature of these texts makes them particularly revealing as articulations of the consciousness of those who produced and consumed them. They are, in Raymond Williams's words, "specific objectifications, in relatively durable material organizations, of what are otherwise the least durable though often the most powerful and affective human moments."[35]

These popular narratives also inhabit both the mythic space and the specific historical space of their compositions. The fact that their dramatis personae are of mythic proportions and that their functions are more or less uniform recalls Propp's characterization of fairy tales. Propp points out that a tale consistently has a small number of functions, whereas the number of personages is extremely large, and that the twofold quality, namely, "its amazing multiformity, picturesqueness and colour, and on the other hand its no less striking uniformity, its repetition," leads to structural homogeneity.[36] Likewise, the *Sim Ch'ŏng* and *Chŏk Sŏngŭi* stories share a plot in which a child takes on a task of enormous difficulty to save his or her parent, but the status, gender, and life situation of the child as well as of the parent differ. Constructed in the manner of a myth, each story produces meaning through the way the limited number of constituent elements is combined.[37] In addition, these works are narrated in an epic mode.[38] They are set either in an indeterminate past, as is *Chŏk Sŏngŭi chŏn* or, as is *Sim Ch'ŏng ka,* in a time meant to stand for the indeterminate past.

Also, these stories embody the consciousness of specific historical moments, and their historicity is encoded in several ways. They articulate a changing worldview in the popular consciousness, a view expressed by the use of cultural symbols. Of course, works of art always make synchronic use of cultural symbols of diachronic origins. What is particularly revelatory in these popular literary works is a crossing of different systems of values and worldviews, between symbols and their meanings, and between signifiers and their significations. *Chŏk Sŏngŭi chŏn* originates from a Buddhist tale. *Sim Ch'ŏng ka* is full of Buddhist and popular religious symbols and imagery. Rather than being used to connote meaning within the value or religious system in which they originate, namely, Buddhism and popular religion, the symbols and imagery are appropriated either to support or reject another—a Confucian—

worldview. The relationship between the earlier stories and the later ones is very complex, involving a process of appropriation and exchange.[39] The transformational significance of these symbols may indicate the historicity of these stories.

Beyond textual and intertextual considerations, I would like to note the social context of these texts.[40] Each story addresses a social issue, indicating its urgency in the popular consciousness of the time. *Chŏk Sŏngŭi* is addressed to the question of primogeniture; *Sim Ch'ŏng* deals with the departure of daughters. It is unknown when these works first appeared. For a long time, it was believed that the earliest extant editions of Korean popular novels dated from somewhere in the mid– to late nineteenth century.[41] Skillend in his 1980 article persuasively argues that one of the two Seoul woodblock editions in the British Museum Library could very well date from the eighteenth century.[42] The earliest editions of *Chŏk Sŏngŭi* are still believed to date from the mid- to late nineteenth century. This does not rule out the possibility that the story might have appeared earlier. In fact, the earliest extant editions of *Hong Kiltong chŏn* (The tale of Hong Kiltong), which is believed to have been written by Hŏ Kyun who lived from 1569 to 1618, also date from the mid- to late nineteenth century.[43] This fragmentary evidence indicates that these works probably appeared well before the nineteenth century, perhaps as early as the seventeenth century, and that they evolved into different texts and even different genres over time.[44]

Although some popular literary works evolved over more than two centuries, one can argue that, as imaginative literature, these works, in their different editions, captured "contemporary structures of feeling"[45] and that, in the cases of *Chŏk Sŏngŭi* and *Sim Ch'ŏng*, the contemporary structures of feeling were engendered by social practices, namely, unequal treatment of sons according to birth order and the separation of daughters from parents. These works voice protest or resistance against such practices, but one senses that the practices were already widespread. We see this phenomenon in the seventeenth-century novel *Hong Kiltong chŏn*. This novel protests discriminating against children born of concubines, a practice already widespread. In fact, different versions of these popular stories can be termed part of the "historical chain of discourses,"[46] and, as such, they were active constitute forces in the evolving ideology of filiality.

Most important, *Chŏk Sŏngŭi chŏn* and *Sim Ch'ŏng ka* are about filial children and signify concepts of filiality. These concepts differ markedly both from those in stories based on alternative worldviews and from the concept of filiality underlying Confucian hegemonic discourse. In the earlier narratives, filiality is much less central to the moral universe. In *Sŏnu t'aeja chŏn* and *Pari kongju*, both religious tales, filiality is not unimportant but it is relegated to a status below compassion for humanity. In *Chŏk Sŏngŭi chŏn* and *Sim Ch'ŏng ka*, on the other hand, filiality is viewed as supreme goodness, even equated with goodness. *Chŏk Sŏngŭi* and *Sim Ch'ŏng ka* also differ from the hegemonic discourse by challenging its ideology concerning filial emotions and filial values, especially the way these notions are related to social norms.

Chŏk Sŏngŭi and the Challenge to Primogeniture

Chŏk Sŏngŭi chŏn is a short vernacular Korean story of about forty pages. In addition to various Seoul and Wanp'an woodblock editions, there are a palace manuscript edition and modern printed editions. I examined three texts. The first two are the Seoul edition and the Wanp'an edition, reprinted in the *Ko sosŏl p'an'gakpon chŏnjip*.[47] The dating of the Seoul and Wanp'an editions is unknown, but similar editions have been dated at sometime in the middle and late nineteenth century, respectively. The third text is a 1925 modern printed edition.[48] These three texts, probably from a time span of over half a century, are remarkably similar in wording and in constituent elements of the story.[49] The only conspicuous differences are that the Wanp'an edition uses more descriptive language and is longer and offers more detail on the protagonist's life after he ascends the throne toward the end of the story.

Chŏk Sŏngŭi chŏn is based on *Sŏnu t'aeja chŏn*, a tale of much earlier date. *Sŏnu t'aeja chŏn* has a complicated textual history. Like many Buddhist tales, the story has foreign origins. It can be traced to a number of Indian sutras translated into Chinese and to some Chinese works as well. In several of them, including the *Poŭn'gyŏng* (The sutra of recompense for kindness), even the name of the protagonist is the same.[50] Its earliest appearance in Korea is as the sixth *jātaka*, a tale of a former life of Buddha, in the series of ten jātaka stories in the collection called *Sŏkka yŏrae sipchi suhaenggi* (Records of the trials of the ten lives of Śakyamuni Buddha), which is believed to have been compiled in 1328. This edition is written in literary Chinese and was reproduced in 1660.[51] These jaātaka stories were translated into Korean, though it is not certain when the translations appeared or whether the Korean translations circulated.[52] Meanwhile, a longer and more embellished Korean-language version appeared. The *Wŏrin sŏkpo* (The lives of Buddha and songs in his praise), a huge collection of Buddhist literature translated into or written in Korean and published under King Sejo's auspices in 1459, includes this story of close to forty pages.[53]

While *Chŏk Sŏngŭi chŏn* is clearly based on *Sŏnu t'aeja chŏn*, there is presumably a gap of several hundred years between the two stories. Many of the symbols in the first story are changed to denote the essentially Confucian tenets of the story. Even the names of the protagonist and the antagonist of each story reveal this. Sŏnu and Agu, their names in the Buddhist story, which mean Good Friend and Evil Friend, are changed to Sŏngŭi and Hangŭi, which mean Achieve Righteousness and Resist Righteousness. Sŏngŭi is a second prince in a fictitious country, Anp'yŏng, supposedly located somewhere in southern

China. Sŏngŭi is virtuous, beautiful, and filial; his older brother Hangŭi is malevolent and violent. The theme is announced at the outset when the story places the protagonist as a person of rank and virtue, but situates him as a second son, someone other than the heir. When one compares this to *Sŏnu t'aeja chŏn*, the point becomes even more clear. In the earlier story, Prince Sŏnu is the crown prince of P'ananal kingdom, the first son born of the first wife, and is the one who is good; the antagonist, Agu, who represents evil, is the younger son, born of the second wife.[54] Thus, one is made aware that the reversal of birth order in *Chŏk Sŏngŭi chŏn* is deliberate and pointed. In the later story, the brothers Sŏngŭi and Hangŭi respectively symbolize filial emotion and the lack thereof, and Hangŭi, the heir, represents the social norm. Responding to their different qualities, the parents love Sŏngŭi more than Hangŭi, and the people of the country also esteem Sŏngŭi above Hangŭi. But it is Hangŭi who is the firstborn. When the parents express a wish to appoint Sŏngŭi as heir-apparent, they meet strenuous objections from the courtiers, who argue that the eldest son should be appointed in accordance with law and that to go against it would lead to social disorder. The parents concede and Hangŭi is appointed heir. Can the unity between emotion and values be maintained under the circumstances and, if so, in what way?

Structurally, the stories share many similarities. The first part establishes the contrasting qualities of the brothers, but in the two stories these qualities are determined by different worldviews. In *Chŏk Sŏngŭi chŏn*, the characters of the brothers are established by their filial responses to their mother's illness. When their mother takes to bed, Hangŭi is indifferent but Sŏngŭi becomes deeply distraught. Tending to her day and night, he prays to Heaven for the restoration of her health. The sincerity of his filial devotion elicits divine assistance. One day, a Taoist immortal appears and tells him about a medicine called *Illyŏngju* which will cure his mother and where he can obtain it. Resisting his parents' pleas not to go, Sŏngŭi departs for the Western Region in search of the magical medicine. Though this is an arduous journey, he receives help at each of his most trying moments from supernatural Buddhist deities who are moved by his "deeply sincere great filial devotion" (*chisŏng taehyo*), and thus he successfully accomplishes his objective. Having obtained the miracle drug, he returns to the place where he left his attendants.[55]

Prince Sŏnu likewise makes a difficult journey, but to the sea in search of a jewel. It is, however, compassion for living beings that prompts Sŏnu to do this. Like Sŏngŭi, he receives divine assistance and obtains the jewel from the dragon king, but the jewel he obtains is not intended to cure a specific person but the disease and hunger of all living beings.[56]

At this point the protagonists in both stories suffer a temporary setback through the evil machinations of their respective brothers. They are both blinded after being struck in the eyes by their brothers' swords. Jealous of the parental love and the adoration of the people that Sŏngŭi receives, Hangŭi has been looking for a chance to harm him. On hearing that Sŏngŭi is returning with the medicine for his mother, Hangŭi resolves to kill him. Under the pretext of going to welcome Sŏngŭi, Hangŭi brings several tens of armed men. Reproaching his younger brother for unfiliality because he has left his parents, Hangŭi strikes him with his sword, throws his body into a river, and returns to the palace with the medicine. Prince Sŏnu is blinded more pacifically— while he sleeps after having entrusted the jewel to his younger brother, who has come to meet him. The protagonists' loss of eyesight signifies the temporary loss of light in the world and the obstruction of justice in society. The antagonists fare somewhat differently. Hangŭi triumphs for the moment but at the expense of his moral legitimacy. His attempted murder of his younger brother violates justice and his victory signifies social and cosmic disorder.[57] In the Buddhist story, Agu steals the jewel from the wounded Sŏnu, but in his hand the jewel loses its benevolent power and becomes malevolent. His parents lose their eyesight as well and Agu is imprisoned.

The second part is devoted to the protagonists' trials abroad, the recovery of their eyesight, and the achievement of Confucian order or the realization of Buddhist paradise. Sŏngŭi's road to recovery is the less arduous of the two. He manages to hold onto a piece of driftwood and arrives at an uninhabited island. At the island, he sorrowfully plays a bamboo flute thinking of his mother. A minister from China passing by in a boat hears his flute playing. Deeply moved, he orders the boatmen to find the flutist. On finding a good-looking blinded youth, he brings him to China and describes him to the emperor. The emperor too is moved by his flute playing. He lets Sŏngŭi stay at the palace, where he becomes the playmate of a princess. One day, a goose arrives with a letter bound to its leg. The princess notices that the letter is addressed to Sŏngŭi. In fact, the letter is written by his mother, who has tied it to the leg of the goose that Sŏngŭi kept and asked the goose to deliver the letter to its master. The princess reads the letter to Sŏngŭi. Tears stream down his face when Sŏngŭi hears his mother's letter. Indeed, he is so moved that, in his desire to see the letter, he attempts to open his eyes and miraculously regains his eyesight. Then, Sŏngŭi passes the civil service examination at the top of the lists and marries the princess. With his bride, he returns to his home for a visit.[58]

But Prince Sŏnu endures much greater suffering. He roams in pain and hunger and enters another country, Isabal, as a beggar. The princess of that country recognizes that he is special and, despite the strong objections of her father, marries him. The couple's fervent prayers are answered and Sŏnu regains his sight. His status as the crown prince of P'ananal is then revealed and he is accepted as a royal son-in-law. With his bride, he returns to his country.[59]

In overcoming their trials, the protagonists display different sources of power. In Sŏngŭi's case, it is the affective power of his emotion, and this power is exactly proportional to the depth of the filial emotion he feels toward his mother. His flute playing moves everyone who hears it because of his depth of feeling. The purity of his filial emotion is so complete that it enables him to transcend physical limits and regain his eyesight. But Sŏngŭi's affective power is a human quality easily perceptible to ordinary mortals of good heart. It is different from Prince Sŏnu's Buddha nature, which is visible only to those who have these godlike qualities themselves. Only the princess of Isabal perceives Prince Sŏnu's superiority, while everyone else, including her father, the king of Isabal, sees only a blind beggar.

This perceptibility or imperceptibility of worth is related to different assumptions about human society. The first assumption is a Buddhist one, that human society is living in delusion and that there is not, and cannot be, a correspondence between a person's worth and his or her social recognition. In fact, the greater a person is, the less likely that his or her true worth will be recognized. In this sense, the hardships that Prince Sŏnu endures only reenforce his greatness. A corollary is the notion that those with vision have to transcend society. Despite her father's objections, the princess of Isabal marries Prince Sŏnu while he is still a blind beggar. This establishes her vision.

The other view is a Confucian belief that there should be a correspondence between one's moral worth and one's social standing and that the social order depends on maintaining it. In *Chŏk Sŏngŭi chŏn*, although Sŏngŭi's goodness rescues him from ill treatment in his years of exile, he is not treated beyond his station. Sŏngŭi can consort with the princess before marriage because he is blind and so cannot see her. This is at least the pretext the princess uses when she invites him to her quarters and, if there is any suggestion of impropriety, it is rectified by their later marriage. To become an eligible suitor, however, Sŏngŭi has first to regain his eyesight and pass the civil service examination, thus overcoming his physical handicap and earning social honor. Only then is he allowed to win the princess's hand. Everyone acts properly, in accordance with social rules and social stations. This leads to a happy ending.

The resolutions of these stories reflect their very different worldviews. The *Sŏnu t'aeja chŏn* is concerned with the Buddhist aim of eliminating human suffering, whereas *Chŏk Sŏngŭi chŏn* is concerned with the restoration of order. Once Prince Sŏnu arrives in his native country, he coaxes his imprisoned younger brother and retrieves the jewel; with it, he restores his parents' eyesight and brings peace and comfort to all living beings.[60] Prince Sŏnu is more than a filial son. His love for his parents is only a part of his concern for humanity. He is a savior; he expects and forgives the transgressions of ignorant, unseeing mortals. He brings light and eliminates the suffering of mankind, not because he has been asked, but out of compassion.

In *Chŏk Sŏngŭi chŏn*, on the other hand, order is restored through the death of Hangŭi. When Hangŭi hears that Sŏngŭi is on his way home, he leaves with armed men to kill Sŏngŭi. Instead, Hangŭi is killed by Sŏngŭi's attendants. Hangŭi's death signifies the removal of a scourge to cosmic justice.

It also prepares for unity between emotion and values. Sŏngŭi has a tearful reunion with his parents. He returns to China and becomes a minister. Then he is appointed crown prince of his home country. After the deaths of the emperor and empress of China and the deaths of Minister Ho and his wife, his parents-in-law and his adoptive parents in China, respectively, he returns home to succeed his father to the throne on the latter's death.[61] By confirming Sŏngŭi within social norms, an accord between his worth and his social standing is reached. Order is thus restored.

It is interesting to note that *Chŏk Sŏngŭi chŏn* displays a certain ambivalence toward Buddhism. Consistent with its origin as a jataka story, all three editions I examined portray Buddhism in a favorable light. It is Buddhist deities who supply Sŏngŭi with the miracle drug. By responding to Sŏngŭi's filial devotion and by using their power to help Sŏngŭi procure the drug, these deities play a supporting role in a Confucian universe. All three editions vehemently reject any suggestion that Buddhism might supplant the Confucian order. When Hangŭi returns with the miracle drug that he has taken from Sŏngŭi by force, he maligns his younger brother to his parents, saying that, though Sŏngŭi had obtained the drug, he had become entranced by Buddhism and so decided to stay in the Western Region to become a monk. In this tale, pursuing the Buddhist way in search of enlightenment and forsaking one's familial role are represented as the antithesis of filiality. In the later part of the Wan'pan edition which describes Sŏngŭi's life on the throne, however, he is presented as being devoted to the Buddhist deity who provided him with the miracle drug. He has a portrait of the deity painted, has it placed in a pavilion, and regularly burns incense before it.[62] This may indicate that the Wanp'an edition, being a provincial publication, displays a more open attitude to popular religious practice. This devotional practice, however, in no way threatens the Confucian order. In fact, his remembrance is presented as having stemmed from his sense of indebtedness to the deity for having provided the drug to cure his mother.

Sŏngŭi's devotion to his imperial parents-in-law and ministerial adoptive parents is also treated in this noncompetitive and complementary manner. He remains devoted to them because they have been good to him and because he is indebted to them. There is no suggestion that they supplant his parents in his affection. Nor is there any hint that he may stay on in China. There is no doubt that, once he has taken care of his affairs abroad, he will return to his home to assume his rightful place there.

That the conflict between filial emotions and filial values is resolved by the death of Hangŭi, however, challenges several assumptions underlying the Confucian hegemonic discourse. The first of these concerns the nature of the power of goodness. Clearly, Sŏngŭi's filial emotion has affective power. The source of his affective power lies in his ability to be affected by others, be it through love or through suffering. "Others" here is represented by his mother.

That he is filial to his mother is sufficient testimony to his goodness. Unlike the filiality of Prince Sŏnu, that of Sŏngŭi is not merely a part of his compassion for humanity, but ultimate virtue in itself. The supremacy of filiality is reenforced throughout the story. Time and time again, supernatural and human assistance is rendered to him because both gods and mortals are moved by his great filial love for his mother. Yet, Sŏngŭi's affective power does not have transformative power. Only those who already have a good heart are moved by Sŏngŭi. Unlike Shun, Sŏngŭi cannot transform his brother. Yet, Sŏngŭi's inability to transform his brother does not diminish his goodness. Rather it accentuates Hangŭi's evil. Hangŭi is evil because he remains beyond the influence of goodness. In fact, just as Sŏngŭi's goodness lies in his ability to be affected by others, Hangŭi's evil rests in the fact that he is devoid of empathetic emotion, thus disconnected from others. This leads Hangŭi to remain unfeeling when his mother becomes ill and makes him oblivious to his younger brother's affective power.

Subtly, but unmistakably, the story redefines the Mencian notion of innate goodness. On the one hand, Sŏngui's character is an exaggerated manifestation of inborn goodness. His greatness rests on the fact that he follows his natural emotion and it is invariably good. This is quite a feat for a young man. After all, Confucius achieved this state only at seventy years of age. On the other hand, the character of the antagonist, Hangŭi, which is devoid of empathy, defies the Mencian notion of the universality of inborn goodness. The story acknowledges that there are evil people such as Hangŭi who do not possess inborn goodness. A natural extension of this is a challenge to the hegemonic ideology which posited that true goodness should have transformative power. The belief in the transformative power of goodness was based on the notion of the universality of inborn goodness, that a man may stray from the proper path but still possess somewhere in his soul the capacity to be transformed by others. Once this possibility was removed, as in the case of Hangŭi, then the possibility of the transformative power of goodness was also eliminated. Goodness had merely affective, not transformative, power. In this sense, the story signifies a somewhat darker vision of humanity.

The next point is that in this story, it is not filial emotion that serves social norms. Rather, social norms are presumed to affirm filial emotion. That Sŏngŭi possesses filial emotions while Hangŭi occupies the position supported by filial values is an imperfection. It is an imperfection because Hangŭi, though born the heir, is undeserving of the status. As long as he remains in that position, he wreaks havoc. He is, in fact, the source of chaos, and this is rectified only when he is eliminated and his younger brother is elevated to heirship. Filial emotion, in this sense, is equated with the social order. This also applies to the parents. It is not only natural to love Sŏngŭi for his goodness and beauty, it is also right to let him inherit the mantle for his superior qualities. Values thus conform to emotions and the social order rests on the unity thus achieved.

It is not difficult to see that by making Sǒngŭi simultaneously the emblem of goodness and the second son, the story challenges the wisdom of primogeniture. One wonders, however, about the implications of its social criticism. What exactly does the story object to and what does it accept? Perhaps a cursory comparison with other second son stories might be useful. Jacob in Genesis, for instance, was made an heir, and eventually his sons became the ancestors of the twelve tribes of Israel. But he tricked his father into blessing him as the heir by disguising himself as his older brother, Esau. For this deception, he spent twenty years working for the crafty Laban before he returned with his wives to the land of his father. In contrast, Sǒngŭi has no ambition to become the heir. In some ways, Sǒngŭi resembles Joseph of the coat of many colors, the favored son of Jacob and his second wife, Rachel. Both were loved by their parents for their beauty and goodness and, for this, both were hated by their brothers, who harmed them. Both had to make their way outside of their homeland. Both attained success in countries more powerful and wealthy than their own, and both took foreign wives.

The resemblance, however, ends here. Joseph was united with his brothers in a famous scene in which he recognized and forgave his brothers, who, reduced to hunger during the seven years of famine that Joseph predicted, came to Egypt. Joseph was restored to the ranks of Jacob's sons and his sons became the ancestors of two of the twelve tribes of Israel. In contrast, Sǒngŭi becomes the heir by replacing his evil older brother, who is killed. In this sense, *Chǒk Sǒng ǔi chǒn* may challenge the importance of birth order, but it seems to accept the idea of a worthy single heir.

In other words, criticism is not leveled at structure but at practice. It redefines the Mencian concept of goodness, but it adheres to the Confucian belief that goodness receives social confirmation. Sǒngŭi's goodness transcends his imperfect status, but the imperfection, such as it is, is in the order of birth, not in parentage. In challenging certain aspects of the society whose general basic constructs it accepts, *Chǒk Sǒngŭi chǒn* reminds one of contemporary fiction in Britain such as *Tom Jones* or *Joseph Andrews*. These eighteenth-century English novels are mildly satirical of prevailing social norms, but they nevertheless support the notion that goodness, birth, and social reward are inextricably linked.

Sim Ch'ǒng and the Departure of Daughters

Sim Ch'ǒng, a filial daughter who sells herself to seamen as a human sacrifice to restore her father's eyesight, is the most famous of Korean filial children. In fact, her name has become an epithet for a filial child in Korea. Just as Ch'unhyang, another heroine of vernacular literature, has become the emblem of a faithful wife, Sim Ch'ŏng has dominated the popular imagination where filial children are concerned. The Sim Ch'ŏng industry, which expanded into several genres, seems to have thrived from the late eighteenth century, if not from a significantly earlier period, until the early twentieth century. During this period, Sim Ch'ŏng's popularity rivaled that of Ch'unhyang. In the twentieth century, Sim Ch'ŏng has conceded first place to Ch'unhyang, but she remains a visible cultural symbol and makes periodic appearances in comic books, videos, and television dramas. But then and now, it is in p'ansori, in which her aria lamenting her fate just before she throws herself into the sea is considered a high point of pathos in the Korean musical repertoire, that Sim Ch'ŏng receives the audience's unrestrained sympathy. It is no accident that Sim Ch'ŏng's greatest popularity coincided with that of p'ansori.

It is significant that a daughter came to personify filial devotion in late Chosŏn Korea. In fact, it is quite extraordinary that Sim Ch'ŏng rather than a filial son came to represent filiality in the p'ansori repertoire. Unlike Western opera or Chinese musical dramas, which have a huge repertoire with many variations on the same themes, p'ansori has a very limited repertoire. During the nineteenth century, there were twelve p'ansori, but only five are extant.[63] They are Ch'unhyang ka, Sim Ch'ŏng ka, Hŭngbu ka (The song of Hŭngbu),[64] Chŏkpyŏk ka (The song of the red cliff), and Sugung ka (The song of the water palace);[65] they dramatize five Confucian virtues: marital fidelity, filiality, brotherly affection, trust among friends, and loyalty to the king, respectively. Given the social norms of the time, that a male should represent fraternal affection and loyalty to the king makes eminent good sense, as does the fact that a woman represents marital fidelity. But that a daughter devoted to her natal parent should represent filiality, a representation in conflict with social norms as well as practice, calls for attention. In Western opera certain roles have been recast in gender to meet the demands or requests of specific singers, but this could not have applied to the case at hand. P'ansori is performed by one vocalist who, accompanied by a drummer, sings and narrates all parts, both male and female. In other words, performers are not restricted by gender. A male singer may gain a reputation for rendering a superb Sim Ch'ŏng ka, and a woman can achieve renown for her performance of Hŭngbu ka.

Nor was it for want of filial son stories. There were stories like Chŏk Sŏngŭi chŏn, transformations into Korean vernacular fiction of jātaka stories with filial themes.[66] Well-known examples include Allakkuk chŏn and Kŭmu t'aeja chŏn.[67] These stories obviously did not capture the popular imagination as Sim Ch'ŏng's did, but nevertheless the existence of various versions and editions attests to the fact that they circulated. Of course, filial daughter stories were not a phenomenon uniquely confined to Korea. China, where Confucian patriarchy and patrilineality has a longer history, for instance, produced a fair number of them, including legends of Miao-shan and Ma Tsu, though these are goddess figures rather than simple filial children. In any case, the preeminent position there should go perhaps either to Shun or to Mu-lien, filial sons who preside over the official and the popular spheres, respectively.

The *Sim Ch'ŏng* narrative is believed to be of purely Korean origin. A great deal has been written on the possible sources for Sim Ch'ŏng, both historical and legendary.[68] Often cited sources include the story of the filial daughter Chiŭn of the Silla dynasty, recorded in the biography section of the *Samguk sagi*. Chiŭn has remained unmarried to support her aged widowed mother. When things become very bad, she sells herself into slavery at the age of thirty-two for ten sacks of rice. Hearing of this event, a *hwarang*, an aristocrat-warrior, sends food and clothing and restores her freedom. The king hears of this and awards Chiŭn and her mother a house and a comfortable livelihood.[69] The same story, in a slightly altered form, appears in the *Samguk yusa* (The legends of the three kingdoms) of the thirteenth century. In this version, the filial daughter is not identified by name, her age is given as around twenty, and her mother is described as blind.[70]

The second source is the founding legend of Kwanŭm Temple in South Chŏlla Province. This legend closely resembles the story of Sim Ch'ŏng. A blinded widower, Wŏn Yang, pledges fifty sacks of rice to a temple to regain his eyesight. On discovering this, his daughter Hongjang sells herself to seamen for fifty sacks of rice. These seamen have been sent by the widowed Chinese emperor to find a new wife, according to instructions he has received in a dream. Hongjang is made empress and Wŏn Yang regains his eyesight.[71]

The third source is *Pari kongju*, an epic shaman song sung as the central chant in a ceremony performed by a shaman to assure the spirit of the dead a safe journey to the next world.[72] Whether the *Sim Ch'ŏng* narrative is directly influenced by *Pari kongju*[73] or, more broadly, *Sim Ch'ŏng* has a shamanistic origin is still being actively debated.[74] The evolving nature of these works and the profusion of texts render it exceedingly difficult to trace the origins of these narratives and the relationship between them. In any case, the oldest transcription of *Pari kongju* dates from 1938, and so it is difficult to make a case that *Sim Ch'ŏng* was influenced by Princess Pari.[75]

Following the 1938 text, which is known as the Akiba and Akamatsu text, Korean folklorists, including Kim T'aegon and Sŏ Taesŏk, have collected many other versions of Princess Pari from different regions. Sŏ notes that there are substantial differences on important points among the *Pari kongju* texts from different regions and even among individual texts from the same region.[76] I have examined about a dozen different texts and have found that constituent elements seem to be similar, although there are considerable differences in details.[77] I have also examined eight editions of the *Sim Ch'ŏng* narrative: four Seoul editions, an Ansŏng edition, and three Wanp'an editions.[78] Two of the Seoul editions are housed at the British Museum[79] and resemble each other; they are distinct from the two remaining Seoul editions, which are also similar.

The Ansŏng edition closely resembles one of the Seoul editions.[80] The Wanp'an texts, supposed to date between 1905 and 1916, are almost identical.[81] The greatest differences are found between the Wanp'an texts and the Seoul texts: the Seoul editions are more laconic than the Wanp'an editions, which insert long tearful or comic scenes. Still, all of these editions share the basic constituent elements of the story until the ending. In the ending, they handle the central issue of a married daughter's filiality quite differently.[82]

Sim Ch'ŏng and Princess Pari are both filial daughters who undertake exceedingly difficult tasks to benefit or save their parents. These two filial daughters, however, preside over separate domains. Sim Ch'ŏng offers a vision of familial happiness in this life, and Princess Pari tends to the dead on their dark journey to the next world. Princess Pari is a goddess who offers solace to every departed soul; Sim Ch'ŏng, for all her power, is no more than a filial child. The protagonist's journeys over metaphoric landscapes in *Pari kongju*, which is after all a religious chant, are narrated in pure epic mode. *Sim Ch'ŏng*, on the other hand, has developed as popular entertainment and has responded to popular taste by incorporating realistic detail. *Princess Pari* provides a useful counterpoint to *Sim Ch'ŏng* in discussing different concepts of filiality in popular religion and in popular Confucianism.

The *Sim Ch'ŏng* story addresses the central issue in the concept of filiality for women. Is a woman's filiality basically the same as or different from a man's? Is her filial emotion transferable? Is there some way to resolve the conflict between the ideal of unity between filial emotion and filial values and the social norms for women which place emotion and values at odds? In other words, is there some way a daughter's filial devotion to her natal parent can be made to encompass filial values? The social norms of the Confucian patriarchal family system do not allow this. Yet the *Sim Ch'ŏng* story clearly gropes for a way to make social norms coincide with a daughter's filial emotion. This theme is announced at the time of Ch'ŏng's birth, which occurs with portents that usually accompany the birth of a hero/ine.

The story begins of course with her parentage. In the Tohwa district of Hwangju, there lives a man named Sim Hakkyu.[83] Sim is descended from a yangban family that has fallen on hard times. To make matters worse, Sim is blinded before he reaches twenty, and so all hopes of attaining an official post, and thus riches and honor, evaporate. Still, his wife, Madame Kwak, is good and wise, and she supports her husband by her needlework. They are reasonably content except for the fact that they are over forty years of age and without issue. They pray and make offerings to every Buddhist and popular religious deity. One day, they have an identical dream in which a fairy appears and announces that she will come to them. In due course, a daughter is born. Madame Kwak is disappointed that the newborn is a girl. Sim, however, is all smiles. He is not disappointed over the gender of his child. He hopes that, if he brings her up lovingly and well, her future husband, out of love for his wife, will be kind to her parents. Thus his grandchildren by his daughter might include him and his wife in their ancestral sacrifices. This is *woeson pongsa,* a practice that existed earlier in the Chosŏn dynasty. In other words, he invests his affection in her, hoping that filial emotion will somehow generate filial values.

His dream of raising Ch'ŏng properly, however, is shattered. His wife develops postpartum complications and dies, leaving him with the infant. Thus, his difficult days of rearing Ch'ŏng begin. He goes to women with infants in his village begging milk for his daughter. The sight of a widowed blind father carrying around an infant moves them to pity and they all contribute.

That the caretaker is a widowed father is not of itself odd. In stories of filial children, a father-daughter dyad is usual, as is a mother-son dyad. The Miao-shan legend is based on a father-daughter relationship, and the Maud-galyāyana (Mu-lien/Mongyŏn) narrative,[84] *Chŏk Sŏngŭi chŏn,* and *Kŭmu t'aeja chŏn* all center around mother-son relations. Nor is Sim's blindness unusual. For some reason, stories concerning filiality often contain parental blindness. The fathers of Oedipus and Shun were both blind, for instance. What makes Sim's case unusual is that he is at once totally loving and extremely inadequate. From the moment of her birth and throughout her childhood when he has to beg for her, he never once sways from his delight with his daughter or from his conviction that she is the best child in the world. Yet he is a most unable caretaker. He is poor, he is blind, and he is gullible. The fact that he is a man emphasizes the hopeless inadequacy of the parent—he cannot even produce milk. He has in fact very little to offer, but he invests all his affection in her.

Princess Pari is situated as a mirror image of Sim Ch'ŏng. She is born to a king and a queen, thus to a most exalted status. Unlike Ch'ŏng, however, her birth is not welcome. Her parents already have six daughters. Her father is so disappointed in the fact that the seventh child is yet another daughter that he orders her cast out.[85] Placed in a jade box, she is thrown into the sea. At this point, one recalls another cast-out child, Oedipus, who is thrown out because of an oracle predicting that he will kill his father and marry his mother. But there is no basis for casting out Pari. The only thing against her is her sex, and even this results from her parents' haste. Just before her father wedded, he was warned by a fortuneteller about the inauspicious timing of the marriage. He was told that were he to wed in the inauspicious year he proposed, then he would have seven daughters, but if he were to wait a year to marry in an auspicious year, then the couple would produce three sons. Despite this warning, he refused to wait. Hence, seven daughters. Unlike Sim, Princess Pari's parents' love for their child does not transcend their disappointment in her sex. Sim is poor and blind, but Pari's parents are equipped to provide their daughter with all of life's comforts. Nonetheless, they reject her.

It is not only her parents who reject Princess Pari because of her sex. Cast into the sea, she journeys beneath the waters, where she meets Śakyamuni Buddha, who is accompanied by two of his disciples, Maudgalyāyana and Kā- śyapa. But he too rejects her on the basis of her sex. Instead, he places her in the charge of two mountain gods, who bring her up.[86] Princess Pari's separa- tion from her parents is also reflected in the separation and disunity among different worlds: the world of her parents, the world of the mountain gods in which she grows up, and the world of Buddha.

When both Princess Pari and Sim Ch'ŏng reach fifteen years of age, they are called on to perform filial tasks of enormous difficulty. Both rise to the challenge. Motivations and circumstances, however, differ. In the case of Prin- cess Pari, the request comes from her father. When her father and then her mother grow ill, they are informed in a dream that they will die of this illness on the same day because of their sin of having cast out their child. They will be cured only if they seek out the discarded child and have her bring back magic water and magic plants from the other world. Their message to Princess Pari asking her to return is delivered. She journeys to this world, the world of her parents, to meet them. Her parents, the king and queen, ask all of their courtiers and their six daughters to journey in search of magic water. One by one, they all refuse. It is rather interesting to compare the way the six (eight, in some versions) daughters refuse in different texts.[87] In many cases, includ- ing the Akiba and Akamatsu text, they plead inexperience or inability to hide their unwillingness to take on a risky task. Typical excuses are, "Even so and so can't go. How can I go?"[88] or "I don't even know how to get to such and such a place; how can I go to that place?"[89] In some texts, however, the reasons these daughters cite have to do with their prior commitments to their married lives. In a version from Andong in Kyŏngsang Province, the reasons cited include a son's wedding, a duty to prepare meals for parents-in-law, an obli- gation to perform an ancestral sacrifice to a parent-in-law, pregnancy, and a husband's death.[90] Conflict between a daughter's filiality to her natal parents and her prior responsibilities to her married life is overtly indicated in this version.

When Princess Pari is asked, she replies: "Although I have not received parental grace from the king and bear him no moral debt, since my mother meritoriously carried me in her womb for nine months,[91] I will go."[92] That is, though she feels no moral debt to her father, who cast her out, depriving her of her place in life, she accepts the request on behalf of her mother, who carried her to term.

This sense that a child is entitled to the proper station in life offered by his or her birth, and that parents do not have the right to deprive their children of this entitlement, is found in other literary works. Ch'oe Koun chŏn, a ver- nacular novel based on the legend of a historical person, Ch'oe Ch'iwŏn of the Silla dynasty, is explicit. After Ch'iwŏn's mother has completed three months of her pregnancy, she is kidnapped by a golden pig. Ch'iwŏn's father, Ch'ung, has had prior warning that this would happen, and so is able to kill the pig and rescue his wife in a few days. Nevertheless, when she gives birth to Ch'iwŏn six months after her return, Ch'ung, fearing that the child might have been fathered by the pig, orders him cast out. The child receives divine protection and survives. When Ch'iwŏn's mother discovers this, she urges her husband to take back the child. He sends a messenger to his son. Ch'iwŏn, however, refuses to come, saying: "My parents have discarded me, believing that I was the son of the golden pig. With what face do they seek me now? If I were the son of the golden pig, with what face would I return to meet them?" Only after Ch'ung comes to him and performs acts of penance does Ch'iwŏn agree to return.[93]

Ch'ŏng, on the other hand, volunteers her sacrifice, but the occasion is brought about by her father. From the time she reached seven years of age, she has taken charge of their livelihood and the household chores. She begs and does errands to support them. By fifteen, she has become a young woman of incomparable goodness and beauty. She has also acquired all the accomplishments of a lady without receiving any instruction. One day, in her absence, Sim has fallen into a ditch. Saved by a passing monk who informs him that he would regain his eyesight if he were to donate 300 sŏk of rice to a temple, he pledges the donation. On hearing of this, Ch'ŏng sells herself to seamen seeking a fifteen-year-old virgin to offer to the sea as a sacrifice. Ch'ŏng entertains no questions over whether or why she should do it. Her devotion to her father, as is Sim's affection to her, is unconditional. What troubles her is how her blind father will fare once she is gone. Earlier, when a widowed woman of prominence and wealth asked her to become her adopted daughter, she refused, saying that she had to care for her father: "I cherish my father even as a mother, and my father trusts me even as a son. If it were not for my father, I would not have lived until now; and if I were gone, my father would have no way to live out his remaining years."[94]

But her determination to sacrifice herself for the recovery of his eyesight overrides her anxiety over his daily life. In what might be the longest succession of arias of pathos, she laments her fate and expresses her concerns for his future and her hopes for his recovery of sight: "I beg you let this body of mine, instead,/ Bear my father's flaw/ And then brighten my father's eyes!"[95]

Then Sim has his scene of wild grief. Although it is his impetuous pledge of donation that has led his daughter to sell herself, Sim, informed of her impending departure, is inconsolable and begs her not to go: "Though I sold you to open my eyes,/What would I open my eyes to see?"[96]

Each daughter's perception of the nature of the task involved is correspondingly different. For Princess Pari, she must make another journey to the netherworld. This is commenced with images of death. "Ah! sad! If those who have died were to follow Princess Pari, then they could attain their wishes to go to the Paradise in the Pure Land of the West, and to reach the Lotus Pavilion as a man."[97] But Princess Pari has done this before. The arduous journey traversing worlds is not new to her. For Ch'ŏng, it is death, pure and simple. She has no knowledge that she will survive it. She believes that she is but a poor fifteen-year-old girl who has sold her self as a human sacrifice. The sacrifice motif in the *Sim Ch'ŏng* narrative bears a resemblance to legends involving Ma Tsu and Miao-shan, the Chinese female deities who perform filial acts of sacrifice. Ma Tsu is a popular goddess revered for protection of sailors and seafaring people.[98] In one version of the Ma Tsu legend, on seeing her father's boat capsized at sea, she swims out to rescue him but drowns.[99] Miao-shan, whose legends describe her as the incarnation of the Bodhisattva Kuan Yin, gouges out her eyes and cuts off her arms to cure her father's illness.[100] Both Ma Tsu and Miao-shan, however, are attributed with divine power. Ma Tsu is said to have gone to Heaven for her meritorious act, where she watches over seafaring people.[101] And when her father embraces her, Miao-shan assumes her original form as the Bodhisattva Kuan Yin with a thousand eyes and a thousand arms.[102] Ch'ŏng, on the other hand, remains resolutely human and does not attain divine attributes.

It is not that divinities do not respond to her filial devotion. In fact, her filial emotion has strong affective power. When Ch'ŏng jumps into the sea with a cry, "Oh, father! I die," her cries shake the whole universe and the divinities of every region come to her rescue. As if even the smallest discomfort to this paragon of filiality would mar the just rule of Heaven, no less than the Jade Emperor of Heaven takes charge of Ch'ŏng and issues orders to all the kings of the nether regions and the Dragon Kings of the seas. She is escorted to the Crystal Palace to stay until she returns to the human world.[103] Thus, what is supposed to be her death turns out to be an interlude between her childhood and her adult life. She suffers no pain. She is feasted daily and entertained most lavishly. Her mother visits her. But even in this tearful encounter, the person Ch'ŏng thinks of is her father.

Divine power also charts her adult life. Believing that this young woman of extraordinary filiality deserves the most exalted position in the human world, the Jade Emperor sends her to the widowed emperor of China (or the king of Yuriguk). She is placed in a huge lotus flower which is plucked by a sailor who presents it to the emperor. On discovering the contents of this exotic flower and receiving a message from the Jade Emperor, the emperor of China marries Ch'ŏng. Thus, a person of superior goodness achieves a social station appropriate to her moral quality through divine intervention. This affirms the harmony between the divine and the social orders. It is interesting to note that a huge lotus, a symbol of enlightenment, is appropriated to denote communication between the ruler of Heaven and the ruler of the human world. It is not individual enlightenment that is at issue here; it is understanding and harmony between the human and divine worlds. What connects them is Ch'ŏng through the affective power of her filial emotion.

The focus of this filial emotion, however, is absent until she is united with her father. Sim has left his village and is nowhere to be found. Ch'ŏng proposes a feast for all the blind men in the country and receives her husband's hearty permission to hold it. There she awaits her father. He finally appears, still blind and still poor. When he hears his daughter's voice, his desire to see her is so intense that he opens his eyes and regains his eyesight. This affective power of emotion is contagious. All the blind men congregated at the party also open their eyes and regain their sight. In his delight, Sim sings: "Ah, lo! People of the world!/More precious the birth of a girl than a boy!"[104] The newly sighted men also sing, praising imperial virtue.

It is interesting to note that another Buddhist symbol of enlightenment—opening eyes—is used to connote the affective power of devotion between father and daughter, and this power extends to all others. This is not Buddhist compassion for humanity. Filial devotion is seen as extending to benevolent rule, thus uniting private emotion to public virtue. That is why the newly sighted sing the praises of imperial virtue. A symbol of enlightenment is employed to signify the affective power of filiality, while the Buddhist concept of compassion is replaced by the benevolent rule of the imperial couple. Another feast is held to celebrate the Great Peace, which is established between the human and divine worlds and among all the different regions of the world. And it is Ch'ŏng who connects these spheres.

Unlike Ch'ŏng, who has been carried by fairies and for whom everything has been done by assisting divinities, Princess Pari has to actually travel and perform arduous tasks to obtain magic water for her parents. On her second journey to the underworld, which she undertakes disguised as a man, she again meets Śakyamuni Buddha, this time attended by the Bodhisattvas Amitābha (Kuan Yin/Kwanŭm) and Kṣitigarbha (Chijang), and this time she receives his help. When she reaches the underworld, she is met by God Peerless, who guards the magic water. When she states her reason for coming, he says, "Let us both pledge a hundred-year troth. How would it be if I gave you seven sons before you go." She agrees, saying, "If this, too, can be considered serving my parents, let us do it."[105] She marries him and draws water for him for nine years, giving birth to seven sons. Then a dream informs her that her parents have died at the same time on the same day. She immediately departs for this world, accompanied by her husband and her sons. With the miracle water she has brought, she revives her parents. When her grateful parents offer her half of their kingdom, she declines, saying: "Since I have not received good food and good clothes under your care, I would rather become a shaman deity." This is the Bakhtinian voice of a dead child. There is no way she can return to the world of the living. Her husband and her sons join her as deities.[106] On this second journey, she makes peace with the world of her parents and the world of Buddha. But she remains separate from them and these worlds exist separate from one another. Unlike the vision offered in the *Sim Ch'ŏng* story, this is a vision of disparate worlds. Princess Pari may travel between them, but she cannot connect them.

Sim Ch'ŏng's and Princess Pari's respective journeys to the underworld signify apparent changes in their lives. For Ch'ŏng, it is an interlude between her childhood and her adult station as a wife and an empress. She attains this new status after her return to this world. It is notable, however, that despite great changes in her outward life—her journey to the other world and her elevated status—Ch'ŏng is not transformed. She has acquired an added role as a wife, but she remains primarily a daughter. With Princess Pari, it is different. She goes to the netherworld a child and returns a married woman with seven sons, and is transformed by this experience. She may have undertaken her marriage to fulfill her filial duty, but one senses that her conjugal life has taken precedence over her filial role in her consciousness. When she realizes that her parents have died, she laments, "No matter how important a couple's love is, my service to my parents has been too late."[107]

Their respective marriages thus hold different significations in terms of filiality. One should note that although both stories deal with the dilemma a woman faces upon her marriage, neither proposes singleness, even as a remote possibility. This differs from the rejection of marriage one finds in the legends of Chinese female deities such as Miao-shan and Ma Tsu. Miao-shan, for instance, earns her father's wrath by refusing to marry. She says, "Empty things come to an end—I desire what is infinite."[108] In one version of the Ma Tsu legend in which she fails to rescue her father from drowning, she resolves never to marry, so that she can devote herself to the care of her mother.[109] This also resembles the story of the Korean filial daughter Chiŭn of the Silla period. In these cases, for a woman, marriage is seen as an encumbrance that obstructs her from complying with her true calling, be it a compassionate act to humanity, a spiritual awakening, or duty to her natal parents.

Although there is no sense that Princess Pari has been diminished by her marriage, her marriage is seen as being in conflict with her filiality.[110] First of all, by marrying God Peerless, the underworld deity, she chooses the other world, not the one that her parents inhabit. This is the world that resembles the one in which she was raised. Moreover, though she ultimately fulfills her filial duty, bringing magic water with the help of her husband, she is detained from accomplishing the filial task for nine years by her marriage. When she completes this task, she again has to leave. Bringing back the magic water is a symbolic act with which she repays her filial debt, but she cannot stay with her parents. The gulf between them is too wide, as wide as that between life and death. She returns to the other world, the world to which she has emotional allegiance. There she presides as guardian spirit to those who embark on a journey to the netherworld when they depart from this life. The underlying motif in the story is the eternal separation between parents and their daughters. In fact, Princess Pari and her parents cannot stay in the same sphere except for brief moments.

Princess Pari as a shaman chant is interpreted as an expression of a filial daughter's guilt for leaving her parents. What could be a worse nightmare for a daughter, ensconced as she is with her marital concerns far away from her parents, than not knowing of her parents' death and arriving too late to participate in their funeral rites? Is there some way, summoning her primordial love for her parents, to bring them back to life? Suppose she is willing to die for them? At least, she can pray for their souls. The chant is a sublimation of a departed daughter's guilt, anxiety, sorrow, and filial love, unfulfilled as it is in real life.

Sim Ch'ŏng's story treats her marriage differently. In the Seoul as well as the Wanp'an editions, a much greater effort is expended in causing social norms to be affirmed in filial emotion. Ch'ŏng's filial emotion is presented as so great that it calls to mind the legendary filial love of Shun. Shun, being a man, however, did not have to transcend social norms. He only had to transform his parents through his filial love. Ch'ŏng is in a worse predicament. The question is whether Ch'ŏng's filial love is seen as so supreme that it is endowed with power to transcend the restrictions posed by her sex and thus by social norms. Ch'ŏng and her father desire this. Ch'ŏng's filial emotion is engendered by her father's parental love. He refuses to withhold parental love because of his child's sex. Her father, especially in Wanp'an editions, has many failings. He is reckless and gullible.[111] But his faults are immaterial. He redeems himself because he is a man of good heart and, most important, a parent who gives unconditional love. Although it is Ch'ŏng who sacrifices her life in the hope of recovering his sight, it is he who, in his desire to see his daughter, opens his eyes. The miracle results not just from her devotion to him but also from his love for her. Treated by her father so lovingly, Ch'ŏng does not acknowledge that filial emotion can be based on sex. The affective power of their mutual devotion leads others to accept their vision of filiality. This is fine while Ch'ŏng is primarily a daughter, but what does this mean when she also has to play the role of wife?

It is in resolving this issue that the Seoul editions and the Wanp'an editions diverge from one another. The two Seoul editions that are believed to have circulated widely evade this issue. They end soon after the father and daughter are reunited and the father regains his sight. Sim is bestowed with honors appropriate to the father of an empress and is provided with a new wife.[112] This ending has its logic, yet stylistically there is a certain abruptness to it. One of the Seoul editions found at the British Museum seems to explain the reason for this.[113] This edition continues with the life that Ch'ŏng and her father lead after their reunion. In fact, the last third of the story is devoted to this account. Ch'ŏng and her father both have sons and daughters, and Ch'ŏng and her stepmother become attached to each other. After twenty-seven happy years, the father dies at the age of seventy-five. His wife dies of grief. Ch'ŏng, after completing mourning, also dies of grief, followed by her husband, the king (in this version). The death toll reaches almost Shakespearian proportions. What is the meaning of these deaths?

Mrs. Sim's death presents no problem. It can be taken as an emblem of conjugal loyalty. But what of Ch'ŏng's and the king's? Unrestrained grief at the death of a parent was an accepted ingredient of exemplary filiality. The morality books are full of filial children who spent decades in mourning and grief for their parents.[114] In some cases, they are so overcome with grief when their parents die that they too die.[115] These extreme manifestations of grief often contain an element of guilt on the part of the mourner. Kao Yü in *Oryun haengsil to* exemplifies this sentiment. Upon his return home from many years of travel in quest of superior scholarship, he finds both of his parents dead. He feels so remorseful when he realizes that he has irrevocably lost the chance to care for his parents that he dies.[116] On hearing of her father's death, Ch'ŏng too becomes wild with grief and is full of self-reproach at her deficient filiality. Her husband, in a mixture of pleading and impatience, asks:

"Why do you neglect the state and think only of your private feelings?" "Your majesty's rebuke," [she replies,] "is to the point, but my father in his last years enjoyed the greatest possible blessing and wealth, except that I, his daughter, could not attend him morning and evening, or perform my duties, wishing him safe sleep and greeting when he woke. Nor was I at his side at his death, and so I cannot justify myself as worthy of his boundless love."[117]

It is, just as it was for Kao Yü, her sense of unrequitedness that she could not render her father daily filial care that is at the heart of Ch'ŏng's grief. In Ch'ŏng's case, however, unrequitedness is brought about by the fact that she is a married woman. She has done everything for her father that she could possibly do, but it is intrinsic to the situation of a married woman who lives with her husband that she cannot attend to her parents day and night as a son might. Could it be that this harks back to the era of uxorilocal marriage? Indeed, that a woman's life consists of different phases, as a daughter, a wife, and a mother, each with its corresponding conflicting demands and allegiances, is seen as tragic. Blame for this tragedy is placed on the dissonance between social norms which require that a woman rearrange her priorities and her inability to shift her emotional attachments accordingly. It is clear that filial emotion, presented as a powerful natural force, is not seen as gender-based. A woman's filial emotion is as powerful and as untransferable as a man's. Feeling as grieved and remorseful as she does, Ch'ŏng has no recourse but to die. This version of the *Sim Ch'ŏng* story clearly denies the possibility of unity between filial emotions and filial values because social norms do not affirm the filial emotions of a woman. The king's death intimates a larger tragedy. His adoration of Ch'ŏng has been based on the fact that she embodies beauty and virtue, of which filiality is a central ingredient. He has not opposed or obstructed Ch'ŏng's filial devotion to her father. Still, he is incapable of saving her from the dilemma of a married woman. Only death can end his remorse.

This tragic vision in the earlier Seoul edition seems to have been a little too distressing for the audience. The result is the popularity of truncated Seoul versions which stop at the conclusion of Ch'ŏng's phase as a daughter. The Wanp'an editions, however, resort to a different solution. They all describe the happy days after father and daughter are reunited. Both are presented as fulfilled in their various roles. When Sim dies at the age of eighty, Ch'ŏng grieves and mourns him for three years.[118] What is emphasized here is that Ch'ŏng has rendered all the happiness, riches, and honors that a child can to a parent. There is very little sense that Ch'ŏng is in any way deficient because of her sex. This version affirms that a woman's filial devotion to her parents is not only rooted in the same natural force as a man's but that it can perform the same service materially and socially as well. Ch'ŏng is the ideal child before and after her marriage. Despite her sex and marriage, her role as a child is sanctioned by social norms. Ch'ŏng observes a three-year mourning period, that expected of a son or an unmarried daughter.[119] She thus fulfills the role of chief mourner. By allowing social norms to be affirmed in her filial emotion, this version confirms the unity between filial emotion and filial value. This unity, however, is achieved by making social norms coincide with filial emotion, which remains supreme and invariable.

In seeing filial emotion as the unvarying element in the balance between filial emotion and filial value, and in proposing that filiality cannot be differentiated by sex, Sim Ch'ŏng ka joins Chŏk Sŏngŭi chŏn in counterhegemonic discourse. The social vision it presents, however, is popular Confucian. It upholds the supremacy of filiality, which is seen as the basis of social and cosmic order. It presents worldly riches and success as ultimate rewards. Vernacular literature including p'ansori is often regarded as a voice of popular resistance against yangban oppression. Because the yangban were a substantial portion of the audience and readership, this may be an exaggeration. Still, in several important ways, it does respond to popular sensibilities. First of all, in proposing such poverty-stricken, socially lowly personages as Ch'ŏng as emblems of ultimate virtue and goodness, Sim Ch'ŏng ka surely redefines the concept of hero/ine. It maintains that it is goodness rather than social status that defines worth. In a way, it pushes to the extreme the idea that social standing should conform to moral worth. In Chŏk Sŏngŭi chŏn, it was a matter of birth order. In Sim Ch'ŏng ka, a beggar girl, though not completely without social pretensions at some point in her ancestral past, becomes empress on the basis of her filiality. It is of interest that becoming an empress is presented as the ultimate achievement and that someone like Ch'ŏng is made to become one.

A more fundamental structure of feeling that *Sim Ch'ŏng ka* captures seems to be the parental, especially the paternal, hope for daughters. In the story, despite unshakable paternal love, parental care is quite insufficient. Parental anxiety and guilt seem to run through the narrative. Could it be that this narrative expresses wistful parental hope? Hope that despite insufficient care, daughters might remain devoted and that their ties might remain unbroken? Perhaps a wistful wish that affection between parent and daughter be empowered to transcend social restrictions?

One still wonders, however, what these stories of filial daughters signify as a social phenomenon. Why should Sim Ch'ŏng have become the ultimate filial child? Or, even more striking, how did *Pari kongju* come to be sung as the central chant in the funerary and shamanic ceremony to assure a safe journey to the departed spirit of the dead?

It is noted that such strong images of women are least expected in a complex, patrilineal, and patriarchal society such as Chosŏn Korea. More usual in such societies are negative representations of women in myth and ritual. This results from the tension between male normative power and female real power and from the male attempt to delegitimate female power.[120] The Chinese conception of pollution is proposed as an example of this phenomenon.[121] Though there may have been quite a few "positive" and strong images of women in Chinese myth,[122] the concept of female pollution seems to have been widespread. Certain dramas such as the Mu-lien dramas, for instance, are performed at a woman's funeral to purify her so that she may enter the pantheon of gods and ancestors. But this can be done only by male descendants, who are not polluted.[123] If we extend this logic, could it be that in Korea, or at least in late Chosŏn Korea, an opposite structure of feeling prevailed? In Korea, women are seen as polluted only temporarily.[124] Perhaps there was a feeling that women and daughters had had power but had lost it, and so, rather than try to delegitimate that power, there was a sense that women and daughters should be compensated for their loss. Could it be that Koreans bestowed power on women in art and ritual for this reason?

Conclusion

Chŏk Sŏngŭi chŏn and *Sim Ch'ŏng ka* are constructed on an appeal to filial emotion. This is not anti-Confucian. Hegemonic Confucian ideology also appealed to filial emotion. In fact, these works must have maintained their influence and affectivity because they used a fundamental assumption of human nature: the affective power of filial emotion. Yet, they also assume the reciprocity and untransferability of filial emotion, which places them in the counterhegemonic discourse. In their sensibilities and worldviews, however, they seem to fall within Confucian discourse. Both narratives are, in this sense, counterhegemonic but within the dominant cultural discourse.

If we accept the notion that these works of popular literature embody the popular consciousness, the question arises of just whose consciousness it is that we are referring to. Do we accept, as is often stated, that it is "people," the nonelite segment of the population, who "produced and consumed" these popular works? But we know that the audience of p'ansori ranged widely in class constituency from the royal court to the peddlers in the marketplace.[125] Taewŏn'gun's patronage of p'ansori, for instance, is well-known.[126] The readership of vernacular novels seems to have ranged less widely, upper-class ladies being the most conspicuous consumers.[127] Evidence seems to suggest that the structures of feeling embodied in these works were shared by those who had to cope with reconstruction and change in the system and that the more widely shared the structure of feeling of a given work, the more widely it would be disseminated. The social logic of the two narratives buttresses this point.[128] The Chŏk Sŏngŭi story remained exclusively in a genre favored by the upper-class public. Conflict concerning heirship would seem to have been most acute among members of the upper class, as it involved wealth and prestige. Separation of daughters from their natal parents, on the other hand, concerned almost all segments of the population, hence, the evolution into different genres and the profusion of texts of the Sim Ch'ŏng story. And almost all segments of the population actively participated in popular discourse on the departure of daughters.

In proposing that the elite class was also engaged in popular discourse, I do not mean to suggest their wholesale flight from the hegemonic discourse. They were the very same people who produced and consumed prescriptive literature. That the same group of people should participate in two discourses of opposite nature is not unusual. In her study of a Bedouin community, Abu-Lughod describes two different, almost opposite, modes of discourse in which the same persons engage depending on the social occasion and company. The first is a discourse of honor which stresses valor, independence, and autonomy. This is maintained in public. The same person will, in the company of close friends, also engage in a discourse of sentiment, allowing the expression of pain and vulnerability. This is done in poetic chants.[129] Rather than see this as a contradiction, Abu-Lughod views these two modes of discourse as complementary, "each providing models of and for different types of experiences." As for the function of poetry, she sees it as a corrective to the "overzealous adherence to the ideology of honor."[130]

Similarly, rather than dividing along class lines, we may see hegemonic and counterhegemonic discourses in Chosŏn Korea as discourses of value and emotion, respectively. Works of popular fiction provided a medium in which people who upheld every tenet of the social order in their public personae could contest and question the social norms, express their pain, and dream of alternative resolutions for their dilemmas. By presenting alternative views of the role of emotion, these popular works posed a counterpoint to the vision of a perfect moral order presented in the prescriptive literature. They imagined possibilities beyond the prevailing norms in arranging social and personal re-lations. As an embodiment of alternate views and sentiments, these works continuously interacted with the prescriptive literature of hegemonic ideology. In the process, they functioned in no way less powerfully as a viable constitutive force in the evolving ideologies and social structures.

NOTES

The author wishes to thank W. J. Boot, Myron Cohen, Martina Deuchler, Teresa Kelleher, Laurel Kendall, Gari Ledyard, Boudewijn Walraven, and Pei-yi Wu for their comments and criticism.

The Chinese and Korean characters in the original version of this essay (*Harvard Journal of Asiatic Studies* 55, no. 1 [June 1955]) have been omitted from this version.

1. See the story of Chiŭn in *Samguk sagi*. Kim Pusik, *Samguk sagi*, ed. and trans. Yi Pyŏngdo (Seoul: Ŭryu munhwasa, 1977), 1.704–5; 2.405.

2. Jürgen Habermas, *Toward a Rational Society* (Boston: Beacon Press, 1970), 95.

3. Martina Deuchler, *Confucian Transformation of Korea* (Cambridge, MA: Harvard University Press, 1993). For a survey, JaHyun Kim Haboush, "The Confucianiza-tion of Korean Society," in *East Asian Region*, ed. Gilbert Rozman (Princeton: Prince-ton University Press, 1991), 84–110.

4. On discriminatory practices against secondary sons and the debates on them, see Martina Deuchler, "Heaven Does Not Discriminate: A Study of Secondary Sons in Chosŏn Korea," *Journal of Korean Studies* 6 (1988–89): 121–64.

5. As for various interpretations of the dominant ideology, see Nicholas Aber-crombie, Stephen Hill, and Bryan S. Turner, *The Dominant Ideology Thesis* (London: George Allen and Unwin, 1980).

6. Yi Tŏkmu, *Sasojŏl*, trans. Kim Chonggwŏn (Seoul: Myŏngmundang, 1985), 185.

7. *Sohak*, 2.37.

8. *Hsiao-ching chu-su* [ch.chor] (Taipei: Kai-ming shu-chu, 1959), 2,2545.3.

9. This hypothesis is made on the basis of his study of the Trobriands. See Mel-ford E. Spiro, *Oedipus in the Trobriands* (Chicago: University of Chicago Press, 1982), 144–80.

10. Melford E. Spiro, "Some Reflections on Family and Religion in East Asia," in *Religion and Family in East Asia*, ed. George DeVos and Takao Sofue (Osaka: National Museum of Ethnology, 1984), 39.

11. Iven Chen, *The Book of Filial Piety* (London: John Murray, 1908), 33–34.

12. This was a famous Korean morality book. It was published in 1797, as a re-publication, with two additions, of *Samgang haengsil to* (1434).

13. See Chen, *Filial Piety*, 37–38. Also *Oryun haengsil to* (Seoul: Ŭryu munhwasa, 1972), 33–34.

14. *Oryun haengsil to*, 40–41.

15. Ibid., 53–54.

16. Paraphrasing from Eve Kosofsky Sedgwick, *Between Men: English Literature and Male Homosocial Desire* (New York: Columbia University Press, 1985), 14. The similar reasoning pertaining to the women's position in the Western family is discussed in Juliet Mitchell, *Woman's Estate* (New York: Pantheon, 197), 152–71.

17. There were several versions of the *Nü ssu-shu*. The Ch'ing version compiled by Wang Hsiang was translated into Korean in 1736.

18. See *Yŏsasŏ* (Seoul: Myŏngmundang, 1987), 115.

19. For examples, see *Oryun haengsil to*, 37–38, 80–82. Also, *Hyŏnbu yŏljŏn* in *Yŏsasŏ*, 195–202.

20. *Oryun haengsil to*, 37–38.

21. *Naehun*, trans. Chŏng Yangwan (Seoul: Hagwŏnsa, 1988), 28–39.

22. Song Siyŏl, *Kyenyŏsŏ*, in *Kugŏ kungmunhak ch'ongnim* (Seoul: Taejegak, 1985), 10.282–83.

23. JaHyun Kim Haboush, ed. and trans., *The Memoirs of Lady Hyegyŏng: The Autobiographical Writings of a Crown Princess of Eighteenth Century Korea* (Berkeley: University of California Press, 1995).

24. JaHyun Kim Haboush, "Dual Nature of Cultural Discourse in Chosŏn Korea," in *Contact between Cultures, East Asia: History and Social Science*, ed. Bernard Hung-Kay Luk (Lampeter, Dyfed, UK: Ellen Mellen Press, 1992), 4: 194–96.

25. Some of the stories derived from novels written in Chinese and some Korean novels were translated into Chinese. Nonetheless, the versions that were widely disseminated tended to be those in Korean.

26. See W. E. Skillend, *Kodae Sosŏl: A Survey of Korean Traditional Style Popular Novels* (London: School of Oriental and African Studies, University of London, 1968).

27. Ibid., 23.

28. Due to the small number of extant editions, the Ansŏng editions have received scant scholarly attention. What we know about Ansŏng editions are that all the titles are also found in Seoul editions and that, in appearance, Ansŏng and Seoul editions closely resemble one another. Kim Tonguk, "P'anbon'go—Han'gŭl sosŏl panggakpon ŭi sŏngnip e taehayŏ," in *Ch'unhyang chŏn yŏn'gu* (Seoul: Yŏnse taehakkyo, 1983, ed.), 385–99; Skillend, *Kodae Sosŏl*, 22–23.

29. Kim Tonguk, "P'anbon'go," 385–99. Only a dozen works can boast of this.

30. Skillend, *Kodae Sosŏl*, 192–93, 128–31. Among premodern vernacular novels in Korean, in number of editions both woodblock and modern printed editions, *Chŏk Sŏngŭi chŏn* is the ninth. Sin Tonguk, "Chŏ Sŏngŭi chŏn," in *Kojŏn sosŏl yŏn'gu*, ed., Hwagyŏng kojŏn munhak yŏn'guhoe (Seoul: Ilchisa, 1993), 517.

31. *Sim Ch'ŏng* as shaman song, like *Pari kongju*, was transmitted primarily through oral tradition until it was written down by anthropologists early in this century. In this essay I do not discuss it.

32. Marshall R. Pihl, *The Korean Singer of Tales* (Cambridge, MA: Harvard University Press, 1994), 82–83.

33. Ibid., 82.

34. Some of these handwritten texts were used exclusively by performers. Ibid., 82–83.

35. Raymond Williams, *Marxism and Literature* (Oxford: Oxford University Press, 1977), 162.

36. V. I. Propp, *Morphology of the Folktale*, trans. Laurence Scott (Austin: University of Texas Press, 1958; 2nd ed. revised and ed. Louis A. Wagner, 1968), 20–21.

37. In discussing this question, Lévi-Strauss's analysis of myth seems useful. Claude Lévi-Strauss, *Structural Anthropology*, trans. Claire Jacobson and Brooke Grundfest Schoepf (New York: Penguin, 1972), 210–11.

38. For a discussion of the epic versus the novel, see M. M. Bakhtin, *The Dialogic Imagination: Four Essays*, ed. Michael Holquist, trans. Caryl Emerson and Michael Holquist (Austin: University of Texas Press, 1981).

39. Greenblatt makes this point concerning the relationship between literary works and society. See Stephen J. Greenblatt, "Towards a Poetics of Culture," in *Learning to Curse* (New York: Routledge, 1990), 158.

40. There is of course active debate on whether there is any need for a separate and independent context other than that already supplied in the text. See Gabrielle M. Spiegel, "History, Historicism, and the Social Logic of the Text in the Middle Ages," *Speculum* 65. 1 (1990): 59–86.

41. Kim Tonguk, "P'anbon'go," 382–83.

42. William E. Skillend, "Puritas Submersa Resurgit," *Asiatische Studien* 34.2 (1980): 131–32.

43. Kim Tonguk, "P'anbon'go," 385–99.

44. It is generally agreed that *Chŏk Sŏngŭi chŏn* appeared as a vernacular fiction sometime in the eighteenth century. In Kwŏnhwan, "*Chŏk Sŏngŭi chŏn* kŭnwŏn sŏlhwa yŏn'gu," *Inmun nonjip* 8 (1967): 318–19; Cho Ch'unho, "*Chŏk Sŏngŭi chŏn* yŏn'gu," *Kugŏ kyoyuk yŏn'gu* 15 (1983): 105.

45. Raymond Williams notes that imaginative literature, more than formal systems, captures contemporary structures of feeling. Williams, *Marxism*, 133–34.

46. The phrase is Roland Barthes's, *The Rustle of Language*, trans. Richard Howard (Berkeley: University of California Press, 1989), 318.

47. Kim Tonguk ed., *Ko sosŏl p'an'gakpon chŏnjip*, 5 vols. (Seoul: Inmun kwahak yŏn'guso, 1973–75), 3.1–49. The same Seoul edition is reprinted in *Han'guk kodae sosŏl ch'angsŏ*, 3. 227–72. The latter is in a bigger print.

48. *Chŏk Sŏngŭi chŏn* (Seoul: Yŏngch'ang sŏgwan, 1925), 111–45.

49. Although the three editions are similar, the Seoul and the modern edition are much closer to each other.

50. In Kwŏnhwan, *Chŏk Sŏngŭi chŏn*, 283–97.

51. Sa Chaedong, "Allakkuk t'aejagyŏng ŭi yŏn'gu," in *Han'guk pulgyo munhak yŏn'gu* (Seoul: Tan'guk taehakkyo ch'ulp'anbu, 1988), 2.100–1.

52. The first printed edition was in 1955. See An Chinho, *Sŏkka yŏrae sipchi haengnok* (Seoul: Pŏbyunsa, 1955).

53. Either some part of *Wŏrin sŏkpo* is lost or the text is quite corrupt. The volume number of *Wŏrin sŏkpo* is not clear, though it is conjectured to be 23. *Sŏnu t'aeja chŏn* runs from 20b to 53b of this volume. For a discussion of this point, see Sa Chaedong, *Pulgyogye kungmun sosŏl ŭi hyŏngsŏng kwajŏng yŏn'gu* (Seoul: Asea munhwasa, 1977), 25–26. Also see Kim Yŏngbae, "Sinbalgyŏn *Wŏrin sŏkpo* hoesonbon e taehayŏ," *Kugŏ kungmunhak* 68/69 (1975): 35–52.

54. Wŏrin sŏkpo, 23(?): 21a–22b, quoted in Sa, Pulgyogye, 51.

55. Chŏk Sŏngŭi in Kyŏngp'an, 1–4; Wanp'an, 13–18; Yŏngch'ang, 113–20.

56. Sa, Pulgyogye, 52.

57. Chŏk Sŏngŭi in Kyŏngp'an, 4–5; Wanp'an, 18–9; Yŏngch'ang, 120–22.

58. Chŏk Sŏngŭi in Kyŏngp'an, 5–12; Wanp'an, 20–47; Yŏngch'ang, 123–42.

59. Sa, Pulgyogye, 52.

60. Ibid.

61. Chŏk Sŏngŭi in Kyŏngp'an, 12; Wanp'an, 45–58; Yŏngch'ang, 142–45.

62. Chŏk Sŏngŭi in Wanp'an, 48.

63. There is one additional extant text, Pyŏn Kangsoe ka (The Song of Pyŏn Kang soe), but the music for it is lost. Pihl, Singer 65. As for the Sin Chaehyo's nineteenth-century texts, see Sin Chaehyo, P'ansori sasŏljip (Seoul: Minjung sŏgwan, 1972). For more recent versions, see Chŏng Pyŏnguk, Han'guk ŭi p'ansori (Seoul: Chimmundang, 1981), 233–466.

64. This is also known as Pak t'aryŏng (The song of sawing the gourd).

65. This is also known as T'obyŏl ka.

66. On the important influence of Buddhist tales on the emergence of the Korean vernacular novel, see Sa, Pulgyogye. For a discussion of a similar phenomenon in China, see Victór Mair, T'ang Transformation Texts (Cambridge, MA: Harvard University Press, 1989).

67. See Kim Kidong, ed., Chosŏn pulgyo sosŏlnon (Seoul: Tongguk taehakkyo pulgyo kanhaeng wiwŏhoe, 1979), 43–71, 119–65. Allakkuk chŏn is based on Allakkuk t'aeja chŏn which appears in worin sŏkpo, 89b–103b. This is translated into English; see Allard M. Olof, "The Story of Prince Allakkuk," Korea Journal 23.1 (1983): 13–20. Allakkuk chŏn also appears as an appendix to the Sŏkka yŏrae sipchi suhaenggi. See Sa, Pulgyogye, 30–42. Kŭmu t'aeja chŏn appears in the main text of the Sŏkka yŏrae sipchi suhaenggi (Ch'ungu, 1660 ed.), 14a–24. See Sa, Pulgyogye, 54–55.

68. Notable publications include Kim T'aejun, Chŭngbo Chosŏn sosŏl sa (Seoul: Hakyesa, 1939), 144–53; Chang Tŏksun, Kungmunhak t'ongnon (Seoul: Sin'gu munhwasa, 1960); Chang Tŏksun, Sŏlhwa munhak kaesŏl (Seoul: Iu ch'ulp'ansa, 1975), 192–207; Kim Tonguk, Han'guk kayo yŏn'gu (Seoul: Ŭryu munhwasa, 1961), 378–82. For scholarship in English, see Pihl, Singer, 69–75 and B.C.A. Walraven, Muga: The Songs of Korean Shamanism (Leiden, 1985), 109–11.

69. Samguk sagi, 1.704–5; 2.445.

70. Iryŏn, Samguk yusa, ed. and trans. Yi Pyŏngdo (Seoul: Kwangjo ch'ulp'ansa, 1972), 466–67. For an English translation, Samguk yusa, trans. Ha T'ae-Hung and Grafton K. Mintz (Seoul: Yŏnsei University Press, 1972), 384–85.

71. Chang Tŏksun, Sŏlhwa munhak, 203–4. Also Pihl, Singer, 73.

72. This ceremony is commonly known as chinogwi kut or ogu hut. It is usually quite elaborate, consisting of many parts. Clark W. Sorenson, "The Myth of Princess Pari and the Self Image of Korean Women," Anthropos 83 (1988): 411–12.

73. Kim T'aegon proposes that Sim Ch'ŏng was influenced by Pari kongju. See Kim T'aegon, Hwangch'ŏn muga yŏn'gu (Seoul: Ch'angusa, 1966), 124–69.

74. Walraven, Muga, 110–26.

75. No one has any idea when the legend began and where it originated. It is assumed that it is very old, but no reference to this legend exists in older texts. Even

if it predates the Chosŏn period, it is apparent that important constituent units were influenced by Chosŏn sensibilities. It is possible that the filial component might have been added during the Chosŏn.

76. Sŏ Taesŏk, *Han'guk muga ŭi yŏn'gu* (Seoul: Munhak sasang ch'ulp'anbu, 1980), 199–252.

77. The texts I examined include *Pari kongju* in Akiba Takashi and Akamatsu Chijō, *Chōsen fuzoku no kenkyŏ* (Tokyo: Osaka yagō shoten, 1938), 1.3–60; *Pari tegi* in Kim T'aegon, *Hwangch'on muga yŏn'gu*, 172–75; *Malmi* in Kim T'aegon, *Han'guk muga chip* (Seoul: Chipmundang, 1979), 1.60–84; *Pari tegi* in Kim, *Muga chip*, 2.29–42, *Pŏri tegi* in Kim, *Muga chip*, 2.125–132; *Ogugut* in Kim, *Muga chip*, 2.335–341; *Ogu* in Kim, *Muga chip*, 3.382–92; *Ch'il kongju* in Kim, *Muga chip*, 3.124–50; and *Pari kongju*, a text in current use in the Seoul area, courtesy of Laurel Kendall.

78. All eight bear the title *Sim Ch'ŏng chŏn*.

79. Skillend first found the two Seoul editions at the British Museum. They are reprinted in *Ko sosŏl p'an'gakpon chŏnjip*, 4.493–505. The rest, except for one Wanp'an edition, are also reprinted in *Ko sosŏl*, 2.105–214. The additional Wanp'an edition is a reprint of the edition at the National Library. *Sim Ch'ŏng chŏn in Kugŏ kungmunhak ch'ongnim* (Seoul: Taejegak, 1986), 71–221.

80. This Seoul edition bears Songdong as the place of publication. Kim Tonguk, *Ko sosŏl*, 2.129.

81. In terms of the names of characters and the places, however, the two British Museum editions differ from the rest. In these texts, the father's name is Sim Hyŏn rather than Sim Hakkyu, the mother's surname is Chŏng rather than Kwak, and Sim Ch'ŏng marries the king of a small kingdom rather than the emperor of China. The name of the heroine, Sim Ch'ŏng, is the same in every text.

82. To avoid confusion, I discuss differences among various texts only to make a point. As basic texts, I use the Akiba and Akamatsu text for *Princess Pari* and, for *Sim Ch'ŏng*, Marshall Pihl's translation based on Wanp'an editions printed between 1905 and 1916. Pihl, *Singer*, 123–233.

83. Pihl, *Singer*, 187.

84. For the translation of the transformation text on this narrative, see Victor Mair, trans. and ed., *Tun-huang Popular Narratives* (Cambridge, MA: Harvard University Press, 1983), 87–121.

85. Akiba and Akamatsu, *Chōsen fuzoku*, 3–27.

86. Ibid., 28–34; Sorenson, "Myth," 413–14.

87. In some texts, these daughters are not asked to go, e.g., the text based on Kim Chu of Kwangju city. See Kim T'aegon, *Hwangch'ŏn*, 262–63.

88. Akiba and Akamatsu, *Chōsen fuzoku*, 34–41; Kim T'aegon, *Muga chip* 2.35.

89. The popular performance text of the Seoul area, 42.

90. Kim, *Muga chip* 2.2330–31.

91. In Korean, she says, "my mother carried me to the tenth month." That is, the Korean manner of enumerating the passage of time is ordinal rather than cardinal, and so this indicates a nine-month term.

92. Sorenson, "Myth," 413; Akiba and Akamatsu, *Chōsen fuzoku*, 41.

93. Kim Kidong, ed., *Chosŏn sidae sosŏlnon* (Seoul: Iu ch'ilp'ansa, 1975), 199.

94. Pihl, *Singer*, 150

95. Ibid., 158.

96. Ibid., 164–65.

97. Akiba and Akamatsu, 42.

98. There seem to be certain similarities between Ma Tsu and Princess Pari. They are both the seventh child and, in North Kyŏngsang Province, Princess Pari is invoked to console the spirit of those who were drowned. Pihl, *Singer*, 72.

99. For a discussion of Ma Tsu, see Judith Magee Boltz, "In Homage to T'ien-fei," *JAOS* 106.1 (1986): 211–32. Also James L. Watson, "Standardizing the Gods: The Promotion of T'ien Hou ('Empress of Heaven') along the South Coast, 960–1960," in *Popular Culture in Late Imperial China*, ed. David Johnson, Andrew J. Nathan, and Evelyn S. Rawski (Berkeley: University of California Press, 1985), 292–324. Also see P. Steven Sangren, "Female Gender in Chinese Religious Symbols: Kuan Yin, Ma Tsu, and the Eternal Mother," *Signs* 9.1 (autumn 1983): 8–9.

100. Glen Dudbridge, *The Legend of Miao-shan* (London: Oxford University Press, 1978), 30–32.

101. Boltz, "Homage," 220.

102. Dudbridge, *Miao-shan*, 32–34.

103. Pihl, *Singer*, 185–87.

104. Ibid., 223–25.

105. Sorenson, "Myth," 413, 415; Akiba and Akamatsu, *Chōsen fuzoku*, 46–47.

106. Akiba and Akamatsu, *Chōsen fuzoku*, 42–54.

107. Sorenson, "Myth," 415.

108. Dudbridge, *Miao-shan*, 29.

109. Boltz, "Homage," 220.

110. Sorenson, however, observes that Princess Pari's marriage, instead of separating her from her parents, becomes a useful contact with which she saves her parents. Sorenson, "Myth," 415.

111. It is his reckless pledge that has driven his daughter to the water palace. After his daughter's departure, he has done miserably. He has acquired some wealth because the villagers have turned a profit on the money that the sailors have entrusted to them on his behalf. This has attracted the slatternly, voracious, and scheming woman known as Ppaengdŏk's mother. She has gone through this money in no time at all and, poor again, they leave the village in search of somewhere else to live. One day they hear of the feast of the blind at the capital and decide to go. On the way, however, the woman runs off with another man. To add insult to injury, his clothes are stolen while he bathes in a stream. He manages to obtain another set of clothing but, once again, he is distracted, this time by women pounding rice with a mortar and pestle. This scene also has some explicit sexual imagery. Thus, it is only on the last day of the feast that he arrives at the palace. Pihl, *Singer*, 116–67, 195–96, 206–20.

112. Kim Tonguk, *Ko sosŏl*, 2.117, 2.129.

113. Skillend proposes that the two editions are based on one Seoul manuscript edition which was probably completed before 1772. One of the two woodblock editions is dated around 1889. This is less corrupt than the other one, but the last pages are missing. The other, believed to have been made between 1850 and 1880, has some corruptions but is complete. Skillend, "Puritas," 127–36. This complete edition is also

included in *Collections of Korean Books in Seven Volumes* at the Oriental Institute of the Academy of Sciences in Saint Petersburg. This collection is signed W. G. Aston and dated October 1881.

114. Several paragons among the twenty-four model filial children did this. Chen, *Filial Piety*, 39–40, 47–48, 53–54. The *Oryun haengsil to* also lists people in this category, 38–39, 55, 70–73, 84.

115. In Chinese compilations, these people are presented as admirable examples of pure hearts. Fang Chung-te, ed., *Ku-shih-pi* (Taipei: Kwang-wen shu-chu, 1969), 2.301–7.

116. *Oryun haengsil to*, 36.

117. Kim Tonguk, *Ko sosŏl*, 4.504. The order between plates 23 and 24 is reversed in this reprint. I followed Skillend's translation with a few punctuation modifications. Skillend, "Puritas," 137.

118. Kim Tonguk, *Ko sosŏl*, 2.177–78; 2.213–14. Also, *Kungmunhak ch'ongnim*, 210–11.

119. In Chosŏn Korea, a married woman was to observe one year mourning for her natal parents but three years mourning for her parents-in-law. See Deuchler, *Confucian Transformation*, 267.

120. Sorrenson, "Myth," 404.

121. Emily Ahern, "Power and Pollution of Chinese Women," in *Women in Chinese Society*, ed. Margery Wolf and Roxanne Witke (Stanford: Stanford University Press, 1975), 193–214.

122. Sangren, "Female Gender," 1–25.

123. Gary Seaman, "Mu-lien Dramas and Funeral Ritual in Puli," in *Ritual Opera Operatic Ritual*, ed. David Johnson (Berkeley: University of California Press, 1989), 155–90.

124. Women are polluted only temporarily during menstruation and for a short period after childbirth. They become ritually clean afterward and resume their ritual activity. Laurel Kendall, *Shamans, Housewives, and Other Restless Spirits* (Honolulu: University of Hawaii Press, 1985), 175–76.

125. Chŏng Pyŏnguk, *Han'guk ŭi p'ansori*, 161–205.

126. Ibid., 207–16.

127. Ōtani Morishige, *Chosŏn hugi sosŏl tokcha yŏn'gu* (Seoul: Koryŏ taehakkyo, 1985), 94–119.

128. I am using the term coined by Spiegel, "History," 77.

129. Lila Abu-Lughod, *Veiled Sentiments: Honor and Poetry in a Bedouin Society* (Berkeley: University of California Press, 1986).

130. Ibid., 258–59.

4

The Philosophical Foundations of Sacred Rhetoric

Debora K. Shuger

In this study of Renaissance sacred writings—works addressing Christian metaphysics, morals, and experience—Debora K. Shuger argues that sacred rhetoric was valued because it was thought to speak to the heart as well as the intellect. The fact that Renaissance rhetorics appealed to emotion to persuade their readers did not undermine their epistemological value, but, rather, enhanced it. Writers of the period did not make the stark separation between objective philosophical pursuit of knowledge and inquiry clothed in religious belief and experience that emerged in the critical works of Enlightenment philosophes (and has been widely embraced since). Reason and passion were not polar opposites in Renaissance rhetorics because, in fact, knowledge itself was "passionate." Shuger presents evidence that writers of the period took belief to be grounded in emotion and that they understood their task to be the uncovering of the most important knowledge—that which was most hidden—precisely through the excitation of emotion through literary images. The sacred rhetorics in this way manifest the "interwovenness" of emotion and reason, belief and knowledge, in the pursuit of truth. Sacred rhetoric, relying on "emotional power" to make its case, presented truth, finally, in a way that was never completely objective, in "nonliteral, nontransparent language" that made probable arguments rather than cases for absolute certainty.

How is emotion defined here? Are certain emotions—love and fear, for instance—more important than others for sacred rhetoricians? What are the implications of Shuger's argument for a history of Western

Debora K. Shuger, "The Philosophical Foundations of Sacred Rhetoric," in *Rhetorical Invention and Religious Inquiry*, ed. Walter Jost and Wendy Olmstead (New Haven: Yale University Press, 2000), 47–64. Used by permission of the publisher.

thought? Does this interpretation of Renaissance rhetorics lead to new views about the history of religion in the West? To what extent have religious discourses been grounded in an appeal to affect? Has emotion played a larger role in theological reasoning than historians have claimed? What are the historical trajectories of the Renaissance valuation of emotion in epistemology?

In a 1990 essay, Stanley Fish suggested that the history of Western thought from Plato through postmodernism could best be understood as a protracted debate between those who seek the truth and the sophists, or as what he terms the "quarrel between philosophy and rhetoric." According to Fish, rhetoric is thus sophistic discourse, at once partisan and playful, and hence doubly "unconstrained by any sense of responsibility either to the Truth or to the Good"; it appeals to the emotions rather than the intellect and strives for victory rather than understanding. Philosophy, conversely, pursues "what is absolutely and objectively true"—real knowledge, "which is knowledge as it exists apart from any and all systems of belief," "knowledge free from doubt, free from metaphysics, morals, and personal conviction." Philosophy is thus serious business, and "from serious premises, all rhetorical language is suspect." Moreover, Fish adds, "Although the transition from classical to Christian thought is marked by many changes, one thing that does not change is the status of rhetoric . . . [as] the force that pulls us away from . . . a foundational vision of truth," whether secular or religious, "and into its own world of ever-shifting shapes and shimmering surfaces. The quarrel between philosophy and rhetoric survives every sea change in the history of Western thought."[1]

This is an old, familiar story. Yet it cannot be the whole story. One need only skim J. J. Murphy's *Renaissance Rhetoric: A Short Title Catalogue* to sense that there must be something wrong with Fish's paradigm. If rhetoric is inherently unserious, amoral, and irreligious, how can we account for the scores of sacred rhetorics—on my count (and Murphy's list is by no means complete), 504 of them, including reprints and reeditions, between 1500 and 1700? Examination of the texts themselves only compounds the problem. The majority of Renaissance sacred rhetorics, both Catholic and Protestant, do not favor a dispassionate, unadorned, "philosophic" language but, quite startlingly, advocate a deeply emotional and richly figured style.[2] In his *Theologia prophetica*, Johann-Heinrich Alsted demands that a sermon "be powerful and strong . . . composed partly of emphatic, weighty epithets and antitheses, partly of passionate figures."[3] Bartholomew Keckermann, like Alsted an early seventeenth-century Protestant, recommends that the preacher dramatize biblical scenes "as in a theater," using prosopopoeia, dialogue, and hypotyposis to place the subject before our eyes "surrounded with various striking details and circumstances, as if we were painting with living colors, so that the listener, carried outside himself, seems to behold the event as if placed in its midst."[4] The great

Spanish preacher and theologian Luis de Granada advocates the grand style because of its "sublimity and power to move souls," this being "the special and distinctive duty of a preacher."[5] These texts unequivocally sanction the emotional power and shimmering surfaces of rhetoric, yet one could scarcely accuse them of being "unconstrained by any sense of responsibility either to the Truth or to the Good." They are simultaneously rhetorical and serious.

Fish's paradigm, which summarizes the standard postmodern understanding of the rhetorical, clearly does not work here. Whatever its overall validity, it cannot account for the ethical and epistemic bases of early modern sacred rhetoric. Yet given the current unimportance of sacred rhetoric, to investigate its premises might be thought a rather specialized project. I am not sure, however, that this is a fatal objection. At least, I argue in what follows that these sacred rhetorics point to key difficulties in postmodernism's "platonic" historiography. In particular, these texts suggest that its central narrative—the quarrel between rhetoric and philosophy—hinges on three deeply problematic claims about what Fish calls "Western thought": that it viewed rhetoric as basically another name for sophistry; that it considered the emotions to be *sub*rational; and that it identified dispassionate, objective inquiry with the pursuit of both Truth and Goodness. I would not for a moment deny that numerous thinkers, from Plato on, make these claims, but not all of them—not even all the important ones. If Renaissance sacred rhetorics retain significance now and for us, it is because they complicate the postmodern account of Western thought and do so in ways that allow the possibility of disavowing Plato without falling into the clutches of Protagoras.

Rhetoric and Sophistic

The contrast between seriousness and play is central to both ancient and Renaissance thought; in each period, however, this contrast does not distinguish philosophy from rhetoric but rather rhetoric from sophistry. Although *sophistic* has more than one sense—humanists tend to use it as a pejorative synonym for scholastic philosophy—both ancient and early modern usage principally associate it with aesthetic pleasure (*delectatio*), playfulness, and the desire for praise. The sophist uses a highly wrought style to impress audiences with his own artistic virtuosity. Ludovico Carbo thus defines *elegantia* as "a harmonious and ornate style of speaking, designed to delight, as was once popular among the sophists." But he immediately proceeds to differentiate this style from that appropriate to rhetoric: "In *elegantia* is a certain power of delighting, in eloquence the power of persuasion. The former shines and sparkles, occupying the senses with trifles; the latter burns and flames in order to move souls." The opposite of sophistic prose in most Renaissance discussions is not an unadorned, "philosophical" style but the conjunction of power and luminosity.

Although Christ did not use "sophistic elegance and a vain rouge of words and delicate harmony," nevertheless his words were "sinewy and splendid . . . suited for teaching and moving, which are the two principal gifts of an orator."[6] Rhetoric is not sophistry precisely because the former is passionate, and hence serious *rather than* playful.

The bifurcation of rhetoric and sophistic rests on the premise that visible art inhibits emotional response. As soon as the audience notices how well something is said, it assumes a position of critical detachment. The delight in language for its own sake thus produces a playful, distanced appreciation that is at odds with the commitment and unselfconscious absorption of strong emotion. The sophist excites applause; the orator, passion.[7] Both ancient and Renaissance rhetorics thus typically render the distinction between sophistic and rhetoric via the paired metaphors of game and battle. Criticizing the sophists of his own day, Erasmus writes that such teachers train their students

> more for the gymnasium than for battle. . . . When they come to se-
> rious matters they seem inept rather than instructed: wherefore
> scarcely any others are more unprepared for real fighting than those
> whose whole lives have been spent teaching and learning the art of
> sword fighting. In their games they know how to slice with a sword
> the arrow hurled at them before it reaches its goal. But in war the
> archer does not warn his victim in advance nor abide by the rules of
> the swordsman's game.[8]

This military imagery can be easily misunderstood. The comparison between the soldier and the orator highlights the vehemence of forensic oratory. More important, however, it picks out the urgency and involvement of all true rhetoric. In this latter sense, rhetoric is not primarily a form of aggression but a kind of commitment to the real issues of human existence, whether political or spiritual. Oratory resembles a battle because both are serious and therefore impatient of virtuoso flourishes and the other self-pleasing refinements of art.[9]

In Renaissance rhetorics, the classical metaphors of oratory as warfare undergo specifically Christian transformations. The contrast between play and commitment, between the shade of the declamatory schools and the sun of the forum, between games and battles, familiar from the ancients, reappears in sacred guise in Nicholas Caussin's attack on florid, "sophistic" preaching:

> The Hebrew women are not as the Egyptian; whereas the latter bore
> children on ivory couches among vain luxuries; the former light-
> ened their womb in the sun and dust, even among their burdens.
> . . . But we by whom the heat of the day and its weight must be
> borne, we who must preach the cross, the cross, who must arouse,
> prick, thunder against all sinners sunk in perfidy by their crimes,
> what have we in common with these luxuries? . . . Who could fight

against sins if tied and bound by the laws of rhythmic speech? What
energy and vehemence will he have who plays with circular periods?
... He does not come to fight, he comes to show off. Do you expect
him to contend? He plans to dance.[10]

Christian urgency opposes the refinements of sophistic eloquence—but it
does so under the banner of rhetoric. Caussin's martial imagery associates
verbal power with spiritual combat, with the agon of Christian existence, not
with the speaker's own aggressive designs on his audience. The sacred orator,
unlike the sophist, does not fight for victory but against sin. As a late sixteenth-
century rhetoric explains, "Because our internal enemies, who treacherously
attack us ... are most strong and fierce, we must move [men's] souls and
arouse them to this inevitable battle, lest careless and asleep they be con-
quered."[11]

As Fish observes, the aesthetic of conversion "is finally an anti-aesthetic.
... It is surely anti-art-for-art's-sake because it is concerned less with the making of better poems than with the making of better persons."[12] But although
Fish regards this attitude as fundamentally unrhetorical, the same anti-
aesthetic suffuses Renaissance sacred rhetoric, which everywhere juxtaposes
the language of ornamental, gratifying self-display with passionate and re-
demptive discourse. The two are incompatible because insofar as language calls
attention to itself as art, it undercuts the possibility of emotional involvement,
which depends on at least the illusion of sincerity and spontaneity. As sincerity
is a necessary condition for passion, the evident playfulness of conspicuous
art defeats the psychagogic and serious aims of Christian rhetoric. Those whose
sermons are "so garnished with quibbles and trifles," the Restoration Anglican
churchman Robert South complains, act "as if they played with truth and immortality. ... For is it possible that a man in his senses should be merry and
jocose with eternal life and eternal death?"[13]

The Revaluation of the Emotions

The sacred rhetorics associate conversion with eloquence rather than dialectic
because the former touches not only the intellect but the heart. Because both
moral and spiritual life are less a matter of theoretical knowledge than of rightly
ordered will, the preacher, Keckermann argues, must concentrate his endeavors on "moving the emotions rather than [on] teaching the minds of his hear-
ers, for men sin more from corrupt emotions than ignorance of the truth."[14]
In his magisterial biblical rhetoric, the early Lutheran theologian, polemicist,
and scholar Flacius Illyricus likewise comments, "Emotion or the movements
of the heart govern practical knowledge and choice ... [and] Holy Scripture
deals not with speculative but practical knowledge, which God wishes to be,

above all else, living, ardent, and active."[15] Sacred rhetoric presupposes an audience at least nominally Christian and therefore less in need of being intellectually convinced than of being moved to embrace what it already believes true.

But these arguments for the efficacy of emotional suasion do not address the problem of its epistemic value; as Fish notes, philosophy mistrusts rhetoric precisely because it muddies objectivity with emotion, or, as John Locke memorably put it, "If we would speak of things as they are, we must allow that all the art of rhetoric, besides order and clearness . . . [is] for nothing else but to insinuate wrong ideas, move the passions, and thereby mislead the judgement."[16] In antiquity, as in the Enlightenment and thereafter, the pursuit of truth was typically (although not invariably) held to require dispassionate, rational inquiry, so that rhetoric's power to move the emotions seemed little else than the power to distort reality and deceive reason.

The polarization of reason and passion, and hence of philosophy and rhetoric, does not seem, however, to have been central to Renaissance thought. Into the seventeenth century, the distinction between rhetoric and philosophy centered on decorum rather than epistemology. Sacred orators and scholastic philosophers shared the same basic doctrines and beliefs. Rhetoric differed from philosophy in being a popular and practical art, more concerned with right action than speculative inquiry,[17] but both disciplines, in the still largely Christian cultures of the Renaissance, assumed and expounded the same Truth. Thus, in contrast to virtually all classical thinkers, Cicero as well as Plato,[18] Saint Augustine repeatedly insists that although a Christian "may be unacquainted with the writings of the philosophers[,] . . . [this] does not mean that he is ignorant of the teaching thanks to which we acquire knowledge of God and ourselves"; rather, Christianity is a "universal way," given "not to a few sages, but to the whole nation, an immense people."[19] George Herbert's "Faith" makes the same point:

> A peasant may believe, as much
> As a great clerk, and reach the highest stature.
> Thus dost thou make proud knowledge bend and crouch,
>   While grace fills up uneven nature.

Because Christianity subordinates knowledge to faith and love, it weakened the classical link between the philosophic quest and the summum bonum. Once gnosis no longer leads to the fulfillment of human existence, it sinks from a divinizing power to a technical specialty. For the mid-seventeenth-century Protestant Johannis Ursinus, in contrast, preaching aims not merely "to arouse a probable opinion but rather divine faith . . . to the glory of God and their own salvation."[20] Insofar as saving faith is more valuable than systematic argument, the superiority of philosophy to rhetoric with respect to either its methods or its ends seemed less evident to early modern Christians than it had to Plato.

The deeply favorable view of the emotions that is characteristic of the sacred rhetorics depends in part on denying reason's exclusive proprietary rights to truth. The emotions present a threat to rational objectivity but not to faith, particularly if one understands faith in the Protestant sense of *fiducia,* or trust. But the principal factor in the legitimation of affect, and hence of rhetoric, was Augustine's sweeping and massively influential rejection in *The City of God* of the classical intellectualist tradition with its hierarchical faculty psychology in favor of a more unified picture of mental activity, one in which feeling, willing, and loving become tightly intertwined. The emotions, Augustine thus argues, "are all essentially acts of the will," for as the will is attracted or repelled by different objects, "so it changes and turns into feelings of various kinds." Volition, subjectively experienced, is emotion, and Augustine uses the term "love" to denote this orientation of the self toward the desired object.[21] Affectivity, instead of being an irrational perturbation, thus moves into the center of spiritual experience.

The Renaissance appropriates Augustine's psychology for rhetorical theory, restoring the connection between the emotions and rhetoric that is fundamental to Aristotle but thereafter largely abandoned. This is particularly true for the sacred rhetorics, for Renaissance Augustinianism belongs to the history of the religious renewal, both Catholic and Protestant, that took place in the sixteenth and seventeenth centuries. Many of these texts, especially the more scholarly ones, contain detailed lists of emotions as part of their emphasis on *movere* and passionate discourse. Almost always the list begins with the love of God and includes hope and sometimes even faith—the Pauline theological virtues—along with spiritual joy, contrition, and desire for God, as well as "secular" emotions like shame and anger. Only the nature of their object differentiates secular from sacred, evil from good emotion. "For the sake of example," Carbo writes, "if desire (*concupiscendi vis*) is directed toward the heavens, it brings forth praiseworthy emotions which move us toward perfect virtues: as weariness of this life, fear of future punishment, desire of eternal beatitude, love of God, contempt of self, and others of this sort."[22] The sacred rhetorics can advocate an intensely emotional style because the whole view of the passions has changed and broadened to include the upper reaches of distinctively human experience. As Philipp Melanchthon writes, "Human emotions—love, hate, joy, sadness, envy, ambition, and the like—pertain to the will. . . . For what is the will if not the fount of the affections? And why do we not use the word 'heart' instead of 'will.' . . . For since God judges hearts, the heart must be the highest and most powerful part of man."[23]

The distance between ancient and Renaissance views of emotion can be measured by looking at a revision of the Platonic tripartite soul found in

Alsted's *Orator*. Alsted starts out like Plato, dividing the soul into intellective, irascible, and concupiscible components—Plato's charioteer, white horse, and black horse. The passage begins normally enough: the intellective faculty is the mind itself, to which Alsted attributes wisdom, prudence, and eloquence. But then the analysis takes a surprising turn. Plato's appetitive horse had been "crooked of frame, a massive jumble of a creature, with thick short neck, snub nose, black skin, and grey eyes; hot-blooded, consorting with wantonness and vainglory; shaggy of ear, deaf, and hard to control with whip and goad." But for Alsted the concupiscible part of the soul contains the love of God and man, love of virtue, zeal for divine glory and the salvation of all men, and so forth. In the irascible part, which Plato associates with courage and a sense of personal honor, Alsted places hope and faith (*fiducia*), fear of God, fortitude, magnanimity, and outspokenness.[24] In the process of Christianizing Plato's model of the soul, Alsted has completely disregarded Plato's rationalism and mind-body dualism, although in some sense Alsted's concupiscible faculty is not unrelated to the Platonic eros, the daimon in the middle space (*metaxy*) between gods and men. But this eros never appears in Plato's analyses of the parts or faculties of the soul; in these the model for appetite is physiological desire (food, sex), which Plato generally perceives as irrational and dangerous. If we might call Plato's model of the psyche, with its internal hierarchical subordinations, polytheistic, then Alsted's is Trinitarian: three coequal faculties subsisting in a single nature.

The evaluation of passionate discourse in Renaissance rhetoric follows from this assimilation of spiritual and affective experience. Movere is no longer thought of as subrational obfuscation. Rather, emotional persuasion aims at the transformation of moral and spiritual life by awakening a rightly ordered love, by redirecting the self from corporeal objects to spiritual ones. But it turns the heart toward spiritual reality by fulfilling, not subverting, the human need for the sensible and corporeal. It gives invisible truth a local habitation and a name through metaphor, symbol, prosopopoeia, and all the figures that create drama, vividness, and force. The criticism of passionate rhetoric as either sophistic play or sophistic deception fails because it ignores the Renaissance's unplatonic view of the seriousness of rhetoric, based on its unplatonic psychology of the emotions and their relation to the *iter mentis ad Deum*.

Passionate Knowledge

The sacred rhetorics (and, in general, Augustinian Christianity) set affective inwardness over dispassionate intellection. Yet—and this is the crucial point—they do so in a way that links rather than opposes emotion and reason. That is, they do not treat rhetoric's power to move the heart and will as separate, or even separable, from the procedures of rational inquiry, as though rhetoric concerned the pursuit of the Good, while philosophy alone directed the search for Truth. Rather, these texts typically insist on the ineluctable "interwovenness" of cognitive and emotional experience. This claim partly derives from the Aristotelian position that emotion is not an irrational perturbation but the offspring of belief.[25] We feel fear, for example, because we judge that danger is imminent. Emotion is therefore bound up with argument; the orator moves by giving reasons. As early modern rhetorics and logics endlessly remark, the loci of dialectic and pathos are identical.[26] Obviously, not all arguments arouse emotion because some subjects have no affective valence, being too abstract, trivial, or logically intricate. Nevertheless, in principle, passion flows from proof, and thus discussions of movere often occur under invention rather than (or as well as) under *elocutio*.

But the link between intellection and affect found throughout the sacred rhetorics has deeper and more complex epistemic premises. These are worth tracing in some detail, for they imply that with respect to the Christian cultures of the Middle Ages and Renaissance, Fish's paradigm rather profoundly misrepresents the fundamental nature of "Western thought": that for these cultures, the distinctive features of rhetorical discourse had an *essential* role in the pursuit of truth and goodness.

Here again, Augustinian theology proves crucial. For Augustine, love and knowledge are tightly interconnected, as the noetic quest begins from and is propelled by love, yet we can love only that which, in some sense, we already know. Rather than undermining rational judgment, love wings the mind's search for God and truth. As Augustine writes in the *Confessions*, "My weight is my love; wherever I am carried, it is my love that carries me there. By your gift we are set on fire and are carried upward; we are red hot and we go."[27]

This erotic epistemology pervades early modern thought. In his *De anima*, Juan Luis Vives writes:

> The object is known so that it may be loved, but the knowledge need only be so much as is sufficient to elicit love. Yet when we are connected to the desired object we know it better and more intimately, and then we enjoy it. Our first knowledge leads us to believe the object is good; in the latter knowledge we feel that it is so. . . . Thus love is the middle point between inchoate knowledge and the full knowledge of union, in which desire always disappears but not love. This rather burns more fiercely, the more and greater the goods found in that union.[28]

The noetic quest begins in inchoate knowledge, in a dim and partially realized faith, which awakens in turn a desire for this faintly glimpsed object. Impelled by desire, the quester strives to apprehend what he loves, which achieved, creates the ardent love of full union. As Edward Reynolds's *A Treatise of the Passions* (1650) explains:

> Love and Knowledge have mutuall sharpening and causalitie each
> on other: for as Knowledge doth generate Love, so Love doth nour-
> ish and exercise Knowledge. The reason whereof is that unseparable
> union which is in all things between the Truth and Good of them.
> . . . The more Appetite enjoyeth of [the Good], the deeper inquiry
> doth it make and the more compleat union doth it seek with [the
> Truth].[29]

In the sixteenth century, this epistemology enters the rhetorical tradition—as,
significantly, a defense of movere. Erasmus's Ecclesiastes, the earliest full-scale
sacred rhetoric, makes the debt to Augustine explicit:

> What Augustine, following Plato, said is true: nothing is loved un-
> less known at least to some degree and again nothing is known un-
> less loved in some respect. . . . In the Hortensius Cicero praised phi-
> losophy and aroused love for it before he taught it. And those who
> undertake to teach a subject first inflame their students, showing
> through amplification how noble it is . . . what great things it prom-
> ises and how useful it will be.[30]

The Hortensius was the book that first stirred Augustine to embrace philosophy. For Erasmus, it was not Cicero's arguments but his encomiastic rhetoric that led Augustine to love a subject he barely knew. Eloquence is not
philosophy; but both, like Dante's Virgil and Beatrice, direct the viator into the
ways of truth. The connection between love and knowledge appears again in
Keckermann's Systema rhetoricae: "Reason and will should be implicit in emotion, and emotions resolve into knowledge and understanding. . . . Will and
emotion derive from reason and knowledge."[31] Here again emotion is bound
up in the larger cognitive process. Our emotions spring from belief and lead
us to further insight.

This sense of the inseparability of love and knowledge found support in
the biblical anthropology of the Renaissance. Both Flacius's Clavis Scripturae
Sacrae (1562) and Glassius's Philologia sacra (1623) point out that the Bible
does not differentiate between knowing and feeling, as classical philosophy
did. Glassius thus comments that in Hebrew, "to know or to think does not
denote simply gnosis but also emotion and affect, . . . or what is the same, it
signifies a living and efficacious knowledge. . . . Thus [in Hebrew] to know is
the same as to love, to care for.[32] Flacius makes the same point: "The Hebrews
attribute the whole psychic life of man to the heart and appear to place the
rational soul completely in the heart, . . . ascribing to the heart the power of
both thought and choice, of wishing and doing. . . . On the other hand, the
philosophers locate the rational soul . . . in the head or brain, leaving only emotion in the heart.[33] Both classical and biblical anthropology coexist up through
the Renaissance, sometimes causing no small inconsistencies. The biblical,

however, dominates what William Bouwsma has called the Augustinian Renaissance, to which belongs most of the period's rhetorical theory and whose ideal was not Jonathan Swift's stoical horses but a passionate and unitive knowledge. Rhetoric on this view participates in the noetic quest; its emotional power does not subvert reason but animates it, drawing heart and mind toward union with the desired object. As Adam says in his conversation with Raphael, "Love thou say'st / Leads up to heav'n, is both the way and guide."[34]

The claim that the emotions, particularly love, span the distance between confused intimation and full apprehension addresses what may be *the* fundamental problem in premodern epistemology: How and to what extent can human minds gain access to that which cannot be perceived by the senses? This is, obviously, a theological matter. But it is also a rhetorical one—as can be seen from Francis Bacon's well-known declaration:

> The duty and office of Rhetoric is to apply reason to imagination for the better moving of the will[,] . . . for the affections themselves carry ever an appetite to good, as reason doth. The difference is, that the affection beholdeth merely the present, reason beholdeth the future and sum of time. And therefore the present filling the imagination more, reason is commonly vanquished; but after the force of eloquence and persuasion hath made things future and remote appear as present, then upon the revolt of the imagination reason prevaileth."[35]

That is, for Bacon rhetoric brings the distant objects of reason imaginatively close enough to seem visible, to seem real. Or, as John Donne remarks in the course of a sermon, "Rhetorique will make absent and remote things present to your understanding."[36]

But this contrast between the remote objects of reason and close-at-hand sensible particulars derives, as Wesley Trimpi has shown, from Aristotle's crucial distinction between two types of knowability.[37] For Aristotle things can be knowable either to us or in themselves: the concrete objects of sense are most knowable to us; that which lies farthest from perception (that is, universals), most knowable in themselves. Because all knowledge derives from sense experience, cognition always involves a movement from that which is knowable to us toward that which is knowable in itself but harder for us to know—a movement from, in Bacon's terms, things present toward things remote.[38]

What is at stake is not merely knowability, inasmuch as those things most distant from us are also more excellent than what we can perceive close up. As Aristotle explains in a remarkable passage from *The Parts of Animals:*

> Other substances constituted by nature some are ungenerated, imperishable, and eternal, while others are subject to generation and decay. The former are excellent and divine, but less accessible to

knowledge. The evidence that might throw light on them . . . is furnished but scantily by sensation; whereas respecting perishable plants and animals we have abundant information, living as we do in their midst. . . . [Yet] the scanty conceptions to which we can attain of celestial things give us, from their excellence, more pleasure than all our knowledge of the world in which we live; just as a half-glimpse of persons that we love is more delightful than an accurate view of other things, what ever their number and dimensions.[39]

The objects least accessible to knowledge are also the most valuable (and vice versa). There thus exists an *inverse* proportion between the excellence of an object and our knowledge of it: an epistemic state of affairs that Trimpi labels the ancient dilemma of knowledge and representation. This issue then becomes finding a way to bring what is remote and yet most worth knowing into some kind of relation with what we can more accurately grasp. Rhetoric, Bacon suggests, does just that by making the distant and remote present to the imagination.

Whereas Bacon would appear to be thinking mainly of secular oratory, the ancient dilemma had perhaps greater significance for the sacred rhetorics. But in the sacred rhetorics, the terms of the dilemma have been reshaped by specifically Christian (and profoundly un-Aristotelian) modes of spanning the distance between the divine and the humanly knowable. To get some idea of these theological solutions, which turn out to be identical to the rhetorical ones, we might look briefly at two early modern English divines, Richard Hooker and John Donne.

Hooker's account of the grounds of faith begins by restating the Aristotelian distinction between two kinds of knowability: "*Certainty of Evidence* we call that, when the mind doth assent unto this or that, not because it is true in itself, but because the truth is clear, because it is manifest to us." The truths of logic and perception are certain because evident to us; we find ourselves, however, painfully unsure concerning the more excellent objects of faith precisely because clear evidence for these is unavailable. Hooker resolves the ancient dilemma by arguing for a second type of certainty, the "certainty of adherence," whereby the person who has once tasted God's "heavenly sweetness" hopes "against all reason of believing." For Hooker faith grasps its object by love, not evidence.[40] Hooker, that is, not only accepts the terms of the dilemma as those relevant to Christian belief but assigns emotion a central role in the act of faith—the same role that the sacred rhetorics attribute to movere in the art of persuasion.

In a somewhat different way, the ancient dilemma also structures Donne's treatment of the Incarnation and sacraments. Here too, the theological attempt to make that which is remote near and hence knowable has rhetorical implications. The parallel is apparent from Donne's phraseology: as rhetoric makes "absent and remote things present to your understanding," so the sacraments bring Christ "nearer [to us] in visible and sensible things." Similarly, the Incarnation brings *the glory of God . . .* within a convenient distance to be seen *in the face of Jesus Christ,"* for Christ "could not have come nearer, than in taking this nature upon him"; he is the "image of the invisible God, and so more proportionall unto us, more apprehensible by us.[41] As "visible and sensible things," image and sacrament thus negotiate the poles of the ancient dilemma, enabling us to bridge the epistemic and ontological distance between the invisible God and the sensory objects knowable to us.

As ways of negotiating the terms of the ancient dilemma, the routes laid down by Hooker and Donne of love and images are fundamental for Renaissance sacred rhetorics. These affirm that the emotions are moved by the conjunction of *magnitudo* and *praesentia,* by the union, that is, of the excellent object with sensuous immediacy. *Magnitudo* and *praesentia* thus represent the polarities that must be brought into relation for the most excellent objects to penetrate our thought and feeling, for as Edward Reynolds notes, the emotions are moved only by the presence of their object.[42] In his *Ecclesiasticae rhetoricae,* de Granada writes, "Emotions are quickened (as philosophers say) both by the excellence of the objects [*magnitudo rerum*] and by placing them, vividly before the eyes of the audience [*praesentia oculis subiecta*]."[43] For the most valuable things or truths to become objects of men's love, they must be brought "near" through the figural techniques for rendering things both large and luminous.

Hence the sacred rhetorics insist on the value of images, whether literal or metaphoric. Because the "deep things of God," according to a late seventeenth-century Protestant, "lye remote from our Understandings (as all Spiritual Objects do)," they need to be "represented under some obvious and sensible Image . . . that so the disproportion between them and our faculties, being qualified and reduced, we may the better . . . converse with them. . . . For as we are more affected when the things of God are brought down to us, under sensible representations, so likewise the things themselves become more intelligible."[44] Images make what is unseen accessible to both feeling *and* thought. Nor are affect and intelligibility unrelated; as we have seen, the sacred rhetorics presuppose the Augustinian dialectic of love and knowledge. Their mutual dependence is likewise implicit in Hooker's claim that love—our love of God's "heavenly sweetness"—creates the certainty of adherence. Love bridges the poles of the ancient dilemma precisely because, as Thomas Aquinas states it brings its object nearer (*propinquius*) to the lover.[45] But love requires the presence of its object, and hence requires images.

The correspondences between religious and rhetorical techniques arise from their common basis in the ancient dilemma. As rhetoric, in Bacon's formulation, makes "things future and remote appear as present," so for Reynolds, "Divine love hath the same kinde of vertue with Divine Faith; that as this is the being and subsisting of things to come and distant in Time; so that is the Union and knitting of things absent, and distant in Place."[46] Whereas in the classical tradition the ancient dilemma is negotiated by *scientia* or discursive reasoning, in Christianity only faith working by love can traverse the distance between God and humans. Saint Thomas thus writes, "By faith we know certain things about God which are so sublime that reason cannot reach them by means of demonstration."[47] This is also Hooker's point: in matters of faith, love outstrips evidence. Renaissance sacred rhetorics build on this theological (that is, philosophic) foundation in their claim that passionate vividness can carry the mind to God while reason flounders in its inevitable limitations. The language of images, which overcomes the distance of both time and place, knits the soul to God, while no amount of argument can enable the intellect to know him. The scared rhetorics lay so much weight on imaginative vividness because it creates both love and faith. In his discussion of hypotyposis, Flacius thus comments that "the Bible employs pictorial language not only to move the stony heart of man more strongly . . . but also to strengthen [it] with greater certitude."[48] Rhetoric in this sense, then, is not below but beyond reason.

Absolute and Objective Truth

Early modern sacred rhetorics thus raise serious doubts about the historical, and hence theoretical, validity of the standard postmodern account of rhetoric. These texts oppose rather than equate rhetoric to sophistic play and skeptical relativism; they do not treat the emotions as subrational; they do not view rhetoric as antithetic—or even as unrelated—to the pursuit of the True and the Good. This much seems fairly obvious; its significance, however, depends on the significance one is willing to accord these obscure, if numerous, works, by no means a clear-cut issue. But the fact that the sacred rhetorics repeatedly and explicitly base their project on philosophic (including theological) axioms points to a further conclusion, on which a good deal hinges. If philosophy is the unvarnished language of objective and absolute rational certitude, as Fish claims, it would seem inherently hostile to rhetoric. And yet the sacred rhetorics defend the use of passionate, figured language on philosophic grounds. That they would—that they could—do this suggests that Fish's notion of philosophy may be seriously inaccurate and hence that the postmodern narrative of the quarrel between rhetoric and philosophy fails not simply because it ignores one subcategory of rhetoric but also because it misrepresents the nature of Western thought *totaliter.*

It is not, first of all, self-evident that philosophy pursues "objective and absolute" truths untainted by "metaphysics, morals, and personal conviction" (this latter category including, one presumes, religious belief). Metaphysics, ethics, and theology have usually been regarded as philosophic concerns, and it seems both likely and proper that what philosophers write on these matters expresses their personal conviction. And although numerous philosophers have held that one truth or another was objective and absolute—the law of noncontradiction, the cogito—few claimed that philosophy deals exclusively, or even primarily, with objectively demonstrable certainties.[49] Aristotle's methodological preface to the *Nicomachean Ethics* has particular interest in this regard: a philosophical analysis, he begins, "will be adequate if it has as much clearness as the subject matter admits of; for precision is not to be sought for alike in all discussions." Ethical and political goods, in particular,

> exhibit much variety and fluctuation . . . for before now men have
> been undone by reason of their wealth, and others by reason of their
> courage. We must be content, then, in speaking of such subjects . . .
> to indicate the truth roughly and in outline . . . for it is the mark of
> an educated man to look for precision in each class of things just so
> far as the nature of the subject admits: it is evidently equally foolish
> to accept probable reasoning from a mathematician and to demand
> from a rhetorician demonstrative proofs.[50]

Moral and political inquiry, that is, seeks to formulate approximate rather than absolute truths; its arguments are probable, which is to say that they are rhetorical. Yet for Aristotle the fact that these subjects use probable (rhetorical) reasoning does not render them unphilosophic.

A second, perhaps equally important problem with Fish's definition of philosophy is that a great deal of Western philosophy—nearly all of it for the thirteen centuries separating Origen from Descartes—is religious. This returns us to the sacred rhetorics. These draw on central philosophic traditions in which the pursuit of goodness is inseparable from love and therefore never wholly objective, in which truth is apprehended by faith and therefore never known with absolute evidential or logical certainty. The same traditions likewise argue that one can only "speak about God" in the language of "figures, tropes, metaplasms and allegories."[51] Aquinas thus defends the radical metaphoricity of the Bible by invoking the Aristotelian postulate that human beings "attain to intellectual truths through sensible things, because all our knowledge originates from sense."[52] Before the Enlightenment, that is, a good deal of Western philosophy makes belief, affect, and nonliteral, nontransparent language central to the pursuit of the Good and the True, and consequently has no quarrel with rhetoric, which is simply language that relies on probable argument, emotional power, and figurative heightening. "Rhetoricatur igitur Spiritus sanctus," as Luther puts it: "And therefore the Holy Ghost," although most certainly not a sophist, "is a rhetorician."[53]

NOTES

1. Stanley Fish, "Rhetoric," in *Critical Terms for Literary Study*, ed, Frank Lentricchia and Thomas McLaughlin (Chicago: University of Chicago Press, 1990), 204–

205, 205–206, 208–209. Considerable portions of this essay offer a revised version of chapters 3 and 5 of my *Sacred Rhetoric: The Christian Grand Style in the English Renaissance* (Princeton: Princeton University Press, 1988). All translations are mine unless otherwise indicated.

2. The distrust of artistic language found in most English vernacular sacred rhetorics, especially those of a Puritan stripe, is atypical; see Shuger, *Sacred Rhetoric*, 50–53, 69–70, 93–95.

3. Johann-Heinrich Alstead, *Orator, sex libris informatus* [1612] (Herborn, 1616), 8. For a general overview of Renaissance sacred rhetoric, including brief summaries of the major texts and information concerning their availability in Tudor and Stuart England, see chapter 2 of Shuger, *Sacred Rehtoric.*

4. Bartholomew Keckermann, *Rhetoricae ecclesiasticae sive artis formandi et habendi conciones sacras, libri duo* [1600] (Hanover, 1616), 27, 44.

5. Luis de Granada, *Ecclesiasticae rhetoricae, sive, de ratione concionandi, libri sex* [1576?] (Cologne, 1582), 328.

6. Ludovicus Carbo, *Divinus orator, vel de rhetorica divina libri septem* (Venice, 1595), 23, 18; see also Johannis Sturm, *De universa ratione elocutionis rhetoricae, libri 4* [1575] (Strassburg, 1576), 665.

7. See, for example, Quintilian, *Institutio Oratoria*, trans. H. E. Butler, 4 vols. (Cambridge: Harvard University Press, 1920); St. Augustine, *On Christian Doctrine*, trans. D. W. Robertson (Indianapolis: Bobbs-Merrill, 1958), 4.53; Didacus Valades, *Rhetorica Christiana ad concionandi, et orandi usum accomodata* (Perugia, 1579); Bernard Lamy, *The Art of Speaking: Written in French by Messieurs du Port Royal: In Pursuance of a former Treatise, Intituled "The Art of Thinking"* (London, 1626); Johann-Heinrich Alsted, *Theologica Prophetica* (Hanover, 1622); and Erasmus, 5:959b, 922d, de Granada, pp. 306–7; Keckermann, *Rhetoricae ecclesiasticae*, p. 110.

8. Desiderius Erasmus, *Ecclesiastes sive concionator evangelicus* [1535], ed. J. Le-Clerc, vol. 5 of *Opera omnia emendatiora et auctiora*, 10 vols. (Leiden, 1703–1706), 5: 849f.

9. See, for example, Lamy, 1.99, 145.

10. Nicholas Caussin, *De eloquentia sacra et human, libri 16* [1617?] (Paris, 1630), 945.

11. Agostino Valiero, *De ecclesiastica rehtorica libri tres* [1575], vol. 1 of *Ecclesiasticae rhetoricae*, 2 vols. (Verona, 1732), 45.

12. Stanley Fish, *Self-Consuming Artifacts: The Experience of Seventeenth-Century Literature* (Berkeley: University of California Press, 1972), 3–4.

13. Robert South, *Sermons Preached upon Several Occasions*, 4 vols. (Philadelphia, 1845), 2:81.

14. Bartholomew Keckermann, *Systema rhetoricae in quo artis praecepta plene et methodice tradunter* [1606], vol. 2 of *Opera omnia quae extant*, 2 vols. (Geneva, 1614), 2: 1392.

15. Matthias Flacius Illyricus, *Clavis Scripturae Sacrae, seu de sermone sacrarum literarum, in duas partes divisae* [1562] (Leipzig, 1695), 1:179.

16. John Locke, *Essay Concerning Human Understanding*, ed. John Yolton, 2 vols. (London: Dent, 1961), 3.10.34.

17. See, for example, Valiero, 95; de Granada, 41–43; Carbo, 187; Keckermann,

Systema, 2:1391–92; Caussin, 12; Niel Hemmingsen, *The Preacher or Method of Preaching*, trans. John Horsfall (London, 1574); Andreas Hyperius, *The Practis of Preaching*, trans. John Ludham (London, 1577); Alsted, *Orator*, 148.

18. Both of whom took for granted that philosophic wisdom differed in substance from popular belief; Jerrold Seigel, *Rhetoric and Philosophy in Renaissance Humanism: The Union of Eloquence and Wisdom, Petrarch to Valla* (Princeton: Princeton University Press, 1968), 9–10, 19–25.

19. Saint Augustine, *The City of God*, ed. David Knowles, trans. Henry Bettenson (Harmondsworth, England: Penguin, 1972), 8.10, 10.32, 10.13.

20. Johann-Henricus Ursinus, *Ecclesiastes, sive de sacris concionibus libri sex* (Frankfurt, 1659), 9; see also François Fenelon, *Fenelon's Dialogues on Eloquence* [1717], trans. Wilbur Samuel Howell (Princeton: Princeton University Press, 1951), 89.

21. Saint Augustine, *The City of God*, 14.6–7.

22. Carbo, 204. See also Caussin, 459–512; Keckermann, *Systema*, 2:1615–31, and *Rhetoricae ecclesiasticae*, 43; de Granada, 83–87; Melanchthon, *Elementorum rhetorices*, 13:425–57, 434.

23. Philipp Melanchthon, *Loci communes theologici*, ed. Wilhelm Pauk, trans. Lowell Satre, in *Melanchthon and Bucer*, 18–152 (London: SCM Press, 1969), 27–29.

24. Alsted, *Orator, sex libris informatus; Phaedrus*, 253–54, 208–209.

25. W. W. Fortenbaugh, *Aristotle on Emotion* (London: Duckworth, 1975), 17, 83.

26. Agricola, 199–200; de Granada, 110–11; Alsted, *Orator*, 91; Carbo, 124–125, 188; Keckermann, *Systema*, 2:1610; Caussin, 552.

27. Saint Augustine, *The Confessions of St. Augustine*, trans. Rex Warner (New York: New American Library, 1963), 13.9.

28. Juan Luis Vives, *De anima et vita* [1538] (Turin: Bottega d'Erasmo, 1959), 178.

29. Edward Reynolds, *A Treatise of the Passions and Faculties of the Soul of Man* (London, 1650), 103–104.

30. Erasmus, *Ecclesiastes sive concionator evangelicus* [1535], 5:952b.

31. Keckermann, *Systema rhetoricae in quo artis praecepta plene et methodice tradunter*, 2:1612.

32. Salomon Glassius, *Philologia sacra liber quintus, qua rhetorica sacra comprensa* [1623] (Frankfurt, 1653), 1053–54.

33. Flacius Illyricus, 1:178.

34. John Milton, *Paradise Lost*, ed. Merritt Hughes (New York: Odyssey, 1935), 8.612–13.

35. Francis Bacon, *The Works of Francis Bacon*, 7 vols. (London, 1826), 1:153–54.

36. John Donne, *The Sermons of John Donne*, 10 vols, ed. Evelyn Simpson and George Potter (Berkeley: University of California Press, 1953–62), 4:87.

37. Wesley Trimpi, *Muses of One Mind: The Literary Analysis of Experience and Its Continuity* (Princeton: Princeton University Press, 1983), 87–129.

38. Aristotle, *The Complete Works of Aristotle: The Revised Oxford Translation*, ed. Jonathan Barnes, 2 vols. (Princeton: Princeton University Press, 1984), *Post. An.* 1.2.71b–72a; *Meta.* 7.4.2–3.

39. Aristotle, *The Parts of Animals*, 1.5.644b, in *The Complete Works*; see also *De anima*, 1.1.402a.

40. Richard Hooker, "Of the Certainty and Perpetuity of Faith in the Elect" in

The Complete Works, [1586], vol. 3 of *The Works of Mr. Richard Hooker*, 469–81, ed. John Keble, 7th ed., 3 vols. (Oxford, 1888; reprinted New York: Burt Franklin, 1970), 3: 470–71.

41. Donne, 5:144, 4:90–91, 125, 2:320.

42. Reynolds, 97.

43. de Granada, *Ecclesiasticae rhetoricae*, 158. The formula likewise appears in Keckermann, *Rhetoricae ecclesiasticae*, 53, 85; Alsted, *Theologica*, 20; Carbo, 208; Valades, 159.

44. Robert Ferguson, *The Interest of Reason in Religion; With the Import and Use of Scripture Metaphors* (London, 1675), 320–23.

45. Saint Thomas Aquinas, *Introduction to Saint Thomas Aquinas*, ed. Anton Pegis (New York: Modern Library, 1945), *Summa*, 1a.2ae.66.6.

46. Reynolds, 96.

47. Aquinas, *Introduction to Saint Thomas Aquinas*, 459.

48. Flacius Illyricus, *Clavis Scripturae Sacrae*, 2:310.

49. The only philosophers to do so who come to mind are the logical positivists and Spinoza, Wittgenstein, and Russell in their early writings.

50. Aristotle, 1.4.1094b.

51. Charles Trinkaus, *In Our Image and Likeness: Humanity and Divinity in Italian Humanist Thought*, 2 vols. (Chicago: University of Chicago Press, 1970), 1:62–63; see also Ferguson, *The Interest of Reason in Religion*, 279–280.

52. Aquinas, *Introduction to Saint Thomas Aquinas*, 16.

53. Martin Luther, *D. Martin Luther's Werke*, 66 vols. (Weimar: Boehlaus, 1883–), vol, 40, pt. 3, 59–60; quoted in Klaus Dockhorn, "Rhetorica movet: Protestantischer Humanismus und karolingische Renaissance" *Rhetorik: Beitrage zu ihrer Geschichte im Deutschland vom 16–20 Jahrhundert*, ed. Helmut Schanze (Frankfurt: Athenaion, 1974), 17–41.

5

Rites of Terror: Emotion, Metaphor, and Memory in Melanesian Initiation Cults

Harvey Whitehouse

In this study of the ordeals endured by initiates in Papua, New Guinea, Harvey Whitehouse explores the way religious experience is constructed in terror, and he remarks on the long-term consequences of that ritual strategy. For Whitehouse, there is an irreducible core to the experience, a complex of interrelated emotional and cognitive elements that cannot be rendered as simple thoughts without doing them irredeemable damage. Presenting the rites in the context of what he terms "the imagistic mode of religiosity," Whitehouse argues that the trauma of the rites is the basis for a unique order of memories about it. Those memories—"flashbulb memories"—are imprinted in such a way that they survive, in strikingly rich detail, for long periods of time. Through the collective experience of the rites of terror, initiates as well as their initiators bond closely to each other, enhancing overall social solidarity in a community that only infrequently engages in the rites. As Whitehouse claims, "Actual persons inhabit these memories" so that "the political and religious community that initiation creates is fixed forever in the minds of novices." Not merely the mastery of a performance script or a schema of actions, the rites of terror loom in memory as profound, lived experience central to the coalescence of social identity in Melanesian males.

What is the relation of emotion to cognition in Whitehouse's presentation of the rites of terror? In what ways is terror itself constructed for the initiates and their handlers? Is a certain order of experience expected by the participants? In what ways, according to Whitehouse, have these

Harvey Whitehouse, "Rites of Terror: Emotion, Metaphor and Memory in Melanesian Initiation Cults," *Journal of the Royal Anthropological Institute* Volume 2, Number 4 (Dec., 1996), 703–715. Used by permission of Blackwell Publishing.

sorts of rites been misunderstood by previous observers? How have those observers reduced religious ritual to other terms? Is Whitehouse correct in claiming that the imprinting of images on the memories of participants is the primary function of the ritual, in social and personal terms? Does Whitehouse's approach to emotion in religion manage to avoid the reductionism that he criticizes in other accounts? What is the place of metaphor in this interpretation?

Terror is an integral component of religious experience in many of the societies of Papua New Guinea. Following a hair-raising account of penis-bleeding among the Ilahita Arapesh, Tuzin observes that the whole ordeal "is carefully and successfully designed to inspire maximum horror in its victims."[1] Barth describes how a Baktaman novice was so terrified by the ordeals of initiation that he defecated on the legs of his elders and had to be excluded from the group of boys being initiated.[2] In his analysis of Orokaiva initiation Schwimmer approvingly cites Chinnery and Beaver's claim that a function of the rites is to instill "absolute and lasting terror in the candidates."[3] In his discussion of Bimin-Kuskusmin initiation, Poole likewise emphasizes the terror of novices, observing that "the piercing of the nasal septa and the burning of forearms . . . created the most trauma, producing overt signs of physical and/or psychological shock in six cases."[4] Examples could, of course, be multiplied. In this region terrifying ordeals are not confined to initiations; they may also be evident in such diverse contexts as mortuary rites, possession, and millenarian activity.[5] It would not be unduly fanciful to describe these sorts of practices as "rites of terror."

The principal dynamics of rites of terror may be identified in the initiation system of the Orokaiva of northern Papua. Schwimmer divides these rites into several phases which do not necessarily occur in a fixed sequence.[6] One phase entails the isolation of novices in a hut where, for several months,[7] they observe a taboo on washing but are generally treated well. During a second phase, the novices, blinded by barkcloth hoods, are herded together in the village and brutally attacked by senior men who assume the guise of spirits (*embahi*). In the course of this ordeal, novices are gradually corralled onto a ceremonial platform. Then there follows a much longer period of seclusion. According to Iteanu, this second seclusion lasts for between three and seven years, during which time the novices must not be seen or heard beyond their place of confinement, on pain of death.[8] During this period, novices learn to play sacred instruments (flutes and bullroarers).

Schwimmer's third phase concerns the debut of the novices, decked out in full dancing regalia. The novices enter the dancing ground in a dense phalanx, brandishing mock spears and stone clubs. A fourth phase involves the presentation of "homicidal emblems" (*otohu*), at which time aged warriors recite the names of men they have killed in battle, before otohu are fastened to the foreheads of the novices. There is a final phase which is not included in Schwimmer's summary, but which Williams and Iteanu regard as indispensable. This phase entails, among other acts, the distribution of amassed wealth. Iteanu stresses the fact that novices are responsible for sharing out cuts of pork from a lofty platform, not unlike the one to which they were earlier driven by the embahi.

All ethnographers of the Orokaiva have stressed the terrifying nature of the embahi ceremony. The early accounts of Chinnery and Beaver (1915), further enriched by Williams (1930), convey a sense of the real panic induced in the Orokaiva novices and the anguish of parents who are witnesses to their suffering.[9] Moreover, as Iteanu more recently observes, there is always a risk that some children may not survive the ordeal.[10] Any thoroughgoing analysis of the ceremony clearly needs to take into account its traumatic and life-threatening character. I examine critically several current approaches to the interpretation of this kind of ritual, arguing that the principal weakness of all of them is that they fail to show how the complex conceptual and emotional aspects of "rites of terror" are interconnected. I then propose an alternative theory, linking the formation of affect-laden memories to the political dynamics of Melanesian initiation.

Current Approaches to Rites of Terror

Bloch has recently used Orokaiva initiation to elucidate what he calls the "irreducible structures of religious phenomena."[11] His starting point is that there is a universal recognition of the biological processes of birth, maturation, reproduction, physical deterioration, and death that characterize the life cycles of humans and many other species. Social groups, however, are not subject to this kind of process; they have a notional permanence, which is unaffected by the arrival and departure of particular members. In a Durkheimian spirit, Bloch argues that ritual provides a way of conceptualizing a timeless social order. Through the caricature and violent negation of biology and process, ritual affirms the transcendent authority of society, represented in the timeless order of the ancestral world.

According to Bloch, the embahi ceremony among the Orokaiva brings into focus an image of transcendental permanence through the symbolic destruction of earthly vitality. The hooded novices are like pigs, insofar as their persecution by the embahi is construed as a hunt, and they are herded onto a platform associated with butchery. With some ingenuity, Bloch argues that pigs represent the biological aspects of humans. Being the only other species of large mammal indigenous to Papua New Guinea, pigs are especially similar to humans in their reproductive characteristics. They are also uniquely associated with humans by virtue of their integration into social life. They are referred to as "children" and their deaths are mourned. Bloch maintains, therefore, that pigs represent the vital or bodily aspects of people.

The embahi, by contrast, are like birds. Bloch argues that the feathers, movements, and vocalizations of the embahi have strong avian connotations. According to Bloch, the bird is symbolically the mirror image of the pig. Birds are linked with an immortal extraterrestrial existence beyond the village world of vigorous activity, birth, and aging. Avian imagery provides a way of conceptualizing the sacred or spiritual side of humanity, which is somehow the opposite of corporeal, transformative experience. In the embahi ceremony, the piglike aspects of the novices are "killed" by the birdlike ancestors. All that remains of the novices is their sacred, transcendental character. This is nurtured during the period of seclusion away from the vitality of village life, where (appropriately enough) the novices are said to "grow feathers."

The ritual could not end at this point, because the aim of initiation is not to "kill" the novices, but to deliver them back into village life as changed persons. This is not simply a matter of recovering the vitality that was earlier beaten out of the novices by the embahi; it is a matter of conquering that vitality, of bringing it under transcendental control. This enables Bloch to account for the triumphant and militaristic tenor of the debut. The brandishing of spears and clubs, the conferral of otohu, and the climbing of the platform in the guise of hunters and butchers rather than prey publicly declares the new role of initiates as killers rather than victims. They are reinstated in the village, the life cycle, and the production process, but they are now more birdlike, more sacred than before. In keeping with Hertz's image of the "social being grafted upon the physical individual," transcendental authority is seen as penetrating more deeply into the fleshly, vital body of the initiate.[12] This is a process that will continue through life until finally, at death, the corporeal shell is utterly consumed.

Bloch's reanalysis of Orokaiva initiation emphasizes certain ideological implications of ritual violence. According to this approach, the most important effect of the embahi ceremony is that the novices are symbolically killed or, more precisely, their vitality is negated so that they become purely transcendental beings. The jubilant return of the novices, which Bloch describes as "rebounding violence," is a way of conceptualizing and instituting a political order that is subject to ancestral authority.[13]

A problem with Bloch's interpretation, as applied to the embahi ceremony or to Papua New Guinea initiation rites in general, is that it does not capture very much of the conscious experience of participants. According to Bloch, embahi violence is part of a bifurcation process, as cognitively simple as it is ideologically powerful. In the context of this irreducible core of religious thought, the terror of Orokaiva novices seems to be superfluous, a mere side effect of the particular choreography that happens to be involved. One gains the impression that an equally satisfactory result could be achieved in the embahi ceremony by symbolically killing the novices *without actually frightening them*. I will try to show that this is not the case. But, before we can understand the role of terror, it is first necessary to appreciate that many of the cognitive processes involved in Papua New Guinea initiation rites are themselves rather disconcerting, and may not fit very easily with the principle of "rebounding violence."

Bloch's hypotheses about the symbolic value of birds and pigs are not substantially derived from Orokaiva statements. This is wholly justifiable in principle, and would be true of any thorough interpretation of the symbolic value of these animals. Whatever understandings are cultivated through the use of porcine or avian imagery in Orokaiva initiation, they are not transmitted in language. Williams commented at length on the absence of exegetical commentary attaching to Orokaiva ritual, and Schwimmer supports his observation that novices are not given verbal interpretations of initiatory symbolism.[14] Even if they were, that would not be the end of the anthropological quest for meaning.[15] In the case at hand, virtually the entire burden of cultural transmission rests on the ritual acts themselves.

Bloch intuits that the revelations of Orokaiva initiation are iconically codified. In his interpretation, the physical and behavioral characteristics of pigs are concrete metaphors for human characteristics. Thus, under certain circumstances, the killing of pigs would imply the destruction or negation of porcine qualities in the sacrifier, in a manner that parallels the symbolic killing of novices behaving like pigs. Contra Bloch, however, novices are not treated in a way that makes them like pigs in general, but in a way that specifically makes them like *wild* pigs. The "hunting" of novices by numerous embahi connotes the collective wild pig drives for which the Orokaiva are renowned.[16] This technique of hunting frequently involves the members of several villages, who set light to the tall blade grass to drive wild pigs and other animals into the hands of their pursuers. The novices in initiation who are similarly herded and hunted do not, therefore, resemble domestic pigs, as Bloch assumes, but *wild* pigs. Domestic pigs are indeed anthropomorphically cognized by virtue of their integration into social life, but the case of wild pigs is rather different. If wild pigs are like people, then this has nothing to do with images of the village world of physical activity, maturation, death, and so on; as Iteanu observes, it is because they are like alien and dangerous human enemies who, prior to pacification, were likewise killed and eaten if encountered in the forest.[17] Insofar as novices appreciate that their senior kinsmen are treating them like quarry and thus repudiating their former nurturant, protective roles, this is likely to stimulate confusion and strong emotion. What sense novices make of all this has never been comprehensively explored by ethnographers of the Orokaiva, but knowledge of other New Guinea religions encourages us to be wary of a simplistic understanding of iconicity.

Bloch's interpretations of porcine and avian imagery in Orokaiva initiation are generated by a highly original and ambitious theory, but this theory seems to bypass much of the intellectually challenging and emotionally stimulating aspects of religious experience. For example, if it is argued that the "core" understandings cultivated in the embahi ceremony are fetched from everyday knowledge, then it is hard to see how initiation might engender revelatory experiences. According to this theory, knowledge that one already possesses about pigs and birds is dramatically re-presented in ritual performance. If there is a sense of "revelation" then it is presumably rooted in an appreciation of the hierarchical relationship between corporeal aspects of humans (their porcine qualities) and immortal ones (their avian qualities). This, in itself, is unlikely to be particularly surprising or impressive, as it is a pervasive aspect of discourse in religious communities everywhere, and not simply an outcome of ritual. This is affirmed by the way Bloch construes iconicity in initiation: that pigs reproduce, mature, and die is known independently of ritual; but so too is the fact that birds do not seem to age and die, the fact that they move in spaces where human bodies cannot go, and so on. These attributes of species are known independently of ritual action and are re-presented rather than created by the embahi ceremony, at least according to my reading of Bloch.

Yet there is also a strand to Bloch's argument that seems to deny the iconicity of avian imagery, by suggesting that immortality is only "thinkable" as a result of a binary logic in which images of the "other world" are constructed out of contrasts with the perceptible, physical world. As Bloch puts it, this is a process by which "a mirror-like alternative existence is set up."[18] A sense of the revelatory character of ritual is thereby rescued, but at a theoretical premium. The recourse to binary or digital codification makes it appear that the "transcendental" emerges as an artifact of the ritual process, rather than of everyday experience. The idea that people's everyday perceptions of birds could imply a world outside biological process becomes theoretically burdensome rather than useful.

It seems to me, however, that these problems do not arise if iconicity is seen to operate in a way that conflicts with everyday attitudes and assumptions. It then becomes possible to explore the revelatory character of initiation rites without seeking refuge in digital operations that reduce religious concept formation to a very simple thought (for instance, that pigs are to birds what bodies are to spirits).

It is necessary to put the Orokaiva material on one side, for the moment, and examine initiation systems that have been more comprehensively studied. Some especially impressive work has been carried out by Barth among the Baktaman, a society in which the power of iconic codification, or of what Barth calls "analogic" codification,[19] lies in the cultivation of paradox, mystery, multivocality, and secrecy.

Barth has shown that Baktaman initiators entertain ambivalent attitudes toward wild male pigs. On the one hand, wild pigs frequently damage gardens and are therefore inimical to the prosperity of crops and banned from initiation ritual. On the other hand, their ferocity and virility (not least the vital service they provide in impregnating domestic sows) exemplify desirable qualities in men. Barth describes how a group of novice warriors carried into battle the mandible of a wild male pig that they had just killed in the act of copulation.[20] Following the success of this raid, the mandible was introduced to the male cult, but an ambivalent attitude to wild boar persisted to the extent that the bones of other specimens were still barred from the temples.

What Bloch has to say about pigs among the Orokaiva might equally be said about pigs among the Baktaman. In both environments, pigs are the only large mammals, both wild and domesticated animals are valued for their meat, and in behavioral and physiological terms their resemblances to human beings are much the same in both societies. There is, however, no reason to privilege the connexion between pigs and ideas of vitality or biological process. The attitudes of the Baktaman toward wild pigs, in the context of everyday life, focus primarily on their destructive habits: "Baktaman men seem to regard themselves as involved in a continuous war with the wild pigs; they spend hours in the men's houses describing their depredations in detail, discussing their habits and individual idiosyncrasies, speculating on their location and next move."[21] A novice confronted with a relic of this public enemy in the context of a fertility cult is likely to experience confusion, and a sense that wild pigs are not the kind of creatures one might suppose. As Barth puts it: "An aura of mystery and insight is created by dark hints that things are not what they appear. That ignorant assumptions are negated by guarded knowledge is the very stuff of mystery cult."[22]

A clue to the meaning of the mandible is likely to be picked up by the novice in contemplating the aggressiveness and virility of wild male pigs. In addition to mulling over the paradoxical character of this revelation, the novice is likely to associate the mandible with other items of temple sacra: the bones of ancestors, and the blackened ceiling of the cult house, which in turn connotes the blackened vine used to tie the novices together—an even more explicit image of male solidarity.[23] Above all, the first encounter with the pig mandible will be associated with the tortures and privations of third-degree initiation, which are among the most terrifying of all Baktaman rites. But here I am jumping ahead of myself.

It is not only in the Baktaman case that porcine imagery lends itself to the cultivation of ideas about masculinity and spirituality. Among the Ilahita Arapesh, initiators use pig incisors to lacerate the glans penises of novices as part of an act of purification and sacralization. Here, it is an attack by a pig rather than by a bird that makes the novice more like an ancestor and less like a worldly, polluting being. Tuzin claims that, at a later stage of initiation, Ilahita Arapesh novices are ritually transformed into pigs, as a result of gorging on pork during the phase of liminality.[24]

The point is that the analogic or iconic principle operates in New Guinea initiations in such a way as to confound everyday understandings and to emphasize the multivocal and multivalent character of revelation. This process is resistant to expression in language and certainly does not emerge out of a simple digital operation or a straightforward re-presentation of everyday understandings.

Where I part company with Barth over his approach to analogic codes is at the point where he turns to psychoanalysis to incorporate the affective quality of ritual symbolism and account for patterns of variation in time and space. Drawing on Noy's classification of the operations of primary process, Barth tries to identify the unconscious generative mechanisms that might produce incremental changes in the feelings, insights, and performances entailed in initiations.[25] It seems odd that Barth should wax Freudian, given the grounds of his aversion to Lévi-Straussian structuralism. Some twenty years ago, he wrote:

> One may be justifiably unhappy about a method where structures or
> patterns must be constructed merely with a view to make all the
> pieces fit together and without opportunity for falsification at any
> stage. The naive question of how much of these thoughts have actu-
> ally been thought by the actors concerned can be raised . . . but not
> resolved in such a structuralist framework.[26]

A more recent quotation will show that Barth's views on the matter have not changed substantially. He writes: "I feel intuitively committed to an ideal of naturalism in the analytical operations I perform: that they should model or mirror significant, identifiable processes that can be shown to take place among the phenomena they seek to depict."[27]

Nevertheless, Barth's appeals to Noy, and ultimately to Freud, seem to violate his empiricist instincts. For, as I have pointed out elsewhere, Barth's insistence on the unconscious nature of culture change is nowhere supported by evidence of such transformations.[28] In fact, all the examples of culture change adduced in Barth's publications on the Baktaman are examples of consciously introduced changes.

The psychological effects of initiation ritual in New Guinea are far wider-reaching than any analysis of the cognitive process entailed in analogic communication could encompass. Psychoanalytic theory, however, presents only one of a range of possible ways of understanding the emotional impact on novices. Another approach, one that has the advantage of seeking to establish the conscious experiences of participants, is suggested by social psychological studies of attitude change among the victims of terrorism. Such an approach is elaborated by Tuzin in his analysis of Ilahita Arapesh initiation, and his conclusions are worth quoting at length:

Under certain conditions the victim of extreme terror, by virtue of what may be called coerced regression, experiences love and grati- tude toward, and deep identification with, his persecutors. During the ordeal, of course, the novice's attitudes are at best highly labile; but immediately following it, the initiators drop their razors, spears, cudgels, or what have you, and comfort the boys with lavish displays of tender emotion. What resentment the latter may have been har- bouring instantly dissipates, replaced by a palpable warmth and af- fection for the men who, moments before, had been seemingly bent on their destruction. As their confidence recovers itself, the novices become giddy with the realization that they have surmounted the or- deal. If there is an element of identification disclosed in this re- markable transformation—and I do not know what other interpreta- tion to place on it—then the terror component may well be essential if the cult, and indeed the society itself, is to continue in its present form.[29]

Tuzin's analysis is quite plausible and, unlike the theory of "rebounding violence," goes a long way toward accounting for the terrifying nature of ini- tiatory ordeals. But, as with Bloch's approach, the "love-of-the-oppressor" par- adigm does not take proper account of the multivocality and multivalence of religious imagery. The alternation between cruelty and kindness in Ilahita Ar- apesh rites would presumably have the same effect on the novices without the complex imagery of the male cult.

Williams would probably have sympathized with Tuzin's approach. The image he held in mind throughout his analysis of the embahi ceremony was one of public school "ragging" rather than terrorist violence, but he preceded Tuzin in stressing the way that novices come to identify with their oppressors.[30] In so doing, Williams sought to redress what he saw as an imbalance in Chin- nery and Beaver's approach, which emphasized the educational value of terror. According to Chinnery and Beaver, embahi violence produced in the novices a "receptive . . . frame of mind."[31] This constitutes one of the earliest attempts to explain the use of terror in New Guinea initiation, but the line of reasoning it suggests has been among the most neglected.

Fears and Flashbulbs

In seeking to bring the cognitive side of Orokaiva initiation rites, exemplified in Barth's theory of analogic codification, into harmony with the affective as- pects of these rituals, and especially the terrifying nature of the embahi cere- mony, I am inclined to return to Chinnery and Beaver's hypothesis. Contemporary anthropology has the advantage of being able to draw on the fruits of a greatly advanced psychological understanding of learning and memory. I focus particular attention on the operations of so-called flashbulb memory in which extreme emotions and cognitive shocks become intertwined.

Flashbulb memories are vivid recollections of inspirational, calamitous, or otherwise emotionally arousing events. Brown and Kulik argue that such memories are generated by a peculiar neural mechanism in which a specific range of details about the event (location, source, affect, and aftermath) is simultaneously encoded.[32] Numerous alternative explanations for the phenomenon, in both biological and psychological terms, have since been advanced.[33] In spite of Neisser's attempts to explain the canonical structure of such memories in terms of the conventions of storytelling, Winograd and Killinger show that the vividness and detail of flashbulb memories are not substantially affected by reminiscence.[34] Thus, the fact that Baktaman and Orokaiva initiates do not converse about their experiences and interpretations of secret cult ritual should not affect the canonical structure of these memories.

Herdt, in his work on the Sambia of the New Guinea highland fringe, has used Brown and Kulik's theory of flashbulb memory to understand the extraordinary experiences of revelation which mark the onset of shamanic powers, and which (as Herdt mentions in passing) may be triggered by the traumas of Sambia initiation.[35] I have also invoked the concept of "flashbulb memory" in connexion with the traumatic ordeals of millenarian ritual among the Baining.[36] An advantage of this theory is that it fits with people's intuitive impressions of how dramatic, frightening, and surprising experiences seem to be "printed" on the mind. There is no need to postulate processes inaccessible to consciousness. What we are dealing with here is a stock of very vivid, disturbing, and perhaps enlightening memories which are consciously turned over in the minds of initiates for years to come, and indeed may accompany them to the grave. When a Baktaman novice first realizes that he is (in some sense) being made into a virile, aggressive pig—a warrior and a father—he is not only struck by the absurdity of his previous assumptions about pigs, but he associates this revelation with the terrifying and agonizing experience of being beaten with stones, whipped with nettles, and dehydrated almost to the point of death. It is this combination of cognitive and emotional crises that produces the distinctive mnemonic effect. As Herdt points out, such memories provide focal imagery for subsequent reflection,[37] and this is how the "fans of connotations of sacred symbols" are elaborated.[38] Initiation rites produce a patterned screen of representations and feelings against which later insights and revelations are projected.

The vividness and detail of people's memories of initiation rites are related in part to the surprising and unexpected nature of revelation and in part to the high level of emotional arousal. For instance, it is relevant that Baktaman esoteric knowledge is surprising to the novices, but the reversal of everyday assumptions about wild male pigs is not in itself sufficiently impressive and memorable to produce flashbulb clarity. Psychologists have shown that surprising events are remembered in greater detail if they are also emotionally arousing.[39] Moreover, at least three studies suggest that the detail of flashbulb recall increases directly with intensity of emotion at encoding.[40] The longevity of such memories is also very striking, as has been demonstrated by victims' detailed and closely matching recollections of atrocities in concentration camps, forty years after these camps were closed down. There is also some evidence that recall of disturbing or traumatic experiences actually improves with time, in contrast with other sorts of memories, which may be subject to decay.[41]

These findings, although they seem intuitively plausible, are at odds with most early hypotheses about the relationship between emotion and memory. Studies based on the "Yerkes-Dodson law," which represented the relationship between mental efficiency and level of arousal or stress as an inverted U-shaped curve, assumed that states of extreme fear impaired rather than improved cognitive processing. Nevertheless, following an extensive review of recent literature on the subject, Christiansen concludes: "The results from flashbulb studies and other studies of real-life events suggest that highly emotional or traumatic events are very well retained over time, especially with respect to detailed information directly associated with the traumatic event."[42]

Memory, Transmission, and Political Association

Now, the *political* implications of initiatory traumas reside partly in the nature of episodic memory, of which flashbulb memory is (in the context of initiation rites) an especially salient manifestation, and partly in the contrived circumstances of transmission. On the latter subject, I have elsewhere written at length and I confine myself here to a summary of four main points.[43]

First, the religious understandings cultivated in initiation ritual derive from collective performances and can only be disseminated among neighboring groups or through the displacement of whole populations. As Barth has pointed out, this helps to explain the fragmentary, localized character of many religious traditions founded around initiation rites.[44] Second, the traumatic nature of these rites, and the secrecy surrounding them, generate intense solidarity among participants, as many writers have observed.[45] Third, this experience of solidarity may be related to the practice of "sister exchange," and it is certainly linked to courage in war, as the foregoing discussion of Orokaiva and Baktaman rites clearly demonstrates.[46] Sister exchange and warfare, meanwhile, are conducive to the autonomy of small local groups.[47]

All these factors encourage a highly fragmented political landscape composed of small, boundary-conscious ritual communities, standing in relations of hostility or rivalry. Internally, the emphasis is on cohesiveness and solidarity. If there is also an egalitarian ethos among adult males, this may be linked to the conditions of religious transmission, in particular to the fact that revelations are not mediated by leaders. In the context of initiation, crucial insights are inferred by participants in a process subjectively experienced as personal inspiration. Nobody comes forward to impart the wisdom of the ancestors, for this wisdom is elusive to language. Religious instruction is therefore a matter of collective revelation, rather than a transaction between teacher and pupils.[48] Admittedly, the authoritarian behavior of initiators instantiates a striking imbalance of power, but once the metamorphosis of the novices is complete, the camaraderie engendered in their common experience of liminality is extended to their initiators. In a real sense initiators and novices undergo the experience together, and share its dramatic consequences.[49] When it is over, they are closer than before, both in status and identity.

People undergo particular initiation rites once in a lifetime. They may participate in or witness such rites again, but never as objects of the performance. In these conditions of infrequent transmission, it is vital that the original impact of the experience endures in memory. An important quality of flashbulb memories is that they are unforgettable, vivid, and haunting. Their potency is a concomitant of the uniqueness and emotionality of the situation that gave rise to them. The solidarity generated among initiates is lasting, but it is also difficult to generalize or extend. This is another factor contributing to the politically bounded character of initiation systems and it is best understood in terms of the mechanics of episodic memory. What is encoded is not a script (as in a liturgical sequence) or a habitual body practice (as in kneeling for prayer), but a set of very particular events, experiences, and responses. In the case of flashbulb memory, these recollections are canonically structured and tied to the actual historical context in which the events occurred. What this means, among other things, is that actual persons inhabit these memories. This is very different from the memories that people have of highly repetitive rituals, involving schemas for general sequences of actions that might be performed by anybody and not a specific set of people.[50] Thus, the political and religious community that initiation creates is fixed forever in the minds of novices. The bonds of solidarity once forged cannot easily be revoked or extended. They encompass those people who actually endured the terrifying experience together, and separate them forever from the rest of humanity.

Conclusion

Certain influential approaches to the interpretation of Melanesian religion do not do justice to the conscious experience of participants. The significance that

Bloch attributes to porcine and avian imagery in Orokaiva initiation would, in the eyes of practitioners, be unrecognizable or (more likely) heretical. This is not to say that the theory of "rebounding violence" does not apply, merely that it excludes a great deal. It could not, even in principle, handle the most striking aspects of this experience from the viewpoints of participants, including the surprising reversal of everyday understandings and the terror induced by the embah.[51] The interpretations suggested by social psychology are better able to make sense of the affective aspects of initiation, but much of the complexity of cognitive processes is excluded. Tuzin's recourse to the "love-of-the-oppressor" syndrome does not interlock with the symbolic richness of Arapesh rites. Novices would identify with their oppressors just as readily if they were simply abused, without being exposed to the complex imagery of the male cult. Barth's use of Freudian insights encompasses more of the ethnographic detail; like Bloch's and Tuzin's approaches, however, it produces an interpretation that fails to engage substantially with the conscious experience of participants. What is clearly required is a way of relating the lived experience of ritual performance, in conceptual and emotional terms, to wider political conditions in a manner that is both generalizable and empirically productive across a range of cultural traditions.

I have suggested that "rites of terror" may be seen as part of a nexus of psychological and sociological processes, in which specific dimensions of concept formation, feeling, and remembering, are linked to the scale, structure, and political ethos of social groups. This nexus is found in a wide variety of religious traditions and not merely in Melanesian initiation systems. In a fuller exploration of its dynamics, I have dubbed this concatenation of features the "imagistic mode of religiosity," mode of "being religious" that has been written about from many angles and endowed with many labels.[52] It has long been appreciated that intense emotional states are a crucial element of the nexus, but (as in the sample of interpretations surveyed in this essay) these states have not been related to the complex conceptual processes that are engendered in "rites of terror" and other "ecstatic" religious practices. An advantage of focusing on the integrity of emotion and conceptual complexity, via a close analysis of the workings of memory, is that it impels us deeper into the ethnography at the same time as it forces us to generalize.

NOTES

This is a revised version of a paper presented in 1993 at departmental seminars at the Universities of Oxford and Manchester and the Queen's University of Belfast. I should like to thank members of the anthropology departments at all three universities for their instructive criticisms. For reading and commenting at length on earlier drafts, my particular debt of thanks goes to Marcus Banks, Maurice Bloch, Bob Barnes, Simon Harrison, and Howard Morphy.

1. D. F. Tuzin, *The Voice of the Tambaran: Truth and Illusion in Ilahita Arapesh Religion* (Berkeley: University of California Press, 1980).

2. F. Barth, *Ritual and Knowledge among the Baktaman of New Guinea* (New Haven: Yale University Press, 1975).

3. E. W. P. Chinnery and W. N. Beaver, "Notes on the Initiation Ceremonies of the Koko Papua," *J. R. Anthrop. Inst.* 45 (1915): 69–78, cited in E. Schwimmer, *Exchange in the Social Structure of the Orokaiva: Traditional and Emergent Ideologies in the Northern District of Papua* (London: Hurst, 1973).

4. F. J. P. Poole, "The Ritual Forging of the Identity: Aspects of Person and Self in Bimin-Kuskusmin Male Initiation," in *Rituals of Manhood: Male Initiation in Papua New Guinea,* edited by G. H. Herdt (Berkeley: University of California Press, 1982).

5. As in Schieffelin's description of the burning Kaluli dancers in E. L. Schieffelin, *The Sorrow of the Lonely and the Burning of the Dancers* (New York: St. Martin's Press, 1976); Williams's account of the injuries caused by supernaturally induced convulsions in F. E. Williams, *Orokaiva Magic* (London: Humphrey Milford, 1928), 67; Elbert and Monberg's transcription of an account of the bloodbaths resulting from a "cargo cult" on the island of Bellona in S. H. Elbert and T. Monberg, *From the Two Canoes: Oral Traditions of Rennell and Bellona Islands* (Copenhagen: Danish National Museum, 1965), 399–400.

6. Schwimmer, *Exchange in the Social Structure of the Orokaiva.*

7. A. Iteanu, "The Concept of the Person and Ritual System: An Orokaiva View," *Man* (n.s.) 25 (1990): 35–53.

8. Ibid., 47.

9. F. E. Williams, *Orokaiva Society* (London: Humphrey Milford, 1930).

10. Iteanu, 46.

11. M. Bloch, *Prey into Hunter: The Politics of Religious Experience* (Cambridge, UK: Cambridge University Press, 1992), 4.

12. R. Hertz, *Death and the Right Hand* (London: Cohen and West, 1960), 77.

13. Bloch, 6.

14. See, for instance, Williams, *Orokavia Magic,* 175–176; Schwimmer, 177.

15. See A. Gell, "Order or Disorder in Melanesian Religions [letter]," *Man* (n.s.) 15 (1980): 735–737; D. Sperber, *Rethinking Symbolism* (Cambridge, UK: Cambridge University Press, 1975).

16. Williams, *Orokaiva Society,* 45–57; Schwimmer, 143.

17. Iteanu, 37.

18. Bloch, 20.

19. Following G. Bateson, *Steps to an Ecology of Mind: Collected Essays in Anthropology, Psychiatry, Evolution, and Epistemology* (Northvale, NJ: Jason Aronsen, 1972).

20. Barth, *Ritual and Knowledge among the Baktaman of New Guinea.*

21. Ibid., 39.

22. F. Barth, *Cosmologies in the Making: A Generative Approach to Cultural Variation in Inner New Guinea* (Cambridge, UK: Cambridge University Press, 1987), 33.

23. Barth, *Ritual and Knowledge among the Baktaman of New Guinea,* 67.

24. Tuzin, *The Voice of the Tambaran: Truth and Illusion in Ilahita Arapesh Religion,* 340–341, 344.

25. P. Noy, "A Revision of the Psychoanalytic Theory of the Primary Process,"

Int. J. Psycho-Analysis 50 (1969): 155–178; P. Noy, "From Creation in Art: An Ego-Psychological Approach to Creativity," *Psychoanalytic Q.* 48 (1979): 229–256.

26. Barth, *Ritual and Knowledge among the Baktaman of New Guinea*, 213.

27. Barth, *Cosmologies in the Making: A Generative Approach to Cultural Variation in Inner New Guinea*, 8.

28. H. Whitehouse, "Memorable Religions: Transmission, Codification, and Change in Divergent Melanesian Contexts," *Man* (n.s.) 27 (1992): 789–791.

29. Tuzin, *The Voice of the Tambaran: Truth and Illusion in Ilahita Arapesh Religion*, 77–78.

30. Williams, *Orokaiva Society*, 197.

31. Chinnery and Beaver, "Notes on the Initiation Ceremonies of the Koko, Papua," 77.

32. R. Brown and J. Kulik, "Flashbulb Memory," in *Memory Observed: Remembering in Natural Contexts*, edited by U. Neisser (San Francisco: W.H. Freeman, 1982).

33. See, for instance, D. Wright and G. D. Gaskell, "The Construction and Function of Vivid Memories," in *Theoretical Perspectives on Autobiographical Memory*, edited by M. A. Conway et al. (Dordrecht, Netherlands: Kluwer Academic, 1992) and H. Whitehouse, "Jungles and Computers: Neuronal Group Selection and the Epidemiology of Representations," *J. Roy. Antrhop. Inst.* (n.s.) 2 (1996): 413–422.

34. U. Neisser, "Snapshots or Benchmarks," in *Memory Observed: Remembering in Natural Contexts*, edited by U. Neisser (San Francisco: W. H. Freeman, 1982); E. Winograd and W. A. Killinger, "Relating Age to Encoding in Early Childhood to Adult Recall: Development of Flashbulb Memories," *J. Exp. Psychol. Gen.* 112 (1983), 413–422.

35. G. H. Herdt, "Spirit Familiars in the Religious Imagination of Sambia Shamans," in *The Religious Imagination in New Guinea*, edited by G. H. Herdt and M. Stephen (New Brunswick, NJ: Rutgers University Press, 1989), 115.

36. H. Whitehouse, *Inside the Cult: Religious Experience and Innovation in Papua New Guinea* (Oxford: Oxford University Press, 1995), 195, 206.

37. Herdt, 115.

38. Barth, *Cosmologies in the Making: A Generative Approach to Cultural Variation in Inner New Guinea*, 31.

39. See, for instance, S.-A Christiansen and E. F. Loftus, "Remembering Emotional Events: The Fate of Detailed Information," *Cognition and Emotion* 5 (1991): 81–108.

40. See S.-A. Christiansen, "Emotional Stress and Eyewitness Memory: A Critical Review," *Psychol. Bull*, 112 (1992): 287.

41. E. Scrivner and M. A. Safer, "Eyewitnesses Show Hypermnesia for Details about a Violent Event," *J. Appl. Psychol.* 73 (1988): 371–377; G. Cohen, *Memory in the Real World* (Hove: Lawrence Erlbaum, 1989), 156–159.

42. Christiansen, "Emotional Stress and Eyewitness Memory: A Critical Review," 288.

43. Whitehouse, "Memorable Religions: Transmissions, Codification, and Change in Divergent Melanesian Contexts", H. Whitehouse, "Strong Words and Forceful Winds: Religious Experience and Political Process in Melanesia," *Oceania* 65 (1994): 40–58; Whitehouse, *Inside the Cult: Religious Experience and Innovation in*

Papua New Guinea; H. Whitehouse, "Apparitions, Orations and Rings: Experience of Spirits in Dadul," in *Spirits in Culture, History, and Mind,* edited by J. M. Mageo and A. Howard (New York: Routledge, 1996).

44. F. Barth, "The Guru and the Conjurer: Transactions in Knowledge and the Shaping of Culture in Southeast Asia and Melanesia," *Man* (n.s.) 25 (1990): 640–653.

45. For instance, Barth, *Ritual and Knowledge among the Baktaman of New Guinea,* 223, 245, 251; D. K. Feil, *The Evolution of Highland Papua New Guinea Societies* (Cambridge, UK: Cambridge University Press, 1987), 231; M. Godelier, "An Unfinished Attempt at Reconstructing the Social Process Which May have Prompted the Transformation of Great-Men Societies into Big-Men Societies," in *Big Men and Great Men: Personifications of Power in Melanesia,* edited by M. Godelier and M. Strathern (Cambridge, UK: Cambridge University Press, 1991), 294; S. Lindenbaum, "Variations on Sociosexual Theme in Melanesia," in *Ritualized Homosexuality in Melanesia,* edited by G. H. Herdt (Berkeley: University of California Press, 1984).

46. The covariance of male initiatory cults and sister exchange is observed by Godelier (e.g., 1991: 227), though I argue elsewhere that his explication of their relationship is not entirely satisfactory (Whitehouse, "Leaders and Logics, Persons and Polities," *Historical Anthropology* 6 [1992] 110–111).

47. N. Modjeska, "Production and Inequality: Perspectives from Central New Guinea," in *Inequality in New Guinea Highlands Societies,* edited by A. J. Strathern (Cambridge, UK: Cambridge University Press, 1982).

48. Cf. Barth, "The Guru and the Conjurer: Transactions in Knowledge and the Shaping of Culture in Southeast Asia and Melanesia."

49. Tuzin, "The Voice of the Tambaran: Truth and Illusion in Ilahita Arapesh Religion," 73–74, 78.

50. See Whitehouse, *Inside the Cult: Religious Experience and Innovation in Papua New Guinea,* 85–86.

51. In talking about "everyday understandings," I am not referring to a universal level of perception (which Bloch sees as being ritually inverted), but specifically to those ideas and attitudes that are culturally emphasized in nonritual discourse, but then exposed as falsehoods in esoteric cosmology. A good example is the marsupial mouse (*eiraram*) which, according to everyday Baktaman understandings, is categorized as "disgusting vermin" but, in the context of the male cult, "is elevated to a sacramental category all of its own: privileged food monopolized by the ancestor" (Barth, *Ritual and Knowledge among the Baktaman of New Guinea,* 82).

52. Whitehouse, *Inside the Cult: Religious Experience and Innovation in Papua New Guinea.* For instance, "dionysian," "effervescent," "charismatic," "ecstatic." For a discussion of the history of these attempts to characterize the "imagistic mode of religiosity," see Whitehouse, *Inside the Cult: Religious Experience and Innovation in Papua New Guinea,* 194–217.

6

The Sacred Mind: Newar Cultural Representations of Mental Life and the Production of Moral Consciousness

Steven M. Parish

According to Steven M. Parish, emotion is sacralized in the religious ethos of Newar culture in Nepal. As Harvey Whitehouse does for Melanesian initiation cults, Parish seeks to approach Newar culture in a way that avoids making a reductive account of person and mind and discloses the ways affective experience is embedded in Newar culture. In observing the Hindu community of Newars, he focuses on their representation of emotion, memory, cognition, and perception by nuga: *or the heart, so that "when Newars speak of the states of the 'heart,' they express their emotional worlds. . . . the discourse of the heart discloses the self." The* nuga: *at the same time is characterized by its shifting and porous nature, its openendedness, as it were, so that it serves as a framework for the merging of the self with the godhead. Moral emotions such as shame and remorse are engaged by a self as both agent and passive experiencer. Most important, moral evaluations are "felt." They are judgments embodied in feeling. Linking emotional experience to cognitions, Parish writes that "in the absence of emotional experience, people in any culture may cognitively know and use the knowledge structures that constitute the moral code" and thus be equipped to respond to social challenges through rehearsals of that code and its application to various instances requiring*

Steven M. Parish, "The Sacred Mind: Newar Cultural Representations of Mental Life and the Production of Moral Consciousness," *Ethos* 19, no. 3 (Sept. 1991): 313–351. Used by permission of the American Anthropological Association.

moral evaluation. However, such behavior remains to a large extent automatic and unengaged. Emotions, as part of the "sacred mind" of the Newars, involve the self more completely in such events, "bringing to life what was known about, in a passive way, but not known in terms of self-experience."

Is emotion constructed exclusively in culture, or are there aspects of emotional life having to do with one's life history or personal psychological details? What does Parish mean in claiming that a moral judgment is embodied in emotion? Does such feeling then have a physical component? Are all emotions moral emotions for the Newars? Are some emotions stronger than others, more refined than others, and therefore more important to moral life? Do certain social situations call for certain moral emotions? Are certain predicaments constructed in culture as scenarios requiring the experience of lajya? *Are there other emotions that might be present that are culturally unmarked? Does Parish's theorization of emotion serve, as he proposes, as a middle ground between bodily experience and cultural commands?*

For the Newars of Nepal, mind, self, and emotion are sacred and moral; the "inner" world is absorbed in a religious ethos. This sacralization of mental life in Newar culture is consistent with the way religious forms—sacred beings and symbols and a moral order based on a religious worldview—provide the fundamental grounds for the Newar construction of reality. Newar life has not been secularized; the world and the mind have not been disenchanted.

The concept of mind Newars bring to the experience of an "inner" life, of mental existence, helps Newars create themselves as moral beings. As Newars evaluate and experience themselves in terms of cultural theories of mental life, they produce states of moral consciousness, ways of knowing themselves as moral agents. Their concepts of mind, formed within a religious and ethical worldview, mediate the development of a "moral self." Their vision of mind sensitizes them to "moral" emotion, shapes insight into self, and structures efforts to alter self. In sum, their cultural concept of mind helps generate what I would term "moral knowing."

My discussion of these processes—the sacralization and ethicization of mind and the production of moral consciousness—underscores the need for more flexible and less reductive accounts of mind, self, and emotion. Some theorists, reacting to a tradition in academic psychology that reduces feeling to a material entity or psychophysiological process, have played down the importance of affective experience, of feeling as a core aspect of emotion, emphasizing instead the way emotions are cognitive and social judgments.[1] While I also view emotions as judgments about the relationship of self to world, and reject theories of emotions that reduce them to nothing but physiological processes, I think we miss something vital if we treat emotions as nothing but discourse. Emotions are social judgments, but judgments embodied reflexively in affective experience.[2] That emotions are affective rather than discursive judgments makes a difference: I may use emotion concepts without feeling them, but when I feel an emotion I am more completely and powerfully engaged with my world. Emotions prepare people to be agents. The experience of emotion mediates engagement with life, priming social actors to find meaning in events and experiences, preparing them to know themselves in certain ways, and readying them to act.[3]

Other theorists ignore the role of culture, stressing instead psychological processes. They view cultural models of psychological experience as unrelated to the processes that generate that experience. For example, the psychologist George Mandler has argued that people's beliefs and intuitions about how minds work have little to do with how minds actually work. He argues that "folk theories" fundamentally misrepresent psychological processes. Indeed, experimental psychologists should probably not look to ordinary language or to culture for "concepts and distinctions" that can stand as "ultimate descriptions" of mind from the point of view of academic psychology.[4] In contrast, it is people's beliefs about mental life that pose fundamental questions for anthropologists. Ethnographic research makes it clear that emotional experience is culturally embedded; it is more than a set of psychophysiological processes.[5] Because emotion has cultural meaning, we are compelled to ask: What place do "folk theories" of mind and emotion have in people's lives and experience? Although cultural concepts of mind may not be "true" from the perspective of experimental psychology, neuroscience, or analytical philosophy, they may reflect significant aspects of social, cultural, and personal reality.

Thus, the ethnographic data to be presented here point out the need to bridge the gap between two opposed approaches to emotion. These opposing approaches force the analyst either to decontextualize emotion or to disembody it. Both strategies are reductive; one severs the connection of emotion with sensation and feeling, with the actual self-experience of human bodies, while the other eliminates the need to explore cultural and social context. As useful as these strategies may be for very limited purposes, I believe the Newar material presented here makes it clear how emotional life is both intricately embedded in culture and dynamically embodied in affective experience. Because people make their lives within the world created by the interaction and interpenetration of culture and experience, it is there that the analysis of emotional life should begin.

The Newars are the indigenous inhabitants of the Kathmandu Valley; the Newar cities of Patan, Bhaktapur, and Kathmandu were independent city-states, ruled by Hindu kings, until their conquest by another ethnic group in the sixteenth century. The basis for the Newar economy is irrigated rice agriculture, which supports a complex division of labor. A range of occupational specialists—Brahman and Tantric priests, artisans and craftsmen, merchants, untouchable sweepers, and others—is organized into a complex caste system.

The informants cited and quoted here are Saivite Hindus, but other Newars are Buddhists.[6]

I describe Newar concepts of mind by presenting and interpreting data from open-ended interviews with Hindu Newar informants.[7] The goal is to show some of the ways in which Newars ethicize and sacralize mind, emotion, and self and come to know themselves as moral beings.

Moral Knowing and Newar Ethnopsychology

Newars take it for granted that people experience mental states something like those indicated by the English words *desire, feeling, emotion, thought,* and *memory;* these are located in the chest, since for Newars the mind is in the heart, not the head.[8] (Some informants mention head and brain as involved in mental processes, especially thinking.)[9] The "heart" (*nuga:*) itself actively feels some things, but it is also viewed as a site that passively houses other mental processes, such as perceptions, memory, emotions, and desires. For Newars, these are obvious "facts" about the inner world.

In Newar culture, a moral god animates the mind, so the efforts of individuals to monitor their inner life often draw on a sense of the presence of a divine agency. This, too, is, for Newars, an obvious "fact" about the inner world.

The Newar idea of a god who inhabits the "heart" is one component in a complex ethnopsychology in which parts of the person may be deified. This inner deity, the "heart god," "god dwelling inside," or "god who dwells in the heart," is thought of as Nārāyana, a form of Vishnu, by Hindu informants. This deity makes possible, or empowers, perception and cognition. A high-caste Newar, Siva Bhakta, stressing the identity of the inner god with the ultimate form of god, puts it this way:

> The god who dwells in the heart . . . is the same as [the god] Bhaga-bān. How do we serve Bhagabān? We chant god's names "Bhaga-bān, Nārāyana" [in prayer]. We pray to the very same god on the outside. We Newars feel [*bhābanā yāi*] that this same god is in our hearts. . . . The god who dwells in the heart, and who, it is said, sees with our eyes, is Bhagabān. Bhagabān is every place. He is here in the heart too.

Here Siva alludes to the idea that the god in the heart makes perception and attention possible. A person sees because the god sees through his or her eyes. Another informant clarified this by giving the example of a person who is not paying attention to what some one is saying. The speaker may "scold" the inattentive listener by asking, "Where is the heart god?" or by remarking that "Your heart god is not still, and so you don't understand." These can be seen as face-saving expressions that slightly redirect responsibility away from the person so addressed by drawing on the idea that mental states and processes have a source beyond the empirical individual in which mental life is embodied.

Asked to explain in more detail what the "god who dwells in the heart" does, Siva Bhakta continues:

> This is your own idea—we think of Bhagabān. Like this [he shuts his eyes]—while our eyes are closed shut—let's say we think of the god Pashupatināth [the god enshrined in a nearby temple]. He has four faces, right? Just like that, if we have our eyes closed, here an image comes. Of that god. . . . With our eyes closed like this—suddenly he comes before us. It does not come before us—it appears in the heart. While our eyes are shut, it appears. Even with your eyes closed, you can still see it. In the same way, I can see your face, your eyes, your nose—inside, with my eyes shut, I can see your features. This is what we call the god who dwells in the heart.

Other Newar informants interpreted this to mean that the power of recall, the ability to see a face in memory or thought, derived directly from this deity. The idea of "god dwelling within" or the "Nārāyana dwelling within" helps explain how the mind works.

Notice how what happens inside the mind is mapped out in terms of what happens outside the self, in the public, perceptible world. D'Andrade notes that cultural understandings of mental life cannot be totally private; if they were, neither children nor ethnographers could learn anything about them.[10] Because they do, there must be public means of identifying mental states and internal processes. Thus, concepts of thinking may be modeled on the public activity of speech; sometimes thinking is analogous to saying something to oneself. Other thoughts are analogous to seeing something. (Seeing may not be a public act in the way that speech is, but it occurs in a public visual world.) The way Newars identify and characterize inner experience in terms of what happens in the shared, external world suggests that access to models of mental experience is given in this way.[11] Newars sometimes talk of the workings of the heart as comparable to sensory processes or public events: when your eyes are closed, images can be seen in the heart. The god who dwells in the heart makes this possible. When you mentally resolve to do something, several informants remarked, you must "say to yourself" that you will or will not do that thing. This is perhaps a special case, as it involves a high degree of self-consciousness. When asked to explain what thought was like, how it was experienced, two Newar informants residing in the United States indicated that thought is sometimes like speech—one said "conversation"—and sometimes like visual imagery, but not exactly like them.[12]

Clearly, the "heart" is the seat of cognition, memory, and perception. Nuga: is also the locus of emotional experience. The heart may be "easy" or "uneasy."

Pain, sadness, fear, and grief are spoken of in terms of a heart in distress: a heart may sink, tremble, throb, flutter, or burn like fire. A heart can feel as if it has been pierced through, or as if it has been torn to pieces. The Newar heart can open and blossom like a flower in joy. It may fly away in fear or confusion, or burst in envy. It can feel pricks of pain or uneasiness for another person's plight. It can be bound and controlled, kept in balance, or stamped with lasting impressions. The heart can weep and be wounded. "My mother's heart went weeping," said one informant, speaking of a family tragedy, "her mind [*citta*] could not be happy." The language of the heart is thus the language of emotional experience, making it possible for Newars to speak of their heartfelt engagement with the social world.

The qualities of the heart also express the moral qualities of a person. To say that someone has a "smooth mouth" or a "smooth face" but a "blue heart" is to warn against impression management that masks malice or manipulation. A cruel person has a hard heart, an evil person is black-hearted. There are persons with small, deceitful, stingy hearts. A person may be made of proper flesh and bone, like everyone else, Newars say, but lack the "heart blood" that animates moral commitments; Newars assert that such individuals do not possess the conviction or energizing feelings needed to do what is right or necessary. Moreover, if persons, viewed as moral selves, are sometimes passively incomplete, they may also be actively wrong in their inclinations, because "sin" (*pāp*) can inhabit the heart. "Who," asked one informant, "will trust a person who speaks with sin in his heart?" But a heart can also be generous and pure, clear and open.

Speaking in terms of the "heart" signals engagement in specialized kinds of discourse. In my view, the Newar "heart" is a multiplex, metonymic sign—a sign of the self. The part stands for the whole; but the whole has many facets— it encloses a range of ways of being and knowing. Thus, talk of the heart helps Newars know themselves by providing ways to formulate and evaluate experience and relationships.

When Newars speak of the states of the "heart," they express their emotional worlds. The heart may be present or absent, intact or incomplete, whole or compromised—the discourse of the heart discloses the self. The feelings, rhythms, movements, conditions, and colors of the heart are cultural ways of speaking of critical aspects of individual experience and agency, of social embeddedness and constraint.[13] The concept of nuga: allows individuals to represent their personal experience—feelings, emotions, intentions—to themselves and others in cultural terms. Thus, the discourse of the heart helps mediate self-awareness and self-identity.[14]

The concept of the heart also helps Newars place themselves within a religiously conceived moral order. The idea of a god who dwells in the heart does more than explain behavior; it represents and invokes the moral order within "the self."

> If you ask, "This Nārāyana who dwells in the heart, what does it do
> to you?—what does it cause you to do?" [the answer is] he is in every-
> thought. He has caused you to act. We think that he causes us to do
> things. We think that. People think to themselves, Our Father, Bha-
> gabān, has caused me to do this. What I am doing now, I was
> brought to this by Bhagabān. [Siva Bhakta]

But the deity may react to wrong actions and reproach the actor:

> You think of the god who dwells in the heart and [you] act. Don't do
> wrong acts. If you do something wrong this Nārāyana who dwells in
> the heart will curse you. The Nārāyana who dwells in the heart will
> curse you. Curse, meaning rebuke. [Siva Bhakta].

The imagery here is of a kind of moral monitor—of an agency paradoxically
identified with, and yet separate from, the self. This dual state of identity and
separation makes it possible for this agency to cause persons to act, yet also to
judge them for those acts.

Newars often speak of an external deity as a moral witness or judge, rather
than of the "god who dwells in the heart." They may assert that Bhagabān
"sees" wrongdoing. When conceived of as Nārāyana, the "god who dwells in
the heart" is also a form of—perhaps the right phrase is "station of"—a transcendent and omniscient deity. God is both immanent and transcendent, at
once part of the self, yet separate, a larger whole in which the self is embedded.
This does not necessarily mean the two forms have precisely the same significance for people (that they feel and think the same things when they invoke
either form of the god). It seems likely, for example, that the immanent, indwelling form relates to concerns within experience; it symbolizes and supports self-monitoring as a moral activity. The idea of a transcendent judge of
a life shifts the scale and focus of moral reflections toward "ultimate" concerns:
the prospects of death and salvation, given the objective existence of a moral
order. Perhaps this idea of a moral watch kept in heaven also helps give shape
to the intuition that a life is a totality, a moral career that is the object of moral
judgment. We can speculate that there is a kind of division of labor that reflects
two orders of biographical time: a life is both witnessed in its passing moments
(by the heart god) and judged in its totality (by the god in heaven).

Cultural Representations and Self-monitoring

In an interview with informant Krishna Bahadur, focusing on the Hindu concept of the soul (ātmā), Krishna introduced the concept of sin (pāp) and invoked
the key Hindu concept of *dharma*, the moral law that constitutes human duties
and obligations. He argued that it is a sin not to believe in the existence of the

gods. Because one can refuse to believe in the gods in the privacy of one's own heart, I asked him, "What if no one knew—would that be a sin or not?" This low-caste Newar replied.

> It is a sin to lie. . . . That the gods do not exist, if we put this in our hearts, the god will know. In the sky, in the domain of Indra, King of Heaven, in the place of Yamarāj [the god of death], and account book is kept. The keeper of this book . . . counts our dharma and our sin. He continually considers and weighs [our acts]. He weighs our dharma, and our sin, in a balance and then records all in this account.
>
> [If I understand this, if no one in society knows, god will know?]
>
> Yes. With us in our heart, soul, is Nārāyana.

The point here is that Newars do speak of behavior and mental acts as being monitored and judged by supernatural agencies—and one of these is imma- nent in the heart, sometimes playing the part of an "ego," sometimes of a "superego."

The god who dwells in the heart seems to be a cultural representation of the way people experience mental processes of self-monitoring. In Western parlance, we might say that the heart is a place where part of the "self" observes and evaluates what an individual thinks and feels, experiences and does. The conscious self does not experience this self-monitoring part of the self as di- rectly under its control. Rather, it may experience this part of the self as virtually an independent agency and itself as the object of the actions of this other part of the mind. Thus, the image of a god immanent in the self at once captures the experience of finding yourself the object of another part of your mind and ethicizes it.

Cultural models take account of the fact that people do not always view their "inner" experiences as part of themselves. The mind can be viewed as divided into parts; only some of these parts may be viewed as self. You may reproach yourself for some act at the same time that some other agency in the inner world reproaches you—and you passively experience this rebuke. Your self-reproach may only be a kind of echo, set off by an unexpected surge of remorse, which you may attribute to a culturally defined entity—the heart-god or the voice of conscience. People sometimes evaluate and interpret themselves spontaneously, despite their expectations, even against their will, as well as volitionally; you do not have to consciously "will" yourself to feel bad when you believe you have done something wrong, though you may consciously resolve to never again do what makes you feel bad. The image of the god who inhabits the heart reflects the way in which some mental processes are not directly controlled by the conscious, core part of the self. Perceptions, feelings, emo- tions, and desires are not willed or directly controlled by the self;[15] the image of the god who dwells in the heart as the source of psychological states explains how processes that happen inside a person "happen to" a person. (There are also ways in Newar culture of explaining how "bad" desires come to a person: for example, a sorcerer may have planted a spell.)

The idea of the heart-god is not "psychological" in a narrow Western sense, as it does not *only* relate self to entities and processes within self; it *also* relates self to entities and processes in the world, and this world is conceived religiously and ethically. The Newar heart-self is permeable, not rigidly bounded, and is not entirely dependent on the senses for knowledge—it has direct, "inner" access to the religious source of moral being. From one point of view, the religious construct, the god, is viewed as projected into the self, where it is held to produce thoughts and feelings. From another point of view, self, the I, is identified with this being—and so transcends the bounds of mind, body, and personal identity as understood in Western terms. But these concepts, although implicit in Newar thought, may not be active in a given person's thinking about self. Much of the time, an individual Newar may be content to live as a "bounded, unique, more or less integrated motivational and cognitive universe, a dynamic center of awareness, emotion, judgment, and action organized into a distinctive whole," as Clifford Geertz has described the Western concept of the person.[16] Newars have a range of ways of viewing self.

In less Western terms, rather than thinking of "parts" acting within a self-contained, bounded whole, we might think of the Newar heart as *a place where* various forces, processes, agencies, essences, and beings meet and interact. The heart provides a location for interactive psychological processes—it is where warring forces of emotion and desire, of thought and understanding, confront each other and are transmuted and redeployed—but it is also a place where self meets with god, where a dialogue with god and self is held. The nuga: is a receptive and permeable field, not a self-contained entity. Furthermore, the Newar heart-self is poised for merging with higher-order reality—the self, through the heart-god, is identified with godhead—even while it enables persons to view and experience themselves as dynamic centers of awareness and as morally responsible agents.

The "god who dwells in the heart" is not always taken by Newars in a literal sense, as an actually existing divine being. Nevertheless, even some of those who do not believe that the "god who dwells in the heart" actually exists say that it represents a psychological truth. In the following quote, for example, a high-caste informant denies that the heart-god actually exists, but maintains that some "part" of the "heart" knows what is going on in the self.

> Although there is no god in the heart, the truth is always spoken in
> the heart. Never is a lie spoken from the heart. If I tell you a lie, I
> will feel with my heart that I am telling a lie. Though the mouth
> tells a lie, the heart tells the truth. Although there is no god dwelling

in the heart, your own ideas and truth are spoken in the heart.
When you feel sad, if you cry, that, too, is in the heart. Since it occurs mentally in this way, there is the idea that, it is said that, there
is a god in your heart. The heart god is *bibek* [discrimination, conscience, reason]. With bibek you think.

This statement suggests that the "god who dwells in the heart" is a cultural
representation of the way "part" of the mind monitors self and is the source
of thoughts and feelings. This informant prefers not to speak of a god within,
but of a more abstract entity that observes and knows what self is thinking and
feeling, bibek. For him, the heart-god is bibek.

In the lexicon, bibek designates discrimination, or the power of discrimination or of reason. In the passage quoted, however, the informant is, I think,
positing the existence of a part of the self that monitors the larger self in action.
Moral judgment is possible because some part of the mind or self knows what
is going on within a person—and so can separate lies from truth. The fact that
"the mouth" told a lie while "the heart" knows the truth indicates that intentional acts are observed and evaluated.

Newar informants often treat bibek as a moral faculty; not only have they
posited a mental agency that engages in self-monitoring and self-evaluation,
they have ethicized it. Bibek, too, prompts moral behavior. One informant told
me that his bibek made him feel "soft" toward others, so that when he saw
them suffering or in need, he would try to help them. Another noted that bibek
makes you think "only good things."

By viewing people as endowed with bibek, a cognitive power, and as having
a moral god immanent in the heart, Newars see people as capable of moral
knowing in a broad sense. Some individuals may be entirely indifferent to
such conceptions, but these ideas can be used to raise the level of consciousness about moral life, to encourage sensitivity to moral norms, and to evoke
commitment to values. These concepts of mental life do not function directly
as moral controls, but provide the foundation for moral controls. They define
persons as moral beings, capable of moral knowing—creating the expectation
that they should act in moral ways.

Cultural concepts such as these introduce a theme, a nuance, into the way
people view themselves and others. The concepts mediate between a postulated
moral order (what is known) and individual consciousness (the knower); they
render the mind capable of the moral knowing required for persons to live a
moral life.

This does not mean that people will behave in a moral way. Newars see
mental life as subject to many different, often conflicting influences, and the
cross-currents do not necessarily result in moral behavior. Newars know this
from what they observe of others and from their own experience. Newar culture
takes account of this and provides ways of thinking about the fact that people

can want and do things that are wrong. As Newars see it, wrongful acts, or sin (pāp), begin in the mind and must be resisted in the mind.

So, while Newars ethicize some mental processes, they see others as morally problematic. Some mental dispositions or desires, for example, should be "tied up" or bound—that is, controlled. Moral controls and the resistance to mental dispositions to sin or to "bad thoughts" are understood to involve psychological states and processes. Cultural conceptions of moral controls and of self-control are based, in part, on understandings regarding the *relations* of different mental capacities, states, and processes.

Moral Emotions

The cultural experience of feelings or emotions—feelings structured in cultural ways—also helps create moral orientations. Newars sometimes say: If you are a person, through shame you must bind yourself (*Manu kha:sā tha:yāta lajyā(n) cī-mā*).

This Newar maxim says something important about the morality of everyday life in Newar society and about the sort of person required by that everyday morality: being a moral person means regulating the self through *sensitivity* to the emotion *lajyā*. Self-control requires the capacity to experience lajyā, an emotion embracing the kinds of emotional experiences and contexts usually designated by the English words "shyness," "embarrassment," and "shame." Although a number of "moral emotions" play a significant role in the everyday morality of the Newars, I focus primarily on lajyā, as it is especially important as a moral control.[17]

Lajyā combines feeling and evaluation; it is an emotion and a moral state. The noun lajyā is used with the verb *cay-gu*, "to feel." Informants report that the feeling of lajyā may be associated with blushing, sweating, altered pulse, and similar psychophysiological phenomena, which are general signs of emotional arousal or anxiety. However, experienced emotion in a physiological sense is not always present. The term may be used coherently in the absence of such states, for lajyā has, as a moral concept, evaluative and social-regulative uses. By showing the contexts in which Newars speak of lajyā, I will show that this emotion—like emotion in general and moral emotion in particular—cannot be reduced to states of physiological arousal. The perceived connection with experienced feeling is, however, central to the larger, evaluative sense of the concept. To disembody lajyā—by identifying it with cognitive and social judgments and treating it as a moral discourse alone, while ignoring the feelings that energize and ground it—would deeply distort what lajyā is for Newars.

The connection with "energizing" feeling seems critical. Even though an actual state of "raw" feeling—the emotional experience—*may* not always be present, the affiliation of lajyā with feeling is crucial to the understanding of the concept in general. A feeling may be understood to supply motive and to animate action. Because feeling is central to lajyā and relates it to action, lajyā can be used to assert a number of things about moral behavior and moral personhood. The person with lajyā (the self, that is, who possesses the capacity to experience shame, who is sensitive to the possibilities of shame) is seen as motivated by lajyā (as feeling) to act in a manner consistent with moral norms. A person who lacks the capacity to experience lajyā is, as Newars often put it, "like an animal." The idea is that animals have no moral standards and do not live in conformity to a moral order. They will "do anything."

Thus, one of the central features of the Newar cultural concept of the moral person is the idea that all people are subject to lajyā as a feeling or emotion. They are potentially sensitive to it. But the capacity to experience lajyā—the disposition to know shame—is conceived to be more developed in some people than in others. A greater degree of lajyā is held to be inherent in the person-alities or natures of women, children, and youths. The assumption is not only that they do have more lajyā than adult males, but that they *should* have more.

As an evaluative concept that expresses disapproval, lajyā is used to point out violations of norms and to affirm standards of behavior in contrast to the violation. When a person does something wrong, disapproval may be expressed by saying that the violator is without lajyā (*lajyā marumha manu*). This assumes that lajyā (as sensitivity to shame) would cause a person to behave in conformity to norms: if one had lajyā, one would behave in a proper way. There are degrees of sensitivity to lajyā. One person might be moved by feelings of shame to stop behaving in a way that violates a community standard. Another would never have begun to behave in a way that would inevitably elicit disapproval, because he or she would anxiously anticipate that such acts would be greeted with shame-inducing criticism.

The kinds of behavior subject to evaluation in terms of lajyā are diverse. One can be ashamed, for example, because one is poor.

> [You sometimes have lajyā?]
> Sometimes.
> [Why?]
> You are a have [literally, you have-person become]. I am a have-not. As you have, so do you eat. I have nothing, there is nothing to eat. I cannot come up to your level. Since there is not enough to eat, there is lajyā ["to eat" has extended meanings of "to have," "to experience"]. If you cannot go in society, it is lajyā, isn't it? [Ganesh Lal, a farmer]

The "shame" of being a have-not has to do, I think, with perceived failure to be the kind of person who is socially valued. It is not just that he is poor, but that being poor points out, for others to see, that he is inadequate, a "failure" as a person—or, as I heard other Newars put it, that he has not yet "become a person"—and that he knows others see this.

Lajyā is said by informants to be elicited as well by the following:

1. To be caught in a lie or deception.
2. To be forced to beg for a living.
3. To be seen eating at the door of a house.
4. For certain parts of the body to be exposed or mentioned.
5. For an unmarried woman to be seen in the company of men.
6. To make a mistake or misspeak in the presence of others.
7. To be seen urinating or defecating.
8. Obscene, rude, or improper language.
9. To fail to show proper respect in speech or action.
10. To be rebuked in front of others.

One basic criterion for inclusion in this list is being seen, being in view, publicity: in each instance, something becomes known to others. Each act is publicly in violation of a norm. The feeling of lajyā is triggered (or at least is most acute) when others become cognizant of or confront a person with a breach. The norms or standards themselves are not of equal importance and have different sorts of meaning; social mistakes and inadvertent mishaps, as well as moral offenses, are grounds for lajyā.

Lajyā has to do with intersubjective integration into public life: lajyā is felt when a person knows that others know that a breach has been committed. When asked if lajyā would be felt if no one would see, a high-caste man replied, "If no one sees, why would they feel lajyā?" Other high-caste informants agreed:

> [If you were at a place where no one else was, and you made a mistake, or did something wrong, but no one would know—would you feel lajyā or not?]
> I would not feel lajyā.
> [What if at that time you thought of others?]
> I would not feel lajyā. I'd be afraid—what if others knew?

Fear is an important moral emotion when it is linked to a set of moral standards. Newars report they worry about the disapproval of others, and the idea of lajyā creates a fear of exposure. This anxiety is one of the main components of sensitivity to shame: one fears that others will know, and this fear acts as a check on behavior. The idea that others "might see" is an important control in Newar culture. As Obeyesekere notes, people may fear exposure even when alone, to fantasized others who are psychologically present.[18]

As a high-caste informant pointed out, sometimes it does not matter what others see or think; what matters is what a person thinks they see or think, or

what a person thinks of self. The informant concluded his argument that lajyā
is internalized by giving this example of a student who cannot come up with
the right answer to a teacher's question:

> When you cannot give your *guru* an answer, you may feel lajyā.
> When someone cannot say something in front of other students, he
> will only feel lajyā himself. The others will not tease him. . . . It is
> not lajyā, except in his own judgment. [He says to himself] "I could
> not do even that much." It is not lajyā, only for himself is it lajyā.

Lajyā here is more like "embarrassment" over a flawed performance than it is
like "shame" felt because others accuse self of a moral transgression. Others
are not holding self to any standard in this example; they do not care. The idea
expressed is that individuals may hold themselves to certain standards and feel
lajyā as a result of their failure to meet these standards.

Lajyā applies not only to social mistakes and lapses or inadequacies in the
presentation of self, but also to serious cases of wrongdoing.

Lajyā as Response to Wrongdoing

How do Newars experience lajyā? Let me take the case, not of minor social
mistakes or lapses in the presentation of self, but of serious transgressions. By
violating important moral norms, people risk their social identities, and they
may seriously complicate their views of themselves. A high-caste informant
makes this point by describing a hypothetical scenario, a situation to which
lajyā applies both as evaluation and as an emotion:

> Let's say that I told you that you owe me money. But you don't owe
> me money. But what I say is, you owe me money. Will you pay or
> not? An argument starts. You do not owe me any money. Without
> justification, I say, "Give the money to me." While we argue, having
> no proof, our friends will ask, "What money?" [That is, they demand
> an explanation.] Since I lied, I now have to make something else up:
> isn't it lajyā? This is a very low thing. If I could, I would have taken
> your money. If I could, I would have taken it by fighting. I would try
> to get it by taking your watch. If I'm stronger than you, I'd take it.
> But my friends and neighbors will ask, "What money?" If I can
> make up some proof, whether it is true or not, I can take the money.
> So I would be a liar. One without lajyā. If someone then says, "He is
> a liar," then I will have lajyā. I am as good as dead [literally, I am
> equal to dead]. A person who lives by lying may as well die, no?

This account shows how lajyā is central to moral discourse. "Shame" is
not only a feeling here; it also organizes and animates moral judgment, helping

to define the wrongfulness of co-coercion, force, and intimidation. It is thus a moral-psychological concept: the evaluative and the psychological senses of the term support each other. The violation the informant gives as an example here is serious; the stakes are high. Lajyā is conceived of as a basic standard of conduct, closely associated with right and wrong (a person with lajyā does what is right, whereas the person without lajyā does wrong); it is viewed as a motive for moral behavior (a person who lies has no lajyā, whereas, by implication, a person with lajyā will not lie, steal, or do "low things"); and it is conceived of as an experienced feeling (a person caught in a lie feels lajyā).

The thread I want to pursue here is the expression "as good as dead," or "the same as dead." By using this expression, Newars say something about the organization and meaning of the experience of lajyā.

Another high-caste informant, commenting on this expression, suggested that persons who lied would feel "as good as dead" because of the "raw" experience of great lajyā. "When people say you have no lajyā, you feel lajyā." The notion of a kind of social death seems appropriate. Newars who ignore standards of conduct risk loss of social standing and prestige (ijjat). They may face ostracism, which can have devastating social and economic consequences. The threat of social death, like the threat of physical death, is a shock; it can cause a derealization of the self, experienced as a loss of meaning, as emptiness, withdrawal, and confusion.

Yet another high-caste informant elaborated on the ideas that a person shamed is "as good as dead" or "already dead" by speaking of the way he experienced lajyā. He said that lajyā felt "cold—like you did not exist." This indicates that lajyā may, in certain situations, have a cold, withdrawn dimension, drawing on, or providing an experiential base for, the death metaphor.

This contrasts with hot, flushed, red-faced feelings of embarrassment that are also part of the experience of lajyā. When the presentation of self as a proper social person slips, not coldness, but blurred perception, a red face, and blushing are attributed to the experience.

The loss of meaning associated with an intense experience of lajyā may be profound. One high-caste informant said:

> As long as you are alive you must do your rituals. The only people
> who don't do rituals are the dead—no one says anything to them.
> So if you are alive and don't do the rituals, you are . . . [drifts off]
> [You are what?] You are the same as dead. You feel that—because
> you know society will say that you are bad. And society won't count
> you as a person. And that is like being dead. Having no significance
> [chu(n) he mahatwa maru].

The combined loss of self-control and social meaning involved when intense shame is induced may result in intense disorientation, because a relationship with the social world and the capacity for intentional action have been called into question by the emotion. The sense of self is threatened; a moral emotion can be a dangerous way to bind the heart.

The Structure of Shame-like Affect

Lajyā seems to involve not one, but several ways of evaluating and experiencing the relationship of self with the social world: the "embarrassment" of social failure or flawed interaction; "shyness" before strangers and "respect" for hierarchical superiors; the "shame," "humiliation," or "social death" of being caught doing wrong or harming others. In a preliminary draft of this discussion, I suggested that a "derealization" dimension might distinguish true shame from embarrassment and shyness, though all three were labeled in Newari by a single word, as they are in some other cultures as well. I still think the shame of transgression involves the most intense experience of derealization in Newar culture, but partial derealization—if not of the moral self, then of part of self, a role-self—occurs when someone errs in social interaction. The shame of wrongdoing can be distinguished contextually from social embarrassment and shyness. The meaning of acts, and the engagement of the self, vary; lajyā is more intense and shame-like in the context of moral transgression and humiliation.

A vulnerability to some manner of derealization of self seems integral to emotions usually glossed as shame in a range of cultures; the exact form this takes seems specific to the emotional meaning system shaping shame-like affect within a particular culture. Geertz says that the Balinese emotion lek, often translated as "shame," is better glossed as "stage fright," because it has "nothing to do with transgressions," but with performance in social interaction that is culturally constituted as depersonalizing "ceremony."

> What is feared . . . is that the public performance that is etiquette
> will be botched, that the social distance etiquette maintains will con-
> sequently collapse, and that the personality of the individual will
> then break through to dissolve his standardized public identity.
> When this occurs . . . ceremony evaporates, the immediacy of the
> moment is felt with an excruciating intensity, and men become un-
> willing consociates locked in mutual embarrassment, as though they
> had inadvertently intruded upon one another's privacy.[19]

This points to a destructuring of the meanings through which people integrate themselves into a public world, introducing an element of incoherency into life and causing a disruption of the sense of public self. To take another example, Keeler has argued that the Javanese define themselves through interaction. Status is fluid, and, in important ways, self-constructed, rather than fixed by social roles or formal attributes. Hierarchical status and a sense of self are mutually constituting, dependent on the display, interpretation, and expe-rience of emotion in social interaction. The operative emotion in this context, *isin*, is similar in some respect to the Balinese lek and the Newar lajyā. In Javanese culture, Keeler says, if a person has status,

> others should feel *isin* to eat or speak too familiarly in his presence.
> If they do not, he feels *isin* because they have shown him incapable
> of arousing fear and respect in them. If his power does not impress
> itself upon those around him, his status has been impugned, and he
> feels *isin*.

Such acts of disrespect threaten a derealization of self. They subvert self-identities within a culturally constituted social order. In Javanese culture, Kee-ler argues, the "awkwardness" that flows from "inappropriate" social behavior does not, as Geertz maintains for Bali, threaten to dissolve a public identity and expose a private self. Instead, Keeler says, "it threatens the dissolution of several people's identities in the collapse of all social order."[20]

The Newar data suggest that a culturally constituted self is vulnerable to derealization in terms of some range of circumstances involving the integra-tion of self into the public world. As we have seen, the meaning of lajyā, and the contexts in which it is imputed or experienced, range from something like stage fright (where the emphasis is on performance in social interaction) to shame (associated with transgressions that threaten the moral order). The dis-turbance of the sense of self varies in intensity: the self may be rendered mildly problematic in embarrassment, or it may be threatened with dissolution and incoherence in more intense states of shame—one may become nothing, "as good as dead," as the Newars put it.

I suspect that some of the confusion and controversy regarding shame has resulted from a failure to recognize the complex structure of the emotion. Thus, Geertz says of lek that it

> is neither the sense that one has transgressed nor the sense of hu-
> miliation that follows upon some uncovered transgression, both
> rather lightly felt and quickly effaced in Bali. It is, on the contrary, a
> diffuse, usually mild, though in certain situations virtually paralyz-
> ing, nervousness before the prospect (and the fact) of social interac-
> tion. . . .
> Whatever its deeper causes, stage fright consists in the fear that
> for want of skill or self-control, or perhaps by mere accident, an aes-
> thetic illusion will not be maintained, that the actor will show
> through his part and the part thus dissolve into the actor.[21]

This exegesis—apart from the underlying dramaturgical metaphor—is not inconsistent with aspects of the shyness or embarrassment dimensions of lajyā. But Geertz denies that lek has anything to do with feelings of shame resulting from transgressions, whereas lajyā encompasses experiences of shame associated with transgressions and humiliation.[22] Unni Wikan challenges Geertz's interpretation of lek on the basis of fieldwork in another part of Bali. She reports that she found that the northern Balinese concept of *malu,* which her informants identified as synonymous with the southern Balinese lek, "does indeed have to do with transgressions and humiliations, not at all lightly felt or quickly effaced in Bali."[23] I suspect that the Balinese terms lek and malu tap an "emotional space" with complex dimensions, as does the Newar term *lajyā.* Stage fright may be an apt description of one dimension of lek, but the context-sensitive emotional meaning system that generates stage fright may also generate shame/humiliation. People—Newars, Balinese, and Australian Aborigines—seem to recognize some kind of family resemblance among shame, shyness, fear-fright, and embarrassment and make use of a single context-sensitive term to refer to a range of related experiences. Perhaps the unity of emotions like lajyā and lek has to do with the vulnerability of the self in a world of others who observe and evaluate self. Within the framework of the public world, self-esteem and self-image are modulated and vulnerable in a number of ways, given the vicissitudes of the flow of social life. The complex structure of vulnerability is reflected in the range of meanings attached to these emotion terms.

The English emotion term *shame* seems peculiar in cross-cultural perspective, because it does not seem to be semantically and socially organized in terms of conceptual links with timidity, fear-fright, and respect in the way that the emotion terms often translated by the English word *shame* generally do. To put it another way, English speakers apparently discriminate lexically what other cultures seem to discriminate contextually—if at all. Wierzbicka, for example, discusses some of the ways the meaning of the English word shame contrasts with Australian Aboriginal emotion concepts, such as *kunta,* often translated as "shame." Wierzbicka asks, "Are the feelings corresponding to concepts such as 'shame,' 'fear,' and 'embarrassment' discrete?" She suggests that if a language does not discriminate between emotions such as shame and fear, then the speakers of that language may not be able to perceive them as two different feelings.[24] This may be true to some extent; linguistic categories can influence cognitive and perceptual processes,[25] but there may be bases for discrimination other than language. Speakers who do not discriminate lexically may be able to discriminate contextually. They also may be able to discriminate cognitively, even when they do not discriminate lexically, if they can tap alternative cognitive schemas or cultural scenarios for a single lexical term, as they do with lajyā. Furthermore, people may experience and express mental states that are not lexicalized; psychological experience is not always mediated by language. People may know more than they can put into words;[26] and there are nonverbal, or partly nonverbal, modalities for socialization, communication, and expressiveness.[27] I have discussed lexicalized emotions here, but although these culturally "marked" and lexicalized emotions are central to Newar moral knowing, I want to stress that there may be other, culturally "unmarked" feelings for which people may have no words but which color moral knowing. Even culturally marked emotions are constantly reforged in terms of life experiences.

It is worth stressing that Newars view the experience of lajyā as painful. It is desirable to have the capacity to feel lajyā, and to lack this capacity is a defect in moral character. The experience of the "raw" sensation of lajyā, in its psychological immediacy, its "pain," is highly undesirable—but essential to moral life. Newar moral and emotional discourse presupposes that moral behavior is grounded in moral pain and in the fear of moral pain. What Newars know, as moral beings, is mediated by this pain and fear. I think it is fair to say that part of the reason moral emotions work as behavioral controls is because they are painful to experience, and that this experience of distress influences how agents place and present themselves in the social world. In my view, hot, flushed, red-faced feelings of embarrassment, and cold, metaphorically death-like, empty feelings of shame, *embody* moral evaluations: to *feel* moral judgments of self in this way alters the way people know moral values and know themselves.

In the absence of emotional experience, people in any culture may cognitively know and use the knowledge structures that constitute the moral code. They can answer hypothetical questions about the moral code, but a cognitive or discursive rehearsal of their moral knowledge may have little impact on how they live their lives and organize their behavior. In contrast, painful emotional experience commands a greater degree of attention and may initiate processes of psychological work, through which a person attempts to reorient the relationship of self to social world, and of self to self. Emotions engage the self more completely and more reflexively, bringing to life what was known about, in a passive way, but not known in terms of self-experience.

Thus, moral emotions are moral judgments; they are not just cognitive judgments. They are, or have the potential for being, *felt* moral judgments. Such judgments have motivational significance. Simply knowing about a moral norm—being cognitively acquainted but not emotionally engaged with it[28]—is not as likely to motivate social action and psychological work as powerfully felt, emotionally embodied judgments are.[29]

Pastāe: Remorse, Regret, Contrition

Lajyā is not the only emotion that a moral person feels. A person with the capacity to feel lajyā will, Newars say, also be subject to *pastāe*. Pastāe, then, like lajyā, is a moral emotion. It is painful to experience and evaluative in nature. Pastāe designates an emotion resembling remorse, regret, or contrition. Like lajyā, pastāe results when a person violates a norm or fails to live up to expectations about his or her conduct. As Ganesh Lal, a farmer, put it, "Pastāe means—if we do something that is not appropriate, we have pastāe." But the concept of pastāe is apparently narrower than lajyā. Pastāe unlike lajyā, is not experienced for mere solecisms or minor improprieties. Acts that result in feelings of pastāe often involve some actual harm or infliction of pain (*dukha*) on others. Informants give examples like lying to someone, or hitting or beating someone, as acts that might produce pastāe.

Unlike lajyā, pastāe seems to be what a person expects to feel *after* doing something wrong; it is not felt in anticipation of wrongdoing. Nor does pastāe establish conventional standards in the way lajyā does. There are separate terms for legalistic "guilt," such as the word *dosh*. It refers to the condition of having violated some norm or law, of bearing the "blame" or "fault" for some act, without having the emotive sense of remorse that pastāe possesses.

Pastāe is not used in reproaching others in the way lajyā is. This may reflect the definition of pastāe as something felt after an act; it lacks the anticipatory value of sensitivity to shame. Informants say you may feel pastāe and lajyā at the same time about the same action. Krishna Bahadur has a keen sense of the pain of remorse and views pastāe as an emotional response to harming others:

> Pastāe means that we for no reason—unnecessarily—do something that gives pain (dukha) to others. We hit them, and then this is a sin. Because you struck them. Pastāe means reviling [yourself]. For no reason you did that—do you have pastāe? If you did not do that, you would not need to have pastāe. You do something wrong, and then have pastāe.

Pastāe, in his view, flows from acts that hurt others, when those acts are not justifiable ("for no reason"). Krishna grounds pastāe in pāp. Pastāe is felt when some act causes pain or injury to another; the act itself is a pāp.

The notion of harm to others is not central to the concept of lajyā. Exposure to the sight and verdict of others, not harm to others, unifies such diverse acts as being seen eating, public nakedness, and other improprieties.

The notion of harm may be picked up in other Newar moral concepts: "If I do dharma," said a low-caste Jugi, "I don't hurt anyone. Only if I sin do I hurt someone." Pastāe conveys, as part of its central meaning, the feeling associated with harming others.

Pastāe often results from actions that were undertaken in the belief that they were warranted, but later were determined to lack justification. "Pastāe means I made a mistake. Later I know my mistake; this is pastāe," reported Krishna. One example cited by several informants is punishing a child in the belief that the child has done something wrong. Should they find out later that the child did not do anything wrong, the informants agreed that pastāe would be experienced. Some reported that they had been in that situation and had

experienced pastāe; others simply maintained it would be the appropriate emotion. Informants pointed out that a person feeling pastāe in these circumstances might feel lajyā as well, if others knew of his or her actions, because
others might call you a bad person for striking a child without sufficient reason.

Pastāe does not always designate a feeling that follows from a perception
of harm done to another. It may be used in the sense of regret where there is
no implication of moral fault, no sense of having done wrong. In such cases,
it sometimes seems to play off a sense of empathy and connection, marking,
not perceived harm to another, but a sense of loss, of diminished relatedness,
perhaps filtered through feelings that self did not do enough to sustain and
nurture the relationship with other.

Despite the power of these emotions, even the fear of shame and the pain
of remorse sometimes fails to inhibit people. At times, there are deeper problems of self-control; some Newars, sometimes, engage in behavior that causes
them deep shame and remorse, but find they cannot help themselves. Cultural
responses to this state of affairs are revealing of further assumptions made
about mental life.

The Problem of Self-Control

> If you can't control your own heart, who can?
> *Tha:gu nuga: thama (n) cii mapha:sā, su-(n) phai?*

Newars have ideas about what causes, and how to respond to, what might in
Western folk models be termed "weakness of will": an inability to do what one
wants, to live up to one's own or others' expectations. For example, sometimes
Newars who drink heavily want to stop but find that they cannot. For this,
Newars propose various cultural remedies. One response, a kind of ritual ther-
apy, involves mobilizing religious ideas to support resolve or to counter desire.

The therapy proceeds along lines consistent with the Newar view of the
nature of mental life. The Newar cultural model of the mind proposes that
desires (*icchā*) are important mental states. Desires are states of wanting, needing, wishing, or liking.[30] These may be seen as arising from within the self,
from feelings, emotions, and thoughts, or as arising from outside the self,
through perceptions and experiences of things in the world. In either case, they
are not fully under the control of the individual who experiences them, though
an individual may be expected to make an effort to control them. In certain
cases, desires may be viewed as entirely outside the control of the individual
and as caused by external forces. If not checked or regulated, desires tend to
cause behavior. If you want to drink, and you let yourself, you will. To control
yourself you have to regulate your desires. Dharma Raj, a Brahman, describes
the process as follows:

You can choose desires [icchā]. Slowly. So here we practice austerities [vrata].[31] [People] are taken to a god place to have these bad desires removed. They enlist the aid of the god or goddess. They
swear, "From now on I truly will not drink alcohol." At the god
place, they say, "Oh Bhagabān, Oh Goddess, I swear not to drink
spirits. If I drink spirits, it will be as if drinking your blood." . . .
And in that same way, to their friends they say, "Friend, if I drink
spirits, it will count as drinking your urine." To the god, it will count
as drinking the god's blood. Drinking blood is a great crime [apar-
ādh]. Drinking a god's blood is an even greater crime. Should I
drink alcohol, it will be as if I committed that crime. They make this
vow.

Viewed as a mental state, the vow expresses a resolution; D'Andrade remarks
that resolutions are "second-order intentions—intentions to keep certain other
intentions despite difficult and opposing desires."[32]

The vow can also be viewed as a social act, as it is publicly declared to
other persons—to friends, family members, or deities (who count as special,
divine persons). Notice the performative utterance: the vow taken is the speech
act of promising. Speech acts may have a close relation to beliefs about mental
states. D'Andrade theorizes that "speech acts are one of the major classes of
public events used as identifying marks of internal states and processes."[33]
What goes on in speech—in acts such as promising, commanding, request-
ing—may map out ideas about what goes on in the mind.

In the resolutions in the above passage, there is more involved than swear-
ing off drink; the speech act, or vow, is followed up by saying that any lapse
will be the equivalent of some socially abhorred act. To drink alcohol is equated
with drinking the goddess's blood, a fearful moral crime, or drinking urine, a
disgusting or degrading act. (There are cultural performances in which ritual
actors drink the blood of animals, so the notion of drinking blood is a familiar
one—but one does not drink the blood of deities.) Drinking alcohol may also
be equated with drinking mother's blood, or people may ask that they be made
to die, vomiting blood, if they drink again. In this way, the "bad" desire is
countered by utterances that express "good" intentions or resolve, and we can
speculate that the added notion of drinking blood is meant to arouse emotions
that will lend strength to the resolution. This corresponds to a proposition in
the cultural model of mind that says that desires reflect emotions or feelings
and that intentions follow from desires. To combat a morally wrong desire, a
person must resolve not to do wrong, and this must be supported by desires,
which develop from emotions. The imagery in the Newar resolutions supplies
emotion; the desire is a desire not to do wrong, which is lent strength, in a
sense, by the desire to avoid committing such an elemental crime as drinking
blood. Arguably, feelings of anxiety and guilt are intensified by equating a

wrongful act (drinking alcohol) with a far greater wrong (drinking blood)—
and by asking to be punished for the former as if it were the latter.

Vows or pledges made to deities thus express "good" intentions or resolutions. The god is the guarantor of the consequences of breaking the pledge;
the person who wishes to stop drinking organizes his or her intentions in the
act of pledging. The equation of drinking spirits with drinking blood heightens
the sense of consequence; it constitutes an effort to frighten self out of the
habit of desire.

There is also, perhaps, an attempt in all this to leverage intentions—to
make them stronger by making them public and linked to consequences so
horrible as to render doing what would engender such grotesque consequences
unthinkable. To increase the severity of the consequences of an action is to
arm a person with counterintentions, with resolve against desire. The more
wrong the consequences of an act, the more wrong the desire to act in that
manner—making self-control more important.

The resolutions of the vow can be viewed in reflexive terms as efforts to
manipulate or manage the mental processes that lead to unwanted behaviors.
The ritualized resolutions presuppose that the mind is organized as an interactive system of different states and processes and that people can willfully or
deliberately influence the mind by formulating different goals. It is from this
perspective that resolutions can be seen as therapeutic discourse.

It is probably unnecessary to say that such procedures do not seem to be
entirely effective.[34] Nevertheless, these procedures do point out what people
believe about minds: the Newar cultural model proposes that there are links
between mental states and processes that result in behavior; these beliefs about
the links among mental states, processes, and behavior are the basis for therapeutic interventions. Self-control means being able to take an intentional
stand regarding mental states (desires) that organize behavior.

Newars, like Americans, believe that one can think about what is thought
and felt, and they believe this capacity to reflect on "inner" experience makes
a difference. They feel that one can act, mentally, to alter the self; in their view,
self-control involves active "deliberations" about mental states and processes.
D'Andrade points out the way the links between elements in the American
cultural model of the mind make possible a concept of self-control:

> The folk model treatment of desire and intention as states that take
> propositionally framed objects or states of affairs means that what
> can be wanted, aimed for, and planned depends on what is known,
> or believed, or understood. . . . Since what is wanted, aimed for, and
> planned are things thought of, one may "deliberate" about these
> wants, aims, and plans. These deliberations may, in turn, lead to
> other feelings, such as guilt or doubt, or other wishes, which may
> counter the original wish, or may involve various second-order in-

tentional states, such as resolution or indecision. Were this feedback loop, in which one can think about what one feels, desires, and intends, not present in the folk model, there would be no mechanism of self-control in the system, and hence we would have no basis for concepts of responsibility, morality, or conscience.[35]

This is a cultural process; the way these deliberations are couched and framed draws on cultural resources. When I asked Krishna, "If you have a bad thought or bad desire, what do you do to stop that bad thought or desire?" he responded by describing how you should deliberate about these bad thoughts or desires and resolve to give them up:

> To unmake a bad thought you have to think, to concentrate in your mind, with your spirit, "I must not do this, it is a sin. If I do that, a great sin will happen to me, a mistake will happen." And if, in this way, we think thoughts of god, then god will be in our minds. . . . If we keep having this kind of mind [wish, desire], this kind of sin in our mind, then we should give it up. Cause ourselves to forget it. And then we decide by our hearts, by our soul, I should not do this, it is not done. Thinking so, we won't commit sins.

The language of self-control here is religious. As we saw in earlier passages from interviews with him, this man believes that inner moral struggles for self-control have a kind of transparency: they are known to god. This transparency—where you know that you are known—perhaps lends something to reflections on what one wants and desires; inner deliberations are undertaken with a sense of the moral presence of god. And for Krishna, the ultimate goals of self-monitoring are religious: to think thoughts that bring god to consciousness, to avoid thoughts that lead to sin.

Newars judge themselves in moral terms. The process of self-judgment is a subjective experience. Inner deliberations may be motivated by moral feelings. I have described how Newars experience what they term pastāe, a concept that designates something like remorse or regret. When I ask Krishna what pastāe is, he speaks of it in terms that weave together psychological, moral, and religious ideas:

> [What is pastāe]
> There is worry.
> [How?]
> By his heart, he knows. Now he has done wrong, made a mistake, and he says to himself, "Oh, my god, damn." [That is, he reproaches self.] So he has worry in his heart. However great their understanding of dharma [the moral law], people sin too . . .
> [What happens inside you when you have pastāe?]
> In the heart there is our Bhagabān, this heart beating. And then

we do wrong; pastāe means a mistake happened. I did wrong, why did I do that . . . so pain comes.

Cultural ideas shape how people view themselves and how they reflect on their moral intuitions and, thus, shape the way they experience themselves, even as what they experience shapes the way they understand culture. That people experience moral pain because they have done something they view as wrong lends meaning to the idea of a knowing heart. But the connection can be traced in the other direction as well: moral knowing grows out of the way culture and experience re-create and animate each other. The idea of a knowing heart, and the concept of a god within, are cultural representations that give meaning to moral experience; they give people's feelings and intuitions explicit ethical significance. Not only are they a way of speaking about what people feel, they articulate personal experience with the idea of a moral person and of a moral order. The Newars, like many people in many cultures, tend to see morality as an objective part of the world, rather than as a human construction: morality reflects natural or sacred law.[36] Newars also see society as ideally embodying this law. We have seen that they also articulate morality with personal, subjective experience. By understanding that the heart knows what is moral, that a witnessing god dwells within the heart, Newars are able to know that they are moral persons, at least in potential, capable of moral feeling and self-judgment. Their morality reaches into the heart.

Agency versus Passive Experiencing

Newars understand and experience mental life in ways shaped by their distinctive cultural tradition; their ethnopsychology is a local form, based on "local knowledge." Nevertheless, some of what Newars say and assume about mental life seems familiar: many of the categories and concepts used by Newars correspond, roughly, to what is designated by such English psychological terms as desire, memory, thought, emotion, shame, intention, and resolution. The social and cultural meaning of the states and processes that correspond to these terms are not precisely the same as in English,[37] but there is at least a family resemblance.

Not just discrete concepts, but also some of what is posited about the organization of psychological experience seem in some ways similar in the American and the Newar models. One interesting cross-cultural parallel is the way that some mental states can be represented either as involving parts of the self or as engaging the core of self.[38] This shapes the ways a self can relate to itself within the bounds of intrapsychic life: people can be seen either as passive experiencers (as the objects of some other part of their minds) or as agents of psychological states (having intentional control over aspects of mental life).

Both Newars and Americans seem to assume that people may experience themselves as the agent of some states of mind, but as the passive experiencer (or object) of other states.[39] Newars do not will themselves to feel ashamed; the emotion originates within them but is experienced by them. It happens to them. When Newars resolve to stop drinking or thinking "bad thoughts," they are attempting to do something to themselves, rather than passively experiencing something happening to them. They relate to themselves as agents in mental acts of intending, deliberating, and choosing.

In Newari, as in English, there are verbal forms and expressions that reflect the distinction between "a passive experiencer," and "an intentional agent." D'Andrade gives the examples of "the thought struck me" versus "I thought" and "I am afraid" versus "I fear." The Newar model seems similar to the American model in that it, too, "treats the self as an area of focus that can expand and contract, but the limit of its contraction lies outside the core act of intending."[40] The core of the self can be experienced as inside or outside an emotion, so that self may be identified with an emotion or viewed as passively experiencing it. For example, Newars seem to sometimes view anger as involving the intentional core of the self, the intending I, whereas at other moments they may conceptualize it as a process happening to a person, in which the intentional core of the self is not (yet) fully engaged—but might become so.

Newars have two ways of speaking of anger. To say "anger came out to me," *ta(n) pihā wala,* is to indicate that a process of anger is happening to self; to say "I felt angry," *ji ta(n) cāyā,* according to some informants, seems to involve more of a commitment of self, and seems to shift the semantic focus from process to action. One informant explained that when a person throws things, or yells, or fights, "he [or she] feels angry," *wa ta(n) cāla,* is the appropriate verbal form; the anger is shown in the actions. This suggests that this expression refers to intentional states. One informant characterized "anger came out to me" as happening before such angry acts; a person might warn another not to speak or do something because "anger comes out to me." This suggests that anger is viewed here as a process happening to the self that might lead to actions; anger is treated as something that is "building up" but has not yet involved the intentional core of the self. When it does, the emotion will be acted on; a shift occurs, so that anger is no longer something happening to the self, but is something self is doing. It becomes intentional.

The conception of anger as something that happens to the self rather than something self does, is perhaps more salient for Newars because frequent or excessive anger is subject to disapproval. Only justified anger is likely to be seen or portrayed as involving the I, the intentional self. Typically, this involvement must be explained. One informant noted that it felt unnatural to say "I felt angry," without giving an account of why you were feeling angry. You would, he thought, ordinarily say why you felt angry and then conclude by saying "and then I felt angry," *ale ji ta(n) cāyā*. When anger is justified, the experience of anger can be reconceptualized: anger happens to the self, but, under some conditions, the intending core of self is identified with the anger. A commitment to being angry arises, and anger becomes an intentional process. The person becomes involved as a whole—as an agent, not just as passive experiencer.

This may hold cross-culturally. For example, Lakoff and Kövecses examine the metaphorical structure of ways of speaking about anger in American English; the "folk" model Lakoff and Kövecses identify resembles the "hydraulic" model of academic psychology in which anger "builds up," creates pressure, and seeks release in an outburst or explosion.[41] I think the metaphorical structure of these models may culturally represent and map out the process-action sequence, that is, the movement from passive experiencing to engagement as an intentional agent. The notion of self-engagement seems equally relevant to alternatives to the "hydraulic" model. Sabini and Silver, for example, discuss the possibility of a "moral account" of anger, where anger (and the shift from process to action) has to do with transgression and retribution, rather than with frustration and aggression.[42] Even more than the hydraulic account, a moral analysis of anger would seem to presuppose some concept of agency.[43]

Thus, I would speculate that the engagement of the "whole person" or "intentional core of the self" is a precondition of moral action, in Newar society and elsewhere. Take the example of shame, or lajyā, as a response to wrongdoing; this feeling seems to happen to a person but also engages the core of the self. Shame is something that happens to the self as a passive experiencer. One does not will shame to happen, and a self does not have direct control over it. And yet shame is not a moral emotion only because it acts as a kind of external force acting on self. People do fear being shamed and feeling shamed; shame does act on the self, producing anxiety and distress. But there is (at least sometimes) a deeper engagement of the self. Although one does not will shame to happen and has no control over it, once shame is *felt*, the person responds not only by avoiding actions that induce shame (making shame a kind of aversive conditioning) but also by intending not to do wrong (making it a matter of self-control). The person can respond with deliberations, reflections, intentions, resolutions—that is, as an intentional agent. The feeling may be unwilled, but the core of the self is involved in taking a stand on the breach of the relationship of self and world that gave rise to the feeling. The distress associated with moral feelings—the pain they cause—pushes the core of the self to respond, to commit itself to a course of action that may resolve difficulties that have arisen in the relation of self to social world.

Diversity

It is worth stressing that any culture may contain a range of ways of knowing self. This is certainly true of Newar culture. Often, postulates about mind that seem to be based on universals can be reframed in more culturally specialized terms; people can shift between models or parts of models. There may be a variety of reasons for having multiple models; the psychological and the social implications of different models are different. For example, Newars see desires as a given of mental life; they assume that desires are part of the ordinary person's mental experience, and they see this as natural and necessary. They can shift perspectives, however, and drawing on their cultural tradition view desire in other ways. "If a man had no desires," I asked a Brahman, "what would he feel?"

> If there were no desires—if a man had no desires—it would be like being sick. There would be hopelessness [*nirās*]. There are two kinds of hopelessness. There is suffering [dukha] and [so] hopelessness develops. There is knowledge and hopelessness develops. A renouncer [*sannyāsi*] is one who experiences hopelessness through knowledge. He has knowledge but he has no hope for the world. A sannyāsi has no hope for the world. It is hopelessness, but even so for the *para-mātmā* [soul, oversoul of which the individual soul is part], there is hope. While a sannyāsi must hope with the paramātma he has no worldly hope. So hopelessness develops. But a sick person, a man who suffers greatly, he despairs because he has no money, no medicine, because he is ill, and has no rest. This too is a kind of hopelessness. In these there are no desires. [The informant qualifies his remarks.] There can be desires in sick people.
> [What is the relationship (of hopelessness) with desire?]
> Desires are for oneself.

In Newar culture, the desire to be without desire makes sense. It is a religious value, even though few Newars desire to be ascetics—or lack the desire to enjoy the world. Even as nonascetics, they see renunciation as radically reframing the way mental life is conceived and giving it a special ethical and soteriological twist. Ordinary models do not apply to special cases. Informants gave the example of world-renouncers as people without desire, but these informants typically insisted that ordinary people, nonascetics like themselves, would have desires. Some informants found it hard to answer the question of what it would be like to be without desires. One informant remarked that even very sick, "hopeless" people have desires: they want to die.

Conclusion

D'Andrade suggests that even if parts of cultural models of mind are based on universal psychological experience, other parts may be related to the ecological and social structure of a community, and still others may be "legacies from the past"—historical formations unrelated either to current conditions of life or to universals of psychological experience.[44] The Newar case leads to similar conclusions. Some elements of the Newar conception of mind seem to be due to social and political factors, and others can be seen as reflecting the cultural history of the Newars, especially the way they have made cultural and religious developments in South Asia part of their own worldview—and cultural selves. Other aspects of the Newar concept of mind seem to reflect universals, near universals, or probable forms of mental experience.

The Newar material suggests that fully understanding how people understand mind (and use their beliefs about mind to understand themselves and others) will involve a range of approaches. It will certainly require examining the local organization of mental life and the way mental experience is grounded in specific historical conditions and cultural frames. In the Newar case, this includes attention to religious and moral ideas. I believe it will also require that this body of data and theory be related to more universal perspectives on mind, which take account of the way mental life reflects transcultural existential, ethical, psychological, and linguistic experiences.

It is easy to slip into a cultural determinism that is as one-dimensional and limiting as psychological reductionism. The fact that emotions are socially and culturally constituted does not necessarily entail the view that social actors are simply "programmed" by culture to have certain emotions. Social actors are not merely passive receivers of emotional discourse, incapable of acting on and restructuring that discourse in any way. They are biographical individuals and cultural selves at the same time—thinking, feeling, *and* cultural subjects all at once. The social and cultural structuring of emotion does not rule out the psychological and biographical structuring of emotion. These can be complementary perspectives.

To point out that models found in different cultures make similar assumptions about the categories or organization of mental experience is not to say that the ways these assumptions are fleshed out, represented, and reconstructed in particular cultures do not make a difference. They do. The Newar concept of mind takes forms of experience and knowing that may be universals and fuses them with culture, developing and shaping them into local forms of experience and knowing. Newar concepts of a psychologically active and morally sensitive "heart," their vision of a moral god animating and inhabiting this heart-mind, and their cultural experience of moral emotions, all help articulate a concept of the moral person. These ideas build on, and elaborate, the notion that self can passively experience—and yet actively evaluate—thoughts and feelings originated by other parts of self. This self integrates a capacity for self-knowledge and self-control (however problematic) with sensitivity to moral emotions. Newar ethnopsychology thus articulates a concept of person as, at once, an agent and a passive experiencer within a complex internal world and places this concept of the person in a religious and ethical context. Newar concepts of mind help Newars know that "the person" is constituted as a moral being, with an "inner" life that participates in the moral and the sacred.

NOTES

I wish to thank Roy D'Andrade, Ernestine McHugh, Daniel Linger, McKim Marriot, Charles Lindholm, and two anonymous reviewers for comments on earlier versions of this article. Portions of this discussion were presented as a paper at the 19th Annual South Asia Conference, 1990, Madison, Wisconsin, in a panel organized by Al Pach.

1. Robert Solomon, "Getting Angry: The Jamesian Theory of Emotion in Anthropology," *Cultural Theory: Essays on Mind, Self, and Emotion*, edited by R. A. Shweder and R. A. LeVine (New York: Cambridge University Press, 1984), 238–254; Fred Myers, *Pintupi Country, Pintupi Self: Sentiment, Place, and Politics among the Western Desert Aborigines* (Washington DC: Smithsonian Institution Press, 1986).

2. Michelle Rosaldo, "Toward an Anthropology of Self and Feeling," in *Culture Theory: Essays on Mind, Self, and Emotion*, edited by R. A. Shweder and R. A. Levine (New York: Cambridge University Press, 1984), 137–157; Robert Levy, "Emotion, Knowing, and Culture," *Culture Theory: Essays on Mind, Self, and Emotion*, edited by R. A. Shweder and R. A. LeVine (New York: Cambridge University Press, 1984), 214–237.

3. Owen Lynch has commented on the tension between approaches that emphasize the cognitive construction of emotions and those that emphasize self-reflexivity. Generally favoring a constructionist position, he notes that "pure cognitivism, in its attempt to distinguish feeling from sensation and to show that feelings, as sensations, do not identify emotions, goes too far in making the self a bodyless, unfeeling purely logical mind." See Owen Lynch, "The Social Construction of Emotion in India," *Divine Passions*, edited by Owen Lynch (Berkeley: University of California Press, 1990), 14.

4. George Mandler, *Mind and Emotion* (New York: Wiley, 1975), 8.

5. Emotion, mind, and self have become important subjects of culture theory, and ethnographic studies have shown how deeply and fundamentally psychological life is embedded in culture. See, e.g., Robert Levy, *Tahitians: Mind and Experience in the Society Islands* (Chicago: University of Chicago Press, 1973) and "Emotion, Knowing, and Culture," *Culture Theory: Essays on Mind, Self, and Emotion*, ed. R. A. Schweder and R. A. LeVine (New York: Cambridge University Press, 1984), 214–237; Catherine Lutz, *Unnatural Emotions* (Chicago: University of Chicago Press, 1988); Catherine Lutz and Geoffrey White, "The Anthropology of Emotions," *Annual Review of Anthropology* 15 (1986): 405–436; Fred Myers, "Emotions and the Self: A Theory of Personhood and Political Order among Pintupi Aborigines," *Ethos* 7 (1979): 75–86 and

Pintupi Country, Pintupi Self: Sentiment, Place, and Politics among the Western Desert Aborigines (Washington DC: Smithsonian Institution Press, 1986); Gananath Obeyesekere, *Medusa's Hair: An Essay on Personal Symbols and Religious Experience* (Chicago: University of Chicago Press, 1981); Geoffrey White and John Kirkpatrick, eds., *Person, Self, and Experience: Exploring Pacific Ethnopsychologies* (Berkeley: University of California Press, 1985). Moral phenomena are also receiving increasing scrutiny in anthropology (Alan Fiske, ed., "Special Issue Devoted to Moral Relativism," *Ethos* 18 [1990]).

6. Robert Levy, *Mesocosm* (Berkeley: University of California Press, 1990); Gerard Toffin, *Société et religion chez les Newar du Nepal* (Paris: Centre National de la Recherche Scientifique, 1984); Gopal Singh Nepali, *The Newars* (Bombay: United Asia Publications, 1965).

7. In my interviews with Newars, I attempted to explore not only what Newars "know about" cultural beliefs and practices (their discursive knowledge of culture), but how they experienced and evaluated culture. Thus, the interviews were person-centered and discovery-oriented. I adapted "clinical" techniques to the task of exploring moral discourse in Newar culture (with its culture-specific repertoire of communicative conventions). Interviews were conducted in Newari, without the help of interpreters, with informants from a number of castes, ranging from Brahmans to untouchables. I interviewed each informant in several sessions (ranging from six to twenty of one hour or more. These interviews took place in a room I rented in a house. The setting ensured the confidentiality of the interviews and made it possible for informants to speak with relative freedom and openness. The interviews were transcribed by a Newar assistant, and translations were made with the help of Newari speakers. I have omitted brief repetitions or asides from the transcript I quote here. I have not amalgamated material from different interviews, or from different parts of a long interview, into continuous passages. Standard ethnographic interviewing and participant-observation provided additional data and shaped interpretation of the material from these person-centered interviews. I have given the informants pseudonyms.

8. I draw here on Roy D'Andrade's ("A Folk Model of the Mind," *Cultural Models in Language and Thought,* ed. D. Holland and N. Quinn [New York: Cambridge University Press, 1987], 112–148) discussion of the nature of cultural models of mind and on his description of the American "folk model" of mind, for comparative insights. A cultural model (a type of cognitive schema) consists of a set of conceptual objects and propositions, and their relationships. Concepts of and propositions about internal states and processes make up the American folk model: *feelings, desires, beliefs, intentions* are among the basic states and processes (115–116). People use them to make inferences and construct scenarios about mental life. The models specify what types of "inner" experience there are (what state and processes exist and how they relate to each other), the origins and causes of mental experience (in terms either of posited causal relations among different states and processes, or of hypotheses about agencies or faculties), and what the implications of mental experience are for behavior. Scenarios can be constructed by filling in the model with referents—by applying it to (real or hypothetical) situations or cases. So if I believe feelings of envy cause people to belittle others unjustly, I may attribute Susan's dismissive criticism of Harry to her envy of his success—she feels bad because Harry, not she, is successful and has what she wants to have. As you can see, this scenario is fairly complex, involving *feelings,*

like *envy*, and psychic states, like *wants*, that can take cultural objects like *success*. Envy embodies—in an *emotion*—some sort of comparative judgment about how much more successful Harry is than self, and the proposition that envy leads to unjust criticism would seem to presuppose another proposition that says envious persons try to diminish or downplay the successes of others—motivated, perhaps, by a *need* or *desire* to preserve their *self-esteem*. Only some of these concepts and propositions are drawn from the model of mind, feelings, wants, and needs. (These seem to be elementary parts of the model; terms like self-esteem and motivation seem more like parts of specialized developments of the model.) The scenario draws on other models or schemas as well; success is a schema having to do, not with mind, but with the social world. Many of the elements of a cultural model or scenario can, themselves, be complex schemas. D'Andrade says, "One consequence of the hierarchical structure of schemas is that certain cultural models have a wide range of application as parts of other models" (112–113).

A cultural model supports evaluations as well as inferences. For example, I may think that envy is a bad thing. Or if I believe that being very angry interferes with good judgment, and if my perception of John is that he is chronically angry, I might be skeptical about his ability to perform certain roles—and oppose his taking on those roles. I might even think therapy was indicated because his chronic anger was disrupting his work and social relations.

The set of concepts, information, and relationships that go into a model, typically, are made entirely explicit; because they are intersubjectively shared, everyone in a group knows the schemas, and there is usually no need to make them explicit. They are taken for granted and "treated as if they were obvious facts of the world" (D'Andrade 113).

9. I am not sure to what extent the idea that the head is the locus of mental states and processes reflects culture change and a "modern" viewpoint influenced by outside conceptions or simply the notion that speech is analogous to thought. Dispositions, attitudes, and more enduring thoughts seem to be located in the "heart." The term nuga: refers to the physical organs of the chest cavity as well as to mental entities and processes. In other ways, it is quite close to the Nepali concept of *man* and the Gurung concept of *sae*, which are also located in the chest and are the seat of intention, cognition, memory, and emotion (Ernestine McHugh, "Concepts of Person among the Gurungs of Nepal," *American Ethnologist* 16 [1989]: 75–86). Although nuga: might be glossed as "heart-mind" or "heart-self," I have decided to follow English-speaking Newars in glossing it simply as "heart," except where it seems useful to emphasize the way uses of nuga: comprehend and fuse together what we would distinguish as "mind" (the entities and processes of psychological life) or "self" (as in *self*-identity, my*self*, and so on).

10. D'Andrade, "A Folk Model of the Mind," *Cultural Models in Language and Thought*, edited by D. Holland and N. Quinn (New York: Cambridge University Press, 1987), 145.

11. Psychological and brain processes that make the acquisition of culture and language possible must be integrated into the mental system that includes language and cultural schemas. But the language used to speak of an inner life must have a public grounding. Striking examples of the process of metaphorically mapping the

perceptible events and forms of the world of the senses into an inner world can be found in works of literature; one of my favorite examples is Thoreau's *Walden Pond*.

12. The informants had some trouble understanding the question, perhaps partly because I did not want to "give away" an answer and, thus, phrased the question in vague terms (What happens when you think? What goes on in your mind?), and perhaps partly because this part of the model is so taken for granted that people do not reflect on it and, thus, have never needed to put it into words.

13. Ernestine McHugh, "Concepts of Person among the Gurungs of Nepal," *American Ethnologies* 16 (1989): 75–86.

14. See McHugh (1989) for a discussion of the analogous Gurung concept of sae. Sae, like nuga:, allows individuals to represent self-experience in cultural terms. As McHugh argues, individuality is not absent in South Asian cultures, but coexists with social embeddedness. Dumont's (1960, 1965, 1986) view that South Asian cultures do not "valorize" the individual fails to take into account cultural modes for representing the significance and value of individual existence such as Sae and nuga:.

15. D'Andrade, "A Folk Model of the Mind," 119.

16. Clifford Geertz, in " 'From the Native's Point of View': On the Nature of Anthropological Understanding," in *Culture Theory: Essays on Mind, Self, and Emotion,* edited by R. A. Shweder and R. A. LeVine (New York: Cambridge University Press, 1984), 126.

17. There is a fair amount on "shame," dating form early attempts to identify and contrast "shame cultures" and "guilt cultures" (Benedict 1946). Singer (in Piers and Singer 1971) argued that such contrast were overdrawn. See also Spiro (1965, ch. 15) and DeVos (1973, ch. 5). In South Asia, Obeyesekere (1984: 499–508) has discussed the shame and socialization of shame in the context of Sinhala culture, suggesting that the particular cultural emphasis on shame makes the Sinhalese vulnerable to the loss or enhancement of self-esteem and highly sensitive to status precedence. He conceptualizes shame in terms of sensitivity to the responses of others, as I do for Newars. Obeyesekere associates a desire to humiliate others, and to become enraged at slights, with the sense of shame. Such themes do not seem to be as pronounced in Newar culture. Other recent discussions of shame-like emotion include Clifford Geertz, *The Interpretation of Cultures* (New York: Basic Books, 1973); Ward Keeler, "Shame and Stage Fright in Java," *Ethos* 11 (1983): 152–65; and Michelle Rosaldo, "The Shame of Headhunters and the Autonomy of the Self," *Ethos* 11 (1983): 135–157. For future inquiry, I would suggest that the relationship of shame and empathy deserves attention. Both seem to involve a dialectical, culturally mediated relationship of self and other (Jean-Paul Sartre, *Saint Genet* [New York: Pantheon, 1963]; Gananath Obeyesekere, *The Cult of the Goddess Pattini* [Chicago: University of Chicago Press, 1984]. On empathy, see Nancy Eisenberg and Janet Strayer, *Empathy and Its Development* [Cambridge: Cambridge University Press, 1987]).

18. Gananath Obeyesekere, *Medusa's Hair: An Essay on Personal Symbols and Religious Experience* (Chicago: University of Chicago Press, 1984), 503.

19. Clifford Geertz, *The Interpretation of Cultures* (New York: Basic Books, 1973), 401, 402.

20. Ward Keeler, "Shame and Stage Fright in Java," *Ethos* 11 (1983): 160, 162.

21. Geertz, 402.

22. Ibid., 401.

23. Unni Wikan, "Public Grace and Private Fears: Gaiety, Offense, and Sorcery in Northern Bali, *Ethos* 15 (1987): 360–361.

24. Anna Wierzbicka, "Human Emotions: Universal or Culture-Specific?" *American Anthropologist* 88 (1986): 592, 593.

25. Roy D'Andrade, "Some Propositions about the Relations between Culture and Human Cognition," in *Cultural Psychology: Essays on Comparative Human Development*, edited by J. Stigler, R. Shweder, and G. Herdt (New York: Cambridge University Press, 1990), 73.

26. Richard E. Nisbett and T. D. Wilson, "Telling More Than We Can Know: Verbal Reports on Mental Processes," *Psychological Review* (1970): 231–259.

27. Charles Briggs, *Learning to Ask: A Sociolinguistic Appraisal of the Role of the Interview in Social Science Research* (Cambridge, UK: Cambridge University Press, 1986). Anthony Forge, "Learning to See in New Guinea," in *Socialization: The Approach from Social Anthropology*, edited by Phillip Mayer (London: Tavistock, 1970), 269–291.

28. Melford Spiro, "Some Reflections on Cultural Determinism and Relativism with Special Reference to Emotion and Reason," in *Culture Theory: Essays on Mind, Self, and Emotion*, edited by R. A. Shweder and R. A. LeVine (New York: Cambridge University Press, 1984), 323–346.

29. Emotions are sometimes constructed as "irrational" in Western culture (Lutz 1988). Mr. Spock of *Star Trek* is perhaps the figure in popular American culture who epitomizes this folk opposition of cold, logical intelligence to hot, wild, irrational passions. This folk dichotomy does not do justice to the actual "intelligence" or "rationality" of emotions. Because they rest on the application of one or another moral value or principle, the moral emotions, at least, are often "intelligent," if by that we mean that people must acquire and activate a great deal of cultural knowledge before they experience emotions in cultural contexts. Then, as I have argued here, emotional experience sustains commitment or engagement with culturally constituted moral objects. This means these emotions have a coherent organization; they are not random discharges, inherently disorganized or intrinsically irrational. Thus, people feel moral anger because they perceive an injustice or a grave violation of moral norms; this typically involves a number of conceptual presuppositions and decisions. To feel angry because the U.S. flag has been desecrated, because the Bill of Rights is being put in jeopardy, or because the right to express political or artistic ideas is threatened presupposes that people know complicated things about flags and rights in order to make the judgment that these should be protected on the basis of some intuited principle (e.g., the flag stands for the country; the flag represents those who served or died for their country; freedom of speech serves to check the powers of government and promotes the development of individuals and society; rights are more important than symbols). People may not be able to give an articulate, reflective account of the ethical principle expressed in some of their emotions, because giving such reflective verbal accounts is a special, learned skill.

30. D'Andrade, "A Folk Model of the Mind."

31. *Vrata* are cultural practices involving worship and austerities of various kinds, including fasts, that Hindus view as means to desired, beneficial ends. Susan

Wadley ("Vrats: Transformers of Destiny," *Karma: An Anthropological Inquiry,* ed. C. Keyes and E. V. Daniel [Berkeley: University of California Press, 1983], 147–162) has termed them "transformers of destiny."

32. D'Andrade, "A Folk Model of the Mind," 117

33. Ibid., 146.

34. Bateson ("The Cybernetics of 'Self': A Theory of Alcoholism," *Steps to an Ecology of Mind* [New York: Ballantine Books, 1972], 309–337) pointed out that people's models or understanding of self-control might, in some cases, be wrong in such a way that efforts to exercise self-control would produce the opposite results: a spinning out of control.

35. D'Andrade, "A Folk Model of the Mind," 126.

36. Richard Shweder, Manamohan Mahapatra, and Joan Miller, "Culture and Moral Development," in *The Emergence of Morality in Young Children,* edited by J. Kagan and S. Lamb (Chicago: University of Chicago Press, 1987), 1–83; John Mackie, *Ethics: Inventing Right and Wrong* (New York: Penguin Books, 1977), 30–35.

37. Wierzbicka, "Human Emotions: Universal or Culture-Specific?"

38. D'Andrade, "A Folk Model of the Mind," 118–119; Levy, "Emotion, Knowing, and Culture," 221.

39. D'Andrade, "A Folk Model of the Mind," 118–119.

40. Ibid.,

41. George Lakoff and Zoltán Kövecses, "The Cognitive Model of Anger Inherent in American English," in *Cultural Models in Language and Thought,* edited by D. Holland and N. Quinn (New York: Cambridge University Press, 1987), 195–221.

42. John Sabini and Maury Silver, *Moralities of Everyday Life* (New York: Oxford University Press, 1982).

43. In my view, a "moral account" presupposes the existence of culturally constituted moral objects and expectations; anger becomes a culturally mediated experience, as when a person or group, hoping to make a political point, "desecrates" U.S. flag (a culturally constituted act on a culturally constituted symbolic object). This act counts as a transgression for others to whom the flag is an object of commitment, and they respond with anger, even though they have not personally been inconvenienced or frustrated. The language of "transgression" and "retribution" in moral accounts of anger would seem to presuppose the possibility of a "self" who may take a stand.

To a certain extent, and in certain ways, the "folk" model of anger explored by Lakoff and Kövecses (1987) seems to allow for either frustration or transgression as a form of experience. The model can generate language consistent with a "moral account" of anger as well as with the "hydraulic account," expressing shifts from experience to engagement, from frustration to aggression, and from transgression to retribution, in terms of culturally constituted objects and contexts. As I have suggested, cultural models are invoked in context-sensitive ways. I was once listing some examples of the kind of metaphors for the experience of anger that Lakoff and Kövecses discuss—such as "I blew my top"—in a seminar, when I looked over at one of my students, who was working on a life history of a woman who survived the Nazi concentration camps. I realized I would now speak of moral anger at the Holocaust in the metaphorical terms I was listing: "I hit the ceiling," "I went through the roof," or "I was steamed." There was an almost cartoon-like quality to some of these metaphors that made them inappropriate as language for expressing moral rage about genocide. Choice of metaphors for (and of models of) emotional experience will reflect a speaker's explicit or tacit goals. I suspect some of the metaphors that Lakoff and Kövecses cite are reconstructive and restructuring devices used in narrative contexts as part of a process of social and psychological distancing from the experience of anger.

44. D'Andrade, "A Folk Model of the Mind," 146.

7

The Function of Ritual Weeping Revisited: Affective Expression and Moral Discourse

Gary L. Ebersole

Weeping is not simple. That is, for Gary L. Ebersole, it is a complex act involving layers of shifting meanings and dynamic ongoing engagements with personal and social contexts of ritual. Criticizing the handling of ritual weeping by historians of religions, Ebersole stresses that the expression of affect is shaped in key ways by culture and that we ought to expect different discourses about weeping in different historical and cultural settings. But Ebersole also argues, with respect to the history of religions, that it is a mistake to assume that ritual weeping—and all of its moral baggage—is reducible to cultural scripts. Weeping, in certain instances, challenges cultural commandments for the expression of emotion. Historical actors are not automatons who respond passively to what custom requires. They are, rather, motivated by aspects of their personal background, and such motivation sometimes leads them into behaviors that defy the dominant social logic and depart from cultural scripts. Ritual weeping can be a moral indictment of an oppressive or unfair social order, as a protest— crying truth to power, as it were—of hierarchical social relationships or power asymmetries experienced as morally corrupt. In some instances, as in the case of ritual weeping at the Shi'ite Muslim festival of Muharram, such a display of feeling can serve as an expression of minority identity. Weeping is "symbolic currency in a moral economy," writes Ebersole, and it can be spent in many different ways, aboveboard or on the black market.

Gary L. Ebersole, "The Function of Ritual Weeping Revisited: Affective Expression and Moral Discourse," *History of Religions* 39 (2000), 211–246. Used by permission of the University of Chicago Press.

What does the study of tears reveal about affectivity and moral discourse? Are there kinds of experiences observable through the study of weeping that are not so easily seen in observation of other kinds of emotional behavior? Is it possible to tell if some tears are largely an automatic response to cultural promptings, whereas others are the direct expression of deep personal feeling? Why have tears been so closely linked to moral discourses? Is ritual weeping a kind of "embodied" judgment of a situation? Does such weeping clearly locate the actor in a matrix of cultural assumptions about tears? How can we tell if ritual weeping transgresses feeling rules or cultural expectations for behavior? Does Ebersole's perspective allow us to universalize the meaning of tears in any way? How does the study of tears provide insight into the ways communities engage in a religious ordering of the universe?

Laughing and crying have long been held in the West to be uniquely human acts. Human beings laugh and shed tears, we are told; animals do not.[1] This claim has shown a remarkable durability, surviving, even flourishing, over the centuries despite major shifts in the understanding of theology, epistemology, and human and animal physiology. In the modern scientific world, the assertion that only humans weep and laugh has gone largely unchallenged, with the notable exception of Charles Darwin's *The Expression of the Emotions in Man and Animals.*[2] Anthropologists and historians of religions have also accepted this assertion and have rarely taken laughter and tears as subjects of study.[3] Indeed, few have taken note of the history of tears—or even recognized that such a history exists.[4] In general, we have been content to presume that (with apologies to Gertrude Stein) a tear is a tear is a tear. Although a few anthropological studies of ritual weeping in individual cultures exist, no broad comparative study has been produced.[5] The situation in the history of religions is even more disappointing. It is telling that the few pages James G. Frazer devoted to an eclectic set of reports of ritual weeping, which remained in his hands uninterpreted, still served as the basis for the brief uninformative entry on "Tears" in Macmillan's *Encyclopedia of Religion.*[6]

In this essay, I argue for the importance of the study of tears for the history of religions. Whether tears are indeed a marker of human nature or not is not at issue here. Although all healthy persons have the ability to shed tears, the "meaning" attributed to specific tears depends on a number of situational elements and on specific sociocultural expectations. To understand the functions and meanings of tears, historians of religions must concern themselves with the diverse religious anthropologies found around the world, myths and folktales involving crying, and the historical, ethnographic, and artistic records of ritual weeping. Instances of ritualized weeping, however, should not be studied in isolation from the religious anthropology of a people, social and political structures, the prevailing value system(s) of the actors, or the local constructions of class and gender. Tears—whether actually shed or withheld, or as they are represented performatively, pictorially, or narratively—must be understood in terms of the local sociocultural "feeling rules," moral values, and the aesthetics and politics of affective display.[7] We must, then, concern ourselves with the cultural poetics of ritual and ritualized weeping.

At the same time, we must resist the temptation to judge all tears in terms of their immediate association with "real" emotions. James G. Frazer, for instance, assumed that every instance of ritual weeping-as-greeting reported among "primitives" was "a simple formality attended with hardly more emotion than our custom of shaking hands or raising the hat."[8] Interpretations such as this, which are all too common, assume that when a formal setting or social script requires a person to cry, the tears shed in such contexts are less than "real" precisely because they are not a spontaneous emotional response. As historians, we need to recognize that this evaluation of tears is based in part on the Western bourgeois sense of the individual; it is not a universal; normative distinction.[9] By universalizing this distinction between real and false tears, such interpretations prematurely foreclose any serious inquiry into either the local discourse about tears or the multiple ways in which specifically (and differently) situated social agents at times strategically manipulate the local sociocultural understanding of tears for their own intents and purposes.

To understand the meaning of specific tears, including those shed in religious ritual contexts, the tears must be considered in association with the broader social discourses in which they participate as affective displays, including discourses of social hierarchy, power, gender, class, race, and morality. Thus, the object of study for historians of religions is not only ritual weeping practices per se, but also the discursive activity in the form of praise, criticism, parody, and so on that takes place around tears more generally. It is not the role of the historian of religions to judge tears to be real or fake; rather, we must pay careful attention to how and why situated individuals cry. In writing the history of tears, another important goal must be to analyze, whenever possible, the process of the discursive "naturalization" of tears and the subsequent internalization of the associated social values and feeling rules, which as a whole produces seemingly spontaneous tears in specific situations. We must also investigate the symbolic fields within which cultural capital can be earned by situated persons shedding or, alternatively, not shedding tears. Finally, we need to take careful note of the transgressive potential of tears and the ways tears frequently participate in moral discourse.

The historian of religions is not interested in all tears, however. The tears produced when dicing an onion, for example, are not of concern because they are a purely physiological response to irritation of the cornea. Our focus must be on "performative" tears (those shed in rituals proper or in ritualized social situations that perform cultural work),[10] as well as on the discursive activity that takes place around tears-as-signs. Such tears serve a variety of social purposes, including marking out social and hierarchical relationships at times, dissolving them at others, inviting or demanding specific social relationships, or marking/protesting the abrogation of social and moral contracts. Crossing the inside/outside boundary of the physical body, tears are available to persons as, to borrow Mary Douglas's term, a seemingly natural symbol of the individual in society. As such, tears have often been found to be an effective means of locating (and, possibly, advancing) one's "self" in society, as well as a potentially powerful vehicle of social, political, and moral commentary and critique.

Blurred Vision and Tears in the History of Religions

If tears represent something of a blind spot in the history of religions, this situation is due in part to the distortions in our vision introduced by the unexamined dual assumptions that only human beings shed tears and that "real" tears are spontaneous emotional responses. These assumptions carry internal contradictions generated by the conjunction of bourgeois individualism and Enlightenment universalism. To claim that real tears are a spontaneous emotional response to some event leads to the position that insofar as ritual tears are "scripted," they are by definition mere formalities, not real tears. But saying this does not so much explain ritual tears as it explains them away. We need to take seriously the fact that people in many other cultures and times have not shared our assumptions about emotions, tears, or the similarities and differences between animals and humans. To cite but one example, when the Toloi, a people from Papua New Guinea, discuss the differences between humans and animals, they do not point either to the ability to shed tears or to the emotions as critical markers of difference. Rather, to the Toloi, it is obvious that a dog experiences emotions such as anger, just as humans do.[11] The crucial difference between dogs and human beings, they say, is that, unlike humans, a dog does not recognize right and wrong, for it lacks the ability to reflect on the moral status of its own actions. For the Toloi, the fact that a dog will copulate with its own mother without shame is clear proof of this.[12]

Carrying into our studies the assumption that only humans shed tears has led to a number of distortions of the historical record available to us. Needless to say, cultures parse the differences between human nature and the natures of nonhumans in diverse ways. Many myths and tales from around the world tell of animals, gods, demons, and other nonhumans weeping. What are we to make of these? If we uncritically take our parsing of human nature to be normative and universal, then the very myths and tales through which other people have posed and explored questions surrounding human and nonhuman nature are perforce dismissed as being little more than the products of anthropomorphic projections, unconscious fantasies of some sort, or the creations of a primitive mentality.

A few of the problems that we have unnecessarily created for ourselves by clinging to the "obvious fact" that only humans shed tears may be illustrated by a close analysis of a recent scholarly (mis)reading of a Japanese religious tale. In an influential study of Buddhism and the literary arts in medieval Japan, William LaFleur introduces the following tale from the *Nihon ryōiki*, a ninth-century collection of wondrous events:

> In Kawachi province there was once a melon merchant whose name was Isowake. He would load huge burdens on his horse, far in excess of what it could carry. Then, if it would not move, he would get furious and drive it on by whipping it. The horse would then move along with its burden, but tears would be falling from its two eyes. When the man had sold all his melons, he would kill the horse. He, in fact, killed a good number of horses this way. Later, however, this fellow Isowake happened to be just looking down into a kettle of boiling water one day when his own two eyes fell out of his head and were boiled in the kettle. Manifest retribution comes quickly. We ought to believe in karmic causality. Even though we look upon animals as mere beasts, they were our parents in some past life. In fact, it is passage through the six courses and according to the four modes of birth that constitutes our real family. Therefore, it will not do to be merciless.[13]

LaFleur proceeds to interpret this tale as follows:

> This account is quite obviously based on a local legend that had probably gained credence through many retellings and become widely accepted as fact. . . . With this story Kyōkai [the compiler/editor and a Buddhist priest] explains a double anomaly. He not only provides an explanation to people who may have wondered what lay behind the extant tale of a man whose eyes fell out (however embellished and far-fetched the original event may have become) but he also explains a much more common but still anomalous phenomenon, namely, that of animals whose eyes ooze with water. Kyōkai's contemporaries would have known well that one of the perceptible differences between man and animal is that beings in the latter category do not weep; pain or emotional distress brings no tears to their eyes. Nevertheless, there are exceptions, animals with eyes that water for reasons we would today describe as medical. Kyōkai's explanation for such phenomena was, of course, not medical but in terms of karma and transmigration. For him, the weeping horse is a clear instance of residual activity from a former incarnation, that is, of the earlier human who is in some sense still "in" the horse making his presence known.[14]

No one, to my knowledge, has challenged LaFleur's reading of this tale. Indeed, at first glance, it seems to be a masterful exercise in logical argument and good sense. Yet, there are a number of peculiarities in this exegesis that bear our attention. First, it is odd that LaFleur, a longtime student of Japanese literature, does not really treat the folktale as a folktale (i.e., as a narrative artifact in its own right). The text he has extracted from the *Nihon ryōiki* consists of the tale proper *and* the commentary by Kyōkai, which begins with "Manifest retribution comes quickly." In eliding the distinction between these in his own metacommentary, LaFleur never acknowledges that the folktale had (and has) its own narrative in tegrity prior to and independent to Kyōkai's commentary. What meaning, one must ask, did the horse's tears have within this narrative when it circulated orally prior to Kyōkai's retelling, which in turn gave it a new and specifically Buddhist interpretation?

LaFleur notes in passing the structural parallelism ("coincidence," in his terms) between the tears falling from the horse's eyes and the eyes of the melon merchant falling out, but he never broaches the issue of the possible significance of this structural element within the tale itself. Instead, he implies that in Kyōkai's hands this coincidence was transformed from little more than a thematic and poetic (fanciful?) element into a powerful illustration of the working of karma. Yet, careful attention to the folktale discloses that the parallelism therein does not require the addition of a Buddhist interpretation in order to make it meaningful. Specifically, the presence of the narrative element of the abused horse shedding tears, coupled with the man who shows no signs of compassion as he works his animals to death, already raises such moral issues as brutal exploitation, gratuitous violence, greed, and the dehumanizing potential of the marketplace.

Let us suppose for a moment that, like the Toloi, the early Japanese took the ability to recognize right and wrong, rather than the mere ability to shed tears, to be the true mark of human nature. In that case, the presence or absence of tears in a morally inflected situation would first and foremost signal a character's moral status rather than whether he belonged to the ontological category of "human" or "animal." As an alternative to LaFleur's reading, I want to suggest that the tears in the folktale proper mark or point to a serious violation of a moral contract, here between the human owner and a beast of burden. More generally, they tell of the failure of the superior party in a hierarchical power relationship to fulfill his side of a reciprocal economic and moral contract. Like human laborers, the horse worked for his master with the expectation of receiving reward and sustenance in return. The folktale makes it clear, however, that the melon merchant brutally drove his horses beyond their limits of endurance. In this situation, the detail of Isowaki's eyes falling out signals his moral blindness and, consequently, his inhumane nature.

Careful attention to other narrative details in this deceptively simple tale will disclose even more meaning. For example, although ignored by LaFleur, the seemingly minor details that Isowake is a melon merchant (*uri-hisa*) and that the weeping animal is a horse, rather than some other animal, are highly significant. In Japanese, a classical oval human face, considered the most beautiful, is called *urizanegao*, literally "a true melon face,"[15] whereas an extremely long face, which departs from the aesthetic ideal, is called *umagao* or *umazura*, "a horse face." Moreover, in the Japanese symbolic and linguistic universe, the valences of "horse" are largely negative.[16] For instance, a fool or dunce is *bakamono* (the Chinese characters read "horse-deer person"), and simpleminded credulity or naïve honesty is *baka-shōjiki* ("horse-deer honesty").[17]

Thus, the precise narrative elements juxtaposed in the tale—Isowaki is a melon merchant and a horse sheds tears—suggest that much more is going on here than La Fleur implies. A simple structural analysis will disclose the symbolic inversions at play. A melon is both like and unlike an ideal human face and head. A melon is like a human face in shape and like a human head in that it contains water (and tears). A melon is unlike a human face/head, though, in not having any apertures such as eyes, from which the liquid might emerge. In contrast, a horse's head is like a human's in having eyes, nostrils, and so on, but it is (usually) unlike it in shape.

If one now returns, with these bits of knowledge in hand, to this "simple" folktale, it will be found to be much richer and more complex, even without Kyōkai's Buddhist commentary, than LaFleur intimates. Remarkably compact, without sacrificing symbolic depth or complexity, this folktale has been carefully crafted by invoking, among other things, cultural associations to and values drawn among facial shapes, horses, melons, and tears in order to reflect on human nature and morality. The structural inversion—tears fall from the eyes of a horse and tearless eyes fall out of the melon merchant's head into a container of a hot liquid—constitutes a fairly sophisticated reflection on human nature. The implication is clear that a moral human nature is not something that is given or inherent in any body; it is achieved by being enacted. That is, the tale suggests that true humanity is realized only through moral interactions with other beings, human and nonhuman.

The melon merchant's loss of his eyes signals that human nature can also be forfeited through immoral actions. Without eyes, the merchant's face is in a superficial sense even more like a melon, but, at the same time, this face, which can shed no tears, reveals his real nature (expressed through his actions) to be far from the human moral ideal. In contrast, while the superficial form of the horse's face departs from the human ideal of beauty, its nature as a hardworking creature of simpleminded and uncalculating honesty transforms the tears it sheds into a powerful moral critique of the inhumane treatment it has received. The crucial issue in this tale for the early Japanese, then, was never whether animals really weep or not, as LaFleur suggests. Rather, it was what a proper moral economy would be like, and what, within hierarchical labor relationships, constitutes humane and inhumane treatment. The anomaly being addressed is not that a horse has shed tears; it is the moral aberration that laborers (animal and human) are mistreated by those with power over them.

This is not the only way the tale-as-a-tale and its narrative representation of tears get short shrift. LaFleur is led into an impossibly convoluted argument precisely because he clings to the unexamined and culturally parochial assumption that it is obvious that only humans shed tears because "pain or emotional distress brings no tears" to the eyes of animals. It is LaFleur's explicit linkage of the shedding of tears with pain and emotions that ultimately drives him to parse the "real" and the fictional in this tale and, thus, in effect, to "correct" the original. On the one hand, he denies that the tale-as-told in the ninth century, with weeping horses and a man's eyes falling out, had a real historical referent, as Kyōhai claims it did ("The account is quite obviously based on a local legend"). At the same time, he assumes, without providing any hard evidence for this position, that the legend itself must have been based on an unspecified "original event," which had long since been narratively "embellished" into its current "far-fetched" and incredible form. On the other hand, LaFleur asserts that the putative tears shed by the horse(s) no doubt had a real referent (animals' eyes sometimes "water for reason we would today describe as medical"), which somehow (he never explains how or why this occurred) had subsequently been misrecognized by the early Japanese and mislabeled as "tears."

In LaFleur's metacommentary, Kyōkai is presented as having brought a rational explanation to this "double anomaly" (i.e., an anomaly first in the real world and again in the tale) by imposing on it the Buddhist interpretive frame of karmic causality and the ontological taxonomy of *rokudō*, the six courses of the chain of being. He stresses that although Kyōkai's interpretive framework is different from our modern one, it is internally rational and consistent and thus carries its own explanatory power. With the addition of karma and rebirth to the textual mix, LaFleur finds it acceptable (rational) to speak of a horse crying tears because the horse now retains a (partial) human nature ("the weeping horse is a clear instance of residual [karmic] activity . . . of the earlier human who is in some sense still 'in' the horse"). Not only that, he assumes that the early Japanese themselves must have also recognized the rational, explanatory power of the Buddhist worldview, which now, for the first time, made sense of the anomaly of water oozing from an animal's eyes. Implicit, of course, is the further assumption that the modern scientific worldview, with its definitive "medical reasons" for this oddity, is even more rational.

The contortions and distortions in LaFleur's reading are, I suggest, symptomatic of the obfuscating power that the dual assumptions concerning tears, noted earlier, continue to exercise over us. In good Enlightenment fashion, LaFleur assumes that we share a common human nature and rationality with the early Japanese, who perforce must have perceived the world and reality just as we do. In his eyes, this assumption justifies the conclusion that, just like us, the early Japanese "would have known well that one of the *perceptible differences* between man and animal" was that members of the latter category did not weep (emphasis added). Yet, he does not (and, perhaps, cannot) explain how and why, even as the early Japanese recognized the "fact" that only humans weep, they nevertheless misrecognized water oozing from animals' eyes as emotional tears. It will be worth our while to pause to reflect further on whose vision is blurred here and why.

Even if we grant LaFleur's argument that in early medieval Japan animals' eyes sometimes watered for medical reasons (as they surely must have), more often than not this condition would undoubtedly have been witnessed by the Japanese in situations where neither emotional stress nor physical pain had been inflicted on the animals. Are we to suppose that in all of these cases, too, the Japanese would have taken such watery eyes to be emotional tears? There is, as far as I know, no historical evidence for an affirmative answer to this question. Why, then, is LaFleur apparently willing to live with the awkward situation of simultaneously claiming that the early Japanese were rational like us and that they could still be befuddled en masse by the watery eyes of animals? The answer, in part, lies in his desire to prove his central thesis that "Buddhism gained ascendancy in medieval Japan largely because it successfully put forward a coherent explanation of the world and of human experience; it was the single most satisfying and comprehensive explanation available to the Japanese people at the time."[18]

Two important points emerge from scrutinizing this statement. First, the implication is unmistakable that the pre-Buddhist worldview was incoherent at certain (unspecified, but critical) points and incapable of explaining certain aspects of "human experience." According to LaFleur, the logic of the theories of karmic retribution and rokudō dispelled any sense of the uncanny emanating from "anomolies" in the world and cleared up the blurred vision (of animal "tears," for example) resulting from an inferior epistemology.[19] Second, he implies that human experience of the world (including, most especially, the crucial "perceptible difference" between animals and humans, that the former do not shed tears) exists prior to or outside of all culturally constructed worldviews. One suspects that, if pressed on this, LaFleur would deny the broader implication I have drawn here from his words. But, if this is the case, it only increases the interest in the question of why, of all things, it was tears that led him into this muddle. I will return to this question shortly.

In the end, the very text LaFleur cites presents intractable problems for him. Not only does the text provide no evidence for the claim that the early Japanese recognized full well that animals do not shed tears, it tells of horses weeping. Moreover, the text does not suggest that these tears were perceived to be anomalous, nor does it register any surprise whatsoever over them. It simply says of the horse, with no emotional inflection, "Tears came out of both eyes" (*futatsu no me ni namida o dasu*).[20] These tears are anomalous, it would seem, in LaFleur's eyes only. Within the narrative world of the folktale, they make perfectly good sense.

As a student of Japanese religion and literature, LaFleur is surely familiar with the many other texts from early and medieval Japan in which nonhumans are portrayed shedding tears. To try to explain away each and every such account of gods (*kami*), buddhas, bodhisattvas, demons, animals, birds, and even fish shedding tears would lead to similar, impossibly convoluted positions. More important, to do so would be to destroy the very documents that can provide insight into the world of meaning of early and medieval Japan. La-Fleur's difficulties stem from the anachronistic projection of his own commonsense assumptions back in time onto a different people. Marshall Sahlins's point, made recently in relation to a different cultural-historical context, is also pertinent here: "[Western] commonsense bourgeois realism, when taken as a historiographic conceit, is a kind of symbolic violence done to other times and other customs. . . . One cannot do good history, not even contemporary history, without regard for ideas, actions, and ontologies that are not and never were our own."[21] LaFleur's reading of this tale illustrates an ever-present danger facing historians of religions. We generously want to assume a universal human nature across time and space, yet precisely when we want to think globally, we often do so with local concepts and assumptions. Tear-filled eyes produce blurred vision; so does projecting our assumptions about tears on other peoples and times.

Tearing through the Medieval and Renaissance Worlds in the West

This critique of LaFleur's reading has revealed some of the mental gymnastics that otherwise good scholars are willing to subject themselves (and readers) to in order to maintain and universalize their "commonsense" view that humans shed tears, and animals do not, because only humans feel emotions. A few examples will demonstrate that this commonsense view has never been as widely held in the West as most people assume. In folktales and myths from around the world, animals and other nonhuman creatures are often portrayed as laughing and weeping. In many different cultures the ontological difference between animals and humans has often been a subject of vigorous debate. One scholar has recently argued, for instance, that in Christianity a major shift in understanding concerning this issue occurred in the twelfth century; at this time the earlier ontological paradigm broke down, and it became more difficult to determine what distinguished the categories of animal and human.[22] Equally important for the history of religions, many people have believed (and some continue to believe) that human beings could assume animal forms and vice versa.[23] The integrity of the human body has also often been felt to be tenuous at best, as many have assumed that it can be invaded, taken over, or possessed by other beings, human and nonhuman. As a result, beings with human forms might actually be other than (or less than) fully human. External form, then, has not always been taken to indicate a being's true nature or identity, nor has the ontological distinction between human and nonhuman always been sharply marked.

Two examples must suffice to suggest something of the real historical effects specific assumptions concerning the etiology of tears have had in European history. When corporeal form was deemed insufficient to establish a person's real identity, at times the presence or absence of tears served as conclusive evidence. In Renaissance Europe, for instance, suspected witches and werewolves were often asked to cry as part of a battery of tests. Those who could not produce tears on command were judged to be nonhuman or to be under the control of a demon. Based on this "proof" of identity, numerous individuals were condemned to death.[24] In France, "suspicion alone was enough to warrant arrest. Not to shed tears while making a confession, looking at the ground, speaking as if in asides or blaspheming was a sign of a witch."[25]

Not all observers accepted the reasoning behind this test, yet in *L'incrédulité sçavante et la crédulité ignorante au sujet des Magiciens et des Sorciers* (1671) Jacques d'Autun still felt the need to argue against accepting the inability to shed tears as proof that a person was a witch.[26] Some physicians, who doubted the existence of the Devil, in arguing for a medical rather than a demonic etiology for the inability to cry, cited the authority of Marcellus of Sidon (second century C.E.). He had diagnosed this inability to be a symptom of a medical condition he labeled *lycanthropia* or *morbus lupinus*.[27] For these writers, the absence of tears made one wolf-like, perhaps, but not a wolf. In 1644, however, the philosopher and physician William Drage held that actual physical metamorphosis could and did occur. Many other religious thinkers adopted a middle position, recognizing the apparent existence of werewolves but denying their reality. Augustine wrote:

> It is very generally believed that by certain witches' spells and the power of the Devil men may be changed into wolves . . . but they do not lose their human reasoning and understanding, nor are their minds made the intelligence of a mere beast. Now this must be understood in this way: namely, that the Devil creates no new nature, but that he is able to make something appear to be which in reality is not. For by no spell nor evil power can the mind, nay, not even the body corporeally, be changed into the material limbs and features of any animal . . . but a man is fantastically and by illusion metamorphosed into an animal, albeit he to himself seems to be a quadruped.[28]

Yet, if Augustine could not accept that the Devil could alter human nature, he had no difficulty believing that the origins of the passions, including those that produced tears, resided in disembodied spirits that had invaded the human body.

In the Renaissance, the meaning of tears (or their absence) was highly contested. While an individual's inability to weep could raise questions about her or his identity or ontological nature, excessive weeping could also attract the attention, scrutiny, and displeasure of ecclesiastical authorities. In fifteenth-century England, for example, church officials placed the mystical laywoman Margery Kempe under surveillance and conducted various tests to determine whether her copious tears were a divine "gift," the result of demonic activity, or simply faked to attract attention.[29] Kempe gained renown (and, in some cases, ignominy) for her bouts of boisterous weeping, which could last for hours or even days at a time. In this case, Kempe's human nature was never in question; rather, the nature of her tears was at issue and this was believed to hinge on their casual source.

Through her scribe, Margery Kempe recalled how others had sought to explain away her tears: "Some said it was a wicked spirit that vexed her; some said it was a sickness [epilepsy?]; some said she had drunk too much wine."[30] On the positive side, appealing to the tradition of tears of compunction going back to the Desert Fathers, some contemporaries interpreted Kempe's tears as spiritual signs. Others attributed them to the stirrings of the soul by the Holy Spirit or viewed them as a necessary part of the female meditative practice of imitating the Virgin and Mary Magdalene at the crucifixion. The example of Margery Kempe helps us to appreciate the fact that in a religious context tears sometimes function as clear signs, but at other times their significance is the subject of dispute. What is clear, however, is that the meaning of such tears is always socially negotiated.

One might have expected historians of religious to have recognized that within any given culture tears have a social history or, perhaps better, histories. Even a preliminary study of the subject will disclose that the meanings attributed to tears change over time, as do the social expectations concerning them (e.g., who can or should shed tears; when, where, why, and how they should be shed; and how long one should weep in specific situations). To be sure, the meaning of tears and "performative scripts" for crying tears vary among cultures and over time, but they also vary within complex hierarchical societies among different classes, gender roles, and age and occupational groups. None of this should be news to historians of religions. Since the work of Émile Durkheim and Marcel Mauss, most historians of religions have accepted that the human body is culturally and historically constructed. So, once again we must ask, Why should tears, a bodily product, be considered by many people to be exceptional in this respect?

The answer may lie in certain developments in the Renaissance. In Renaissance Europe the ever-growing flood of reports from around the world concerning the diverse religious beliefs, rites, and social customs of different peoples provoked renewed and intense discussion of what constituted human nature. Significantly, the subject of tears factored heavily in these discussions, which drew on classical and medieval sources, as well as contemporary accounts. According to one scholar, "among the favorite subjects of discussion by Renaissance writers on the affections were laughter and weeping."[31] Building on the work of Norbet Elias, Stephen Greenblatt has noted in passing that in the Renaissance tears came to hold a unique, class-inflected status: "Eventually, all the body's products, *except tears*, became simply unmentionable in decent society."[32] Unfortunately, Greenblatt does not pursue the reasons why tears came to have this unique status, nor does he address the significance of this fact. Below, I will venture a preliminary answer.

If Marcel Mauss was the first comparative sociologist to demonstrate that the human body is not merely a physical reality but is also a symbolic vehicle carrying cultural meanings, which are constructed and represented through bodily techniques,[33] Elias was perhaps the first to reveal the central importance of culturally constructed bodily techniques to the "civilizing process" in the Renaissance.[34] As a part of the civilizing process, specific social forces in the Renaissance solidified as "common sense" the two assumptions concerning tears that continue to haunt us: tears mark a fundamental difference between humans and animals, and "real" tears are spontaneous signs of an internal emotional state. These two assumptions generate two sets of binary oppositions, which can be represented, with their categorical differences, as follows:

humans/animals :: shed tears/do not shed tears
true tears/false tears :: spontaneous/simulated emotional expression

As we saw above in our discussion of the tale from the *Nihon ryōiki*, however, the binary opposition human/animal is not an ironclad dichotomy. Rather, to mark out differences within each category, mixed forms are generated, such as a weeping horse and a man who cannot shed tears.[35] We should not be surprised, then, to find a third mediating form—an animal that sheds tears—in the Renaissance as well. I refer, of course, to the imaginary creature behind the telltale phrase "crocodile tears," a being that bears comparison with the weeping horse in the *Nihon ryōiki*. Whereas the crocodile sheds tears calculated to mislead others, the horse, being honest to a fault, sheds morally justifiable (i.e., true) tears.

In Europe, reports of weeping crocodiles go back to the Middle Ages. One of the most famous is found in a twelfth-century Latin bestiary, which, after presenting a fairly accurate description of a Nile species, proceeds to compare certain human beings with it: "Hypocritical, dissolute and avaricious people have the same nature as this brute—also any people who are puffed up with the vice of pride, dirtied with the corruption of luxury, or haunted with the

disease of avarice—even if they do make a show of falling in with the justifi-
cations of the Law, pretending in the sight of men to be upright and indeed
very saintly."[36] The author continues in this vein, associating the crocodile with
hypocrisy and dissimulation. The crocodile was purported to move only its
upper jaw, while the bottom one remained motionless; this "fact" made it a
perfect symbol of dissimulation. Mention must also be made of Richard de
Fournival's *Bestiary of Love*, which compared in unflattering ways women and
the love of women to a long series of animals, including the crocodile.[37]

One of the first explicit references to a crocodile shedding hypocritical tears
is the report in *Mandeville's Travels* (ca. 1357–58) of a creature that wept when
it killed and ate men.[38] Over the centuries, *Mandeville's Travels* circulated widely
in various forms and in many different languages, spreading the tale of this
calculating animal. Crocodile tears were again attested to in a travel account
of the sixteenth-century slave trader and explorer Sir John Hawkins (1532–95),
who wrote of a peculiar species of crocodile whose "nature is even when he
would have his prey, to cry and sob . . . to provoke them to come to him, and
then he snatcheth at them." This sort of intertextual borrowing or quotation
over the years is typical of medieval and Renaissance textual practices.

How are we to understand these literary and pictorial representations,
spanning several centuries, of a weeping animal? Writing of a twelfth-century
Bestiary, Joyce Salisbury cautions us that "while the work was intended to be
a 'scientific' study of animals, it was not scientific in the same way we understand the term. The author was less interested in [accurately] describing an
animal than in using the animal as a vehicle for understanding religious truth,
the 'science' the author was ultimately studying."[39] The weeping animals in
such works, then, were not (and should not be) taken only as accurate depic-
tions of "anomalies" in the natural world, but also as metaphors or as images
to be understood allegorically. With the "discovery" of the New World and the
receipt of startling reports of its wildly diverse and bizarre animal species,
however, some Renaissance readers no doubt accepted reports of weeping animals as reliable.[40] After all, in the seventeenth century, a supposed siren (half
woman, half fish) was captured off Brazil by Dutch merchants and carried to
Leiden, where it was dissected by a professor of anatomy. It then found its way
into a private natural history collection and, through engraved illustrations,
into the public's ken. Even in the eighteenth century, noted English physicians
and intellectuals were easily convinced that a woman from Surrey had given
birth to rabbits.[41] Such credulity is an indication that the dividing line between
the ontological categories of animal and human was not absolute.

Yet, ultimately, the cultural significance of the Renaissance reports of
weeping crocodiles is not to be found in terms of natural history, but in the
way this imaginary creature provided Europeans with a shorthand image of,
and label for, human beings whose "nature" was deceitful and insincere. No
single meaning, though, can encompass the alterity of a weeping animal,

which in the shifting contexts of its usage sometimes moves closer to and sometimes more distant from categories such as "human," "moral being," or "authentic self."

Elias, Greenblatt, and others have convincingly shown that in the Renaissance the popularity and proliferation of books of manners, which instructed bourgeois readers on how to act like persons of class, signaled an expanded awareness that the social self could be consciously fashioned. In other words, the writers and readers of such how-to books recognized that the social self was (in part, at least) constructed, not an innate inheritance.[42] The very suggestion that distinctive manners and emotive displays, among other things, could be learned and then enacted by almost anyone called into serious question the social fictions that class privileges and prerogatives, the unequal distribution of wealth and power, and the existing hierarchical social systems were all "natural" due to the distinct ontological nature of members of these groups.

It is in this contentious discursive context concerning manners and emotions, then, that we must understand the Renaissance-era reception of tales of weeping crocodiles and the subsequent uses of the image of "crocodile tears." Dissimulation and simulation were important topics of discussion among theologians, philosophers, and political theorists in the Renaissance.[43] By the time Hawkins's account was put in circulation, Machiavelli had already penned *The Prince* (1513), the classic primer on the political uses of deception, dissimulation, and simulation, including emotional displays. A successful prince, he maintained, needed to be a *gran simulatore e dissimulatore*.[44] Similarly, *The Book of the Courtier* (1528), by Baldassare Castiglione, included clear instructions on how a courtier should learn to cover the artifice of his style and manners by playing the part effortlessly. Others held that gestures, demeanor, and other external signs must be controlled in order to communicate one's real self. James I (ruled 1603–25), for instance, wrote that a virtuous king must carefully choreograph his gestures and actions because "they interpret the inward disposition of the mind, to the eyes of them that cannot see farther within him, and therefore must only judge of him by the outward appearance."[45] But then, readers of the King James Bible also had, in the person of King David, a paradigmatic master of the "politics of tears."[46]

The reports of weeping crocodiles, as well as the widespread quotations they spawned, suggest that a deep anxiety in relation to tears surfaced in the Renaissance. Many persons had (and have) a widespread desire for transparent social relations in which the feelings, intentions, and motives of others would be clear and unambiguous. Yet, social relations are never truly transparent, because feelings and intentions can be (and are) hidden behind masks, silence, or lies, and feelings can be simulated and false intentions feigned. In spite of this, at times the phenomenological character of tears has seemed to offer a glimmer of hope that another person's true feelings could be known unambiguously. As drops of clear liquid falling from the eyes (the windows into the soul), tears cross the bodily boundary of interior/exterior and invisible/visible. The symbolic associations of tears with the eyes may explain, in part, the unique position that tears came to hold in the Renaissance among all bodily products.[47]

Such an appeal to the timeless phenomenological character of tears alone, though, cannot explain the sociocultural and historical specificity of tears shed or represented in the Renaissance. Nor can it begin to deal with the sociohistorical consequences of the growing public recognition that tears could be faked. In the cases of witchcraft and werewolf accusations, superficial appearances were not always held to be sufficient to determine the real identity of somebody. Contestation arose over what kind of tears one was dealing with in a given instance or what kind of person had shed the tears. Some authors implied that tears could be shed for strategic purposes, but only by beings whose very nature was duplicitous. These authors drew a dichotomy between true and false tears and, like the author of the twelfth-century bestiary cited earlier, assigned these to constitutionally honest and dishonest beings, respectively. It was a short but momentous step from this point to correlating real/false tears with other binary oppositions from the age: civilized/primitive, human/less than fully human, and male/female. Those persons who cried crocodile tears were discursively constructed as the opposite of the civilized white male. As the Renaissance contest over tears-as-signs was played out in both domestic and foreign arenas, these Others came to include weird animals (like weeping crocodiles), half animal–half human beings, bizarre persons of color in far-off lands, and, closer to home, women.

Shakespeare, among others, genders crocodile tears, as when Othello says of Desdemona, "Oh devil, devil! / If that the earth could teem with woman's tears, / Each drop she falls would prove a crocodile" (4.1.244–46). Shakespeare also blends the ancient Greek humoral theory of how tears are produced, shared with most of his contemporaries, with his gender-inflected understanding of emotions. The following lines from *King Henry VI, Part 3* are spoken by Richard, who has just learned the details of his father's murder:

> I cannot weep; for all my body's moisture
> Scarce serves to quench my furnace-burning heart;
> Nor can my tongue unload my heart's great burthen,
> For self-same wind that I should speak withal
> Is kindling coals that fires all my breast,
> And burns me up with flames that tears would quench.
> To weep is to make less the depth of grief:
> Tears then for babes; blows and revenge for me. (2.4.79–86)

Here, Richard willfully refuses to weep in order to stoke his anger and his desire for revenge. In humoral theory, women are more humid than men and, thus, more susceptible to bouts of weeping. But Shakespeare suggests that

adult women can, like men, control their tears—but with a significant difference. Whereas men restrain their tears, women learn to shed tears at will. The copious tears of a woman such as Desdemona do not disclose her real feelings precisely because they are shed at will, rather than spontaneously. Real tears reveal one's inner emotional state; crocodile tears are designed to mislead others about that state. When discovered for what they are, crocodile tears reveal only one's deceitful nature. In contrast, the morally justifiable (real) tears of a man like Richard, which by sheer force of will are restrained, are transformed into pure acts that express his moral character, authentic nature, and masculinity. We can draw the following implied oppositions:

child/adult :: unable to control tears/able to control tears
adult female/adult male :: shed tears at will/restrain tears at will
crocodile tears/pure acts
  of moral retribution :: conceal ulterior motives/ reveal interior tears

The Blurred Vision of Ritual Weeping in the History of Religions

This brief foray into crocodile and gendered tears may help us to understand certain modern treatments of ritual weeping. Scholars have long recognized that acts of European discovery, exploration, and conquest were often represented in gendered terms (e.g., white males "possessing" the New World, itself portrayed as a reclining and inviting female). Similarly, much has been written about the effects of the primitive/civilized dichotomy. Yet, no one has connected these accounts with the depiction and interpretation of ritual tears in the scholarly literature of the past three hundred years. Here I confine myself to a glance at the treatment of the tears of primitives found in the works of Joseph François Lafitau, Durkheim, A. R. Radcliffe-Brown, and Frazer.

Lafitau's *Moeurs des sauvages amériquains comparées aux moeurs des premiers temps* (1724) is notable for its time in arguing that it was unacceptable to judge other peoples by European manners and customs.[48] Lafitau proposed a comparative "science of the manners and customs of different peoples," based on carefully assembled concrete facts, which he believed would reveal the universal elements of human culture and religions. He also believed that rituals were the key to unlocking the truth symbolically encoded in myths. No matter how diverse, irrational, or grotesque rituals appeared to be, he felt they conveyed a natural symbolic truth, which could be deciphered through his comparative science. In part, Lafitau's positive evaluation of *les sauvages amériquains* sprang from his dual assumptions of "the uniformity of sentiments of all nations" and of the notion that all societies passed through the same developmental stages. He felt justified in comparing the customs and affective expressions of the

"contemporary primitives," whom he knew firsthand from living among them for five years, with reports of early Greek customs and with biblical accounts.[49] In significant ways, his comparative method presaged that of W. Robertson Smith in the late nineteenth century. How ever, Lafitau arranged his materials topically to demonstrate the uniformity of human nature, rather than using them to develop a theory of sociocultural change.[50]

Lafitau records a custom among the Huron and Iroquois, which he terms the "death cry." A returning party of warriors gives out a distinctive cry ("very piercing and sad") to announce the warriors' return and any casualties. Villagers rush to receive them, but social protocol governs their affective responses:

> [The American Indians] have such respect for each other that, however complete may be their victory and whatever advantage they may have gained from it, the first sentiment which they show is that of grief for those of their people whom they have lost. All the village has to participate in it. The good news of the success is told only after the dead have been given the first regrets which are their due. This done, everyone is warned anew by a second cry. They are given a share in the advantage which they have gained and freed to express the joy which the victory has merited.

Characteristically, Lafitau does not question the authenticity of the emotions expressed or the tears shed in this ritual. Indeed, in referring later to the ritual lamentations of native women, he speaks of their tears as "genuine tears which the women have always at hand."[51] Unlike many later scholars who would maintain that ritual tears have no real connection with felt emotions, Lafitau implies that even mandatory tears are authentic. While he assumes that there is a universal human emotional response to death and a grieving process that all must go through, he also recognizes that any given death does not affect all members of a society in the same manner and to the same extent. As a result, he suggests that some ritual tears are shed out of grief, others out of "respect" and "courtesy." Mourning is a universal "mark of reciprocal tenderness" among human beings and "should be regarded as a duty founded on nature." One of the functions of mourning ritual ("law") is, he suggests, to temper and limit temporally the emotional outbursts of those most deeply affected by a death. In a unique argument, he suggests that this is also done as "consolation for those who were weeping only as a sham and through courtesy, rather than through a real regret."[52]

Lafitau clearly recognizes here that after a death certain social expectations guide the actions and affective expressions of the members of any society, yet even those tears shed "only as a sham and through courtesy" are not hypocritical, for they have their own social rationality and utility as signs of respect. No doubt Lafitau's years living among Native Americans allowed him to recognize what today we would call the social construction of emotions and the

scripting of affective expressions. In characteristic fashion, Lafitau moves back and forth seamlessly from a present-tense ethnographic account of the funerary practices of the Huron and Iroquois to a learned survey in the past tense of reports of similar customs in ancient Rome, Egypt, Libya, and Greece; in contemporary rural France; and as found in the Bible. Like many others, he uses the customs, dress, and so on of contemporary primitives to help fill out written accounts of ancient peoples assumed to be at the same primitive stage of development. Thus, after describing the ritual tears and laments of female mourners among the Indians, Lafitau argues that such ethnographic data are of important for classicists and biblical scholars alike:

> When the body is dressed and put into place, the tears and laments which the mourners have had to restrain until this moment then begin with order and cadence. A woman who replaces, on this occasion, what the Romans call *praesica,* or the weeping woman, intones the first part of the tune. All the other women chant after her, keeping the same measure but applying it to different words suitable to each person according to their [sic] different degrees of relationship with the deceased. . . . This artful and systematic way of weeping merits particular consideration. It serves to make us understand what the funeral dirges of the ancients were.[53]

Perhaps, as a Catholic, Lafitau was more open to accepting the authenticity of affective expressions in rituals than were Protestant writers, who had a deep suspicion of "empty ritual." Be that as it may, it would be a long time before anyone attained Lafitau's level of appreciation of the complexities of ritual weeping.

Durkheim's treatment of ritual weeping, offered in a few pages near the end of *Les Formes élémentaires de la vie religieuse* (1912), is, without a doubt, the single most influential statement on the topic.[54] Unlike Lafitau, Durkheim was an armchair anthropologist who based his comments on ritual tears exclusively on ethnographic reports (e.g., those of Baldwin Spencer and Francis Gillen, Alfred Howitt, and Brough Smyth) concerning mourning rites among aboriginal peoples. Much of this ethnographic information was gathered—indeed, generated—under the long-distance guidance of Frazer and his questionnaires on totemism and other topics. The ethnographic scenes of mourning were stereotypically informed by the civilized/primitive dichotomy.

Durkheim's treatment of ritual weeping was, in part, dictated by the form and quality of his "data," his selective use of his sources, and a number of cultural assumptions of the time. Most notably, of course, the extension of Darwin's theory of the evolution of species to the domain of theories of social development, coupled with the work of Frazer and others on totemism, influenced Durkheim's choice of his object of study. Like Lafitau, he assumed that the study of contemporary primitives would shed light on the past of higher civilizations. After a six-page review of reports of aboriginal mourning rites, Durkheim asks rhetorically how they are to be explained, then provides the answer to this question.

> One initial fact is constant: mourning is not the spontaneous expression of individual emotions. If the relations weep, lament, mutilate themselves, it is not because they feel themselves personally affected by the death of their kinsman. Of course, it may be that in certain particular cases, the chagrin expressed is really felt. But it is more generally the case that there is no connection between the sentiments felt and the gestures made by the actors in the rite. If, at the very moment when the weepers seem the most overcome by their grief, some one speaks to them of some temporal interest, it frequently happens that they change their features and tones at once, take on a laughing air and converse in the gayest fashion imaginable. Mourning is not a natural movement of private feelings wounded by a cruel loss; it is a duty imposed by the group. One weeps, not simply because he is sad, but because he is forced to weep. It is a ritual attitude which he is forced to adopt out of respect for custom, but which is, in a large measure, independent of his affective state.[55]

Durkheim's central conclusion—"[ritual] mourning is not the spontaneous expression of individual emotions"—sets up the implicit contrast with "real" emotional tears, which we have seen before. As an armchair anthropologist, he was dependent on the ethnographies at his disposal; however, he did not always give his sources equal weight.[56] Indeed, at times he used his sources selectively to build his own artifice of theory-generated proof. For example, in a footnote after the admission that "in certain particular cases, the chagrin expressed is really felt," he writes: "This makes Dawson say that the mourning is sincere. But Eylmann assures us that he never knew a single case where there was a wound from sorrow really felt."[57] Without telling the reader why Eylmann should be considered a more reliable source than Dawson, Durkheim simply asserts that the latter's report concerned an exceptional case.

Durkheim read thousands of pages of ethnographic reports on aboriginal peoples, but he showed a total lack of interest in individual natives. This is not surprising when one realizes that he assumed that individuals as such did not exist among primitive populations.[58] Personal feelings and differences are summarily declared to be virtually nonexistent in ritual contexts: "The only forces which are really active [in mourning rites] are of a wholly impersonal nature: they are the emotions aroused in the group by the death of one of its members." This claim is based on a peculiar permutation of Lockean sensory psychology and epistemology, which had come to inform the civilized/primitive dichotomy. Primitives, it was believed, experience and represent the world through objects presented to their senses, which create sensate "impressions" in their minds; in contrast, the minds of civilized people also store ideas and judgments. Thus, according to Durkheim:

> The foundation of mourning is *the impression of a loss* which the group feels when it loses one of its members. But *this very impression results in bringing individuals together* in putting them into closer [physical] relations with one another, in associating them all in the same mental state, and therefore in *disengaging a sensation of comfort* which compensates the original loss. Since they weep together, they hold to one another and the group is not weakened, in spite of the blow which has fallen upon it. . . . communicating in sorrow is still communicating, and every communion of mind, in whatever form it may be made, raises the social vitality.

Durkheim's longest passage on ritual mourning is revealing insofar as he presents the reader with a scene of wild wailing, frenzied acts of self-mutilation, and bloody violence—all stereotypic elements of the idea of "the primitive."[59] For Durkheim, if you have seen (or read about) one rite of mourning, you have seen them all: "Practices of this sort are general in all Australia. . . . the real ceremonies of mourning repeat the same theme everywhere; the variations are only in the details."[60]

Yet, Durkheim can claim uniformity of thought and feeling among the ritual actors only by ignoring evidence to the contrary. For instance, he notes that the specific acts and deprivations required of the ritual participants (weeping, diverse forms of self-mutilation, the cutting of hair, imposed silence, and so on) vary according to each individual's age, gender, and social relationship with the deceased, yet he does not follow up this lead.[61] Nor does he seize on the single ethnographic passage he includes where snatches of the actual voices of aboriginals can be heard.[62] Instead, he makes much of Spencer and Gillen's description of the mourners becoming at one point an indiscriminate mass ("we could see nothing but a struggling mass of bodies all mixed together")—a description that privileges the vantage point of the external observer while ignoring that of the ritual participants, who are reduced to being mute actors or to emitting incoherent cries and groans.

The metaphor of ritual as theater is central to Durkheim's argument that the acts and affective expressions of the ritual actors are dictated (or "scripted") by social custom.[63] Even if the action appears chaotic and frenzied at times, it is nevertheless controlled, although not by the actors themselves.[64] Although the natives feel compelled to come together, to weep, and to mutilate themselves, they misjudge the true source of this compulsion (society) when they posit the existence of invisible spirits. Although Durkheim rightly recognized that death triggers ordered and scripted acts among the living, in refusing to accept that these actors feel any personal emotions, he turns them into passive figures, mindlessly moved to perform ritual actions.

Durkheim's understanding of ritual weeping was largely accepted in Radcliffe-Brown's *Andaman Islanders* (1922), although the latter allows sentiment a larger role. Indeed, he argues that "the social function of the ceremonial customs of the Andaman Islanders is to maintain and to transmit from one generation to another the emotional dispositions on which the society (as it is constituted) depends for its existence." When a member of the group is removed, through death or some other cause, from an important affective bond, the requisite emotion must find expression in collective ritual activity of some sort, which will restore the affective bond. After noting several principal occasions in Andamanese social life that require ritual weeping, Radcliffe-Brown repeats Durkheim in part: "The weeping . . . is . . . not a spontaneous expression of individual emotion but is an example of . . . ceremonial customs. In certain circumstances men and women are required by custom to embrace one another and weep, and if they neglected to do so it would be an offence condmned by all right thinking persons."[65]

Radcliffe-Brown also notes that there are two distinct varieties of ritual weeping: one in which both (or all) parties are active, and another (not considered by Durkheim) in which one person is passive, while another weeps over him or her. Finally, in addition to Durkheim's social function, Radcliffe-Brown offers a psychophysiological explanation of ritual weeping, suggesting that it provides relief for individuals from emotional tension. Even when sorrow, grief, or joy as such are not present, there is always "a condition of emotional tension due to the sudden calling into activity of the sentiment of personal attachment."[66]

All of these explanatory elements are then applied to ritual weeping-as-greeting, the peace-making ceremony, the wedding rite, initiation ceremonies, death rites, and secondary burial among the Andamanese. I will confine myself to Radcliffe-Brown's interpretation of ritual weeping-as-greeting:

> When two friends or relatives meet after having been separated, the social relation between them that has been interrupted is about to be renewed. . . . The weeping rite . . . is the affirmation of this bond. The rite, which . . . is obligatory, compels the two participants to act as though they felt certain emotions, and thereby does, to some extent, produce these emotions in them. When the two friends meet their first feeling seems to be one of shyness mingled with pleasure at seeing each other again. . . . Now this shyness (the Andamanese use the same word as they do for "shame") is itself a condition of emotional tension, which has to be relieved in some way. The embrace awakens to full activity that feeling of affection or friendship

that has been dormant and which it is the business of the rite to renew. The weeping gives relief to the emotional tension just noted, and also reinforces the effect of the embrace.[67]

Radcliffe-Brown's treatment of ritual weeping is superior to Durkheim's in several ways. First, he recognizes that individuals—and individual emotions—exist among "primitive" peoples and that their emotional lives are complex like our own. Moreover, he assumes that there are "fundamental laws regulating the affective life of [all] human beings."[68] Second, by focusing on the full range of ritual occasions in which ritual weeping is found, he is able to demonstrate that ritual tears are not associated with only one emotion. Finally, he is able to discern a common element among all of the different ritual occasions, from weddings and initiations to funerary rites: ritual weeping either restores an affective relationship or creates a new one in the light of changes in the participants' social positions or roles.

Nevertheless, Radcliffe-Brown's work still has some limitations. Like Durkheim, he assumes that in any given ritual, weeping always works in the same way, so he feels no need to study individual ritual performances in detail, nor does he focus on individual participants. As a result, he misses the ways individuals at times use or manipulate the social expectations and ritual requirements surrounding ritual weeping for their own intents and purposes. Moreover, he overlooks the ways tears mark out moral relationships.

Earlier, we noted that Frazer wrote that ritual weeping-as-greeting "is often a simple formality attended with hardly any more emotion than our custom of shaking hands or raising the hat." He clearly differentiates "natural" (i.e., real) expressions of emotion from conventional or empty ritual expressions. The latter, he suggests, are especially common "among races at a lower level of culture." Although he implies, à la W. Robertson Smith, that the ancient Hebrews may be included in this group, all of the examples of weeping he cites from the Hebrew Bible are asserted to have been authentic emotional tears.[69]

One of the reports of ritual weeping Frazer cites is of special interest insofar as it illustrates how, for Europeans, ritual weeping was, to use Greenblatt's phrase, one of the "filthy rites" of primitives. For Frazer, however, it was one thing for Europeans to observe rites that offended their sensibilities, but it was quite another to be forced to participate in them. With a few value-laden editorial comments, italicized below, Frazer summarized an early report from North America:

A Frenchman, Nicolas Perrot, who lived among the Indians for many years in the latter part of the seventeenth century, describes how a party of Sioux, visiting a village of their friends the Ottawas, "had no sooner arrived than they began, in accordance with custom, to weep over all whom they met, in order to signify to them the sensible joy they felt at having found them." Indeed, the Frenchman

> himself was more than once made the object, *or rather the victim,* of the like doleful demonstrations. . . . A French historian [Claude Charles Le Roy La Potherie] has described the meeting of ["Ayeo," or Iowa] Indian ambassadors with *poor Perrot.* They wept over him till the tears ran down their bodies; they *beslobbered him with the filth* which exuded from their mouths and their noses, smearing it on his head, his face, and his clothes, till he was almost turned sick by their caresses, while all the time they shrieked and howled most lamentably.[70]

Reports similar to this abound in the early ethnographic literature. Although they tell us little about the cultural meaning of such instances of ritual weeping for the natives, they tell much about the sensibilities of Europeans at specific moments in history. In the seventeenth century, the Europeans' ignorance of native anthropologies and values militated against a full appreciation of the meaning of native rites. How discouraging, though, to discover the situation unchanged in the twentieth century. While Frazer gathered dozens of ethnographic accounts of ritual weeping from around the world, he made no effort to understand the natives' points of view. The civilized/primitive dichotomy encompassed differences in sensibility, so Frazer was secure in his sense of superiority: something was inherently repulsive when he felt it to be so. As a result, his comparative survey of ritual weeping produced little more than the old, tired, and wrongheaded dichotomy of real tears/ritual tears.

When Perrot was wept over by the Iowa, this was part of an adoption ceremony. The weeping, along with the Calumet of the Captain ceremony that accompanied it, signified that Perrot was recognized as a reincarnation of a deceased chief who was being welcomed back. Moreover, precisely because the bodily fluids (tears, mucus, and saliva) rubbed on his face, head, and clothing could be used by an enemy in magic rites to cause the individuals they came from to become ill or even to die, presenting them to Perrot in this fashion served as a public declaration of the trust and friendship among those involved.[71]

Revisiting Ritual Weeping

In this essay I have demonstrated that historians of religions, among others, have all too often misunderstood tears and ritual weeping. The critical analysis of LaFleur's reading of a ninth-century Japanese text reveals the danger of carrying some of our commonsense understandings back into the interpretation of narratives from other times and places. Our glance at witchcraft and werewolf trials illustrates how the cultural assumption that only humans shed tears was at times used to test the real identity of individuals. A brief look at Renaissance reports of weeping crocodiles discloses that these are best understood not so much as would-be contributions to natural history but as symptoms of a growing dis-ease in some sectors of society over challenges to claims of "natural" or innate class distinction. It was, I argued, no accident that references to crocodile tears began to appear at the same time as the proliferation of books of manners. Similarly, a cursory review of selected interpretations of cases of ritual weeping-as-greeting discloses additional problems that result from making too much of the fact that ritual weeping is not a spontaneous emotional response, while ignoring the natives' point of view. The history of the interpretation of ritual tears and tales of weeping animals is one of repeated misunderstandings, but in the course of this essay, we have also found some hints as to how these topics might be usefully revisited. A detailed treatment of this subject will have to await a full-length comparative study, but a few preliminary pointers may be offered by way of a conclusion-as-prolegomenon:

1. It is essential that historians of religions abandon the dual assumptions that all real tears are spontaneous emotional responses and that only humans shed tears. Instead, ritual weeping should be regarded as symbolic activity that marks out the existence or the breach of social and/or moral relationships between beings (human, animal, or suprahuman).

2. Narratives and other representations of weeping animals need to be approached as such, not as the products of misrecognition. Moreover, full attention must be paid to the local religious anthropology, the cultural-symbolic complexes surrounding specific animals (and other creatures), gender constructions, class distinctions, and so on.

3. We need to study individual performances of ritual weeping rather than only "standard" scenarios. At the same time, we must consider the relative social positions of the ritual actors, their audience(s), their interdependencies, and their respective goals. Doing these things will allow us in our analyses to restore historical agency to the ritual actors, rather than ascribing the motivating force to amorphous "customs" or impersonal social forces.

A few examples will illustrate the advantage of this approach and alert us to the politics of ritual weeping. Let me begin with two biblical examples of ritual weeping performed by King David. The first (2 Samuel 1) is more Durkheimian insofar as it describes ritual weeping as marking a rent in the social fabric due to a death, yet the motivation behind David's weeping is anything by impersonal. David is described mourning the death of Saul on the battlefield: "Then David took hold of his garments and tore them, and all the men with him did the same. They mourned and wept and fasted until the evening for Saul and his son Jonathan, for the people of Yahweh, and for the House of Israel" (11–12). David also performed a lament for Saul and Jonathan (19–27), which he then ordered to be circulated among all the people of Judah.

There was a calculated political motivation behind David's leading these mourning rites. Through his ritual weeping, David publicly displayed his social proximity and fidelity to Saul, even though the king had long sought to have him killed. David also presented himself as close to two polities, whose support would be crucial if he was to accede to the throne of Judah and, later, to become the king of all Israel. In this instance, then, by leading the ritual weeping, David was able to reposition himself symbolically. In and through the ritual scenes of public mourning, he represented himself as a bridge between the past and the future.

Compare this to the report of David's subsequent ritual weeping for his young son by Bathsheba, where the primary audience is not human but divine. When his son fell gravely ill, seemingly fulfilling Nathan's prophesy, "David pleaded with Yahweh for the child; he kept a strict fast and went home and spent the night on the bare ground [weeping], covered with sacking" (2 Samuel 12:16). Yet, seven days later, as soon as he was informed that his son had died, he

> got up from the ground, bathed and anointed himself and put on fresh clothes. Then he went into the sanctuary of Yahweh and pros-trated himself. On returning to his house he asked for food to be set before him, and ate. His officers said, "Why are you acting like this? When the child was alive you fasted and wept; now the child is dead you get up and take food." "When the child was alive," he answered, "I fasted and wept because I kept thinking, Who knows? Perhaps Yahweh will take pity on me and the child will live. But now he is dead, why should I fast? Can I bring him back again?" (20–23)

Nothing could be clearer than this passage: King David's tears were not spon-taneous emotional responses to his son's death; he could turn them on and off at will. But it is also clear that David was not compelled to weep by an impersonal and unconscious force. To understand the logic behind his behav-ior, we need to consider the cultural complex of ritual weeping, moral contracts, and the ancient Middle Eastern concept of kingship.[72]

The first point to note is that this is an instance of ritual weeping-as-appeal. In such cases, a relatively powerless person throws himself or herself on the mercy of a hierarchically superior and powerful figure. In the ancient Near East, widows, orphans, and other helpless figures could obtain a hearing from a king by throwing themselves weeping on the ground in front of his proces-sion. A moral contract, if you will, obtained between the king and his subjects such that he was to be the final protector of those who had no others to offer them protection. Given this general understanding, a king who did not pause to listen to the plaint of such an individual risked being branded as a bad king. Here, ritual tears shed by the lowly are, to borrow a phrase from James C. Scott, weapons of the weak, which could at times coerce a social superior to play his or her part in a sanctioned social and moral relationship.

When King David ritually weeps in the case above, however, he adopts the inferior position of the prostrate weeping petitioner before Yahweh. Insofar as relations with Yahweh were imagined and acted out as analogous to those that obtained between human kings and their subjects, the same symbolic logic and social rationality was at work. Before Yahweh, David adopts a humble ritual position (and sheds all the markers of his own kingship) in the hope that his tears might move the deity to pity him, forgive his sin of having caused Uriah's death, remove His curse, and, finally, spare his child's life. His weeping is part of a calculated, but not failsafe strategy ("Who knows? Perhaps Yahweh will take pity on me"). When this ritual appeal fails, however, David immediately ceases his mourning because it no longer serves a rational purpose.

One would be right, then, to note that these ritual tears are not a spontaneous expression of the emotion of grief. Yet, even if David's actions offend our own sensibilities, a little reflection on the politics of the case will allow us to understand why, even if he actually felt grief, this emotion would probably not have found extended public ritual expression. David's political power was in no way threatened by the death of this son. The child's mother did not come from a family or tribe whose political support was critical for him and, more important, the child had never figured in David's dynastic hopes. Although some of his staff wondered about his response to the news of his child's death, David observed a distinction between his public and private personae, which included his expression of emotions. Had he continued to mourn for this son, he may well have opened himself to a whispering campaign suggesting that he was overly emotional and weak, too enamored of Bathsheba, and so forth. If his tears were not spontaneous expressions of emotion, this was because there was a rational political calculus at work.[73]

Not only kings weep ritually, of course. In many societies, weeping is identified as a female activity,[74] yet their ritual tears are equally political, albeit at a different level. To demonstrate this, it is important that we look at specific cases of ritual weeping by ordinary women to correct the assumption that this activity serves one general social function. A number of recent studies of female mourning practices in rural Greece provide exemplary material for this purpose. In her study of oral laments, Anna Caraveli has shown that lamentation provides Greek women with a potential vehicle of social protest and for presenting a "self" or a social identity to the world that differs from that which others (read "society" in Durkheim's sense) would impose on them. "Lamentation," she writes, "becomes for the singer an avenue for social commentary on the larger world, rather than an instrument of restriction and isolation."[75] This is the case because, although all rituals are scripted to a large extent, in mourning rites there is still room for conscious improvisation or "ad-libbing." Moreover, precisely because mourning rites are scripted as emotionally charged, they can at times provide "cover" for individuals to transgress or violate normal social expectations and prohibitions without fear of serious reprisals. In some displays of mourning, the ritual actor behaves as if beside herself. She loses control of herself—tears her hair or clothing, appears in public with disheveled hair, covers herself with ashes or filth, slashes herself, and so on. In her grief, whether real or feigned, she is not held to be responsible for her actions or words—and, thus, within certain ritual boundaries, she is free to say what otherwise could not be voiced publicly. Numerous examples of this from Greece and elsewhere have been recorded.[76]

Ritual weeping is also found outside religious rituals proper, but such "ritualized" tears also participate in a shared moral discourse. Margaret Egnor, for instance, has shown how untouchable women in Tamil Nadu employ an oral genre known as "crying songs" to express publicly "some grievance the singer has against some particular person of higher status than herself" or some egregious inequity in the social system. In these songs, sung while tears flow down the singer's cheeks, she describes her social situation, her moral purity, the wrongs she has suffered, and her emotional state resulting from these. Significantly, the singer always casts herself in an inferior social position vis-à-vis the object of her criticism. In Tamil Nadu, as in most cultures, hierarchical social relationships and relationships of dependency carry certain social and moral expectations and responsibilities with them. The thrust of crying songs is that these have been violated. "[The aggrieved woman] calls herself a lily, a lotus, gold, paddy, gram, fresh green herbs; she is deserving of protection. The kinship term she uses for herself is 'younger sister.' But her perfection has brought her harm, through no fault of her own."[77]

The tears shed while singing a "crying song" publicly mark the breach of a moral contract, but they can also offer a critique of the oppressive aspects of the social system. Crying songs "protest not only the personal sufferings of the singer, but the rules of hierarchy themselves."[78] Similar ritual tears, which seek to implicate superiors in a moral economy, will be found in many other cultures as well. Such rituals may serve to (re)create a communal identity, but this is frequently a subgroup or minority identity within a larger society. To move outside gender relations for a moment, the public ritual weeping at the center of the Shi'ite Muslim festival of Muharram, memorializing the massacre of Hussain and his family, is a striking example of how this collective expression serves to recreate a minority identity within a larger religious tradition.[79]

As a form of symbolic currency in a moral economy, the shedding of ritual tears can also be used to "buy" social status and prestige. For instance, in many cultures, a woman who weeps for her deceased husband, a relative, or a neighbor thereby displays that she and/or her family embody specific cultural and moral values associated with being a proper wife, mother, and so on. In rural

Greece, "the lamenter honorably represents her family at village death rites. . . . Women are responsible for every phase of the care, grieving, and commemorization of the dead. Just as they nurture bonds among the living, they are expected to extend the connection of *ponos* (caring, yearning, pain) to family beyond death through adherence to mourning practices."[80] Just as in life a man's honor (*timí*) is dependent in part on the behavior of the women of his family, his posthumous honor is dependent on his wife and female relatives offering laments and tears for him. For a woman, engaging in ritual weeping also serves as a mark of her changed social status. Her mourning cohorts, usually postmenopausal women, have all suffered the pain of numerous deaths. In this situation, a young widow is an especially tragic figure, prematurely thrown into this social and ritual status. Older women, however, gain respect and, at times, a far-flung reputation by participating in collective rites of ritual weeping. Historians of religions need to pay attention to the potentially multiple (and occasionally contested) meanings of specific instances of ritual weeping.

One final example must suffice to suggest how the social expectations placed on ritual actors can be strategically violated to offer a powerful moral indictment of another person. Gail Holst-Warhaft has recounted the story of a striking, transgressive ritual act of a Greek woman, known as Koundounara, who afterward became a famous lamenter in the late nineteenth and early twentieth centuries. The tale, which still circulates orally today, over a century later, complete with her words, merits citation at length:

> Koundounara's husband came from the village of Layia. He took his [younger] bride by force and shut her up in his house. She soon became pregnant and gave birth to a son. The child was born a little before Easter, the time of the *Epitaphios* ceremony in which women play a major part. Koundounara's husband said to himself, "Since she's given birth she won't leave me." So he let her go to the church, to help the other women with the preparations for the ceremony, but she took the opportunity to escape to her father's house, abandoning her child. When her husband went to fetch her back Koundounara refused to go with him saying: "If you want me to come back to your house and remain your wife, you'll have to bring back a heifer with a bell on it and you'll come through this door on your knees." Her husband found the heifer, put a bell around its neck and went to fetch his wife. She came back to him as she had promised, but to avenge himself he poured scalding oil over her, burning her badly. When her husband died Koundounara sat at the wake with her relatives. Suddenly she took a small lamp, lifted her skirt and stood astride his coffin reciting this little verse: "Look Dimitri / at the little plaything [the word λαλό, meaning a child's toy or

game is used here to refer to her own vagina] you scalded / once upon a time. / Dimitri, I straddle you / and may my plaything make you jealous."[81]

This is a perfectly transgressive act: not only does the newly widowed woman not offer the expected ritual tears for her deceased husband, but she exposes the long-hidden truth of his horrific physical abuse by exposing her scarred body to the world. The boundaries of public and private are transgressed precisely to reveal the husband's past moral transgressions. In straddling her husband's corpse, Koundounara reverses the "normal" sexual positions and the gender expectations of their relative positions of power. The younger wife now "rides" her husband and taunts him that she will go on to enjoy sexual pleasures now denied to him. Not only that, she transforms her scarred body into a site of pleasure at once denied to her husband and scandalously offered to others. This tale (her-story) has been preserved for over a century, passed down over the generations and circulated among women far beyond the immediate area in which the events took place. It has served, no doubt, as a cautionary tale for men, warning that they cannot always count on a woman to shed ritual tears to witness their good nature and bring them honor. It may also serve as a cautionary tale for historians of religions, reminding us that more than "custom" motivates ritual actors to weep or to withhold their tears. Ritual tears—both shed and unshed—are telling. As historians of religions, we must develop new ways of listening carefully for the tales that they tell.

NOTES

1. A few examples of the myriad instances repeating this "universal truism" must suffice. "Throughout the history of humankind, tears have been intertwined with the very essence of the human heart, for the ability to shed emotional tears—psychogenic lacrimation—seems to be one of the few physiological processes which separates humans from other animals" (William H. Frey II, with Muriel Langseth, *Crying: The Mystery of Tears* [Minneapolis: Winston Press, 1985], p. 4). In her foreword to Helmuth Plessner's phenomenological study, *Laughing and Crying: A Study of the Limits of Human Behavior* (Evanston, Ill.: Northwestern University Press, 1970), Marjorie Grene writes, "Laughing and crying are not 'intentional' actions, like speaking, walking, or tacitly giving a sign, say, nodding one's head or smiling in assent. They belong . . . to the Aristotelian class of 'involuntary actions.' Yet neither are they the sort of things that other animals do; only human beings laugh and cry" (p. xi) Later Grene refers to "that strange pair of human monopolies, laughter and tears" (p. xiii). Note that she ignores ritual weeping, which would clearly qualify as an intentional action. On laughter, a historian of religions has recently asserted that "laughter is a universal human expression, restricted to humans and therefore understood as a dividing line between humankind and animals" (Ingvild Sælid Gilhus, *Laughing Gods, Weeping Virgins: Laughter in the History of Religions* [London: Routledge, 1997], p. 2).

2. Charles Darwin, *The Expression of the Emotions in Man and Animals* (London: Murray, 1872). A recent work, which argues that animals experience emotions much as humans do, is Jeffrey Masson, *When Elephants Weep: The Emotional Lives of Animals* (New York: Delacorte Press, 1995). Masson's work is driven by a strong animal rights agenda, and the evidence produced to justify his claims is largely anecdotal in nature. A much better study is Donald R. Griffin, *Animal Minds* (Chicago: University of Chicago Press, 1992).

3. An exception is Gilhus's *Laughing Gods, Weeping Virgins*. Despite the title, weeping is not really treated.

4. The phrase "the history of tears" has been used by literary historians such as Anne Vincent-Buffault, *The History of Tears: Sensibility and Sentimentality in France* (London: Macmillan, 1991); Sheila Page Bayne, *Tears and Weeping: An Aspect of Emotional Climate Reflected in Seventeenth-Century French Literature* (Tubigen: G. Narr, 1981); and Fred Kaplan, *Sacred Tears: Sentimentality in Victorian Literature* (Princeton, N.J.: Princeton University Press, 1987). Although scholars of European and American literature from the seventeenth to the nineteenth centuries have produced some excellent studies, no one has undertaken a history of tears along the lines of Philippe Aries's studies of death, childhood, and privacy in the West. For examples of Aries's work, see *Centuries of Childhood: A Social History of Family Life* (New York: Knopf, 1962), *A History of Private Life*, ed. Philippe Aries and Georges Duby, 4 vols. (Cambridge, Mass.: Belknap Press of Harvard University Press, 1987), *Western Attitudes toward Death: From the Middle Ages to the Present* (Baltimore, Md.: Johns Hopkins University Press, 1974), and *The Hour of Our Death* (New York: Oxford University Press, 1991).

5. A book I am now working on, tentatively entitled *Telling Tears: A Comparative Study of Ritualized Weeping*, would be the first such interdisciplinary comparative study. A few of the best anthropological studies of ritual weeping include Charles L. Briggs, "Personal Sentiments and Polyphonic Voices in Warao Women's Ritual Wailing: Music and Poetics in a Critical and Collective Discourse," *American Anthropologist* 95, no. 4 (1993): 929–57, and " 'Since I Am a Woman I Will Chastise My Relatives': Gender, Reported Speech, and the (Re)production of Social Relations in Warao Ritual Wailing," *American Ethnologist* 19 (1992): 337–61; Anna Caraveli, "The Bitter Wounding: The Lament as Social Protest in Rural Greece," in *Gender and Power in Rural Greece*, ed. Jill Dubisch (Princeton, N.J.: Princeton University Press, 1986), pp. 169–94; William A. Christian, "Provoked Ritual Weeping in Early Modern Spain," in *Religious Organization and Religious Experience*, ed. J. Davis, ASA Monograph no. 21 (London: Academic Press, 1982), pp. 97–114; Loring Danforth, *The Death Rituals of Rural Greece* (Princeton, N.J.: Princeton University Press, 1982); and Steven Feld, *Sound and Sentiment: Birds, Weeping, Poetics and Song in Kaluli Expression* (Philadelphia: University of Pennsylvania Press, 1982).

6. See Beverly Moon, "Tears," in Mircea Eliade, general ed., *Encyclopedia of Religion*, 16 vols. (New York: Macmillan, 1987), 14: 360–61. Frazer's collection may be found in *Folk-Lore in the Old Testament*, 3 vols. (London: Macmillan, 1918), and in the abridged one-volume edition, *Folk-Lore in the Old Testament* (New York: Macmillan, 1923), pp. 238–43.

7. On "feeling rules," see Arlie R. Hochschild, "Emotion Work, Feeling Rules, and Social Structure," *American Journal of Sociology* 85 (1979): 551–75, and *The Man-*

aged Heart: The Commercialization of Human Feeling (Berkeley: University of California Press, 1983).

8. Frazer, *Folk-Lore in the Old Testament,* abridged ed., p. 238.

9. For a trenchant critique of the essentialist position on emotion, see Catherine A. Lutz, *Unnatural Emotions: Everyday Sentiments on a Micronesian Atoll and Their Challenge to Western Theory* (Chicago: University of Chicago Press, 1988).

10. I use "ritualized" to include not only social and religious ritual proper, but also the more mundane forms of patterned social interaction that are informed by cultural values. The phrase "cultural work" is borrowed and adapted from the work of Jane Tomkins, *Sensational Designs: The Cultural Work of American Fiction, 1790–1860* (New York: Oxford University Press, 1985).

11. Due to the constraints of space, I am bracketing here the issue of the differences in the cultural definitions of emotions such as shame, as well as the issue of differences in their forms of expression. Thus, the issues of "translation" are not addressed.

12. A. L. Epstein, *In the Midst of Life: Affect and Ideation in the World of the Tolai* (Berkeley: University of California Press, 1992), p. 63. A dog expresses a sense of shame only after it has been chastised by a human. In this, a dog is like a human child who must be taught such emotional responses. For instance, when a child has done something inappropriate, he is often told, "You should be ashamed [embarrassed]."

13. This translation is William LaFleur's from *The Karma of Words: Buddhism and the Literary Arts in Medieval Japan* (Berkeley: University of California Press, 1983), pp. 36–37. For a complete translation of this collection, see Kyoko Motomochi Nakamura, *Miraculous Stories from the Japanese Buddhist Tradition: The "Nihon ryōiki" of the Monk Kyōkai* (Cambridge, Mass.: Harvard University Press, 1973). The original tale may be found in *Nihon koten bungaku taikei,* vol. 70, *Nihon ryōik,* ed. Entō Yoshimoto and Kasuga Kazuo (Tokyo: Iwanami Shoten, 1967), pp. 120–21.

14. LaFleur, p. 35.

15. Japanese melons are oval in shape, not elongated like the common watermelons in the United States. An alternative compound noun *urizanegao* is written using a different middle Chinese character, which means "seed [of a fruit]," yielding the literal reading "melon seed-[shaped] face."

16. A glance at any Japanese dictionary will disclose that almost all compound words or phrases incorporating the character for "horse" have a negative valence and imply stupidity, dimwittedness, silliness, excessive credulity, and obstinacy (which, interestingly enough, we would call "pigheadedness").

17. Interestingly, in George Orwell's twentieth-century novel *Animal Farm,* a horse figures as the prime example of a simpleminded, good-hearted, gullible, and brutally exploited laborer.

18. LaFleur, p. 26, emphasis added. This sentence, which opens his essay on the *Nihon ryōiki,* taken in conjunction with LaFleur's statement cited earlier on tears as the obvious "perceptible difference" between humans and animals, suggests some slippage in his understanding of the relationship of the world, sensory perception, and epistemology. Regrettably, I cannot address this complex issue here.

19. In *The Karma of Words,* LaFleur does not address the reasons why Mahayana

Buddhism eventually lost its epistemological hegemony in Japan, but one senses that, were he to do so, he would continue to apply Thomas Kuhn's concept of paradigm shifts. Insofar as modern Japanese share LaFleur's assumption that the oozing of liquid from the eyes of animals has a medical etiology, this explanation represents an improvement over that offered by Buddhism.

20. *Nihon koten bungaku taikei*, 70: 121.

21. Marshall Sahlins, *How "Natives" Think: About Captain Cook, for Example* (Chicago: University of Chicago Press, 1995), p. 14.

22. See Joyce E. Salisbury, *The Beast Within: Animals in the Middle Ages* (New York: Routledge, 1994).

23. One need only think of the texts on metamorphosis from the classical world, but there are also modem reports of humans turning into animals. See, e.g., the report collected in the 1970s in rural Ireland by Henry Classic, which suggested that a woman transformed herself into a hare to steal the milk from a neighbor's cows (*Passing the Time in Ballymenone: Culture and History of an Ulster Community* [Bloomington: Indiana University Press, 1982], p. 536).

24. The literature on witchcraft is too voluminous to cite here. On werewolves, see Charlotte F. Otten, ed., *A Lycanthropy Reader: Werewolves in Western Culture* (Syracuse, N.Y.: Syracuse University Press, 1986); Caroline Oates, "Metamorphosis and Lycanthropy in Franche-Comte, 1521–1643," in *Fragments for a History of the Body*, ed. Michel Feher, pt. 1 (New York: Zone, 1989), pp. 305–63; and D. Kraatz, "Fictus Lupus: The Werewolf in Christian Thought," *Classical Folia* 30 (1976): 57–79. For a psychological interpretation of religious lycanthropy, see Daniel Merkur, "The Psychodynamics of the Navaho Coyote-way Ceremonial," *Journal of Mind and Behavior* 2 (1981): 243–57.

25. Julio Caro Baroja, *The World of the Witches* (Chicago: University of Chicago Press, 1964), p. 118. See also Oates, pp. 327–38 and 342.

26. Cited in Lynn Thorndike, *A History of Magic and Experimental Science*, 8 vols. (New York: Columbia University Press, 1923–58), 8: 569.

27. Those suffering from *lycanthropia* were described as "pale and sickly to look at, they have dry eyes and cannot cry. Their eyes are hollow and their tongue is dry; they do not salivate and are very thirsty" (cited in Oates, p. 322).

28. St. Augustine, *De Spiritu et Anima*, chap. 26, cited in Otten, p. 6.

29. The rediscovery of *The Book of Margery Kempe* earlier in the twentieth century has provoked a flurry of work on this laywoman. For the work itself, see *The Book of Margery Kempe*, ed. Sanford B. Meech and Hope Emily Allen (London: Oxford University Press, 1940); and *The Book of Margery Kempe*, trans. Barry A. Windeatt (New York: Penguin, 1985). For an important feminist study, see Kanna Lochrie, *Margery Kempe and Translations of the Flesh* (Philadelphia: University of Pennsylvania Press, 1991). Also useful is Clarissa W. Atkinson, *Mystic and Pilgrim: The Book and the World of Margery Kempe* (Ithaca, N.Y.: Cornell University Press, 1983). On the ecclesiastical surveillance of Kempe, see Meech and Allen, p. 69.

30. Meech and Allen, p. 69.

31. H. M. Gardiner et al., *Feeling and Emotion: A History of Theories* (Westport, Conn.: Greenwood Press, 1970), p. 137.

32. Stephen Greenblatt, "Filthy Rites," *Daedalus* 3, no. 3 (1982): 10, emphasis added.

33. See Marcel Mauss, "Techniques of the Body," *Economy and Society* 2, no. 1 (1973): 70–88.

34. See Norbert Elias, *The Civilizing Process*, 2 vols. (New York: Pantheon, 1982).

35. See Baroja, pp. 36–37, for a similar argument.

36. T. H. White, trans., *The Book of Beasts* (London: Jonathan Cape, 1954), p. 50.

37. See Richard de Fournival, *Master Richard's Bestiary of Love and Response*, trans. Jeanette Beer (Berkeley: University of California Press, 1986).

38. See M. C. Seymour, ed., *Mandeville's Travels* (Oxford: Clarendon Press, 1967), p. 208. The image of a man-eating crocodile shedding tears after consuming a human represents a complete inversion of a second-century report from Aelian that "the people of the City of Apollo . . . catch crocodiles in a drag net, and having hung them up on persea-trees, they beat them with many blows and flog them as men are flogged, while the animals whimper and shed tears; then they cut them down and feast on them" (cited in White, p. 159, n. 1).

39. Salisbury, p. 110. Ian Macleod Higgins, a perceptive student of *Mandeville's Travels*, has recently offered a similar cautionary note about the danger of imposing our own categories and textual expectations (in this case, "plagiarism") on texts from another time. "The Mandeville author," he writes, "is not a plagiarist, for *The Book* is not a mindless compilation; it is rather the product of a considered, engaged, and sometimes inspired overwriting of its sources that offers readers an often compelling account of matters pious and profane, historical and scientific, mundane and marvelous. . . . [It] represents a kind of [discursive] field where asynchronous or contradictory cultural forces and elements manifest themselves and where critical analysis will detect a mixture of the residual, dominant, and emergent elements of a given cultural formation" (Ian Macleod Higgins, *Writing East: The "Travels" of Sir John Mandeville* [Philadelphia: University of Pennsylvania Press, 1997], pp. 12–13).

40. It is worth mentioning that reports of weeping crocodiles were often found in first-person travel accounts, an important genre of the age, which, by its very nature, lends the narrator's voice a heightened authority. Then, too, it is important to note the purported social status of these reporters, for in legal proceedings and scientific salons of the period, the weight given to the testimony of an individual depended in large part on her or his social identity. Steven Shapin, for instance, has convincingly demonstrated how in seventeenth-century England, scientific "truth" was largely determined by the investigator's social class and the presumption that persons of class were by their very nature trustworthy (see Steven Shapin, *A Social History of Truth: Civility and Science in Seventeenth-Century England* [Chicago: University of Chicago Press, 1994]). Thus, a report from someone like *Sir* John Mandeville would have been granted extra credence by some.

41. On this celebrated case, see Dennis Todd, *Imagining Monsters: Miscreations of the Self in Eighteenth-Century England* (Chicago: University of Chicago Press, 1995).

42. See Stephen Greenblatt, *Renaissance Self-Fashioning: From More to Shakespeare* (Chicago: University of Chicago Press, 1980); and Frank Whigham, *Ambition and Privilege: The Social Tropes of Elizabethan Courtesy Literature* (Berkeley: University of California Press, 1984).

43. For an overview of the subject, see Perez Zagorin, *Ways of Lying: Dissimulation, Persecution, and Conformity in Early Modern Europe* (Cambridge, Mass.: Harvard

University Press, 1990), pp. 1–37; also, more generally, Sissela Bok, *Lying: Moral Choice in Public and Private Life* (New York: Vintage Books, 1978).

44. Significantly, modern ethologists have come to refer to the ability of animals, birds, insects, and so on to employ strategies of deception within their species and with others as "Machiavellian intelligence." See Richard Byrne and Andrew Whiten, eds., *Machiavellian Intelligence: Social Expertise and the Evolution of Intellect in Monkeys, Apes, and Humans* (Oxford: Clarendon Press, 1988). Some scholars have resisted using the term universally, arguing that among humans "self-monitoring" can be used in positive ways as well (e.g., to align oneself with social expectations or to avoid conflict). See Mark Snyder, *Public Appearances, Private Realities: The Psychology of Self-Monitoring* (New York: Freeman, 1987), p. 26. The work of Erving Goffman is also pertinent here.

45. *Basilikon Doron*, cited in Katherine Ersaman Maus, "Proof and Consequences: Inwardness and Its Exposure in the English Renaissance," *Representations* 34 (1991): 29. Surprisingly, Maus never mentions tears in this insightful essay.

46. See Zagorin for many examples of this.

47. It also helps us to understand the voluminous lachrymose literature produced in (and productive of) the "sentimental culture" of the late seventeenth to nineteenth centuries in Europe and America.

48. For a brief but useful assessment of Lafitau, see Anthony Pagden, *The Fall of Natural Man: The American Indian and the Origins of Comparative Ethnology* (Cambridge, UK: Cambridge University Press, 1982), pp. 198–209.

49. Lafitau writes of his comparative method, "I was not content with knowing the nature of the Indians, and with informing myself about their customs and practices. I sought in these practices and customs vestiges of the most remote antiquity. I read carefully the works of the earliest authors who dealt with the customs, laws, and usages of the peoples with whom they had some acquaintance. I compared these customs, one with the other; and I confess that whereas the ancient authors have given me some light to support several happy conjectures concerning the Indians, the customs of the Indians have provided me with light for understanding more clearly and for explaining several things which appear in ancient writers" (Lafitau, *Customs of the American Indians Compared with Primitive Times*, ed. William N. Fenton and Elizabeth L. Moore, 2 vols. [Toronto: Champlain Society, 1977], 1:27).

50. Ibid., 1:xliv.

51. Ibid., 2:150, 2:222. In spite of his generally liberal spirit, Lafitau in many ways still shared the prejudices of his time, including many of the gender assumptions. He believed, for instance, that women have always and everywhere been more given to shedding tears than men have. When he nevertheless has to deal with instances of men ritually weeping, in histories, ethnographies, or his own experience living among the American Indians, he cannot resist implying that they are somehow "naturally" different. Thus, he writes, "The men . . . mourn their dead but in a noble manner and one which has not weakness in it" (ibid., 220).

52. Ibid., 2:241–42.

53. Ibid., 157–58, 218–22, 218.

54. See Emile Durkheim, *The Elementary Forms of the Religious Life* (New York: Free Press, 1965), pp. 434–61.

55. Ibid., 442–43.

56. For a recent critical evaluation of the classical ethnographies of the Australian Aborigines, see Sam D. Gill, *Storytracking: Texts, Stories, and Histories in Central
Australia* (New York: Oxford University Press, 1998).

57. Durkheim, p. 442, n. 27. Note, too, the limiting and delegitimating effect of
Durkheim's redundant adjectives here: "in *certain peculiar* cases, of course, the chagrin expressed is really felt" (emphasis added). The texts in question are Erhardt Etylmann, *Die Eingeborenen der Kolonie Sudaustralien* (Berlin: Reimer, 1908), on peoples
of the Western Desert area; and James Dawson, *Australian Aborigines: The Languages
and Customs of Several Tribes of Aborigines in the Western District of Victoria, Australia*
(Melbourne: Robertson, 1881). Neither work is considered to be very reliable today.
Tony Swain suggests Etylmann's study is only of historical interest, and Dawson's is
"predictably superficial" on religion (see Swain, *Aboriginal Religions in Australia: A
Bibliographical Survey* [Westport, Conn.: Greenwood Press, 1991], pp. 210 and 259).

58. See Durkheim, p. 18, for a clear statement to this effect.

59. Ibid., 447, 447–48, emphasis added; 435–36, citing Baldwin Spencer and
Francis Gillen, *The Northern Tribes of Central Australia* (London: Macmillan, 1899),
pp. 516–17. Richard Huntington and Peter Metcalf cite this same passage in their
comparative study of funerary ritual, calling it "vivid" twice and "startling." Surprisingly, they do not question the veracity of the description at all. Indeed, they find it to
be strong both "rhetorically and sociologically," because "one can readily accept that,
at a time of death, some people genuinely feel the great emotions that are expressed."
Yet, this is precisely what Durkheim denies elsewhere. See Richard Huntington and
Peter Metcalf, *Celebrations of Death: The Anthropology of Mortuary Ritual* (Cambridge,
UK: Cambridge University Press, 1979), pp. 31–33.

60. Durkheim, pp. 437–38.

61. Compare "If mourning differs from the other forms of the positive cult,
there is one feature in which it resembles them; it, too, is made up out of collective
ceremonies which produce a state of effervescence among those who take part in
them" (ibid., 445).

62. Ibid., 438–39, where he cites Alfred W. Howitt, *The Native Tribes of South-
East Australia* (London: Macmillan, 1904), p. 459. There Howitt records a few of the
cries of relatives of the deceased (e.g., "Why did you leave us?" and "My child is
dead"), which served to intensify the grief of the others.

63. The connection between ritual and theater was, of course, central to the
"myth and ritual school" (Jane Harrison et al.) and, later, in a different fashion, to the
work of Victor Turner. I am, for the moment, skirting the issue of the signal importance of the ritual-as (or, out of)-theater equations in the history of the academic
study of religion. The topic deserves to be studied carefully and fully, going back to
the debates over the theater in the Enlightenment (Diderot, Rousseau, and so on) and
among the Romantics. Suffice it to say that in relation to the passage from Spencer
and Gillen, it is correct to say that the natives "scripted" the mourning rites, but it is
equally the case that this discursive "scene" was rescripted by Durkheim to serve the
overarching purposes of his study.

64. Compare "Howsoever great the violence of these manifestations, they are
strictly regulated by etiquette" (Durkheim, p. 436).

65. A. R. Radcliffe-Brown, *The Andaman Islanders*, expanded ed. (Cambridge, UK: Cambridge University Press, 1933), pp. 234, 286, 239–40.

66. Ibid., 240–41. Other modern authors have also offered psychosomatic explanations of the function of tears, including Frey and Langseth, and Ashley Montagu, "Natural Selections and the Origin and Evolution of Weeping in Man," *Journal of the American Medical Association* 174 (1960): 392–97.

67. Radcliffe-Brown, p. 24.

68. Ibid., 246.

69. Frazer, *Folk-Lore in the Old Testament* abridged ed., p. 238–39.

70. Ibid., 242, emphasis added.

71. On this topic, see Robert L. Hall, *An Archaeology of the Soul: North American Indian Belief and Ritual* (Urbana: University of Illinois Press, 1997), p. 14. For an anthropological study of similar ritual weeping practices among a contemporary South American Indian people, see Charles Wagley, *Welcome of Tears: The Tapirapé Indians of Central Brazil* (New York: Oxford University Press, 1977).

72. The literature on ancient Middle Eastern kingship is voluminous. On ritual weeping and kingship, see the following selected works: Richard Nelson Boyce, *The Cry to God in the Old Testament*, SBL Dissertation Series no. 103 (Atlanta: Scholars Press, 1988); Paul Wayne Ferris, *The Genre of Communal Lament in the Bible and the Ancient Near East* (Atlanta: Scholars Press, 1992); Flemming Friis Hvidberg, *Weeping and Laughter in the Old Testament: A Study of Canaanite-Israelite Religion* (Leiden: Brill, 1962); and Cheryl Meinschein, *Cries of the Brokenhearted: A Study of Laments in Scripture* (Minneapolis: Augsburg Fortress, 1988).

73. In *Ritual Poetry and the Politics of Death in Early Japan* (Princeton, N.J.: Princeton University Press, 1989), I showed that ritual funeral laments and mourning practices in the ancient Japanese court displayed a similar pattern. Laments and rites for those in line to succeed to high positions of power were more elaborate, involved extended public rites, invoked mythic images, and styled the rent in the social fabric in cosmic terms, whereas laments and rites for members of the imperial family far removed from the succession were more personal in imagery and tone, focused on the personal grief of the surviving spouse, and were more cursory in form and performance.

74. See Paul Rosenblatt et al., *Grief and Mourning in Cross-Cultural Perspective* (New Haven, Conn.: Human Relations Area File Press, 1976), p. 11.

75. Caraveli, p. 191. See also Anna Caraveli-Chaves, "Bridge between Worlds: The Greek Women's Lament as Communicative Event," *Journal of American Folklore* 94 (1981): 129–57.

76. Compare C. L. Briggs, " 'Since I Am a Woman I Will Chastise My Relatives' "; Michael Herzfeld, "In Defiance of Destiny: The Management of Time and Gender at a Cretan Funeral," *American Ethnologist* 20 (1993): 24–55; C. Nadia Seremetakis, *The Last Word: Women, Death, and Divination in Inner Mani* (Chicago: University of Chicago Press, 1991); and Jane H. Hill, "Weeping as a Meta-Signal in a Mexicano Woman's Narrative," *Journal of Folklore Research* 27 (1990): 29–49.

77. Margaret Egnor, "Internal Iconicity in Paraiyar 'Crying Songs,' " in *Another Harmony: New Essays on the Folklore of India*, ed. Stuart H. Blackburn and A. K. Ramanujan (Berkeley: University of California Press, 1986), pp. 297, 303.

78. Ibid., 334.

79. Compare Mary-Jo Delvechio Good and Byron Good, "Ritual, the State, and the Transformation of Emotional Discourse in Iranian Society," *Culture, Medicine, and Psychiatry* 12 (1988): 43–63; David Pinault, *The Shiites: Ritual and Popular Poetry in a Muslim Community* (New York: St. Martin's Press, 1993); and Vernon James Schubel, *Religious Performance in Contemporary Islam: Shi'i Devotional Rituals in South Asia* (Columbia: University of South Carolina Press, 1993). Schubel shows how the public rites of weeping also function to create local identities within a city, as different groups of young men compete against each other for acclaim as ritual performers.

80. Susan Auerbach, "From Singing to Lamenting: Women's Musical Role in a Greek Village," in *Women and Music in Cross-Cultural Perspective,* ed. Ellen Koskoff, Contributions in Women's Studies, no. 79 (New York: Greenwood Press, 1987), p. 28.

81. Gail Holst-Warhaft, *Dangerous Voices: Women's Laments and Greek Literature* (London: Routledge, 1992), pp. 63–64.

8

Krishna's Consuming Passions: Food as Metaphor and Metonym for Emotion at Mount Govardhan

Paul M. Toomey

In analyzing the association of emotion with food in local Hindu ritual, Paul M. Toomey provides fresh insight into the worldviews of three bhakti traditions. Toomey demonstrates the manner in which emotion comes to be represented by food in the language of religious devotionalism, and then analyzes how emotion is objectified and linked with a variety of practices associated with eating. Exploring emotion as it is embedded in local culture, Toomey argues that we "will better understand the complex phenomenon of emotion, not by searching for universal features, as many earlier studies do, but by documenting the diverse means by which emotion is culturally constructed and symbolically mediated to actors in specific social and cultural contexts." In demonstrating how culinary metaphors represent various aspects of the devotion to Krishna at Mount Govardhan, Toomey also observes how three different sects there stress three different emotions from among the five that are central to bhakti. Each tradition offers a distinctive conception of emotion and a full script for its enactment through the representation of emotion in ritual food practices. The worship of Krishna in these settings accordingly is cast as an instance of how distinctions between rational cognitions and irrational feeling, conscious and unconscious, individual feeling and collective emotion, and embodied emotion/spiritualized emotion are

Paul M. Toomey, "Krishna's Consuming Passions: Food as Metaphor and Metonym for Emotion at Mount Govardhan," in *Divine Passions: The Social Construction of Emotion in India*, edited by Owen M. Lynch (Berkeley: University of California Press, 1990), 157–181. Used by permission of the publisher.

Western inventions bearing limited relevance, if any at all, to Indian religious experience.

In what ways does food signify emotion? Can religious emotion be clearly distinguished from everyday emotion in the devotions at Mount Govardhan? Does food represent each equally well? What are the different kinds of emotion that the three bhakti sects emphasize, and how much do they differ? Are there overlapping meanings among the three sects? What does it mean to say that emotion is objectified as food? Could this be the case in other traditions where consumption of food is understood to uphold the religious life of the community and sustain devotion? Is there a distinctly moral element to the representation of the divine in food and food practices? How is the emotion of religious devotion related to emotion as it is represented in explicitly moral discourse? Is there ambiguity in the association of emotion with food? To what extent is emotion made the central object in "transactions" between devotees and their god? Is the objectification of emotion and its valuation in ritual a rendering of it as a commodity?

> Here we have a representation of highest art. This beautiful image shows us the principle of nourishment, on which the entire world relies and which penetrates all nature.
>
> —Goethe, "Concerning Myron's Cow"

South Asianists have recently begun to look more closely at categories of emotion and emotional experience in general in Indian *bhakti* traditions.[1] In this essay I examine similarities and differences in the way emotions are culturally constructed in three such traditions at Mount Govardhan. Govardhan is a major pilgrimage center in Mathura District, Uttar Pradesh, that area of North India renowned as the birthplace and earthy pastureland of Lord Krishna (hence the name *Braj*, or "pastureland," which Hindus give to this region). The traditions are the Vallabhite and Chaitanyaite sectarian traditions and the nonsectarian Braj folk tradition.[2] This discussion follows in part directions of other anthropologists who have used a cultural constructionist approach to study emotional life in settings outside India.[3]

Bhakti devotionalism presupposes a culturally specific ideology of emotion, one adapted by medieval theologians from the *rasa* theory of emotion.[4] Bhakti selects out of rasa emotional theory only those emotions that are patterned after identifiable human relationships (e.g., mother-child, lover-beloved, fraternal love). Devotees' experience of Krishna is therefore conceived in terms of one or another of several possible dyadic human relationships; each expresses love and reciprocity. Much has been written about the function of these emotions as aesthetic structures in Braj drama and poetry,[5] but there are far fewer explanations of their meaning and significance in the everyday lives and social experience of Krishna worshipper.[6]

Efforts of South Asianists to account for the historical significance of bhakti emotionalism rely heavily on the motivational explanations of Freud and other psychoanalytic theorists.[7] In their view emotionalism represented a response by Hindus—a retreat into either collective fantasy or subjective mysticism—to Muslim control of more rational forms of social and political power in North India. This sort of social psychoanalysis overlooks entirely the problem of how the indigenous system of emotions operates in this cultural context. This analysis not only focuses on the latter as a problem for discussion, but also accepts the constructionist view, put forth by Rosaldo and others,[8] that emotions are culturally constituted, shared, generalized in a social network, and reflective of a cultural knowledge system through which actors in a particular cultural milieu interpret experience.

Of particular interest in the following discussion is devotees' use of food as signifier for emotion. In this culture food is closely tied to sociability within religious communities and to devotees' relationship with the deity. Many vocabulary words for emotion are gastronomic terms. Food metaphors and images, which proceed logically from these key words, also conceptualize emotion. These meanings are then produced and reproduced in cultural practices such as the ritual act of offering food to Krishna. This connection between food and emotion is undoubtedly subject to a greater degree of elaboration at Govardhan than at other Braj pilgrimage places because food and food symbolism play central roles in the myth associated with the hill and the practices of pilgrims who visit the site.

The first section of the essay explores this link between food and emotion in key words for emotion and in metaphors and images common to Krishna stories and legends. Analysis turns to food rituals in the second half of the essay, most specifically to the manner in which the emotion favored for worship in each tradition shapes the pragmatic codes and aesthetic parameters of its food rituals. Data presented should indicate that food beliefs and practices objectify emotion and, as such, constitute emotional experience for members of this culture. This premise follows Bruner's remark that experience structures expression and expressions in turn structure experience.[9] Applying this insight to the present case, I further conclude that just as culturally constructed emotions act as sensibilities that inform ritual expressions, so, in the final estimate, they cannot be experienced without these same sensorial expressions.

The Setting

Mount Govardhan, whose name literally translated is "increaser of cattle," is a small hillock some five miles long and only one hundred feet high. The hillock is located in the southwest corner of Braj, the pilgrimage region just south of Delhi celebrated as the birthplace of Lord Krishna and the location of his childhood play on earth (*līlā*). The hill is worshipped by pilgrims as Krishna's natural form (*svarūpa*) and is a central attraction in the 168-mile pilgrimage route (*Caurāsī Kos Parikramā*) that encircles the region. A large number of towns, shrines, and natural sites, arranged along this route, commemorate the deity's miraculous exploits.[10] This proliferation of sites and the active and colorful pilgrimage culture that continues in the 1980s have their beginnings in the devotional resurgence that swept North India in the sixteenth century. As a result of this resurgence, local Braj culture was profoundly influenced by the languages and cultures of distant regions whose saintly representatives came and settled here in the late medieval period.

Because the hill was one of the few identifiable markers of Krishna's divine play on earth, as it was described in textual accounts, it attracted numerous philosopher saints who sought to establish and strengthen Vaishnava sects (*sampradāya*) by visiting the region. In the sixteenth century, Vallabha from South India and Chaitanya from Bengal came to Govardhan, where they established sectarian enclaves at either end of the hill.

The Vallabhite sect, which continues to maintain an active center at Jatipura to the south of the hill, is a householder sect, with no ascetic subbranches. *Gosvāmīs,* the sect's preceptors, are lineal descendants of Vallabha, the founder saint; with few exceptions, most are Tailang Brahmans from Andhra Pradesh. Initiates in the sect are also householders, many of whom belong to the predominantly mercantile castes of Gujarat and adjacent areas of western India and whose families have had connections with the sect for several generations. The sect has evolved a highly ceremonial style of devotional worship that focuses on iconic images of Krishna housed in special temples (*haveli*). Haveli are also believed to be the homes of gosvami preceptors, with whose persons temple images are closely linked in sectarian ideology. Because the sect's preeminent icon, Srī Nāthjī, appeared to Vallabha at Jatipura, this town is especially sacred in the sect. Even after the icon was removed to Nathdwara in Rajasthan, following the emperor Aurangzeb's sack of Braj in A.D. 1670, Jatipura remained an important center of pilgrimage for members of this sect. A lengthy stop at Jatipura and the presentation of resplendent offerings of food at the side of Mount Govardhan is one highlight of the sect's pilgrimage through the region each year.

By contrast, the Chaitanyaite sect in Braj, and elsewhere in India, exhibits tension in its internal social organization between householder and ascetic ritual specialists in the sect, both of whom can be found at various places around Braj. Although the sect's householder Brahmans, also known as gosvamis, preside over the lavish ceremonial temples in nearby Brindaban, Radhakund, to the north of the hill, had historically been the provenance of the sect's many ascetics and monks, who have lived there in retreat since Chaitanya discovered the town beneath paddy fields. Addressing the issue of structural tensions in a sect with a comparable social organization to Chaitanyaites, the

Swaminarayan sect of Gujarat, Williams concludes that it is not uncommon for sects that have both householder and ascetic ritual specialists in their folds to develop different, often competitive, factions over time. Added to this, the presence of an international movement such as ISKCON (International Society for Krishna Consciousness), with links to the Chaitanyaite sect and a large modern temple in Brindaban, makes the Chaitanyaites considerably more heterogeneous than the Vallabhites.[11]

The town of Radhakund clusters on the banks of two holy ponds (*kuṇḍda*) believed to have hosted an aquatic tryst by Krishna and his principal consort, Radha, whose love relationship is the focus of worship in the sect. Pilgrims come to Radhakund for extended periods of time to chant, to listen to textual accounts of Radha and Krishna's love play, and to meditate with the large number of monks and widows who live there. Icon worship and large temples are not noticeable features in the style of worship practiced in this Chaitanyaite center.

Popular, that is nonsectarian, worship of Krishna is carried on by local Brahman priests (*paṇḍā*) and pilgrims in Govardhan town, at the hill's mid point. This, the largest of the hill's three main towns, with a population of twelve thousand, is conveniently located on the major bus route running from Mathura to Dig. The popular tradition cuts across the sectarian traditions in many respects; thus, neither pilgrims nor local priests formally belong to any sect. According to local tradition, ritual worship of the hill is the exclusive domain of resident Brahmans, and pilgrims who belong to sects, much like other pilgrims, have their own priests in the town for this purpose. The only exception to this are Vallabhites; they prefer to worship the hill down the road at Jatipura where local Brahmans are initiates of their sect.

Food as Metaphor and Metonym for Emotion

On a linguistic analogy, A. K. Ramanujan describes bhakti as a series of religious shifts that ultimately dominated, crossed, and transformed older linguistic and cultural forms.[12] There were shifts from noniconic to iconic worship; from rituals, in which a plot of ground was cordoned off and made into sacred space by Vedic experts in a consecration rite, to worship in temples localized, named, and open to almost the entire range of Hindu society; from belief in a nonpersonal absolute to the gods of mythology with faces, complexions, families, and feelings; and from passive modes like hearing and watching to active modes like speaking, dancing, touching, singing, and eating. *Prema*, "other serving love," the final goal of which is rasa, a bliss-filled union with the divine, replaced the earlier *maryādā*, concerned with intellectual knowledge and ritual propriety. In Vaishnava thought and practice, Krishna became the integrative center of an aesthetic worldview that called for devotees' emotional involvement in Krishna's eternal pastimes (*lila*) recounted in sacred texts. As the focus of worship, Krishna is a personal, absolute being who manifests himself in mythic exploits with other players—his foster parents, friends (*gopā*), and female consorts (*gopī*)—in temple images (*mūrti*), in the many pilgrimage places that dot the Braj landscape, and in the human heart.

The Vaishnavite theory of emotional religious experience is based on an ingenious adaptation by Rupa Goswami and others of the rasa theory of Sanskrit poetics[13] Rasa theory, as put forth by Bharata and Abhinavagupta, is a poesis aimed at "emotion recollected": according to this notion, the poetic word has a suggestive power capable of transforming *bhāva*, basic human moods or sentiments, into rasa, emotions evoked in a listener or spectator that are aesthetically distanced and more pristine and rarefied than any feeling derived from direct sensual perception or experience.[14] In Krishna bhakti, bhava, and rasa are reinterpreted, shorn of their aesthetic distance; emphasis is placed, instead, on emotional experience of Krishna and its spontaneous expression (*rāgānugābhakti*) in the devotee's life. Bhava then becomes the devotee's worshipful attitude; rasa is the joyful experience of the love relationship between a human being and Krishna. Krishna is conceived of as the fount of rasa: he is the object that is relished (rasa), the subject who relishes (*rasika*), the embodiment of all moods, and the giver of the experience of moods to others.[15]

The nine emotions of classical aesthetic theory[16] are collapsed into five: where the devotee views Krishna with awe and humility in *śānta bhāva*, he is the supreme being; in *dāsya bhāva*, a lord and master to be served; in *sakhya bhāva*, cowherder friend and equal; in *vātsalya bhāva*, a child to be adored and cared for by its mother; and in *mādhurya bhāva* (also referred to as *śṛṅgāra bhāva*, the sweet emotion), a female cowmaiden enraptured by Krishna's seductive beauty. The devotee chooses, in accordance with his emotional capacities and the help of a guru,[17] to emulate the emotions of one or another of the characters who participate in Krishna's mythic play. Most worshippers at Govardhan identify with the maternal and erotic sentiments; sentiments of reverential awe and slavish love are more characteristic of Shrivaishnavas and Ramanandis, relatively small sects in Braj. It is difficult to convey through simple and misleading English terms the complex meanings assigned to both the identities of mother, female lover, slave, and so on in this culture and the manner in which each form of person hood is conceived, constituted, and experienced emotionally. Moreover, a systematic play of differences (or *différance*, to borrow Derrida's phrase) works in the various interpretations folk and sectarian traditions give to the same set of emotions. To cite but one example of this, in the case of the erotic emotion, the Radhavallabha sect, based primarily in Brindaban, believes that Radha is Krishna's own wife (*svakīyā*), whereas, for Chaitanyaites, a fundamental aspect of Radha's love stems from the fact that she is married to someone else (*parakīyā*) but is irresistably drawn, against all social conventions, into an amorous liaison with Krishna.

Metaphors and metonyms that allude to food and the sense of taste play an important role in conceptualizing emotion and emotional experience.[18] Many key terms in classical aesthetic theory and medieval devotional theory patterned after it are derived from gastronomy. Lakoff and Johnson's experientialist theory of metaphor takes the position that many abstract concepts such as time and emotion are grasped by other concepts understood in clearer, more palpable terms, by means of spatial orientations, objects, or, in this case, food.[19] Metaphors, these authors conclude, enable speakers of a linguistic culture to understand one domain in terms of another. Although most of the authors' illustrations are drawn from English and other Western languages, their explanation may nevertheless help us to understand better the use of culinary metaphors and ritual food practices in bhakti to generate emotional experience.[20]

Let me review briefly some culinary metaphors implicit in Krishna ideology and the entailments that follow from them. First, the term rasa itself means juice, sap, or liquid. In the broad semantic sense, rasa refers to the flavor, taste, or essence of something that can be extracted and experienced in various ways. Devotees consistently make statements of the sort, "I hunger after the sweet nectar of devotion." Here a simile likens devotional experience to a fruit filled with nectar (rasa) that is drunk by those connoisseurs (rasika) who have acquired a taste for the beautiful (bhāvuka); Krishna himself is often said to be raso vai saha, the consummate experiencer of his own essence, which is rasa. Here, as in gastronomy, whence the terms rasa, ruci (taste or liking, used in this context to refer to a person's spiritual inclination) and rasika (meaning both gourmet and a sensitive person, a connoisseur) derive, experience is in the experiencer.

Vaishnavas also believe that just as hunger is a necessary condition for the enjoyment of delicious food, so is the desire for rasa a necessary condition for its enjoyment. Krishna's ever-growing desire for relishing new forms of rasa, which is believed to set the devotional drama in motion, is not symptomatic of imperfection but flows spontaneously from his full, generous nature. The notion that love is of necessity spontaneous—and cannot be achieved solely through the traditional paths of knowledge or ritual discipline—is expressed through culinary metaphors and images in a number of places in Krishna mythology and folklore. In stories of famous saints, for example, Krishna usually makes initial contact by appearing to the saint in a dream, sharing food, and leaving behind an image or icon. Saints are usually simple people (more often than not of the lower castes), but Krishna prefers their victuals—given in a sincere, straightforward manner—to the offerings of sanctimonious Brahman priests serving in his temples. Strains of this same antiritualism come through in episodes of Harirāy's Vallabhite chronicle Śrī Govardhannāthjī ke Prākaṭya kī Vārtā, where Krishna runs away from the majestic splendor of his temple/palace to eat with cowherders and saints living alone in the wilds of

Braj.[21] In stories surrounding the miraculous appearance of Krishna's icons, the whereabouts of images are often signaled to locals by the strange behavior of cows who shed streams of milk on the ground beneath which the images lay hiding.[22] Finally, in Krishna myths and legends the spontaneous outpouring of love between Krishna and his devotees is frequently symbolized by milk, a signifier for rasa. However angry Yashoda might be with her foster son, Krishna, she cannot stop her breasts from overflowing with milk at the sight of him; this poignant image is found is much Braj poetry.

The entailments of these and similar metaphors are too numerous to explore here, but I will mention a few salient examples. For example, theologians explain the manner in which Krishna's divine energy is refracted in different basic human emotions by comparing it to the different tastes rainwater produces when mixed with different substances: "Rainwater mixed with milk tastes sweet, with āmalakī (a fruit of the tree Emblic Myrobolam) sour, in some vegetables salty, in pepper pungent, with other substances bitter and astringent, and so on."[23] Another, more common metaphor likens the devotional path to a churning process, wherein the devotee's constant faith is transformed into sattva (defined as essential spiritual purity), in much the same way that butter and curds are churned from milk.[24] Following along in the same symbolic line, a cluster of metaphors surrounds Krishna in his identity as butter thief (māk-hancor). This image is a mainstay of popular iconography in Braj, represented in sculpture, painting, music, and poetry. This image makes a metaphor of Krishna stealing butter with his thievery of the human heart in religious devotion. In these terms then, Krishna's pilfering is a metaphoric guise for the unlimited creativity by which he takes back in devotion what is his to begin with: rasa, signified in this iconic instance by milk, butter, and curds.[25] Hawley's study of the butter thief theme in Braj poetry traces this cluster of metaphors back to a basic correspondence in the mythology itself, a correspondence between the milk-based economy of Braj and the "economy of love" that circulates freely between Krishna and his playmates in the Braj lila.[26]

These culinary metaphors have an interpretive function insofar as they provide worshippers with understandings of some complex notions involved in devotion. Key transformations in food ritual, however, have a metonymic rather than metaphoric structure. The same is true of the Govardhan myth, which recounts in distinctly Braj terms how food first came to be offered to Krishna. Thus, both food ritual and the associated food myth establish a metonymy between love, a gift given to devotees through Krishna's grace, and food, a concrete means of experiencing and reexperiencing this gift, thereby keeping it in circulation.[27]

Food offerings are present in nearly all Vaishnavite worshipping, from the intimacy of the household shrine to the more public setting of the temple. The central transformation in food ritual occurs when food, called bhoga (literally, pleasure or sensual enjoyment, anything that can be enjoyed by the senses), is set before Krishna's image and Krishna himself is believed to consume it, usually through the image's eyes.[28] In this act of consumption bhoga is metonymously transformed into more love-laden *prasāda* or consecrated food. Bennett draws a homology between this culinary transformation and an equivalent transformation on the emotional level: in his analysis, bhoga (food offerings) is to bhava (the devotee's worshipful emotion) as prasada (consecrated food offerings) is to rasa (Krishna's blissful nature).[29] In light of the data presented here, one might go one step further and say that these are metonymic correspondences, not merely homologous ones, as Bennett suggests.

In the Govardhan myth Krishna persuades the Braj cowherds to make their annual harvest offering to Govardhan hill instead of to the god Indra. Once the offerings are mountainously piled in front of the hill, Krishna jumps into the hill, saying, "I am Govardhan; Govardhan is me." He then sucks in the food through a crack in the hill (known locally as *mukhāravinda*, lotus mouth), metonymically linking himself, the hill, and the mountainous pile of food (*Annakūṭa*).[30] Pictographs of this mythic event, sold throughout Braj, show this metonym clearly. Krishna appears in two places at once in the illustration: standing within a square niche inside the hill, and outside, kneeling to the left of the hill with hands folded in prayer beside his brother, Balarama, and other cowherds. This iconography represents the processual structure of food ritual and the love relationship it signifies: the gift of food-love moves in a circle, from the cowherds to the hill Krishna-Govardhan, and back to Krishna and the cowherds once more. Thus, the food-love metonymy substantiates the circular process underlying devotional experience: Krishna, it is believed, creates devotees through his grace, in order that he might reflexively experience through their loving feelings his own blissful and loving nature (*ānanda*).[31]

This metonymy is objectively inscribed in ceremonies that mark Govardhan Puja in the Hindu calendar. This festival takes place on the day following Diwali, the "Festival of Lights," associated with the goddess Lakshmi and the start of the new business year for Hindus. On this day, the first day of the second fortnight of *Kārtika* (October–November), at Govardhan and throughout this region of North India, two food rituals take place. The twin rituals are grounded in contrasting social settings—one public and community-oriented, the other private and domestic—and draw on different sorts of experiences in the participants' emotional lives. The first rite, performed in the afternoon in Vaishnavite temples by members of the same sect or, in the cases of the folk tradition, by residents of the Brahman neighborhood, expresses solidarity in these communities; the second, celebrated at twilight in each household courtyard, expresses emotional relationships in the joint or extended family.

In the temple ritual known as *Annakūṭa* (the Mountain of Food), a large mound of rice, sometimes weighing thousands of kilos, is constructed in the temple courtyard, facing the sanctum where the deity resides. Sweets and tarts, made from flour and stuffed with raisins and other condiments, and other vegetable and grain dishes are artistically arranged around this central pile. Pilgrims come specially to Govardhan to view these displays. The proceedings often end on a raucous note. In one temple at Jatipura, a Brahman dressed in a cowherd's costume jumps into the rice pile from a balcony above the court-yard; in other temples, pilgrims are permitted to dismantle the display by rush-ing in and, like the mischievous butter thief, grabbing as much food as they can take away with them. Informants explain that Annakūta departs from nor-mal temple etiquette in several important respects. First, in daily worship boiled rice is usually handled according to strict pollution rules and shielded from public view when offered to the deity; here it is openly displayed, even played with by pilgrims, in the temple's most public area, those courtyard. When asked what they were feeling at the time of the ritual, those present said that the mountainous food offering was Krishna's loving body, free to be en-joyed by all in the spirit of *lila*. In their words:

> After a time temple ritual gets stale, bogged down in repetition and priestly details. Going through the routine of daily worship we some-times forget the spirit [bhava] behind the offering. In Annakuta we relive the Govardhan lila. Priestly rules are put to one side, and pil-grims play a key role in the joyous festivities. On this day pilgrims are just like Krishna's friends, able to fool and play with him with-out the restraint normally called for in the temple. We offer moun-tains of food to remind ourselves that Krishna is king of Braj [*Braj Rāja*], that he gives us everything we have, and that his love is as vast and never-ending as a mountain. There is plenty of food to go around in Annakuta, and in sharing this food everybody present gets to share all of this love. We never sell food in our temple on this festival. This loving food is free for all who come here. We try to make certain that there is plenty of food and love to go around.[32]

The domestic ritual, celebrated later in the day, contrasts with the boister-ousness and spectacle of the temple rite. This rite expresses the family's wishes for prosperity in the year to follow and stirs up feelings of dependency and intimacy within the household. One must remember, as Trawick and Vatuk also point out, that feelings of dependency and intimacy associated with family relationships, especially those between parents and children, have different meanings in the Indian family and, thus, make the emotions categorized by these words quite different in the Indian context. This background cultural meaning itself partly constitutes what participants experience emotionally in the rite. Therefore, sensations or feelings of dependency and intimacy do not dictate these experiences, but rather the culturally constructed emotional cat-egories themselves do.[33]

At the time of the ritual a small anthropomorphic figure of Krishna-

Govardhan, made of cow dung, is built in each house. The figure, with a concave naval at its midriff, is enclosed in rectangular walls, said to represent mountains. Within these walls are placed cow dung figurines of cattle, ploughs, and butter churners. Assisted by women and older children in the family, small youngsters place sweets, sugarcane, and other harvest goodies into the naval of the figure. All circle the figure, joining hands and singing folksongs in praise of Krishna in his form as the holy hill. Folksongs recall the ancient myth and beseech Govardhan, as "King of Hills" (*Girirāja Mahārāja*), to bring good fortune in the year to come. Children delight in the ritual and listen with rapt attention to instructions on correctly sculpting the image and making the offering. After the ritual is completed, the family enjoys a meal of harvest grains. Older family members then entertain the children with local legends of Govardhan's might. Stories tell of treasures and good fortune that befall staunch devotees of Krishna-Govardhan. Even adult males, who usually frequent the bazaars at night, stay at home this evening to enjoy the quiet intimacy of the occasion and the tender bonds it celebrates. According to local tradition, crops harvested in this season cannot be eaten until this ritual is first performed. The rite, then, is an act of thanksgiving to Krishna for providing the ecological conditions, symbolized here in the harvest bounty, on which family life depends.

Emotion Objectified in Food Ritual

I turn now to consider sources of variation between traditions. Sects have a different view of emotion than does the popular tradition. In sectarian traditions the five basic emotions of bhakti are sorted out and codified, and one emotion is generally chosen above others for worship in the sect; in the popular view, emotions are fickle and change, depending on where one is in Braj and what the festive occasion might be. Food rituals in each tradition provide a setting that must be culturally comprehended or appraised; that is, comprehension *is* the experience that constitutes the emotion in question. As I show in greater detail below, emotion is constructed in food ritual through certain performance codes, which vary from tradition to tradition. Examples of performance codes include foods themselves (their variety and amounts), whether these foods are visually displayed in the temple, the nature of the culinary art in the sect, and the degree of culinary change and elaboration across the festive cycle. Additional factors to be considered are the identity of cooks (Brahmans or ascetics), the attention given to purity rules in cooking, the presence or absence of food categories based on a scale of purity, and the importance given to food vis-à-vis other forms of sensory expression in the sect.

The Vallabhite Sect and Maternal Emotion

The maternal love (*vatsalya bhava*) of Krishna's foster mother, Yashoda, is the favored emotion for Vallabhites.[34] Worship centers on icons of two- or four-armed Krishna or of Krishna as a crawling toddler with one arm upraised, butterball in hand. Icons are housed in temples (*haveli*) whose interiors and ritual artifacts theatrically recreate the Braj of Krishna's childhood down to the most minute detail. Considerable attention is lavished on cuisine in the sect, and Vallabhites are the undisputed gourmets of Hinduism.[35] Sumptuous offerings play off against other sensory media in worship (e.g., painting, flower arrangement, music, and poetry). This array of ritual and ceremonial forms is thought to manifest outwardly an inner emotion, namely maternal love, and offer an incentive (*bhāvanā*) to developing this inner emotion in all who practice devotion.

Conceptions of motherhood and the experience of motherly love in the sect are modeled on cultural definitions of motherhood in the Indian kinship system. In their analysis of the latter, Vatuk and Das explain that biological ties between a mother and her child are backstaged, that is, not given public expression, in the conduct of Indian family life.[36] So as not to seem too possessive of her child, and hence perceived as self-centered by other members of her husband's family, a woman is expected to deindividualize her relationship with her child to the extent that any member of the family can be entrusted with its care.[37] Thus, everyday behavior in Indian families self-consciously recognizes the fact that the process of mothering, unlike the process of childbearing, can involve any number of surrogates in addition to, or instead of, the real mother. In Vatuk's words, "In family life the tasks of mothering should be shared, as food and space and intimacy are shared, among all of its members according to their needs and inclinations."[38]

What it means to be a mother in India and to experience motherly love are clearly constituted by a quite different set of cultural criteria than they are in the West. What is more, Vallabhites transpose this familial model, in a number of interesting ways, to social and affective relations in the sect. For example, the sect refers to itself as Vallabha's family, *Vallabha-kula*. Caste and lineage ties are strongly emphasized in the sect's leadership; cooks, for example, must belong to specified Gujarati Brahman castes (*jāti*). Devotees' identification with Yashoda (who is, after all, Krishna's adoptive mother rather than his natural one) metaphorically extends the notion, put forth in the kinship system, that maternal love is something anyone, male or female, in the family sect can experience. Last, ritual, so central to the sect's ideology, is conceived in terms of a culinary metonym: *puṣṭi*, or nourishing grace;[39] another name of the sect is *Puṣṭi Mārga*, the Way of Grace. Pusti refers to a grace that nourishes, supports, and strengthens the souls of devotees. As the transactional focus of Vallabhite ritual practice, food is perhaps the chief means by which emotion is experienced in the sect. In devotees' minds the devotional process consists in nourishing the infant icon in the temple (or in one's personal possession, as the case may be) and being nourished by him in return. Thus, icons, it is believed, return the maternal affection stored up in food offerings by showering these same offerings with pusti and keeping the ritual process in motion.

Similar attitudes are reflected in the sect's food practices. Food offerings are prepared in vast amounts and with such attention to ritual detail that they are said to reflect a mother's watchful eye for her child. "Attention means care," priests remarked, "a mother's care." And the purity rules observed by cooks and priests in this sect are far stricter than those in the other two traditions at Govardhan. Temple cuisine—an amalgam of Gujarati, Rajasthani, South Indian, and Braj cuisines—is sweet or bland, for the most part; salt and spices are kept to a minimum because these are believed injurious to Krishna's sensitive child's palate. Krishna is fed eight times daily in the temple, from the time he is awakened in the morning until he is serenaded to sleep at night. Large food festivals are another specialty in the sect. Best known of these is *Chappan Bhoga* (the "Fifty-Six Delicacies"), one showpiece of the festive year at Jatipura.[40] Fifty-six recipes, prepared five or six ways from items such as chickpea gram, flour, milk, dry fruits, and other grains, are called for in this offering. Fifty-six baskets of each dish are, in turn, offered, bringing the potential number of offerings to 21,952 ($7 \times 56 \times 56$). The sizable offering is displayed in a temporary enclosure at the side of the hill. A theatrical backdrop is set up on the hill, and one Govardhan stone, decorated with enamel eyes and made up to resemble Krishna's face, peers out from a hole in the painted scenery. Symbolism of the number fifty-six directly relates to maternal love, for devotees say that, like Yashoda, they show their untiring love by providing Krishna with round-the-clock nourishment: eight times a day, seven days a week.[41]

In the Vallabhite system, Krishna's experience of his own rasa crystallizes in temple ritual. In this highly metaphoric system material acts of worship are metonyms for the love-filled emotions they express. The central metonym, pusti, makes nourishment a critical quality of the love or grace that flows between devotees and Krishna. In this way, maternal affection is conceived and experienced as a grace-filled emotion that nourishes devotees' hearts in much the same way that food nourishes their bodies. In this sect food offerings objectify the closely welded domains of heart and body, spirit and matter. To conclude, many features of the Vallabhite system—its ethos of maternal love and the metonymically related realms of the physical-material and the spiritual-emotional, distinctive to the sect's ritual practices—are nicely summarized in the following remarks by a member of this sect. (To savor some implications made in this section, I suggest that the reader go over the statement several times, substituting at appropriate places the word "love" for the words "wealth," "money," or "food" in the original statement.)

Whenever we visit a place of lila in Braj, we offer Krishna what his cowherd friends [gopa] and cowmaiden consorts [gopi] offered him. In our sampradaya we are admonished not to hoard wealth. Money needs to be in constant circulation, to be shared with as many others as possible. Unfortunately, we can hold on to money, but food cannot be hoarded. It will spoil if it is not shared. A single person can only eat so much food, the rest needs to be shared or it will spoil. Food, then, is the most shareable form of wealth. Food is the best thing that we can offer to god. Whatever we think is best, we offer to Krishna as bhoga. Money is not a form of bhoga. Krishna is a child. If you give him sweets, milk, or other such things, he will be pleased. Bhoga is defined as those things that give pleasure to the lord. Our sect's wealth is concentrated in food. In the Shastras it states that whatever god gives us, we must give back in return, as an offering. Food should never be prepared for its own sake; to do so is a sin. Why? Because everything we see belongs to god—it cannot be enjoyed by us unless it is first offered to him. Prasada or food is the grace by which Krishna helps us to live our lives. Next to air and water, food is the most essential thing in life. All our necessities, luxuries, everything, in short, must first be offered to Krishna, as they rightfully belong to him. We use Krishna's things through his grace.[42]

The Chaitanyaite Sect and the Amorous Emotion

If Vallabhites frame the human: divine relationship in familial terms, then Chaitanyaite ascetics at Radhakund can be said to frame devotees' experience of this same relationship in terms of an emotion that violates domestic order: *madhurya bhava*, the illicit love between Krishna and his consort Radha.[43] Icons of Krishna as a comely adolescent flute player, symbolically if not visually linked in some way to Radha, replace icons of the mischievous child in this sect.[44] Radha and Krishna's passionate love disrupts the ordered relations normally expected of men and women in Hindu society. Madhurya bhava is characterized by eroticism and ambiguity, both of which are delineated for devotees in ways specific to this cultural group. Equally critical to our understanding of the love experience in this sect is the notion of *viraha* (love-in-separation). For devotees the purest form of love is incomplete or frustrated love—the same love experienced in myths by suffering and forlorn gopis who have been separated from Krishna after partnering him in one of his many amorous exploits. Thus, for Chaitanyaites, the frustration of the emotions' desire for immediate union with Krishna (a condition theoretically impossible in this philosophical system) becomes the closest possible encounter with the divine.

This complex emotion is open to a wide range of interpretations in different sects and/or regions of India where it appears, even, in this case, between householder Brahman priests and ascetics in the same sect.[45] Chaitanyaite worship practices at Radhakund reflect a decidedly ascetic view of the erotic emotion.[46] Each *āśrama* (monastic dwelling) in the town has an image of Radha-Krishna in its shrineroom; beside the images are placed bits of Govardhan stone (whose natural coloration is said to represent the divine pair) and votive pictures of Chaitanya and his disciples, Nityanand and the Six Goswamis of Brindaban. But ascetics emphatically state that the amount of attention given to icon worship—relative to chanting and other more aural forms of worship such as listening to readings of sacred texts—is a matter of personal choice. In other words, icon worship is not as central a focus in the worship style followed by ascetics as it is in the householder branch of this sect. Something of this ambivalence toward icons comes across in the following anecdote, told by a *sādhu* at Radhakund:

> If a family is involved in worship, it becomes more elaborate, takes more pleasure in display and other worldly things. As a rule, we sadhus are not interested in the outward show of worship, such as one might find in temples at Brindaban, Mathura, and other places in Braj. A classic case of this involves Sanatana Goswami, himself a renouncer [virakta] and one of the six *ācārya* of our sect, who founded the temple of Madan Mohan in Brindaban. One of his disciples, an elderly lady from Mathura, asked him to take on the worship of her family deity, a splendid image of Madan Mohan, after her death. Sanatana Goswami agreed hesitantly, saying: "I am a sadhu and do not have time to look after this little tyke's every wish. Whatever I beg in the way of food, I will share with Madan Mohan. If he is pleased with this meager amount, then I will take him into my charge." Hearing this, the deity agreed, but after several weeks of dry, stale bread, Madan Mohan called to Sanatana: "You bring *roṭī* without so much as salt. Please bring back some salt from your begging rounds, or maybe even a few sweets which I also crave." Sanatana went to his disciples and complained—"This naughty fellow is trying to kill by *bhajana*. Today he asks for salt and sweets. Next time he will ask for *chattīsa vyañjana* [a large feast calling for thirty-six different dishes, elaborately prepared and offered before the deity]." When Sanatana left Brindaban and retired to Govardhan later in his life, he handed over Madan Mohan to one of his lay followers, in whose family it remains to this day.[47]

According to ascetics, icon worship is a personal, private act conducive to an idiom of purity stressing intimacy and closeness with the deity. These same ascetics define purity as an inner state where intention precedes the manipulation of physical substances in a controlled ritual environment. Absent entirely

are large food displays and the separation of foods into ranked categories during cooking and offering, both characteristic of Brahmanical temple cuisine.[48]
Offerings are fairly simple, consisting mostly of rice, spiced pulses and other
grains, and stewed vegetables. Sweets, the mainstay of other traditions around
the hill, are seldom offered. Last, food offerings are not parceled out to devotees, common practice with most temple prasada; rather, they are shared by
devotees as a feast or common meal (vaiṣṇava sevā), after participating in long
hours of group chanting and other strenuous devotional activities. In short,
more sensual and visual forms of ritual expression (i.e., changing the image's
clothing or food offerings on a seasonal basis) are left unstressed in this tradition, and the food offering itself takes on aspects of a feast, rather than a
sweet or other culinary souvenir to be taken away from the temple by pilgrims.

Attitudes toward food offerings at Radhakund are similar in several respects to those described by Audrey Hayley for Vaishnavas in Assam.[49] First,
rice (called *anna*, life's breath, that on which life depends), which is given high
moral evaluation in the eastern states of India, is the food offering par excellence in both religious communities. Second, they share the view that the
collective religious experience itself is the living body of Krishna, superior not
only to his iconic representation but even to the god himself. This collective
experience is embodied in food offerings that have been transformed by sound
into the four constituent parts of worship: god, name, guru, and devotee. In
this view, the food offering reconstitutes the central importance of the devotional act itself and the devotees who perform it. Food offerings therefore make
substantial the spiritual intentions behind devotional acts; concomitantly, consumption of these offerings is believed to sustain devotees in further acts of
community worship.

Emotion in the Folk Tradition at Mount Govardhan

In the Braj folk tradition I find not one or two emotions, emphasized over the
others, but an amalgam, a medley of emotions playing harmoniously off
against one another as one moves across the sacred landscape. Moodiness and
sentimentality permeate Braj culture, giving the region an ambience of sweetness and solitude in some places, of boisterousness and prankish good humor
in others. Entire towns are said to be saturated with one emotion or another,
depending on the emotional tones of the lila that took place there. Residents
of certain towns are accorded masculine or feminine qualities by virtue of their
association with gopas or gopis who lived there before them. As a key or dominant symbol in Braj cosmology, Mount Govardhan is thought to preside over
and enfold within itself the many teeming emotions of Braj lila.[50]

Govardhan hill means many things to many people. To members of the
Vallabhite sect, the hill is especially sacred because their principal icon, Sri
Nathji, sprang from one of its cracks at Jatipura; to Chaitanyaites, the hill still

resounds with the echo of Krishna's flute and the memories of his afternoon love play with Radha and the other cowmaidens. In the folk conception, shared by sectarian groups as well, the hill connects a wide array of referents: it is alternately Krishna's natural body, a mountain of food (*Annakuta*), a bestower of boons, and the source of the region's agricultural growth and renewal. The hill is semantically open, capable of exegesis at various levels, from that of sectarian literati to the views of simple peasants who come on pilgrimage here every full moon (*pūrṇamāsī*) to pledge their devotion to the mountain in return for good fortune and prosperity. Devotees of all persuasions agree that Krishna-Govardhan condenses into one ritual object both Krishna's many visual images, referred to by hundreds of thousands of melodious-sounding names or epithets, and the welter of emotions stored up in these images. Depending on one's perspective, Krishna is seen in the stones in different ways. In just one example, peasants who come to Govardhan regularly see the hill as a folk deity: the "king of hills," the protector of cows, and the provider of boons and bounty (*dānīrāya*).

Food ritual in the folk tradition is relatively fluid and unsystematic when compared to sectarian practices. In Govardhan's main temple, the place where locals say the hill's mouth (*mukharavinda*) is located, the temple image is composed of two Govardhan stones, treated half like a temple icon and half not.[51] For most of the day the stones are left unadorned so that pilgrims can enter the temple and feed them directly with their own hands. Local Brahmans act as guides in this process, in contrast to the way officiants might be expected to act in temples that house consecrated icons. Foods offered are simple sweets and milk—not the products of a sophisticated temple cuisine, but foods bought in the marketplace and associated with feelings of pleasure, well-being, and auspiciousness (*śubha*), in the festive and ceremonial cycle of North India.[52] Folksongs and pilgrimage ditties, like the *Govardhan Cālīsa* (a forty-line prayer sung by pilgrims), mention foods by name and express the idea that Krishna is a simple peasant who shares pilgrims' food in a spirit of joyous, easy reciprocity.

This same flexibility is demonstrated in numerous other local food practices. Priests and pilgrims generally admit to a relaxed view of ritual: "Ritual implies a distance of some sort between man and god. This distance has no place at Govardhan, where both man and god are part of nature. Images in this temple are *svayaṃ prakaṭ*, that is, spontaneously manifested in nature, without need of priestly intervention to establish them in the temple or to maintain their sanctity in the future."[53] Practices in the local temple attenuate the daily format followed in iconic worship. Unlike icons, which are dressed first thing in the morning and served eight or so daily meals, the mukharavinda temple's stones are dressed only after four o'clock, when the heaviest hours of pilgrimage traffic are over. Only then do the stones appear as anthropomorphic likenesses, with enamel eyes and artificial limbs attached, wearing brightly colored clothes, crowns, and silver jewelry. Similarly, the eight meals of standard temple worship are abbreviated to three: sweets in the morning, a noontime meal of grains and pulses, and warm milk and more sweets at night. The temple does not have kitchen facilities per se; meals are purchased from vendors in the market and offered by pandas without any provisions to shield the images from public view.

Pilgrims are allowed considerable latitude in how they choose to worship in the temple. Those who can afford it bring clothes and jewelry for the temple images and worship them with large amounts of rich and varied foods, pails full of milk, incense, fresh flowers, and so on. Others, with less means at their disposal, offer small clay thimbles of milk and popcorn-size bits of puffed sugar with cardamom seed centers. Finally, as I mentioned earlier in connection with the Annakuta celebration, the aesthetic environment in local temples is particularly charged on festival days. For commercial reasons, temples are draped in strings of colored bulbs on these occasions. With their varied and extravagant food displays and the many songs and performances all around, these festivals create, through a pleasant blend of music, food, and pageantry, a savory experience of Lord Krishna for pilgrims.

Conclusion

My approach in this essay accepts the constructionist view that affects correspond with the societies within which actors live and that they can best be explained with reference to cultural scenarios and associations. The foregoing analysis described the overlapping cultural meaning systems through which emotions are constituted in three devotional groups at Mount Govardhan. Such an approach differs, in several important respects, from standard assumptions about emotion in Western academic psychology: that it is possible to identify the essence of emotion, that emotions are universal and hence easily translatable across cultures, and that they are separable from their personal and social contexts.[54] In contrast, here one faces a complex system of symbols, values, and definitions, which are culturally specific and in terms of which emotions are conceptualized and interpreted by Krishna worshippers. My point is that the culturally appropriate categorization of emotion within a whole context of implicit meaning allows members of each tradition to know what their experience of emotion is and even how to feel it and to know what they ought to experience in it. The task has been to examine what devotees say and do in everyday life to express, enact, and interpret emotions. Findings indicate that emotions such as maternal and erotic love are clearly constituted within a different framework of social relationships and cultural knowledge than emotions referred to by the same name would be in contemporary American society.

If one accepts, then, that there is no single universal mode of appraisal for such cultural features as emotion, one might want to conclude by making some general remarks about the system of appraisal described in this chapter and how this system differs from certain preconceived Western notions. First, in bhakti, emotion is constituted through interactions and transactions of various sorts: between man and god, between members of the same sect, and so on. At times human-divine relationships are conceived in idioms borrowed from family and social life; at other times, they are conceived in opposition to these same idioms, as in the case of the illicit love of Radha-Krishna. Second, this interactive focus also presupposes an enduring cultural concern with reciprocity as a process that animates life. Love, in these terms, has nothing static about it, nor is it based on fixed bonds; rather, it is effective in the experiential sense only when constantly circulating.

Perhaps the most notable aspect of this cultural system is the way these properties of emotion are objectified or substantialized for devotees through food symbols and practices.[55] In the Western cultural formulation emotion is conceived as an inherently irrational aspect of life and talked about in metaphors that center on ideas of chaos. In contrast, Hindu metaphors for emotion center on food and semantic similarities between emotion as an experience and the bodily experiences of eating and nurturing. Actors' understandings of emotion in Braj are not shaped, as they are in the West, by dichotomies between the head and the heart, between conscious and unconscious mind, or between the psychology of individuals and the shared psychological experience of social groups.

And last, can one identify the essence of an emotion? Is there, for example, some identifiable aspect of biological motherhood that can be said to inform the experience of motherly love in all cultures? The data presented here indicate that cultural definitions of emotion are highly variable, even within the confines of a single location or homogeneous religious setting like Govardhan. What makes comparison of these three traditions so exciting—but difficult, alas, to describe with complete coherence—is the quality of difference that underlies the system as a whole. First, the traditions have contrasting social contexts (attitudes toward caste, asceticism, and so on), historical backgrounds, and ties to different regions of India. Second, their views on many finer points of emotional theory, even in regard to emotions bearing the same name, are not parallel in many instances. And finally, though one discerns the same set of culinary metaphors and metonyms (themes derived from rasa theory, for example, and the Govardhan myth) weaving through all three traditions, each tradition is nevertheless equally distinguishable by the model of emotional experience it favors and the stories and rituals it employs to shape this experience for devotees. In my opinion, anthropologists will better understand the complex phenomenon of emotion, not by searching for universal features, as many earlier studies do, but by documenting the diverse means by which emotion is culturally constructed and symbolically mediated to actors in specific social and cultural contexts.

NOTES

Data on which this chapter is based were gathered at Mount Govardhan in 1978–80 under the auspices of an American Institute of Indian Studies Junior Research Fellowship. I have benefited from comments made by Peter Bennett, Veena Das, Alan Entwistle, Jack Hawley, R. S. Khare, Pauline Kolenda, and Arvind Shah on earlier versions of this essay. I am especially grateful to Owen Lynch for the tremendous amount of time he has given in helping me edit and refocus arguments in this chapter.

1. Owen M. Lynch, "The Mastram: Emotion and Person among Mathura's Chaubes," in Owen M. Lynch (ed.), *Divine Passions: The Social Construction of Emotion in India* (Berkeley: University of California Press, 1990), 91–115; Friedhelm Hardy, *Viraha--Bhakti: The Early History of Krsna Devotion in South India* (Delhi: Oxford University Press, 1983).

2. These sects (sampradaya) are known by a variety of names in Western sources. Vallabhites, or Vallabacaryis, as they have been called by Weber, refer to their sect as Pushti Marg. Chaitanyaites, referred to as Bengali Vaishnavas in a now familiar work in English by De (Sushil Kamar De, *Vaishnava Faith and Movement in Bengal* [Calcutta: Firma Mukhopadyay, 1961]), refer to themselves as Mddhaa-Gaufya-Vaisnaaa. This title refers to the fact that these Vaishnavas are most commonly found in Gauda country (Bengal) and follow the philosophy of the South Indian saint, Madhva. Given the complex comparative framework of this chapter, for the sake of convenience, I go back to an earlier scholarly convention of referring to the sects by the names of their founder-saints, Vallabha and Chaitanya.

3. Lila Abu-Lughod, *Veiled Sentiments: Honor and Poetry in a Bedouin Society* (Berkeley: University of California Press, 1986); Catherine Lutz, "Ethnopsychology Compared to What? Explaining Behavior and Consciousness among the Ifaluk," in Geoffrey M. White and John Kirkpatrick (eds.), *Person, Self, and Experience: Exploring Pacific Ethnopsychologies* (Berkeley: University of California Press, 1985), 35–79, and *Unnatural Emotions: Everyday Sentiments on a Micronesian Atoll and Their Challenge to Western Theory* (Chicago: University of Chicago Press, 1988); Sulamith Heins Potter, "The Cultural Construction of Emotion in Rural Chinese Social Life," *Ethos* 16 no. 2 (1988): 181–208; Michelle Rosaldo, *Knowledge and Passion: Illongot Notions of Self and Social Life* (Cambridge, UK: Cambridge University Press, 1980); Edward L. Schieffelin, *The Sorrow of the Lonely and the Burning of the Dancers* (New York: St. Martin's, 1976).

4. V. Raghavan, *An Introduction to Indian Poetics* (Bombay: Macmillan, 1970) and *The Number of Rasa* (Bombay: Macmillan, 1976); see also the following chapters in Owen M. Lynch (ed.), *Divine Passions*: Owen M. Lynch, "The Social Construction of Emotion in India" (3–36); Peter Bennett, "In Nanda Baba's House: The Devotional Experience in Pushti Marg Temples" (182–211); Frédérique Apffel Marglin, "Refining the Body: Transformative Emotion in Ritual Dance" (212–238); Charles R. Brooks,

"Hare Krishna, Radhe Shyam: The Cross-cultural Dynamics of Mystical Emotions in Brindaban" (262–286).

5. Kenneth E. Bryant, *Poems to the Child-God* (Berkeley: University of California Press, 1978).

6. Peter Bennett, "Temple Organization and Worship among the Pustimargiya-Vaisnavas of Ujjain" (PhD dissertation, School of Oriental and African Studies, University of London, 1983).

7. A. W. Entwistle, *Braj: Centre of Krishna Pilgrimage* (Groningen: Egbert Forsten, 1987), 96–103; Norvin Hein, "Comments: Radha and Erotic Community," in John Stratton Hawley and Donna Marie Wulff (eds.), *The Divine Consort: Radha and the Goddesses of India* (Berkeley: Berkeley Religious Studies Series, 1982), 116–124 and "A Revolution in Krsnaism: The Cult of Gopala," *History of Religions* 25 no. 4 (1986): 296–317; Joseph T. O'Connell, "Caitanya's Followers and the Bhagavad Gita," in Bardwell L. Smith (ed.), *Hinduism: New Essays in the History of Religion* (Leiden: E. J. Brill, 1976), 33–52.

8. Michelle Rosaldo, "Towards an Anthropology of Self and Feeling," in Richard A. Shweder and Robert A. LeVine (eds.), *Culture Theory: Essays on Mind, Self, and Society* (Cambridge, UK: Cambridge University Press, 1984), 137–157; Catherine Lutz, "Emotion, Thought, and Estrangement: Emotion as a Cultural Category," *Cultural Anthropology* 1 no. 3 (1986): 287–309.

9. Edward M. Bruner, "Experience and Its Expressions," in Victor W. Turner and Edward M. Bruner (eds.), *The Anthropology of Experience* (Urbana: University of Illinois Press, 1986), 1–16.

10. Owen M. Lynch, "Pilgrimage with Krishna, Sovereign of the Emotions," *Contributions to Indian Sociology,* n.s. 22 no. 2 (1988): 171–194; Prabhudayal Mital, *Braj ka Samskrtik Itihasa* (Delhi: Rajkamal Prakasan, 1966).

11. Raymond B. Williams, *A New Face of Hinduism: The Swami Narayan Religion* (Cambridge, UK: Cambridge University Press, 1984). Charles R. Brooks, "Hare Krishna, Radhe Shyam: The Cross-cultural Dynamics of Mystical Emotions in Brindaban," in Owen M. Lynch (ed.), *Divine Passions: The Social Construction of Emotion in India* (Berkeley: University of California Press, 1990): 262–286.

12. A. K. Ramanujan, *Hymns for the Drowning: Poems for Vishnu by Nammalvar* (Princeton: Princeton University Press, 1981).

13. De.; Raghavan, *The Number of Rasa.*

14. James L. Masson and M. V. Pathwardhan, *Aesthetic Rapture* (Poona: Deccan College Post Graduate and Research Institute, 1969).

15. James Redington, *Vallabhacarya on the Love Games of Krsna* (Delhi: Motilal Banarsidass, 1983), 11.

16. Raghavan, *The Number of Rasa* and *An Introduction to Indian Poetics.*

17. David Haberman, "Entering the Cosmic Drama: Lila-Smarana Meditation and the Perfected Body," *South Asia Research* 5 no. 1 (1985): 49–53.

18. J. David Sapir, ("An Anatomy of Metaphor," in J. David Sapir and J. Christopher Crocker, (eds.), *The Social Use of Metaphor* (Philadelphia: University of Pennsylvania Press, 1977), 3–32 explains that the contrast between metaphor and metonym represents, at the level of figurative language, a contrast between paradigmatic replacement (for metaphor) and syntagmatic continuity or combination (for metonymy).

The same author also says that, with respect to the notion of a shared domains or a common ground, metonymy can be taken as the logical inverse of metaphor. Metaphor is the relationship of two terms from separate domains that share overlapping features; metonymy is the relationship of two terms that share a common ground but do not share common features. Metonymies are usually identified by their substitution of one cause for another: agent for act, cause for effect, container for contained.

19. George Lakoff and Mark Johnson, *Metaphors We Live By* (Chicago: University of Chicago Press, 1980); Johannes Fabian, *Time and the Other: How Anthropology Makes Its Object* (New York: Columbia University Press, 1983) incisively attacks the use of visual metaphor in anthropological discourse. He contends that persistent recourse to visualization has denied ethnographers understanding of more temporal aspects of the cultural Other, such as might come about through increased sensitivity to language.

20. Stephen Tyler, "The Vision Quest, or What the Mind's Eye Sees," *Journal of Anthropological Research* 40 no. 1 (1984): 23–40 provides examples of gustatory tropes in Standard Average European thought and language. For instance, we "ruminate," "digest thoughts," "chew the cud," and even find some thoughts "hard to swallow." Tyler also alerts us to the fact that one major verb for knowing in the Romance language is *sapere*, "to savor, or taste." This he attributes to the well-known Latin and Gallic preference for gustatory sensation.

21. Hariray (Gosvāmī Harirīy), *Śrigovardhannathjī ke Prākatya kī Varta*, edited by Mohanlāl Visnulā Pandya (Bombay: Śrīvenkateśvar Yantrālaya, 1905). See Charlotte Vaudeville, "The Govardhan Myth in North India," *Indo-Iranian Journal* 22 (1980): 1–45 for more examples of these episodes. This author hints at the deconstructionist possibilities inherent in sectarian literature, where, through a number of insertions and deletions, the sectarian view of Sri Nathji as a pampered and worldly prince is undermined by folk conceptions of him as a local ruffian. Thus, Krishna's princely and knavish sides often appear incongruously juxtaposed in the same episode of a sectarian text.

22. The *Govinda Deva* icon of the Chaitanyaite and the *Sri Nathji* icon of the Vallabhite sects were both manifest in this way. In Braj folklore, streams of milk are said to miraculously appear in Govardhan's main bathing pond, Manasi Ganga, during full moon. Folk beliefs in the auspicious qualities of milk are reflected in the pilgrimage practice of walking fourteen miles around the hill, dripping a continuous stream of milk from a hole bored in the bottom of a vessel. The vessel needs to be constantly refilled by one's priest, who ambles alongside for the entire journey.

23. O.B.L. Kapoor, *The Philosophy and Life of Śrī Caitanya* (Delhi: Munshiram Manoharlal, 1977).

24. There is a compelling illustration of this in Govardhan lore. Govardhan hill, it is recounted, was so devoted to Krishna during his lifetime in Braj that it turned into a lump of butter. This is why imprints of his footprints, crown, mouth, and so on can still be seen today as geomorphic impressions in the hill's stones.

25. In his childhood Krishna steals milk and curds from his mother and other women in the neighborhood of Braj. Later, the comely adolescent taunts the milk-maids for their dairy products in the familiar episode known as the *danghdta-lala*. In this lila Krishna masquerades as a toll collector to trick the unwitting maidens as they

take their wares to market. At the height of the fun, he unmasks himself, smashing all the pots and drenching the revelers in milk, butter, and curds. This festive event is reenacted from time to time at Barsana, another popular pilgrimage town in Braj reputed to be Radha's birthplace.

26. John Stratton Hawley, *Krishna, the Butter Thief* (Princeton: Princeton University Press, 1983).

27. Lewis Hyde, *The Gift: Imagination and the Erotic Life of Property* (New York: Vintage Books, 1979).

28. Seeing is an extrusive process for Hindus, an outward-reaching process that in one way actually engages (in a flowlike manner) the object seen (Lawrence A. Babb, "Glancing: Visual Interaction in Hinduism," *Journal of Anthropological Research* 37 no. 4 [1981]: 47–64). See Lynch, "Pilgrimage with Krishna, Sovereign of the Emotions," on further aspects of darśana as seeing and its relationship to bhāva, bhāvanā, and rasa in Braj pilgrimage.

29. Informants say that prasada is actually heavier than bhoga because it has added to it the weight of the lord's sweet love. Pious devotees are reputed to be able to tell the difference between potential offerings and those that have already been offered to and consumed by Krishna through "feeling tones" in the food itself. Peter Bennett, "In Nanda Baba's House: The Devotional Experience in Pushti Marg Temples," in Lynch, *Divine Passions*, 182–211.

30. These metonymies take the form of synecdoches: the trope formed when a part is substituted for the whole. In speech, the names Krishna and Govardhan are used interchangeably to refer to both Krishna and the sacred hill. In ritual, a single stone from the hill often substitutes for the whole. Synecdoche is also characteristic of other sorts of ritual practices. For example, only a portion of food cooked each day in temples is actually offered in front of the temple image. After it is offered, prasada is then mixed with the remaining cooked food, transforming it, by contact, into *firasada*.

31. Ramanujan, *Hymns for the Drowning*, maintains that this circular motif is common in Hindu myth and ritual. He refers to it as an act of "mutual cannibalism," wherein the eater is eaten and the container contained, in a repeated metonymy.

32. Babu Lal Sharma, Das Bisa Mohalla, Govardhan, interview, October 22, 1979.

33. Richard C. Solomon, "Getting Angry: The Jamesian Theory of Emotion in Anthropology," in Richard A. Shweder and Robert A. LeVine (eds.), *Culture Theory: Essays on Mind, Self, and Society* (Cambridge, UK: Cambridge University Press, 1984), 238–254; Margaret Trawick, "The Ideology of Love in a Tamil Family" in Lynch, *Divine Passions*, 37–63; Sylvia Vatuk, " 'To Be a Burden on Others': Dependency Anxiety among the Elderly in India," in Lynch, *Divine Passions*, 64–91.

34. See Richard Barz, *The Bhakti Sect of Vallabhacarya* (Delhi: Thompson Press, 1976) and Redington, *Vallabhacarya on the Love Games of Krsna*, for differing opinions on bhava in this sect.

35. Bennett, "In Nanda Baba's House"; Paul M. Toomey, "Food from the Mouth of Krishna: Socio-Religious Aspects of Food in Two Krishnaite Sects," in R. S. Khare and M. S. A. Rao (eds.), *Food, Culture and Society: Aspects in South Asian Food Systems* (Durham, NC: Carolina Academic Press, 1986), 55–83.

36. Sylvia Vatuk, "Forms of Address in the North Indian Family: An Explanation of the Cultural Meaning of Kin Terms," in Akos Ostor, Lina Fruzzetti, and Steve Barnett (eds.), *Concepts of Person: Kinship, Caste, and Marriage in India* (Delhi: Oxford University Press, 1982), 56–98; Das.

37. This process of deindividualization is rather strikingly reflected in Hindi kinship terminology, where the use of the mother term (*mā*) is reserved, not for the natural mother herself, but for a senior woman of the family, usually the mother-in-law. Vatuk notes that this strategic pattern of address mitigates against the possibility of a mother-child unit asserting its independence against the family as a whole.

38. Vatuk, 95.

39. Bennett, "Temple Organization and Worship among the Pustimargiya-Vaisnavas of Ujjain."

40. Prabhudayal Mital, *Braj kī Kalaom kā Itihāsa* (Mathura: Sāhitya Samsthan, 1975); Raghunath Śivajī (ed.), *Vallabha Pusti Prakāśa* (Bombay: Laksmivenkateśvar Steam Press, 1936).

41. Another interpretation has it that the number fifty-six symbolizes all possible food in the cosmos. By their reckoning there are fourteen worlds (*lokas*) in the universe and four basic substances-beverages, foods that do not require chewing, foods that are chewed, and those that are licked.

42. Goswami Krishnajivanji, interview at Jatipura, September 14, 1979.

43. Sudhir Kakar, "Erotic Fantasy: The Secret Passion of Radha and Krishna," in Veena Das (ed.), *The Word and the World* (New Delhi: Sage Publications, 1986), 75–94.

44. In some representations (e.g., *Jugal Kiśor, Śyāma-Syām, and Lārilī-Lāl*) Radha and Krishna are conjoined in a single icon; in others, a small icon of Radha is placed at the side of Krishna, who stands in the classic *tribhangi* posture (his body bent in three places, with his head to one side, his upper body twisted, and his right calf crossed in front of his left with the ball of his right foot resting on the ground); in still further variants, Radha's presence is signified by her name or a coronet only, placed on a cushion beside Krishna's solo image (Entwistle, 79).

45. A study of these two very different interpretations of the same emotion and their effect on ritual performances in each branch of the sect would make an interesting topic for future study. For example, large food offerings and displays are found in temples run by Chaitanyaite gosvamis in Brindaban, something one might never see among ascetics at Radhakund. In one such temple, Brindaban's Radharaman Temple, the largest food offering is the "Thirty-Six Delicacies" (*Chattisa-Vyanjana*), a feast described in Braj poetry inspired by the erotic sentiment. In this offering, a carved wooden figure of each gopi is displayed holding a dish in hand; thus, each cowmaiden is believed to provide Krishna a unique and different amorous experience, here expressed in gastronomic terms. See Frédérique Apffel Marglin, "Refining the Body: Transformative Emotion in Ritual Dance" in Lynch, *Divine Passions*.

46. Lynch, "The Mastram: Emotion and Person Among Mathura's Chaubes."

47. Narayana Maharaj, interview at Radhakund, January 12, 1980.

48. Compare Eliot Singer's "Conversion through Foodways Enculturation: The Meaning of Eating in an American Hindu Sect," in Linda Keller Brown and Kay Mussell (eds.), *Ethnic and Regional Foodways in the United States* (Knoxville: University of

Tennessee Press, 1984), 37–52 data on food categories and the semiotic structure of meals in an ISKCON temple in metropolitan Philadelphia.

49. Audrey Hayley, "A Commensal Relationship with God: The Nature of the Offering in Assamese Vaishnavism," in M.F.C. Bourdillon and Meyer Fortes (eds.), *Sacrifice* (London: Academic Press, 1980), 42–62.

50. This point is rather nicely illustrated in the popular image of Krishna as "mountain holder" (*Govardhannāth* or *Giridhārī*), one of the first images to appear in Krishna iconography. This image derives once again from an episode in the Govardhan myth. Briefly summarized, after Annakuta was offered, the Vedic god Indra, for whom the offering was originally intended, felt insulted and pelted Braj with rain for seven days and nights. To protect the locals, Krishna held the mountain aloft on his fingertip, umbrella-style, above the entire region. The notion that the hill encompasses all emotional experience is visually reinforced in this important and widely revered image of Krishna.

51. Local pandas explain that one stone is standing Krishna, with impressions of Krishna's crown (*mukut*) in it; the second, a low-lying stone, is said to be Mount Govardhan, complete with the imprint of a mouth. Reflected in this ritual image is the same bifurcated image alluded to in the Govardhan myth. The two stones are seen as one, each a devotee of the other: standing Krishna as devotee of the lower stone, Govardhan hill, and vice versa. They are dressed as mirror images each afternoon, with identical faces, costumes, and jewelry. The fact that these twin images are located in a large pond at the center of the hill further enhances this mirror effect. Sylvia Vatuk and Ved Vatuk, "Chatorpan: A Culturally Defined Form of Addiction in North India," in Ved Vatuk (ed.), *Studies in North Indian Folk Traditions* (Delhi: Manohar, 1979), 177–189 discuss the symbolic importance of sweets in the social and ritual life of North India: "The role of sweets in lubricating all types of social intercourse in this part of India, and the mental association created by this role, have been discussed here to demonstrate that frequent and heavy consumption of sweets is conceived of, in this culture, as an activity of very positive value and, in fact, as an obligatory activity in terms of the individual's successful participation in his community's social and ritual life."

52. T. N. Madan, *Non-Renunciation: Themes and Interpretations in Hindu Culture* (Delhi: Oxford University Press, 1987), 48–71.

53. Shrivatsa Goswami, interview at Jaisingh Ghera, Brindaban, January 30, 1979.

54. Lutz, "Emotion, Thought, and Estrangement: Emotion as a Cultural Category," and Lynch, "The Social Construction of Emotion in India."

55. Clifford Geertz, *Local Knowledge: Further Essays in Interpretive Anthropology* (New York: Basic Books, 1983), 94–120.

9

Emotion in Bengali Religious Thought: Substance and Metaphor

June McDaniel

The bhakti *traditions of Bengal sacralize emotion, encouraging its culti-*
vation through various devotional practices, seeking to deepen it because
they hold that intense emotion is a pathway to God. Approaching Ben-
gali religious life from an ethnopsychological perspective, June McDaniel
observes that although the traditions of Vedanta and Ayurveda value wis-
dom over feeling, much Indian religion, especially in modern India, is
emotional. Focusing on the language of emotion in Sanskrit and Bengali,
she outlines the various meanings of bhava, *stressing that it refers to "an*
emotional complex, a form of experience" associated with religious ecstat-
ics and their followers. Especially important in the Bengali understanding
of emotion are metaphors of heat and water, which variously nuance pas-
sion, desire, pain, and joy. The raw emotion of bhava *can be transformed*
into a more refined essence, rasa, *which is represented as sap, juice, or*
taste, and to some extent objectified, treated as a distant or separate phe-
nomenon, a person "feeling as if he or she felt the emotion but not being
involved enough to feel it directly." Emotions are often known through
bodily changes such as trembling, fainting, paralysis, and weeping, and
the overall tendency in Bengali understanding of emotion is to view it as
substance, as part of the ocean of all that the universe is, that can be
accessed and used to strengthen the self or to build an alternate personal-
ity. Emotions are not experienced passively, but willfully and creatively
disciplined, arranged, and combined to shape a perfected spiritual self.

How do Bengali ideas about emotion differ from those held by Westerners? What role do emotions play in Bengali religion? In what ways do the transformation of the self and the refinement of emotion proceed apace in Bengali devotionalism? How is emotion represented as both spiritual essence and material substance? Is emotion intertwined with cognition in Bengali religious thought? Can one both distance oneself from the experience of emotion and at the same time claim it, as in the case of rasa? How does this understanding compare with Western thinking about the self and emotional experience? How does the Bengali trust in the active participation of the person as agent in creating and governing emotional life differ from Western ideas about emotion as passively experienced?

[Emotions in India] are more likely to be objectified or substantialized, than somatized as in China, or internalized, as forces, drives, or instincts [as] in the West. . . . Contrary to Western stereotypes about India, and contrary to the Western devaluation of emotion in the face of reason, India finds emotions, like food, necessary for a reasonable life, and, like taste, cultivatable for the fullest understanding of life's meaning and purpose.

—Owen Lynch, *Divine Passions*

This essay focuses on Bengali ethnopsychology and some indigenous understandings of emotional events. The ethnological goal is not to relate or reduce the indigenous model to other theoretical perspectives but rather, to examine how cultural and folk models interpret and express experience.

Emotion is variously viewed in both positive and negative ways in the Indian religious and philosophical traditions. In those traditions that are ascetic and emphasize mental control, emotions are distractions that need to be stilled. In those traditions emphasizing love of a deity, emotions are valuable but they must be directed and transformed.

This essay begins by presenting background on some early Indian traditions that understand emotion to be a distraction from clear perception and that also form a foundation for the "fluid" understanding of the world shown by later devotional traditions. It then surveys some of the major Sanskrit and Bengali terms used to express emotion. The essay then moves to a description of the Alaṅkāraśhāstra[1] and the Bengali Vaiṣṇava and Sahajiyā devotional traditions and comments on some differences between the Indian and Western approaches to emotion.

There is a stereotypical view in the West that Indian religion opposes emotion. This is because some of the oldest traditions in India Vedanta, Yoga, and Āyurveda hold this position. However, it is important to note that these traditions are not dominant in modern India and have not been dominant for centuries. I briefly discuss their views, however, to use them as background material.

Vedanta is the philosophy of the Vedic and Upanishadic texts. According to the *advaita* or monistic form of Vedanta, the ultimate state is a world-ground, a tranquil ocean of consciousness. It is disturbed by illusion (*māyā*), by the world of names and forms, which creates ignorance. Emotion is a part of that world of becoming, that changing universe which does not allow the person to perceive things as they really are, merged in *brahman* (infinite reality, knowledge, and bliss). The Vedantin seeks wisdom (*jñāna*) to the exclusion of emotion and renounces attachment to the illusory world. Emotion muddies the waters, disrupting awareness and distracting the sage.

A second ancient tradition is the classical yoga of Patañjali. In *sūtra* I.2 of the *Yoga Sūtras*, Patañjali gives the definition of yoga: "*Yogaś citta-vṛtti-nirodhaḥ*" (Yoga is the control or dissolution of the fluctuations of the mind).[2] The mind is understood as a field or ocean of consciousness (*citta*), which is ideally peaceful and still. However, in most human beings it is full of changes, waves, and eddies. These changes, or fluctuations, are the *vṛittis,* which disturb the clarity of the mind. Some changes are of external origin, from the physical world, and some are internal, arising from memory and impression (*saṃskāra*).

According to Patañjali's yoga, these memory impressions may become inclinations or propensities of the personality (*vāsanās*), accompanied by repeated habits of thought. The associated mental fluctuations become laden with emotion and are called *kleśhas*, impurities or afflictions. There are five kleśhas: ignorance, desire, hatred, fear (especially fear of death), and pride (the sense of the self as an individual entity).[3] These should be avoided: the yogi should control his emotions, withdrawing his perceptions and concerns into himself as a turtle pulls his legs inside of his shell.

The mind is often compared to a river or ocean. According to the commentary of Vyāsa on Patañjali's *Yoga Sūtras* "The river called mind flows in two directions": toward the world of desire (*saṃsāra*) and toward the world of peace (called *kaivalya,* or isolation from the turbulence of daily life). The mindstream, or river of consciousness (*citta-nadī*), needs to be directed and one-pointed, and one way to direct the river is to dam it through dispassion (*vairāgya*).[4]

A third source is Āyurveda, the medical tradition of India, which is based on the balance of the three humors in the body.[5] When these liquids have left their normal channels, they become imbalanced (and are then called faults, *doṣas*), and the person becomes ill. When the flow is imbalanced, the mind can become intoxicated by these humors, and passions and mental disorganization may result.

According to Caraka, one of the most important writers in the *Āyurvedic* system, the person is born with three basic desires: the desire for life (self-preservation), the desire for wealth, and the desire for a good afterlife. Other emotions (envy, grief, fear, anger, pride, hatred) are due to confusion or perversion of the understanding (*prajñaparādh*). Confusion, when combined with lack of self-control and lapse of memory, causes humoral imbalance and mental and physical illness. The humors then attack the heart and obstruct perception and sensation. This causes emotional disturbance and insanity, with their hallucination, delusion, and maladjustment to the social environment. Such disturbance may also be caused by strong desires that are unfulfilled. Whereas dejection and grief aggravate disease, joy and contentment cure it.[6] Pleasure comes from organic equilibrium, and pain, from organic disequilibrium. Liquids link the system together, keep the bodily channels running smoothly, and balance the various aspects of the person.

These three traditions provide a basis for the negative view of emotion in India—a view that is different from that held by the popular culture and devotional religions of West Bengal.

The Language of Emotion

> The process of coming to understand the emotional lives of people in different cultures can be seen first and foremost as a problem of translation. . . . The interpretive task, then, is not primarily to fathom somehow "what they are feeling inside," . . . but rather to translate emotional communications from one idiom, context, language, or sociohistorical mode of understanding into another.[7]

Translation and interpretation between cultures, and between systems of thought and belief, are difficult endeavors. This section does not deal with all of the complexities of hermeneutics and cross-cultural communication, but focuses on language and how it expresses the nature of emotion.

In the Sanskrit and Bengali languages, there is no exact term for emotion. The term used most frequently for it is *bhāva* or *anubhāva* (the physical expression of the state of bhāva). Sometimes the terms *rāga* or *ābeg* are used, which refer to intense emotions or passions. In the yogic literature we see the term *vedanā*, of Pali origin. It refers to a feeling, usually of a negative kind, such as pain or sorrow.

The term bhāva has many referents: the Monier-Williams *Sanskrit Dictionary* has four large columns of definitions for bhāva, and the *Bāngālā Bhāṣār Abhidhān* dictionary has two columns. Definitions in the *Samsad Bengali-English Dictionary* include mental state, mood, emotion, condition, love, friendship, ecstasy, rapture, passion, inner significance, essence, and existence—thus covering a wide range of phenomena.

Bhāva is an emotional complex, a form of experience, with connotations of associated perception, thought, movement, and expression. It is a way of being, a sense of identity which may be individual or shared. It is believed in many of the Bengali devotional traditions that religious ecstatics can create waves of bhāva (bhāva-taranga), which can spread through crowds of people, causing them all to share in the ecstatic's intense emotions.[8] The person who is bhāvāveśh is possessed by bhāva, either intensely emotional or taking on the bhāva (the emotion and identity) of a deity or other being. The person may be bhāva lāgā (affected by an emotion or idea), bhāva prabaṇ (emotional, senti-mental, maudlin), or bhāva bihbul (overwhelmed with emotion or ecstasy). As terms derived from bhāva, bhāvana is thought, meditation, creation, and vi-sualization, and bhāvanā is thought and contemplation but also worry and anxiety (the term is used in the Indian medical tradition for the repeated mac-eration, pulverization, and purification of herbal medicine—an interesting metaphor for analytic thought).

While doing fieldwork in West Bengal, in eastern India, from 1983 to 1984, I asked informants for definitions of bhāva. Some of these popular definitions follow:

Bhāva is that aspect of mind which deals with emotion and experi-ence; it is a result of culture and personality. It is only emotion—it does not include images, which are only fantasy. Yogis may develop stages and faculties of bhāva. Any experience can be called a bhāva, but the highest bhāva, is brahmabhāva, a state of realistic expecta-tions, a poise in which a stable equilibrium is established. (Psychia-trist)

Bhāva is sentiment or emotion. It depends on the context—it may be used for poetry and art or for people—dujon bhāva, they are close. After fighting, children clasp fingers and say, "Bhāva, now we are friends." Bhāva is also inspired thought. (Grant administrator)

Bhāva has a material and a spiritual meaning. Its material meaning is love between a man and a woman, but spiritual bhāva is love of God by a devotee with all his mind and heart. (Insurance salesman)

Bhāva is very deep thought, deep in the heart, until one is lost within the self. The person becomes explosively pure in heart—he sees persons as other persons, such as all women as mother or sis-ter. There are three stages of bhāva in the worship of Śakti [the God-dess] bhāva, possession by bhāva [bhāvāveśh], and deep trance [bhāva samādhi] In bhāva, one becomes lost in memory and emotion. In possession by bhāva, one becomes lost from the material world and sees the heaven world. In the deepest trance of bhāva, one roams in the absolute [ātman]. (Travel agent)

Bhāva is when different parts of the person come together, as when cooking Kashmiri chicken. Different spices are blended together to create a taste. In love affairs [premer bhāva], the parts of the soul are mixed together like spices. The soul and mind consult each other, along with the body, to decide about loving. Good worship [pūjā] creates good bhāva between the devotee and the goddess, if the person believes 100 percent. There is a relation of soul between the deity and the worshipper—they share the same actions, and adjust to each other, even if there was conflict between them at the beginning. (Store owner)

Informants show an understanding of various stages or levels of bhāva, usually shifting its focus (from worldly goals to divine ones) and its degree of intensity (from lesser to greater passion). All of these are understood to be forms or transformations of emotional states.

In the Bengali and Sanskrit languages, terms for emotion and thought, mind and heart, are not opposed. Indeed, most frequently the same terms are used for both. A term often heard, *mana,* means both mind and heart, as well as mood, feeling, mental state, memory, desire, attachment, interest, attention, devotion, and decision. These terms do not have a single referent in English, and must be understood through clusters of explicit and implicit meanings.[9] Verbs based on mana include *mana kara* (to make up one's mind, to resolve or agree); *mana kāra* (to captivate the mind or win one's heart); and *mana kholā* (to speak one's mind or open one's heart).

A term used less frequently by informants, *hridaya,* means the heart as both organ and inner seat of feeling. The heart may be melted (when a play is *hridayadravakara,* touching or evoking pathos) or broken (the heart is pierced, *hridayabhedī*), and may overflow with an outburst of emotion (*hridayochvāsa*). A person unaffected by emotion may be called unfeeling or heartless (*hridaya-hīn*). The heart is also understood as a space or locale, in which persons or deities may dwell. Thus, we see the heart called a canvas for painting (*hridaya-paṭa*), a shrine or temple (*hridayamandir*), a seat for a loved one or deity (*hridayāsana*), or a space as broad as the sky (*hridayākāsh*). As one informant described it, his heart was an empty box that needed to be filled. In poetry, the loved one may live in the heart as in a garden; in worship, an aspect of the god may live there enthroned, surrounded by the devotee's love like an aura of light. The poet Rāmprasād Sen spoke of the "burning ground of the heart," and had visions of the goddess Kālī dancing there.[10] In *kuṇḍalinī yoga,* the heart is a doorway to the worlds of the spirit, as the *anāhata chakra* (heart center).[11]

There are several other terms often used in discussing emotion. *Rāga,* a term more well-known in the West as a mode of Indian classical music, also means passion, ranging from love and attachment to anger and rage. It has the meaning of dye or color (especially red), the soul is understood to be "dyed" by passion, which permeates it like a dye permeates cloth.[12] *Kāma* is desire, lust, and pleasure; *prema* is selfless or spiritual love. *Ābeg* means tremendous force, passionate outburst, intense feeling, uneasiness, and suspense; *anubhāva* refers to both power and physical expression of emotional states (such as tears and sighs). Yet emotion is *sūkṣmatā* (subtlety, delicacy, invisibility to the senses) as well as *komlatā* (gentleness, tenderness, softness). As *anubhuti*, it is both perception and intuition, realization and feeling.

The terms for thought, or cognition, often imply emotion. We have the word *cinta*, meaning thought, idea, and cogitation, with associated meanings of anxiety, worry, and fear. *Dhāraṇā* means idea, conception, memory, belief, impression, as well as feeling, and is associated with the term *dharana*, the act of holding, catching, wearing, carrying (thought is "borne" in the mind). *Anubhāva* means knowledge, perception, and realization but also feeling, and *kalpanā* refers to thought and imagination.

We see in these terms and definitions that emotion is a powerful force which is at the same time subtle and delicate, invisible to the senses yet capable of generating physical expressions, associated with perception, intuition, and realization. There is no sharp distinction between emotion and cognition. Thought is associated with knowledge and discrimination, and the mind grasps and holds memories and ideas. Yet thought is associated with feelings, especially anxiety,[13] as well as imagination.

Bhāva in itself is a complex term with a range of meanings, from a broad understanding of experience and identity (bhāva as a way of being) to a specific bhāva, an emotion or thought that is clearly defined. Using the same term for these events shows that the range of experience—emotion, mood, identity, mental state—is understood as a continuum rather than a collection of distinct and opposed categories. Both emotion and thought are part of the wider category of bhāva.

The Metaphors of Emotion: Fire and Water

> Swept away by rivers of love
> (swelling floods of their desire)
> Torrents dammed by their elders
> (propriety all parents require)
> Close they stand, anxious but still
> (hiding passions, restraining sights)
> Lovers drink nectars from the blossoms
> (the love that pours from lotus eyes).
>
> —Amaruśataka[14]

Metaphorically, emotion has been linked with both fire and water in Indian religious literature. I think that a brief exploration of these metaphors would give some insight into the nature of emotion in the Bengali devotional traditions.

The metaphor of emotional heat is an old idea in India, going back to Vedic times (2000–1500 B.C.E). Vedic sages, or *ṛiṣhis*, sought to control *tapas* (the universal energy of creation and destruction). Tapas comes from the Sanskrit root *tap*, whose most literal meaning is "to be hot" or "to create heat."[15] The heat of tapas could transform both the world and the person, and its dynamic forms include lustful heat, jealous heat, devotional heat, sorrowful heat, and the heat of hatred and anger. The sage was believed to be capable of burning animals and people with his glance if angry—the emotion would return to its original form as heat. Tapas is also the heat of the sacrifice and the force behind creation, linking together the divine and human worlds. In the Vedic creation hymn, the "Nāsadīya Sukta" (*Ṛig Veda* X.29.4), desire (kāma) is born out of tapas.

While the energy of tapas is closely linked with desire and emotion, the term also refers to an ascetic practice used to suppress emotion. Ascetics try to "burn away" their emotional lives in the heat of tapas generated by mediation, and their worldly feelings are given up into the fire of the "inner sacrifice." Thus, they accumulate tapas as transformed emotion, and this tapas can give power, energy, and religious experience. The practice of tapas enables the sage to be indifferent to desire. Even today, some practitioners walk naked and cover themselves with ash from the burning ground to show how their emotions have been burnt away.

In the later *bhakti* (devotional) traditions, passion is said to burn the hearts of devotees, causing the person to be "on fire" for the god. Some saints have stated that their body would burn with fever for the deity for months or years on end. Rāmakṛiṣhṇa Paramahaṃsa, a recent Bengali Śhākta[16] saint, could not touch other people during his meditation on the deity, because his body was physically burning from passion, and he had to wear a sheet when approaching others. The Vaiṣhṇava saint Vijayakṛiṣhṇa Goswāmin, who rebelled against a Western education to return to yogic and devotional practices, felt unbearable heat during meditation. The desire for insight showed itself as *nāmāgni* (the fire of the Name of God), which he said caused his body to burn and his limbs to separate off and later return together. Saints in meditation are said to be "heated"; Ānandamayī Mā's disciples reported that her body caused great heat wherever she sat.[17]

The physical body is understood to be subject to mental and emotional heat. The Vaiṣhṇava saint Siddha Kṛiṣhṇadās was a visionary for whom the world of Kṛiṣhṇa's paradise was more real than the physical world. He would often see Kṛiṣhṇa's consort goddess Rādhā in visions, but when she refused to appear to him anymore, out of intense sorrow and force of will he set his body on fire.[18] We see a similar theme in the idea of *satī*. Many people in the West have heard of the Indian ritual in which the widow climbs on the funeral pyre of her husband, to die with him in the flames. In several early variants of the mythic story, the woman Satī was intensely angry and sorrowful over her father's poor treatment of her husband, Śiva, and she set herself on fire solely by yogic power. In this case, the visible fire was the expression of her inner emotions.[19] The chaste wife also has this power: in the Tamil story of Shilappadikāram, a woman whose husband was wrongfully prosecuted, caused the city to burn down.[20]

There are many folk beliefs that link emotion and heat. However, we also see the development over time of a link between emotion and liquid. The heart burns but it also melts; the person is on fire but softens. In the *Ṛig Veda*, rasa can be any fluid, but it is especially the fluid of life, associated with sexuality, passion, and blood.[21] The Vedantic "ocean of consciousness" uses a watery metaphor, as does the yogic "river of mind." As the tradition of bhakti grew up, heat became associated with the pain of separation, and water, with the joy of love in union. Remedies for the "burning sorrow" of separation included garlands, wet compresses, moist sandalwood paste, and cool breezes. The beloved "cooled the heat" of the lover, and the waves of love represented the forces that drew the lovers together. Whereas earlier metaphors of emotion focused on heat, the focus later shifted to water and/or liquid, which came to be seen as an emotional vehicle in its own right.

The Nature of Emotion Bhāva and Rasa

> Having thoughts of intense passion about you [Kṛishṇa], the deer-eyed woman is immersed in an ocean of passionate bliss [rasa] fixed in meditation.
>
> —Jayadeva, *Gīta Govinda*, VI.10

The most extensive analyses of emotion in Indian religion and philosophy have probably come from the writers of the Alaṇkāraśhāstra, the Sanskrit literary tradition that focuses on aesthetic experience, and from the Vaiṣhṇava tradition, which emphasizes religious emotion. For both traditions, aesthetic emotion is rasa, which is experienced by the person of taste (*rasika*) during identification with a dramatic character or situation. According to the Alaṇkāra, the spectator is totally involved in the dramatic event and feels an emotion that is powerful, extraordinary (*alaukika*), yet impersonal and generic. It is joyful rather than pleasant or painful, and brings a sense of wonder. In some ways, it is similar to the religious goal of realization of Brahman. Viśvanātha writes that aesthetic enjoyment requires subconscious impressions (*vāsanās*) which support an emotional disposition.[22] Aesthetic emotions have a variety of effects on consciousness.[23]

The writers of the Alaṅkāra describe permanent emotions and temporary ones. They base their organization of emotions on those of Bharata in his *Nāṭyaśhāstra:* love, mirth, grief, anger, energy (zeal), fear, disgust, and wonder.[24] These permanent emotions (*sthāyibhāva*) are dominant and cannot be suppressed by other emotions. According to Śiṅga Bhūpāla's *Rasārṇava sudhākar,* "They are permanent emotions, which transform other emotions into themselves, even as the ocean transforms the waves into itself." The transitory emotions (*vyabhichāribhāva*), according to Śāradātanaya's *Bhāvaprakāśhana,* appear and disappear within the permanent emotions as waves appear and disappear in the ocean, contributing to its excellence.[25] They are like bubbles in the ocean or like beads or flowers of a garland, and they help, promote, and strengthen the permanent emotions they ornament. Some of the transitory emotions include shame, exhilaration, dejection, eagerness, apathy, ferocity, and anxiety.[26] In the first chapter of his *Nāṭśhāstra,* Bharata compared the aesthetic experience to eating: as spices add flavor rasa to the main dish, which is enjoyed by the gourmet, so the permanent emotion in drama is spiced with transitory emotions and literary ornaments, to be enjoyed by the connoisseur rasika.

The sentiment of rasa is a transformation of the basic, more "concrete" emotion of bhava. The term rasa means sap, juice, liquid essence, and taste, and is often translated as flavor, relish, mood, and sentiment. Emotional rasa can be tasted and appreciated.[27] When emotions become rasas, they may be viewed as art objects and combined in aesthetic fashion. They may blend harmoniously with each other (*sandhi*), arise and disappear, or conflict with and inhibit one another. This conflict is called *rasābhāsa,* and is understood to result in a semblance or imitation of a true emotion. It is a damaged, inferior, or incomplete sort of emotion, tainted by pride or power or generated by some inappropriate source. The conflicts that may generate such a damaged emotion could include the clash between parental and erotic love or the emotions of disgust and fury combined with the attitude of loving service. They are called "compound emotions" when several transitory emotions arise in quick succession, especially when some are inhibited by others.

From this perspective, the bhāva is a "raw" emotion, not cooked or transformed into an aesthetic emotion. To transform the emotion, an internal distancing is needed from the emotion, so that the experiencer also becomes an observer, in some ways a "witness-self," as described in Vedantic philosophy.

Rasa is characterized by impersonality or generalizing (*sādhāraṇikārana*), the distancing of the person from both the object and his or her own emotions. In bhāva, the person experiences emotions directly; in rasa, he or she empathizes and observes the emotion and situation, feeling *as if* he or she felt the emotion but not being involved enough to feel it directly. It is impersonal, generic, the experience of a type.[28] As De states, "Generality is thus a state of self-identification with the imagined situation, devoid of any practical interest and, from this point of view, of any relation whatsoever with the limited self, and as it were impersonal."[29]

The feelings of the poet or actor are also excluded from the aesthetic experience. The elements of particular consciousness are expunged in order to create generalized emotion, valuing universals more than particular acts. Emotions are not undergone; instead, the aesthete is both observer and participant.

Bhāva is a personal emotion: rasa is an impersonal or depersonalized emotion, in which the participant is distanced as an observer. Why is a depersonalized emotion considered superior to a personal one? Because the aesthete can experience a wide range of emotions yet be protected from their painful aspects. Emotion is appreciated through a glass window, which keeps out unpleasantness. Though the glass is clear, thus allowing a union of sorts with the observed object, the window is always present, thus maintaining the dualism. This becomes important for the religious dimensions of rasa, where the duality between the worshipper and the god (an important concept in bhakti devotion) must always be maintained.

The Bengali Vaiṣṇavas also value rasa, but they emphasize its religious aspects. In the Vaiṣṇava understanding of emotion, bhāva becomes *bhakti rasa* (devotional sentiment). The religious goal is not liberation but love, and the devotee must go beyond dramatic emotion to become filled with religious emotion. The connoisseur (the rasika or *sahṛidaya*, the person with heart), who can truly appreciate the fine points of the arts, becomes the devotee (*bhakta*), tasting the forms of joy brought by the god Kṛiṣhṇa. He or she is both observer and participant. The aesthetic experience is universal, *bhedābheda*, simultaneously individual and eternal, material and spiritual, impersonal and passionately involved.

In bhakti yoga, emotion becomes discipline; the emotions are generated and transformed consciously, especially in that form of practice known as *rāgānugā bhakti sādhana*.[30] There is a sort of "ladder of emotion" that one must climb to the highest emotional states, and it is described in two important texts, the *Bhaktirasāmṛitasindhu* and *Ujjvala-Nīlamaṇi* of Rūpa Gosvāmin. The former text (*The Ocean of the Nectar of Devotional Love*) looks at the earlier stages of religious emotion and its transformation; the latter text (*The Blazing Sapphire*—a pun on the god Kṛiṣhṇa) focuses on the more advanced states of mystical love.

The *Bhaktirasāmṛitasindhu* has the devotee begin with ritual action (*vaidhi bhakti*) and progress to ritual emotion (*rāgānugā bhakti*). Through physical action and imaginative visualization, the devotee builds a soul, a spiritual body composed of love, which can experience emotion more intensely than can the ordinary personality. The bhāva becomes deepened, and the heart is softened. Emotion becomes intense love (prema), and there is continual focus of attention on Rādhā and Krishna the divine couple. The highest state, called the "greatest emotion" (mahābhāva), has the person experience all possible emotions simultaneously, including the opposite emotions of separation and union, in passionate delirium (mādana). As O. B. L. Kapoor states, "Mādana has the unique capacity of directly experiencing a thousand different kinds of enjoyment of union with Krsna. . . . It presents these multifarious experiences of union simultaneously with multifarious experiences of separation (viyoga) involving craving (utkanthā) for union."[31]

The "ladder of emotion" includes sneha (a thickening of spiritual love, when the emotion gains a consistency and taste like clarified butter or honey); māna (sulking and hiding emotion); pranaya (deep sharing and confidence); rāga (intense passion, also defined as the person being totally concentrated on the desired object); anurāga (in which the beloved appears eternally new); and mahābhāva (the experience of emotion so intense and complex that all extremes of emotion are felt at once). In the orthodox Bengali Vaishnava tradition, only Rādhā may experience the state of mahābhāva, though her companions and their handmaidens may share in her emotional states. Indeed, these handmaidens (mañjaris) are said to feel Rādhā's emotions a hundred times more intensely than she does, for they are not as personally involved (selflessness is understood to increase sensitivity to the divine).[32] The devotee may also share in these states by visualizing the mythical situations and characters in which they occur.[33]

These states of intense emotion are expressed by ecstatic bodily changes (the sāttvika bhāvas or sāttvika vikāras). There are eight of these: trembling, shedding tears, paralysis, sweating, fainting, changing skin color, faltering voice, and hair standing on end. Like the transitory emotions, these symptoms are understood to develop and intensify the permanent emotions, and they are an extreme form of emotional expression (anubhāva).[34] The term bhāva is also used for the five basic roles, or emotional relationships, through which the devotee may relate to the deity: through friendship, parental love, service, peace, and erotic love. Among the Bengali Vaishnavas, bhāva is the emotional ground for subtler and more complex emotional states.

But it is among the Sahajiyās, the unorthodox, tantric branch of Vaishnavism, that we find the most literal notion of emotion as substance. Sahajiyās also value rasa, but their understanding of the term is different from the more traditional Bengali Vaishnavas. They practice sexual yoga, literally living out the relationship of Krishna and Rādhā, the deity and his consort, in order to share in their emotions and experiences. Such practice involves maintaining dispassion within a setting of greatest passion, "diving deep without getting wet." By such rituals, lustful and earthly emotion is transformed into spiritual love. The process has been compared to cooking:

To find nectar
Stir the cauldron
On the fire—
And unite the act of loving
With the feeling of love.
Distill the sweetness
Of the heart
And reach the treasures.[35]

Here rasa is a literal fluid, which is heated, stirred, and concentrated, a fluid of pure emotion which is condensed during the practice—the sexual fluid, which can be transformed into new life or spiritual love. There is less focus on observation and more on practice. All other emotions are secondary to those of love, which is viewed as the basic, or primordial, emotion. The emotional fire in the woman ripens the liquid rasa in the male; as the *Vivarta Vilāsa* states, "Now hear about the nature of (the physical) woman. Just as milk is usually boiled with the help of fire, so the Gosvāmis have utilised the fire that is in woman (for the purpose of purifying the passion)."[36]

As S. B. Dasgupta states, the Sahajiyās believed rasa to flow "perpetually from the eternal Vṛindāvana to earth, manifested as the stream of *rasa* flowing to and between men and women." Sexuality and love linked the devotee with the heavenly Vṛindāvana, and passionate emotion showed the presence of heaven on earth. As milk is churned into butter, so the rasa of love for Rādhā and Kṛiṣhṇa is churned by sexuality into more intense and condensed states, becoming a pure substance of joy. As the *Premānanda lahari* states, "If there is no *rāga* [passion], there can be no union."[37] Emotion is directed and transformed.

Thus, in these three traditions we see an evolution of ideas about emotion: it has changed from an abstract aesthetic principle to an intense style of relating with a deity to a sexual fluid that is the essence of God.

Conclusions

Bhāva is like filling a pail full of tap water: when it fills up, the sound will be changed. The body is a vessel which can understand things, and whenever you feel or understand something, you have a sort of bhāva. But it is not called bhāva until it is overflowing. . . . When the pail flows over, the eight *sātivikā bhāvas* emerge—the eight ways of overflowing. These are divine, supernatural events. Bhāvas are temporary because the body is full of pores. It is like a beautiful glass with holes in it—there is leakage. You put water in it and it comes out. The body is made in such a way, that whatever you fill it up with, it will come out.

> Feelings [bhāvas] and highest feelings [mahābhāva] come out
> through the pores of the body. But the memory is an energy that
> remains. (Interview, Śākta practitioner, Calcutta)

There is a wide range of theory in Indian philosophical and religious thought on the nature of emotion. However, if we wish to generalize, there tends to be a different understanding of the nature of emotion in India from that held in the West. Emotion, like consciousness, tends to be substantial rather than conceptual, more like the early Christian notions of *ousia* (being or essence), the transformation of a common substance.

In the bhakti traditions of Bengal, emotion is the path to God and is thus sacred. Rather than trying to eliminate emotion, the goal is to intensify that emotion until it becomes powerful, overwhelming, the center of the devotee's being. There is a natural tendency for that love to increase, "as the ebb tide rises into high waves at the rising of the moon." Human emotion is transformed into divine emotion: it is boiled, thickened, purified, and redirected. Emotion is a means to an end, and often it does not matter which emotion is being emphasized. Hatred of the god (*dveṣa-bhāva*) gives the same focus on the deity as loving like a parent (*vātsalya-bhāva*), and both emotions can bring the devotee to paradise.[38] Indeed, powerful enough emotion can influence the deity's will, even bring him to earth, for love can control the gods and make them slaves of their devotees.

Traditionally, the body has been compared to a vase or pot, and the soul (*jīva*) is incarnate within it. Emotion occurs within the soul but can be manifest in the body. It is inward (*antar* or *mānasa*) when not expressed and outward (*bāhya*) when shown by the physical body. As the Śākta practitioner stated in the quotation above, the body is like a pail that can be filled up with bhāva. The body as vessel of the soul is an old idea in both East and West. The practitioner later stated that the pores can be "plugged" by concentrating on love of the Goddess and chanting mantras, which maintains the intensity of the emotion.

We have looked at a wide range of beliefs about emotion in religion and folklore, and we can ask, What is the value of emotion? Let us examine some ideas from this essay.

1. Bengal tends to study emotions in ways that the West does not. The aesthetic and devotional traditions focus on intense emotions and the disciplines that generate them. Emotion is a sea rather than a puddle or a few stray droplets, and it is studied by participant observation, by disciplined individuals who view emotion from the "inside." From the perspective of rasa, it is best understood in its pure and intense forms, whereas Western philosophy tends to focus on

secular, everyday emotion rather than ecstatic or extreme emotion (though William James comes to mind as an exception). If we accept the liquid metaphor, one is more likely to understand fluid dynamics by the study of water in oceans and lakes than by studying puddles and droplets.

2. Emotion is identified by metaphors of both substance and space. It can be intensified, shared, transferred, deposited in physical locales.[39] Emotion is neither an involuntary response nor cognition and belief, but a transformation of the substance of consciousness. The Indian universe is a fluid one, a complex network of interactions among various forms of substance, according to many modern anthropologists. As Marriott states:

Matter that is subject to such variations may well be called "fluid," and indeed Hindus generally refer to the world they must live in as "(that which is) moving" (*jagat*) and as a "flowing together" (*Samsāra*). . . . It and its inhabitants are generated by, and constituted of, more or less malleable substance that is continually moving in and out of them.[40]

Mind and emotion are no exception to this "wholly substantial and fluid world," and they tend to be understood through metaphors of flowing and water. They may also be located spatially, such as in the "space of the heart," as a throne or box or shrine. As substance, emotion is accessible to mind and heart, and there is no absolute separation between aspects of the self. Substance gives access, for viewing emotion as intangible and invisible also makes it inaccessible.

3. Emotion can act as an aid to concentration, helping to focus the mind rather than acting as a distraction. Passion can direct the mind and fasten it upon its object. In the stories of Kṛiṣhṇa and the *gopīs*, or milkmaids, who loved him, their fascination for him is often described as meditative, and Rādhā's passion for Kṛiṣhṇa is often compared to yogic concentration. The love object is the focus of the mind, for there is no split between thought and feeling. Remembrance (*smaraṇa*) involves mana, which is both mind and heart, and it is directed to a single end, so that even thinking of anything else becomes difficult. Depending on how it is used, the same emotion can distract from concentration or be a means of mental control and limit or increase knowledge.

4. The "hydraulic model" of emotion is differently understood in Bengal than in the West. Superficially, it is much like Freud's notion of the id, whose energies overflow into the conscious mind. A good

Bengali description of bhāva using the hydraulic model was given by a woman ecstatic to describe her own experiences:

When something is boiled in a closed vessel, there comes a stage when the vapor will push up the lid and, unless force is used, the vessel cannot be kept covered anymore. In a similar manner, when, while being engaged in *japa* (chanting) or some other spiritual exercise, a wave of ecstatic emotion surges up from within, it becomes difficult to check it. This ecstatic emotion is called *"bhāva."* It emerges from deep within and expresses itself outwardly.[41]

Her description follows Robert Solomon's rendering of the "hydraulic metaphor," in which emotion is a force within the person, filling up and spilling over. It is based on theories ranging from the medieval humours, animal spirits, and bodily fluids, to the Freudian theory of the dynamic and economic forms of psychic equilibrium within the person, where the ego holds back the repressed libidinal forces pushing for release. He finds that, in Western philosophy, this approach has served to limit the range and importance of the emotions, for it relieves the person of responsibility. The emotions are inflicted by causes beyond human control or are bottled up like volcanic lava, and they render the person passive. As he states, "The key to the hydraulic model is the idea that emotions and other passions (or their determinants) exist wholly independent of consciousness, effecting (or "affecting") consciousness and often forcing us to behave in certain discernible ways."[42]

In Bengal, however, the hydraulic model has opened and expanded the concept of emotion, for it has been tied in with spirituality. The key statement might be rephrased: The emotions are normally independent of consciousness, but the person may gain access to the sources of emotion and direct them to gain certain discernible ends. Unlike Freudian psychology, the Bengali model does not understand the psyche as a closed system. People may undergo emotions but also generate, control, and share them, to gain access to the emotional sea that lies beneath the conscious mind. Different emotions may be combined or many experienced simultaneously. Because the person has access to the source of emotion, there can be no freedom from responsibility or use of emotion as an "excuse" for unacceptable behavior.

5. Emotions can be controlled and combined to become something analogous to art objects. Rather than passions or disturbances, emotions may be aesthetic objects, which are arranged as dominant and transitory, central and peripheral, clashing and ornamental, as an artist might arrange different color relationships on a canvas. Emo-

tions are, in a sense, colors (rāga), which define and structure experience as art. During the dramatic performance, the emotions represented by the actor are experienced by the observer, who is simultaneously a participant. As the trained observer is aware of the subtlety and interplay of emotion, he or she becomes involved in what might be called "performance art." It is a conscious awareness of his or her own shared dramatic experience, which is paradoxical because it is both close and distanced. Raw, "concrete" emotions can be transformed into aesthetic and religious ones.

6. Disciplined emotion can generate new personalities which are highly valued. The person may not be able to determine his or her secular personality, based as it is on past events, but he or she can build a soul, a spiritual body that is sculpted out of emotion. This alternative personality, or "subtle body," is composed of the emotions of love and represents the person's ideal self.

The idea of such a self has often been dismissed as "split personality" or multiple-personality disorder by Western observers. However, it is interesting to note that, in the West, the focus on alternate selves has been on multiple-personality disorder generated by trauma, by abuse or events too painful for the person to bear, and, earlier on, demonic personalities that possess the person involuntarily.[43] The *DSM III* psychiatric manual's description fits the Indian case in many ways:

A. The existence within an individual of two or more distinct personalities, each of which is dominant at a particular time. B. The personality that is dominant at any particular time determines the individual's behavior. C. Each individual personality is complex and integrated with its own unique behavior patterns and social relationships.[44]

The Western alternate personalities are considered to be pathological, a result of trauma. Emotion cannot be deliberately used and controlled to create a new personality; such generation is an involuntary and unconscious event.

From the Indian devotional perspective, developing an alternate self based on emotion is a creative act, building a spiritual body made out of overflowing love. This *siddha deha* (perfected body) or *prema deha* (body of love) becomes the true self of the person, and is believed to continue after the death of the physical body. The alternate self is generated by will rather than by pain, and emotion is utilized rather than repressed or endured. In this understanding, emotion is the foundation of identity, the substance from which it is constructed.

Thus, emotion is a means to an end in the Bengali aesthetic and devotional traditions, and that end is the good life. Emotion is not a passive response but an active eros, involving meaning, beauty, and creativity, which structures both self and world.

NOTES

Epigraph is from Owen M. Lynch, "Introduction: Emotions in Theoretical Context" in Owen M. Lynch (ed.), *Divine Passions: The Social Construction of Emotion in India* (Berkeley: University of California Press, 1990), 22

1. Note on transliteration: the Indian terms in this paper have been written in Sanskritized Bengali, to make them more accessible to Hindi and Sanskri speakers. However, as the audience for this article will not be made up primariy of Indologists, I transliterate terms as phonetically as possibly (rather than follow the Sanskrit conventions). I retain the diacriticals, however, for those who wish to research the Sanskrit and Bengali etymologies. Thus, Krsna becomes Krishna, *rsi* becomes *rishi, Alankāraśhāstra* became *Alankāraśhāstra,* and so on.

2. See Pandit Usharbudh Arya, trans. and commentary, *The Yoga-Sutras of Patanjah, with the Exposition of Vyasa* (Honesdale, PA: Himalayan International Institute of Yoga Science and Philosophy, 1986), *Yoga Sutras* 1.2.

3. Ibid., 11.3. It is debated among scholars whether the sense of individuality is more a problem of ignorance (as personality and individuality are no ultimate truth) or of pride (too much focus on the illusion of individuality).

4. Ibid., 1.2, 1.12, Vyāsa's commentary.

5. The three humors or basic elements (*dhātus*) of Ayurveda are *vāyu, pitta,* and *kapha.* Vāyu, or *vāta,* is associated with movement, nerves, and muscles; pitta with enzymes, hormones, digestion, and temperature; and kapha with liquids and plumpness. Kapha also regulates the other two humors. Imbalance of humors may be endogenous (due to such factors as heredity and degeneration) or exogenous (from such causes as drugs, poison, accidents, unclean food, and animal bites).

6. R. K. Sharma and Vaidya P. Dash, trans., *Caraka Samhita* (Varanasi: Chowkhamba Orientalia, 1983), *Caraka Samhita,* 1.11.20, 1.7.38, 11.7.4, 1.11.45, 1.25.40.

7. Catherine A. Lutz, *Unnatural Emotions: Everyday Sentiments on a Micronesian Atoll and Their Challenge to Western Theory* (Chicago: University of Chicago Press, 1988), 8.

8. Such waves are described in many Bengali biographies of *siddhas,* or saints. For example, the Vaisnavite saint Vijayakrishna Gosvāmin and his devotees were described as dancing in waves of bhāva, which became a "sky-high typhoon." See his biography in June McDaniel, *The Madness of the Saints: Ecstatic Religion in Bengal* (Chicago: University of Chicago Press, 1989).

9. The following terms and definitions come from the *Samcad Bengali-English Dictionary* (Dasgupta, 1983).

10. In India, the dead are not buried but, rather, are burned at the *śmaśāna,* or burning ground. To compare the heart to a burning ground means that all earthly

concerns have been left behind, as the corpse is left behind by the spirit, and a total devotion to the goddess has taken their place.

11. In the meditational system of *kundalinī yoga,* the person is understood to have a body composed of energy (*śhakti*), which exists invisibly within the physical body. This body is composed of seven centers (*chakras*), which are located along the spine and are foci of meditation. These centers are interpreted in different ways by different practitioners, but the heart center is usually associated with emotion, compassion, and respiration.

12. We see a similar range of meanings of the term rāga in the Japanese term *iro* (Chinese *se*). Iro means color and sensual pleasure, among other things, and includes such derivatives as *irogonomi* (sensuality, lust); *iroke* (coloring, shade, passion, romance); *irozome* (dyeing, dyed); and *irokoi* (love, sentiment). See the term iro in Andrew N. Nelson, *The Modern Reader's Japanese-English Character Dictionary* (Tokyo: Charles E. Tuttle, 1974).

13. There is a special kind of madness in Bengal, colloquially known as study-*pāgal,* or study-insanity. Informants told me that too much thinking is dangerous, that it upsets the balance of the mind, and that it could result in grave mental and physical illness. I was told quite firmly that I needed more emotion and less thought in order to be healthy. This is the "folk" view, which separates thought and emotion and finds emotion to be especially important in women.

14. Lee Siegel, *Fires of Love, Waters of Peace: Passion and Renunciation in Indian Culture* (Honolulu: University of Hawaii Press, 1983), *Amaruśataka* 104.

15. Walter Kaelber, *Tapta Marga: Asceticism and Initiation in Vedic India* (Albany: State University of New York Press, 1989), 3.

16. *Śhāktas* are worshippers of the Goddess in West Bengal, primarily the goddess Kali in her form of Mother of the Universe.

17. Heat is often colloquially associated with negative emotion. In the Indian tradition of touching the guru's feet, the devotee is understood to get rid of his bad karma, the guru's feet absorb it like a sponge. When gurus have been touched by people with strong anger, hatred, or desire, they will often complain that their feet are burning from the passions of their devotees. Several gurus in Bengal mentioned this to me as one of the problems of the profession.

18. This story was told to me by an informant. There are many stories of Vaishnava devotees who burned themselves while serving Krishna and Radha in their paradise and who returned to their physical bodies and saw that their physical hands were burned.

19. Variants of the story of Satī are found in the *Mahābharata* and in the *Devībhāgavata, Kālikā, Matsya, Padma, Kūrma,* and *Brahmanda purānas,* though the most well-known version comes from Kālidāsa's *Kumārasambhava.* These variants are discussed in D. C. Sircar, "The Śakta Pīthas," *Journal of the Royal Asiatic Society of Bengal* 14, no. 1 (1948).

20. As the story describes it: "Suddenly, with her own hands, she twisted and tore her left breast from her body. Then she walked three times round the city, repeating her curse at each gate. In her despair she threw away her lovely breast, which fell in the dirt of the street. Then before her there appeared the god of Fire, . . . and the city of Madurai . . . was immediately hidden in flames and smoke." Prince Mango

Adigal, *Shilappadikaram* (*The Ankle Bracelet*), trans. Alain Danielou (New York: New Directions, 1965), 131–32.

21. For a description of the role of the fluids, see the chapter titled "Sexual Fluids in Vedic and Post-Vedic India" in Wendy Doniger O'Flaherty, *Women, Androgynes, and Other Mythical Beasts* (Chicago: University of Chicago Press, 1982).

22. Viśvanātha Kavirāja, *Sāhityadarpana*, as cited in Jadunath Sinha, *Indian Psychology, Emotion and Will*, vol. 2 (Calcutta: J. Sinha Foundation, 1961). It may be noted that Viśvanātha felt that philosophers were incapable of aesthetic enjoyment, as they are devoid of innate emotional dispositions. Dharmadatta echoes this opinion, persons devoid of emotional dispositions cannot appreciate art: they are "as good as a piece of wood, a wall, and a stone in the theatre hall" (Sinha, 166).

23. According to Dhanañjaya's *Kāvyasāhityamīmāmsā*, erotic and comic emotions cause the blooming (*vikāśa*) of consciousness; emotions of courage and wonder bring about the expansion (*vistāra*) of consciousness; horror and fear cause the agitation (*ksobha*) of consciousness; fury and pathos produce the obstruction (*viksepa*) of consciousness (Sinha, 169).

24. The *Natyashāstra* is usually dated not later than the sixth century C.E., but may have elements as old as the second century B.C.E. (Edwin Gerow, *Indian Poetics* [Wiesbaden: Otto Harassowitz. 1977], 245). Such divisions of basic emotions are also seen in Western thought, for example, in Silvano Arieti's concepts of first- (protoemotions), second-, and third-order emotions. He includes tension, fear, appetite, satisfaction, and rage as first-order emotions. See "Cognition and Feeling," in Magda B. Arnold (ed.), *Feelings and Emotions: The Loyola Symposium* (New York: Academic Press, 1970), 135–43.

25. Cited in Sinha, 175, 207.

26. Rasa theory also describes the causes and effects of emotion in great detail. Briefly, the dramatic emotions contain several aspects. The *vibhāva* is the stimulus or cause of emotion (such as persons and events presented); the *anubhāva* is the involuntary reaction or physical effect of emotion; and the *vyabhichāribhāva* is the associated, temporary feeling or transitory state that may accompany the permanent emotion (*sthāyibhāva*).

27. According to Bharata, the moment of gustatory rasa occurs when the eater rests after the meal with a smile of satisfaction, appreciating the individual tastes merging into a general mood of happiness. This is similar to the aesthete appreciating the different aspects of a drama, which merge together.

28. The bhāvas and rasas relate as follows:

Bhāva	Rasa
love	erotic
humor	comic
grief	tragic
anger	furious
energy	heroic
fear	fearful
disgust	terrible
astonishment	marvelous

A ninth, peaceful emotion has been added to this list by later writers, though it has been much debated (as insufficiently intense).

29. See S. K. De, *Sanskrit Poetics as a Study of Aesthetics,* with notes by Edwin Gerow (Berkeley: University of California Press, 1963), 21.

30. This practice involves imitation of the anubhāvas to generate passionate feelings within the practitioner, based on the emotions of the original Krishna devotees of Braj. The goal of the practice is the generation of a new identity—that of a handmaiden of Krishna's consort Radha—composed of emotion (selfless love, or prema). For a detailed analysis of this practice, see David L. Haberman, *Acting as a Way of Salvation: A Study of Rāgānugā Bhakti Sādhana* (New York: Oxford University Press, 1988).

31. O. B. L. Kapoor, *The Philosophy and Religion of Sri Caitanyai* (Delhi: Munshiram Manoharlal, 1977), 210.

32. According to the *Govinda-lilamrta* of Krishnadās Kavirāj, the companions (*sakhis*) of Radha are "like flowers and buds of the vine of love which is Rādhā," and when Rādhā experiences the joy of Krishna's love, her companions' experience of that joy is one hundred times greater than her own. See Krsnadās Kavirāj, *Govinda-līlāmrta* (Navadvīpa: Haribol Kutir, 463 Guarabda). Because they are detached from ego and desire, they are more open to deeper forms of love, and can experience these intensely. Thus, detachment (from ego and desire) paradoxically leads to intensity.

33. There are special meditations that lead to experience of these intense emotional states. In the *manjari sādhana,* the devotee identifies himself with one of Radha's handmaidens, and in the *gaur līlā sādhana,* he identifies himself with the servants of Caitanya Mahāprabhu, a fifteenth-century Bengali saint believed by devotees to be a joint incarnation of Krishna and Rādhā. See McDaniel.

34. They differ in that the *sāttvika bhāvas* are composed only of *sāttva guna,* and, as such, are purely spiritual emotions. There may be one or two at a time, or more than five may manifest themselves at once (in this case, the sāttvika bhāvas are said to be blazing, or *uddīpta*). Although some of these may be caused by other events (such as sweating caused by heat or fear), the more of these bodily changes that appear, the greater the likelihood that the person is experiencing intense emotion.

35. Erfan Shah, *Songs of the Bards of Bengal,* trans. Deben Bhattacarya (New York: Grove, 1969, 55).

36. Quoted in Manindra Mohan Bose, *The Post Caitanya Sahajiya Cult of Bengal* (Calcutta: University of Calcutta Press, 1930), 76.

37. Cited in E. C. Dimock, *The Place of the Hidden Moon: Erotic Mysticism in the Vaisnava-sahajiya Cult of Bengal* (Chicago: University of Chicago Press, 1989), 168, from the *Śrirādhār-krama bikāśa;* 195.

38. Probably the most famous example of *dvesha-bhāva* is King Kamsa, the god Krishna's evil uncle and sworn enemy. He ended up going to Krishna's paradise because of his great passion for the god (even though that passion showed itself by threats on Krishna's life). The evil wet nurse Pūtāna was also blessed, though she put poison on her breast to kill the infant Krishna. When anger, pride, lust, and the like are directed toward the deity, they are purified and eventually transformed into love. The attention is more important than the ethical considerations.

39. There is a set of folk stories (told to me by several informants) that speak of

a sage meditating in a cave who has tried for decades to gain intense love for the deity but leaves discouraged. A new young sage comes into the cave, begins to meditate, and is overcome by love and gains enlightenment in a short period of time. He has gained the love and dedication of the previous sage, who left them in the cave.

40. McKim Marriott, "Constructing an Indian Ethnosociology," in McKim Marriott (ed.), *India through Hindu Categories* (New Delhi: Sage, 1990), 18.

41. Ānandamayī Mā, in Bhaiji, *Sad Vani* (Bhadaini: Shree Shree Ma Anandamayee Charitable Society, 1978), 68.

42. Robert Solomon, *The Passions* (Garden City, NY: Anchor/Doubleday, 1976), 146.

43. In multiple-personality disorder, the selves are highly segregated dissociative states, developed during childhood as a response to severe trauma, usually repeated child abuse. Research indicates that the trauma must occur relatively early and that emotion and memory retrieval are bound to these dissociative states (thus protecting the child from a flood of painful memory and emotion). The most frequent alter-personalities are frightened children, though the most common chief complaint is depression. See Frank Putnam, "The Switch Process in Multiple-Personality Disorder and Other State-Change Disorders," *Dissociation* 1 (1988): 24–32; B. G. Braun and R. G. Sachs, "The Development of Multiple-Personality Disorder: Predisposing, Precipitating, and Perpetuating Factors," in R. P. Kluft (ed.), *Childhood Antecedents of Multiple Personality* (Washington, DC: American Psychiatric Press, 1985).

44. See *Diagnostic and Statistical Manual of Mental Disorders*, 3rd ed. (New York: American Psychiatric Association, 1980).

10

Weeping, Death, and Spiritual Ascent in Sixteenth-Century Jewish Mysticism

Elliot R. Wolfson

In Elliot R. Wolfson's commentary on sixteenth-century Jewish mysticism we see how investigation of emotional performance—in this case, ecstatic weeping—can be oriented toward disclosing the cultural framework that determines a specific emotional behavior to be valuable. Wolfson's analysis, which identifies weeping as a technique by which Jews excited mystical experience and advanced in knowledge, uncovers the rich matrix of ideas that made weeping religiously precious in the first place. Wolfson shows how the experience of ecstasy in weeping was grounded in attitudes and ideas relating to sleep, death, vision, sexuality, and gender, and he demonstrates the interaction between Jewish theological discourse and the craving for highly emotional experience. Central to Wolfson's analysis is the implicit claim that emotional life is represented in a vast and interlocking set of symbols. This symbolic system is strikingly revealed precisely through the focus on the reported emotional experiences of Jewish mystics. Moreover, it is the fact of the cultivation of the emotional mystical experience specifically through engagement of symbols in the performance of religious ritual that is clarified in this study. Cognitive aspects of religion are joined with emotional in the devotions of the mystic, and seemingly contradictory experiences—life and death, for example—are linked in weeping.

How does Jewish understanding of the experience of the mystic rely on translation of ecstasy into other terms? To what extent do those terms ground mystical experience in physical reality? In what ways do they

Elliot R. Wolfson, "Weeping, Death, and Spiritual Ascent in Sixteenth-Century Jewish Mysticism," John J. Collins and Michael A. Fishbane, eds., *Death, Ecstasy and Other Worldly Journeys* (Albany: State University of New York Press, 1995), 209–247. Reprinted by permission.

point to a joining of physical and spiritual realities? How is gender given expres-
sion in the symbology of weeping? How is the emotional experience of the mystic
cognized? That is, how are emotional experiences represented in ideas about the
body, soul, light, sleep, ascent, and so forth? Does weeping bring about a spiritual
vision or is intense emotion the result of the vision? Is emotion actively cultivated
or experienced passively? Where is the self located in the performance of the mystic
rites? How does the soul or self survive the peak of emotion depicted as death?

In the sixteenth century, in the wake of the expulsion of the Jews from Spain in 1492, a spiritual renaissance of sorts took shape in a small community in the Galilean town of Safed in northern Palestine. In a wonderfully written essay, full of both learning and pathos, Solomon Schechter captured the mystical animus of this community of Kabbalists, preachers, poets, and moralists.[1] To be sure, there is historical evidence that from at least the later part of the thirteenth century Safed was a center for Jewish mystical activity, and indeed many of the trends that informed the leading kabbalists in the sixteenth century find their expression in sources deriving from authors inhabiting that city at earlier times.[2] One can, therefore, legitimately speak of a continuity of mystical traditions in that locality. Moreover, the view espoused by Scholem that only in Safed of the sixteenth century do most of the mystical rites described in earlier texts, principally the *Zohar,* become enacted in the realm of performative ritual,[3] has been challenged by recent scholarship that has focused more on the wider range of human experience and behavior to which the earlier textual sources attest as well as on the possibility that behind the fictional fellowship described in zoharic literature is an actual group of mystics who lived and functioned as a society.[4] Thus it is no longer sufficient to view the history of Kabbalah in a linear fashion as a transformation from esoteric doctrine (*torat ha-sod*) to a living religious teaching (*torat ḥayyim*). Still, something distinctive occurred in the sixteenth century, a confluence of socioeconomic, political, and religious factors (including, of course, an intensified messianic enthusiasm that may have erupted on account of the expulsion of Jewry from the Iberian Peninsula at the end of the fifteenth century and the consequent migration of Jews to North Africa, Italy, and the Ottoman Empire[5] resulting in the formation of a major center of Jewish mystical activity at this time and in this place. The impact of this circle on world Jewry was decisive, especially in the area of religious customs (*minhagim*), many of which were either instituted or transformed in light of kabbalistic principles.

One of the characteristic features of the spiritual revival initiated by the kabbalists in Safed was a renewed interest in the cultivation of revelatory experiences or mystical illumination.[6] Thus, in striking contrast to the general trend in the history of Jewish mysticism to avoid writing first-person accounts of mystical experiences,[7] we find a proliferation of reports of dreams and angelic visitations in the sixteenth century.[8] Various examples could be given to illustrate this point, but here I will only mention some of the better known ones: the *Maggid Mesharim* of Joseph Karo, which is the record of his conversations with his angelic mentor (*maggid*), the *Sefer Gerushin* of Moses Cordovero, the record of the forced banishments of the kabbalists which resulted in inspired exegesis;[9] the *Milei de-Shemaya* of Eleazar Azikri, a book of ethical-pietistic teachings rooted in heavenly revelations;[10] and the *Sefer ha-Hezyonot* of Hayyim Vital, the mystical diary that registers his many visions of angels, the prophet Elijah (in different forms), and communications with souls of departed saints.[11] There is, additionally, sufficient evidence to show that the idea of an ecstatic journey of the soul to the heavenly realms, known from the ancient apocalyptic and hekhalot literature as well as from classical works of medieval kabbalah (e.g., the *Zohar*), was once again appropriated as a desired goal of the *via mystica* by the sixteenth-century kabbalists.[12] In this material the ascent is referred to as *'aliyyat neshamah,* thus conveying the belief that the soul under goes the heavenly journey and ecstatically leaves the body. As is discussed more fully below, it is evident that these older traditions concerning ascent are recast in light of contemporary the osophical assumptions, but the fact nevertheless remains that these mystics demonstrated a keen interest in the spiritual journey to other realms of being, an interest that colored their theosophical systems in a fundamental way.

The interest in the cultivation of ecstatic experience is also attested by the fact, noted by various scholars, that Abraham Abulafia's meditative method of inducing the prophetic state by the technique of permutation and combination of Hebrew letters informed many of the kabbalists in sixteenth-century Safed, including Judah Albotini, Moses Cordovero, and Hayyim Vital.[13] There is yet another vantage point that allows us to appreciate the centrality of revelatory experience in the sixteenth-century mystical revival. As has been noted in the scholarly literature, in the history of Judaism—especially of the apocalyptic and mystical varieties, but in more normative sources as well—there is a long-standing tradition that upholds inspired exegesis or pneumatic interpretation as a legitimate mode of reading Scripture. Rather than representing distance from God or a substitute for direct revelation, the interpretative process (*midrash*) is predicated precisely on a reenactment of the state of prophetic inspiration or revelation characteristic of the text in its compositional layer.[14] In the specific case of Vital there is sufficient textual evidence to support the view that he posited a clear nexus between prophecy (understood by him to entail mystical or contemplative illumination) and comprehension of the secrets of Torah.[15] (Needless to say, Vital draws on earlier sources, some of which he cites explicitly in the fourth part of his *Sha'are Qedushah.*) The human capacity to understand mysteries of Torah is related proportionally to the prophetic influx that one receives from one's soul-root in the sefirotic realm.[16] The point is epitomized in the following passage from *Sha'ar Ruah ha-Qodesh,* which un-

derscores the significance of the meditative practice of contemplative unifications (*yiḥudim*)[17] as a higher form of worship than normative Torah study, for
these unifications facilitate communion with the departed souls of the righteous and the drawing down of the efflux of light from the supernal realm,
although the ultimate purpose of this mystical praxis is not realization of personal spiritual fulfillment but rectification of the upper realms of being:

> Know that if the souls of these righteous ones who were mentioned
> are revealed to a person who is from the root of their soul, his com-
> prehension increases wondrously. . . . Know that if a person who has
> begun to unify these unifications abstains from unifying he brings
> about great harm . . . for he causes those souls who wanted to be
> united with the person to withdraw and be separated from him. Do
> not say that the engagement with [study of] Torah is greater and it is
> not appropriate to abolish it, for the matter of the unifications that
> has been mentioned is greater than the engagement in [study of] To-
> rah, for he unifies the upper worlds. [This activity] is called engage-
> ment in [study of] Torah and unification; it is all one. Even if the
> souls are not revealed to him well he should not worry nor cease
> from the unification. His intention should not be only to dray down
> to himself that soul but rather to rectify the upper worlds.[18]

In the parallel passage in *Sha'ar ha-Yiḥudim*, which represents part of the
corpus of Vital edited by Jacob Zemaḥ, the illuminative nature of this praxis is
emphasized as well:

> Know that the one who knows how to unify the upper unifications
> but abstains from performing them causes those righteous ones
> who want to be impregnated[19] by him to assist him in the [study of]
> Torah and the [fulfillment of the] commandments to withdraw from
> him and he brings about great harm upon himself. . . . The reason
> is that involvement with the unifications is greater than engagement
> with the Torah for the unification is engagement with the Torah.
> Further, he who unifies the worlds merits a great reward. Thus it is
> good to unify these unifications constantly every day, for this will
> help him more than engagement with Torah. Moreover, by means of
> this he will draw down upon himself the souls of the righteous who
> want to be impregnated by him for they very much desire these uni-
> fications for they too are unified and cleave to that unification, and a
> great light extends to them. From that great light which extends to
> them on account of that unification they divide and give a portion to
> the person who performs the unification, and they reveal to him the
> mysteries of Torah, and especially if the person intends to elevate
> them by the secret of the female waters.[20]

The concluding statement alludes to the fact that a consequence of the technique of *yiḥudim* is the heavenly ascent of the adept in consort with the soul of the righteous that he has brought down through contemplative meditation. Both souls function as the "female waters" (*mayim nuquin*)[21] that rise to stimulate the unification of the lower male and female aspects of the Godhead (*Ze'eir 'Anpin* and *Nuqba' di-Ze'eir*), a motif to which I return below.

It is well-known that, according to Vital, the authority accorded to his master, Isaac Luria, derived from the fact that he received his Kabbalah from Elijah through the Holy Spirit (*be-ruaḥ ha-qodesh 'al pi 'eliyahu*).[22] That Luria's knowledge of theosophic matters was attained through a revelation of Elijah (*gilluy 'eliyahu*) is considered to be the greatest of his spiritual or mantic powers. On one level the revelation of Elijah, an idea found in earlier rabbinic and mystical texts, is meant to legitimate or privilege Luria's teachings when compared to other kabbalistic trends of sixteenth-century Safed. Thus, in the introduction to his *Sha'ar ha-Haqdamot*, Vital relates that from Naḥmanides, who lived in the thirteenth century, until Luria in the sixteenth, there were no authentic kabbalists, for all kabbalistic works composed during this period were based on speculation rather than an oral reception from a master.[23] (For Luria, of course, the *Zohar* was a work of R. Simeon bar Yoḥai, and therefore it belonged to the second century.) Luria revived the "tradition" for he received kabbalistic secrets directly from the mouth of Elijah, as did R. Simeon according to the *Zohak*,[24] as well as some of the first known kabbalists according to the chain of tradition (*shalshelet ha-quabbalah*) reported by various kabbalists living in the latter part of the thirteenth and early part of the fourteenth century.[25] Yet, on another level, as may be gathered from Vital's writings, the motif of the revelation of Elijah indicates that Luria received esoteric matters in an inspired, indeed ecstatic, state of mind. Thus Vital, in the introduction to his large anthology of Luria's teachings, duly warns the reader that the "sermons and the words themselves in this composition of mine attest and declare that deep and wondrous words such as these are not in the power of the human intellect to compose, if not by means of the influx of the Holy Spirit through Elijah, blessed be his memory."[26] This accords well with the view of Vital, mentioned above, that one can comprehend mystical secrets only to the extent that one receives the prophetic influx from above. In one of the introductions published in his *'Eṣ Ḥayyim*, Vital cites the following in the name of Luria:

> Whenever a person is occupied with this wisdom [i.e., Kabbalah] with all [of his] concentration and strength, and [he is scrupulous with respect to] the fulfillment of the commandments, and he is on guard against any sin, even if he is a servant or the son of a maidservant, the Holy Spirit rests upon him and Elijah the prophet, may his memory be blessed, is revealed to him, and [this revelatory state] does not cease as long as he is involved with it.[27]

In a similar vein Solomon Shlomeil of Dresnitz relates in the first of his five extant letters (written in 1609) that the secrets revealed by Luria "could not be comprehended by any being except by means of the appearance of the Holy Spirit from above and through Elijah, blessed be his memory. . . . Even though there is no prophet or seer after the destruction [of the Temple] the spirit of the living God is not prevented from hovering upon those who are worthy of it."[28] Both Luria and Vital function as the prototype for the mystic visionary, as numerous examples are offered to show that when they studied or expounded kabbalistic truths they had revelatory or ecstatic experiences. To cite in this context one illustration: in *Sefer ha-Ḥezyonot* Vital reports that one Sabbath morning he was delivering a sermon in a synagogue in Jerusalem, and a certain woman, Rachel, the sister of R. Judah Mishan, related that the whole time that Vital was expounding the text she saw a pillar of fire above his head (from other passages it is evident that the pillar symbolizes the Presence) and Elijah to his right helping him out. When Vital completed the textual exposition, the pillar and Elijah vanished.[29] This incident is indicative of a larger assumption in Vital's worldview, namely, the activity of *derashah* as an occasion for revelatory experience, including especially the appearance of Elijah.

Here I would take issue with a comment of R. J. Zwi Werblowsky, who utilized Rudolf Otto's distinction between mysticism and theosophy to characterize the nature of ecstatic experience formulated in the sixteenth-century kabbalistic literature. That is, according to Werblowsky, ecstatic experiences cultivated by kabbalists served only as a means for gnosis or esoteric knowledge. Generalizing from this observation Werblowsky contests the view expressed by Gershom Scholem that "under the cover of the bewildering and often bizarre theosophical speculations of the kabbalists there hides a genuinely mystical life."[30] Werblowsky offers the following critique, focusing primarily on Lurianic Kabbalah: "The fact remains, nevertheless, that the discursive and even dialectical elements are so prominent in kabbalistic literature that we may almost speak of an intellectualistic hypertrophy. . . . More often than not kabbalistic literature is less the record of the *cognitio experimentalis dei* than the substitution of a theosophical *pilpul* for the halakhic one of the rabbinic lawyers."[31] Scholem's formulation is closer to the mark, although he himself was not always consistent on this point.[32] It is misconceived to isolate in the kabbalistic tradition in general, and in Lurianic Kabbalah in particular, theosophic gnosis from mystical ecstasy. In my estimation Vital is clear on this issue: study of Kabbalah is commensurate with prophetic illumination. More than that, the literature of the kabbalists, especially the disciples of Luria, is precisely what Werblowsky says it is not, namely, the record of their experiential knowledge of God. To the outsider it may appear that the Lurianic texts are an exercise in kabbalistic dialectics, a thicket of theosophical ruminations that conceal the living face of divine reality. However, to the initiate these texts constitute the map of the divine world such that textual study itself provides the occasion for mystical illumination.

In the remainder of this study I would like to concentrate on one specific ecstatic technique, that of weeping, which appears a number of times in the writings of Vital. This technique, as I presently show, is viewed as a means for either comprehension of esoteric wisdom or heavenly ascent that occurs specifically while one is asleep. At the outset it behooves me to acknowledge that Moshe Idel has recently discussed weeping as a mystical technique in Jewish texts from apocalyptic sources to Hasidism of the eighteenth and nineteenth centuries. More specifically, Ideal distinguishes two types of weeping in the relevant literature: "mystical weeping," which involved the "effort to receive visions and information about secrets as the direct result of self-induced weeping," and "theurgical weeping," which "intended to induce weeping above—internal processes within the Divine triggered by the shedding of human tears." Within that framework Idel discusses some of the relevant material in sixteenth-century Kabbalah, including the works of Vital.[33] I do not intend to go over the entire historical range that Idel has already covered but concentrate rather on the sixteenth-century material, for there are aspects of the weeping technique in this body of literature that still need to be explained and located within a broader phenomenological and hermeneutical context. Whereas Idel approaches the topic diachronically, as part of his grand effort of reconstructing ideas in Jewish mysticism on the basis of intertextual links, I am attempting a synchronic analysis to shed further light on the phenomenon as it presented itself in Safed.

Let me begin by citing the key text from Vital's *Sha'ar Ruaḥ ha-Qodesh:*

The matter concerning a person's comprehension of wisdom [i.e., kabbalistic lore] entails several conditions. The first condition is silence. One should limit one's speech as much as is possible, and one should not sing any idle song. This is the meaning of [what the rabbis], blessed be their memory, said: "A fence around wisdom is silence."[34] The second condition is that with respect to every word and every matter in the Torah or the *Zohar* that one does not understand, one should think [about them] and weep over them, and as much as one can, one should augment one's weeping. This [tradition] is from R. Abraham ha-Levi [Berukhim] who heard it from the Rabbi [Isaac Luria], blessed be his memory. Moreover, [with respect to] the ascent of the person's soul (*'aliyyat nishmat ha-'adam*) at night after he lies down to sleep, he should not meander about in the follies of this world, but rather immediately he should ascend to the place that is appropriate for him. All this depends on weeping, he should weep during the time of sleep, and sleep from the weeping.[35]

It is evident that two separate traditions (both of which ultimately may be derived from zoharic literature) are conflated in Vital's text, the one, attributed to Abraham ben Eliezer Halevi Berukhim, concerning weeping as a propaedeutic for comprehension, and the other, apparently his own, which links weeping to the nocturnal ascent of the soul separated from the body.[36] Interestingly enough, in his aforementioned survey of weeping as a mystical technique in Jewish sources, Idel notes that weeping results in (1) revelatory or visionary experience, occasionally of the chariot, and (2) comprehension of esoteric matters. It is no accident that Vital adds to the first tradition the one that underscores the connection between weeping and heavenly ascent. Indeed, as I set out to illustrate, the mechanics of the two are quite similar.

The tradition reported in the name of Abraham ben Eliezer ha-Levi Berukhim is repeated with some slight modification in a second passage in *Sha'ar Rauḥ ha-Qodesh:* "R. Abraham Halevi, may God protect and preserve him, told me that my teacher [i.e., Luria], blessed be his memory, gave him advice to attain comprehension, and it is that he should not make idle conversation, and that he should rise at midnight and weep over [his] lack of knowledge. He should study much *Zohar* alone, in a rapid reading without going into too much depth."[37] In one of the introductions to *Sha'ar ha-Haqdamot* Vital combines the various views that were circulating among the disciples of Luria:

> Comprehension of wisdom (*hassagat ha-ḥokhmah*): The first condition is that one should limit his speech and be quiet as much as is possible so that he will not produce idle conversation, in accordance with the saying of the rabbis, blessed be their memory, "A fence around wisdom is silence." Furthermore, another condition: concerning every matter of Torah that you do not understand you should weep over it as much as you can. Also the nocturnal ascent of the soul to the supernal world, so that one does not wander about in the vanities of the world, depends on one's going to sleep through weeping and in bitter sadness, especially to comprehend wisdom for nothing prevents wisdom more than this. Moreover, with respect to man's comprehension there is nothing that helps like purity and ablution[38] so that a person will be pure all the time.[39]

In yet another version of this tradition, extant in manuscript, weeping as a means to attain mystical gnosis (*hassagat ha-ḥokhmah*) is placed in the context of both prayer and study: "The second condition: in all your prayers, and in every hour of study, in a place that is difficult for you, where you cannot understand or comprehend your studies (*ḥokhmat ha-limmudim*[40]) or some secret, arouse yourself to bitter weeping until your eyes shed tears, and the more you can weep, you should do so. Increase your weeping for the gates of tears are not closed[41] and the supernal gates will be opened to you."[42] The juxtaposition of these different motifs, weeping, prayer, and the comprehension of secrets, is attested as well in the following account of Luria given by Solomon Shlomeil of Dresnitz:

> He would tell his students that he would cry as many tears as the [number of] hairs of his beard with respect to each and every secret that was revealed to him from heaven. Similarly, when he wanted to reveal a secret to his disciples they did not want to give him permission until he prayed countless prayers and cried as many tears as the [number of] hairs on his head.[43]

Finally, this tradition is mentioned in another context, the *Sha'ar ha-Yihudim*: "I have found in a manuscript of R. Hayyim Vital: It is good for the one who wants to apprehend [wisdom] to increase his silence as much as is possible, as well as his weeping on every matter that he does not know. . . . Each night he should also place a stone under his head and contemplate the Tetragrammaton [spelled YWD HH WAW HH = 53] which numerically equals [the world] *'even* [i.e., stone = 53]."[44] The placing of a stone under one's head in order to meditate on the divine name is related to a well-known magical technique in Jewish sources, the dream-question (*she'elat hlom*): by placing a parchment with God's name under one's head one could adjure the angel of dreams to answer a query posed in the waking hours.[45] Knowledge of the name confers the capacity for receiving prophetic and visionary illumination.

The full force of the function of weeping in this context can be appreciated if we pause and consider the first specified condition to attain mystical comprehension, namely, silence or refraining from idle conversation.[46] The notion that silence is a prerequisite for the attainment of esoteric truths is expressed, for instance, in the kabbalistic-ethical compendium, *Reshit Hokhmah*, written by another sixteenth-century kabbalist, Elijah de Vidas, one of the students of Cordovero. Commenting on the same passage from the mishnah *'Avot* mentioned by Vital, "a fence around wisdom is silence," de Vidas notes that

> by means of one's silence one is removed from the six extremities [i.e., the six lower emanations], which are the voice and speech [respectively, *Tif'eret* and *Shekhinah*], and ascends to the place of silence, which is thought, the secret of wisdom.[47] . . . Another explanation of the matter is that when a person is silent he makes himself into a chariot for the place of silence, and he merits that secrets of Torah will flow upon him, for they are in silence, as permission is not granted for them to be revealed.[48]

Although the tradition of Abraham ha-Levi reported by Vital does not explicitly mention the theosophic transformation of the rabbinic idea that we find in the case of de Vidas, it is plausible to assume that this is precisely what underlies the former text as well. Silence, therefore, functions as a kind of magical device to draw down the influx from above, a process that Vital elsewhere, perhaps influenced by the anonymous Abulafian work written at the end of the thirteenth century, *Sha'are Ṣedeq*, calls "*hamshakhat ha-maḥshavah*,"[49] drawing down of thought, by means of proper intentions and unifications (*kawwanot weyiḥudim*).[50] It seems to me that in the teaching attributed to Abraham ha-Levi the silence also assumes a specifically magical role as a technique for drawing down the life force from the upper recesses of the Godhead.

This point is important, for it holds the key to understanding the significance of weeping in this context as well. That is, the weeping serves as the means by which the individual can directly effect the divine, specifically by opening up the highest channels to overflow in a way that parallels the shedding of tears below. This is alluded to in one of the formulations of Abraham ha-Levi's teaching to the effect that an increase of weeping opens the supernal gates, which may be interpreted as a reference to the upper emanations. In the case of some kabbalists, the *sha'are dim'ah*, gates of weeping, correspond to the forty-nine gates of *Binah* (understanding), the third emanation. Such a usage is found, for example, in the following comment from the unpublished part of Cordovero's encyclopedic work, *'Elimah Rabbati:*

> When a person desires to perform some unification . . . it should be by means of tears, for the heart does not cleave to the desire of the soul except through weeping. The tears are from the heart, therefore it is proper that when one unifies [the name of God] he should contemplate through weeping. The tears cause the cleaving of the person (*devequt ha-'adam*) . . . and he opens the gates of *Binah*. . . .
> Therefore one must open the gates of weeping to open the gates [of *Binah*], and from there all the other gates are opened.[51]

For Cordovero, as in the other material that I have mentioned, the weeping serves simultaneously as a mystical technique and a theurgical device. It is virtually impossible in this context to keep the issues entirely distinct. In the case of the tradition reportedly going back to Luria, the weeping is presented as a means to attain mystical comprehension, but the latter is depicted as an opening up of the supernal gates. The comprehension of esoteric matters proceeds from an influx of divine light, an influx that can overflow only through the proper magical devices. In yet another context Vital explicitly states that the function of shedding tears below is to ameliorate the forces of divine judgment above. This is formulated, following the zoharic precedent, as a kabbalistic recasting of the rabbinic mythos concerning God's shedding two tears into the great sea when he recalls the suffering of Israel in exile.[52] According to Vital, the weeping below corresponds to the shedding of tears above from the supernal wisdom[53] to the lower wisdom, that is, the Presence symbolized as the great sea; hence, the talmudic gates of weeping, *sha'are dim'ah*, are identified as the aspects of *Neṣaḥ* (endurance) and *Hod* (majesty) within *Hokhmah* (wisdom).[54] From this context, then, we again see that the Lurianic kabbalist conceives of weeping as a theurgic means to open the highest channels of the sefirotic world.

There is another dimension here as well that is not openly stated but may be reconstructed on the basis of various other comments in the relevant literature. That is, the weeping of the eye symbolically displaces the seminal discharge of the phallus. Given the relative neglect of scholars to pay attention to the phallic symbolism of the eye in Lurianic Kabbalah (although, as I show in more detail below, the eyes properly speaking represent not the phallus but rather the testes or at least an aspect of the upper dimension of the Godhead that corresponds to the latter), it seems to me warranted to enter here into a discussion exploring the various facets of this matter. As is the case with so many ideas and motifs in the complex Lurianic system, so too with respect to this particular symbol Luria and his disciples draw on many earlier texts. The correlation of the eye and the phallus is an old one in Jewish sources, perhaps suggested by the fact that the word *ʿayin* connotes both the eye and a spring or fountain, the latter being a rather obvious phallic symbol.[55] The upward displacement of the phallus by the eye, and the philological connection with *ʿayin* in the double sense of eye and spring, is attested in many rabbinic texts, both classical and medieval. Perhaps the most obvious example is found in the interpretation (attributed to R. Abahu) of Joseph's blessing in Gen. 49:22, "Joseph is a fruitful bough, a fruitful bough by a spring" (*ben porat yosef ben porat ʿale ʿayin*). According to the rabbinic reading, the blessing guarantees Joseph immunity against the evil eye.[56] The key expression *ʿale ʿayin*, "by a spring," is thus read *ʿule ʿayin*, "above the eye," that is, beyond the reaches of the evil eye (*ʿeinaʾ bishaʾ*), which refers specifically to sexual desire.[57] This euphemistic usage of the word is implied in the talmudic dictum, "a person should not drink from this cup and cast his eye upon another cup."[58] The phallic symbolization of the eye also seems to underlie various rabbinic passages that deal with the seeing of the divine Presence,[59] especially the midrashic reading of Exod. 24: 11, which contrasts the brazenness of the sons of Aaron, Nadab, and Abihu, who loosened their head-coverings and feasted their eyes upon the Presence, with the modesty of Moses, who hid his face in his visual encounter with the Presence.[60] As I have argued at length elsewhere, the act of gazing in this context likely implies some sexual activity, with the eye functioning as a phallic symbol.[61] Drawing on this midrashic motif, kabbalistic sources, particularly the zoharic and Lurianic materials, refer to the state of union between male and female potencies as a face-to-face glance (*histakkelut panim be-fanim* or *hashgaḥah panim be-fanim*).[62] A later attestation of the correlation of the eye and phallus is evident from the comment of Maimonides that semen is the "light of the eyes."[63] This correlation plays an instrumental role in several kabbalistic sources from the classical period of the development of Spanish Kabbalah in the thirteenth century. Here I provide a modest sampling of the relevant references. The phallic symbolization is evident in a number of zoharic passages, of which I mention one in this context:[64] the wise man, described as one who is filled with eyes, is said to cast his open eye (*peqiḥu de-ʿeinaʾ*) upon the hidden secrets of Torah, which are revealed from beneath its garments, that is, the literal sense of Scripture.[65] As I have suggested elsewhere, it seems that the open eye of the sage corresponds to the phallus (or fulfills a function that is phallic in nature) and the Torah, which is parabolically depicted as the beautiful maiden without eyes, is the feminine Presence.[66] The casting of the open eye, therefore, is erotically charged for it bestows upon that which is seen. To cite one other example, Joseph Angelet comments as follows on the verse, "The eyes of all look to You expectantly, and You give them their food when it is due" (Ps. 145:15):

> The "eyes of all" refer to the seven eyes[67] that are comprised within the attribute of All [*middat kol*], for the world stands upon seven pillars and all of them stand upon one Ṣaddiq [i.e., Yesod][68] . . . and the Ṣaddiq is called All, and all things comprised in him are called the "eyes of All" [which] "look to You expectantly," to that supernal anointing oil that flows from the brain, the most hidden of all that which is hidden, to the All. Then, "You give them their food when it is due." What is "when it is due" [*be-ʿitto*]? This refers to Ṣedeq [*Malkhut*] and she is filled like a container that is filled of all good things, and she overflows to the lower entities in accord with what is decreed in the supernal constellation [*mazzal*] for[69] children, livelihood, and sustenance derive from there.[70]

The seven eyes are thus seven attributes that are comprised within *Yesod*, which is designated as the All (*kol*). Further on in the same context, Angelet specifies the identification of the eye and *Yesod* more precisely: "He will be a 'fruitful bough by a spring' (Gen. 49:22), this refers to the eyeball (*ʿeina de-galgalaʾ*), for the whole sphere depends upon it. Thus he is the eye for all six [emanations], three from the right and three from the left, and he corresponds to the Sabbath, the seventh."[71]

The correlation of the eye and the phallus also underlies a theme repeated on various occasions in the zoharic literature to the effect that the punishment for the sin of onanism is not seeing the face of the divine Presence, that is, according to the principle of measure-for-measure, the eye substitutes for the phallus: the sin is committed through the latter and the punishment affects the former.[72] Based on these associations there develops within later kabbalistic literature the notion that the rectification of sexual sins (*pegam ha-berit*) is achieved through perfection of the eyes (*tiqqun ʿeinayim*), and especially through the shedding of tears. Thus, for example, de Vidas writes:

> All aspects of perfecting the eye (*tiqqune ha-ʿeinayim*) . . . are rectification of the sign of the covenant (*tiqqun le-ʾot berit*), for Joseph

[symbolic of *Yesod*, the divine attribute that corresponds to the phal-
lus] holds on to the eyes, as it is written, "Joseph is a fruitful bough,
a fruitful bough by a spring" (Gen. 49:22) [the last words *'ale 'ayin*
being here read as a reference to the eyes]. . . . In particular, the semen is the light of a man's eyes, and since he sinned with respect to
the semen, he sheds tears from his eyes, and the tears lessen the
semen . . . for the tears too are the light of the eyes.[73]

Similarly, Eleazar Azikri writes that "the waters of the eyes atone for the semen
spilled in vain."[74]

In neither the passage from Cordovero cited above nor the Lurianic material is the explicit connection made between weeping and the spilling of
semen in vain, or, more generally, between the eye and the male genitalia.
Nevertheless, it seems to me that some such correlation is tacitly implied by
these texts: by weeping one cleaves to the sefirotic realm, and as a result of
this cleaving the channels above—corresponding to the eyes below—are
opened and overflow to the individual, enabling him to comprehend secrets
that he did not comprehend before. It is through the weeping that one cleaves
to the divine light and thereby receives the influx from above. That this explanation is valid can be supported by any number of texts in the Lurianic corpus
that are predicated on a correlation of the eye and the male genitalia. Thus, for
example, in *Sha'ar ha-Kawwanot* Vital offers the following explanation for the
gesture of shutting the eyes[75] that is required when the *Shema'*, the traditional
proclamation of divine unity, is recited:

Before you say "Hear O Israel [the Lord, our God, the Lord is one]"
[Deut. 6:4] you should close your two eyes with your right hand and
concentrate on what is written in the[zoharic section] *Sabba' de-
Mishpaṭim* [regarding] the beautiful maiden who has no eyes.[76] We
have explained in that context that the meaning [of this expression]
is Rachel, who ascends at this point [of the prayer] in the aspect of
female waters in relation to the Father and Mother.[77]

To appreciate the complex symbolism underlying this comment it is necessary
to bear in mind that, according to the Lurianic interpretation of the liturgical
order, the mystical significance of the *shema'* is "to raise the female waters from
the Male and Female to the Father and Mother so that the Father and Mother
will be united and the [efflux of the] consciousness (*moḥin*) will come down to
the Male and Female."[78] The worshipper thus joins the feminine hypostasis so
that he may rise with her in the aspect of the female waters to facilitate the
union of the lower two masculine and feminine configurations (*parṣfim*) in the
Godhead, *Ze'eir 'Anpin* and *Nuqba' di-Ze'eir*, which, in turn, stimulate the union
of the upper masculine and feminine configurations, the Father (*'Abba'*) and
Mother (*'Imma'*).[79] The latter union results in the overflowing of the male wa-

ters (*mayim dukhrin*) from *Ze'eir 'Anpin* to *Nuqba' di-Ze'eir* during the moment
of coupling. What is most significant for this discussion is the fact that the
male adept ritually covers his eyes to transform himself into that divine grade
that is symbolized by the zoharic image of a beautiful maiden without eyes,
namely, *Nuqba' di-Ze'eir*, the aspect of the configuration (*parṣuf*) that corresponds to the last of the ten *sefirot*, the *Shekhinah*. It may be concluded,
therefore, that there is here a process of effeminization of the male, a motif
that has not been sufficiently noted in discussions of Lurianic symbolism and
ritual. Indeed, the whole question of sexual transformation in kabbalistic literature has not been adequately studied by scholars of Jewish mysticism. Yet,
this thematic is critical for a proper assessment of the role accorded to gender
and body symbolism in kabbalistic thought in general and Lurianic Kabbalah
in particular. It lies beyond the concerns of this discussion to engage this
important topic in full, but it is necessary to remark that the motif of the males
becoming integrated in the female waters is part of this larger phenomenon
of gender metamorphosis.[80] To be sure, the union of the righteous souls with
the *Shekhinah* is facilitated by the fact that the former correspond to the male
aspect of the divine par excellence, the *membrum virile*. However, once these
souls enter into the *Shekhinah* they become integrated as part of her and constitute the female waters that further stimulate coitus in the divine realm. It is
evident that the Lurianic teaching concerning the female waters is based on
the physiological model of the vaginal secretions that the woman discharges
during foreplay preceding sexual intercourse.[81] Again, for the immediate focus
of this discussion it is essential to note that the assimilation of the male into
the female is characterized as the male closing his eyes in emulation of the
beautiful maiden without eyes. The ritual gains its mystical valence from the
fact that the eyes function as a symbol for the male genitalia while still remaining eyes or, to put the matter somewhat differently, the eyes are the aspect
in the head that function like the genitals in the lower region of the body.
Hence, the female persona of the divine is depicted as the beautiful maiden
without eyes for the latter function as the symbolic correlates of the masculine
reproductive organs.[82] The male worshipper must partake of the character of
the feminine by emasculating himself, a procedure that is ritually fulfilled
through the shutting of the eyes. The interpretation that I have offered is con-
firmed by a second passage in *Sha'ar ha-Kawwanot* that deals more generally
with the closing of the eyes during prayer. In this text Vital has imputed new
theosophic valence to an established prayer-gesture that has as its purpose the
augmentation of intention during worship:[83]

> You should shut and close your eyes during the morning and after-
> noon prayers only at the time of the *'Amidah* [the silent, standing
> prayer of eighteen benedictions] and in the evening prayer close
> your eyes during the whole prayer from the blessings of the recita-

tion of *Shema*ʿ until the [conclusion of the] ʿ*Amidah*. The secret of
the shutting of the eyes is alluded to in what is written in the [zo-
haric section] *Sabbaʾ de-Mishpaṭim* . . . "Who is the beautiful maiden
who has no eyes?" The explanation of this passage is that it is speaking about Rachel, the feminine of *Zeʿeir ʾAnpin*, for she is called the
beautiful maiden. . . . But she has no eyes for her [corporeal] stature
(*shiʿur qomah*) is from the chest and below of *Zeʿeir ʾAnpin*. There is
no aspect of the eyes of *Zeʿeir ʾAnpin* corresponding to her to draw
down from him to her the aspect of the eyes as well. But Leah has
eyes according to the secret, "Leah had weak eyes" (Gen. 29:17), for
the place of Leah is above in the place of the head of *Zeʿeir ʾAnpin*
where there is an aspect of the eyes of *Zeʿeir ʾAnpin*, and from there
their illumination goes forth in Leah who corresponds to them. He
created and formed in her the aspect of the eyes as is not the case
with respect to the lower Rachel.[84]

In still other places within the Lurianic corpus it is evident that the eyes
represent the male potency. Thus, for example, this is the underlying symbolism of the ritualistic requirement to look at the cup of wine during the recitation of the *qiddush*, the prayer of sanctification of Sabbath. Building on the
rabbinic idiom cited above concerning the casting of one's eye on a cup, which,
as I noted, has obvious sexual connotations in its original context, Vital applies
this imagery to the specific rite of *qiddush*:

In another pamphlet I have found that all this should be intended
by the glance of his eyes upon the cup of wine, for by means of this
he draws upon her the aspect of the crown as has been mentioned
above.[85] In another pamphlet I have found [it written that] on the
Sabbath when one casts his eyes upon the cup of wine as is known
he should intend another, different intention from that of the week.
He should intend the name Yah Adonai for five times Yah Adonai is
numerically equal to *bat ʿayin*[86] concerning which the rabbis, may
their memory be for a blessing, said "and one places one's eyes
upon the cup."[87]

The masculine symbolization of the eyes is evident as well in the following
anonymous Lurianic text:

The female has nothing from the house of the father, for the father
is not responsible for the sustenance of his daughter. However, in
order that the matter not be trivial in his eyes, he gives her a
dowry.[88] The matter concerns the fact that she [*Nuqbaʾ di-Zeʿeir*] has
no eyes, but *Zeʿeir* [ʾ*Anpin*] glances with [his] eyes upon his chest
and from there the light is transmitted to her so that she has eyes.[89]

Implicit in the above passage is a motif that recurs in Vital's own writings: the ocular glance (*histakkelut ha-'ayin*) is endowed with generative power.[90] Thus, for example, in the description of the different parts of the face of the Primordial Anthropos (*'Adam Qadmon*) and the respective senses to which they are correlated, it is said that the glance of the eye (which corresponds to the *sefirah* of *Ḥokhman* and the soul of the soul, *neshamah la-neshamah*) on the other three aspects of soul that compose the *'olam ha-'aquddim* (*neshamah*, which corresponds to *Binah* and the ears; *ruaḥ*, which corresponds to *Tif'eret* and the nose; and *nefesh*, which corresponds to *Malkhut* and the mouth) creates the vessels of the points (*ha-kelim shel ha-nequddot*) that eventually shatter because they were not potent enough to hold the lights that stream forth from the eyes. The aspect of the lights that emerge from the eyes of the Primordial Anthropos emanate in an atomized form and are thus designated the "world of points" (*'olam ha-nequddim*), also referred to as the "world of chaos" (*'olam ha-tohu*) insofar as the cataclysmic shattering of the vessels is said to occur at this stage of the unfolding of the divine.[91] A special relationship, therefore, pertains between the points and the eyes.[92] It would appear, moreover, that the former too function phallically in this mythical theosophy, that is, the *nequddim* (or sometimes referred to as *nequddot*) represent the feminine potencies of the Godhead that emerge from the phallus (if not, more specifically, the drops of semen itself)[93] associated with the aspect of *Ḥokhmah* (symbolized by the permutation of the Tetragrammaton, whose sum tallies 63).[94] To underscore the generative power of the eyes, Vital provides the following example: the ostrich hatches its eggs by looking at them. This indicates that there is "actual power in the glance of the eyes" (*koaḥ mamashit be-histakkelut ha-'einayyim*).[95] Vital applies this dynamic to the Godhead—by means of the glance the eyes produce the sphere of being called the world of points:

> From the aspect of this glance of the eyes (*histakkelut ha-zeh shel ha-'einayyim*) the points emerge. Through this you can understand what is written in the *Tiqqunim*, tiqqun 70[96] . . . concerning the form of the [name] YHWH depicted in the form of eyes through points,[97] according to the secret, "and their rims were covered all over with eyes" (Ezek. 1:18), for the aspect of the eyes is the points. . . . The eye has an aspect of the final *he'* and the first *he'* [of the Tetragrammaton], and this is the secret of what is written in the *Tiqqunim* [regarding the verse] "I was asleep" (Cant. 5:2), corresponding to the final *he'*, for with the abolition of the light of the points [the consequence is] "I am asleep," according to the secret of sleep. Further, "I am asleep," [the word] *yeshenah* [asleep] has the letters of *sheniyah* [the second], for *Ḥokhmah* is the first *he'* and it is second to *Keter*. It is known that the cantillation notes correspond to *Keter*, the vowel-points to *Ḥokhmah*, the crownlets to *Binah*, and the letters to the

lower seven [*sefirot* from *Ḥesed* to *Malkhut*]. Thus, the eye is the aspect of *Ḥokhmah* that consists of the points, and this is the reason that the sages of the community are called the "eyes of the community."[98]

In the continuation of this passage Vital remarks that these points compose the aspect of the Edomite kings who died,[99] that is, the primordial forces of judgment that are also connected with the verse, "And the earth was unformed and void" (Gen. 1:2). "The earth," writes Vital, "is the final *he'* that is the aspect of the eye."[100] This implies not that the feminine aspect of the Godhead, symbolized by the earth, is the eye but only that it partakes of divine wisdom, which is, as I indicated above, represented by the eye. Therefore, it is appropriate to apply the symbol of the eye to the final *he'* of the Tetragrammaton, which represents the female configuration of the Godhead. The roots of divine judgment lie within the eyes of the Primordial Anthropos, which constitute elements of *Ḥokhmah*, and they are expunged as the light points that come forth from the eyes. This is also expressed in terms of the description of the circular nature of the lights that emerge from the eyes in contrast to the linear nature of the lights that emanate from other parts of the head, to wit, the ears, nose, and mouth.[101]

> In the beginning of the emanation the points emanated exclusively in the aspect of their circles (*'iggulim*) without the linear (*yosher*), and these are the aspect of the soul of the points (*nefesh shel ha-nequddim*). . . . Therefore they were shattered because they only emerged in the aspect of their soul, for they are circular, and they were incapable of receiving the supernal light. Consequently, there was the aspect of the death of the kings and their abrogation.[102]

When the shattering of the vessels will be rectified, then the light again will stream forth from the eyes in the dual aspect of the circle and the line, the former corresponding to the lower aspect of the soul (*nefesh*) and the latter to the higher (*ruaḥ*). Hence, Vital characterizes the *tiqqun* by citing the following biblical texts: "God said: Let there be light, and there was light" (Gen. 1:3) and "Open Your eyes and see our desolation" (Dan. 9:18). The opening of the eyes represents the (masculine) overflow of the divine influx. That the emanation of the circular lights from the eyes involves a process that parallels or resembles the emission of semen is implied in the following comment of Vital: "With this you will understand how the eyes allude to *Neṣaḥ* and *Hod* for the light of *Neṣaḥ* and *Hod* of this *'Adam Qadmon* went out from the eyes; thus *Neṣaḥ* and *Hod* allude to the eyes."[103] That is, the eyes correspond to the aspects of the divine, *Neṣaḥ* and *Hod*, that are generally depicted as the testes that generate the semen that pours forth from *Yesod* to the *Shekhinah*.[104] It follows, therefore, that the eyes must serve a similar function. The punctiform lights that come forth from the sockets of the eyes are thus comparable to the drops of semen, an interpretation that is enhanced by the connection made by Vital between those light points and the letter *yod*.

I have embarked on a rather lengthy digression to show that the eye and ocular activities in Lurianic Kabbalah assume a phallic or masculine character. It is beyond the scope of this essay to discuss in any more detail the central importance of this symbol, but it should be evident from my remarks that it is indeed crucial for understanding several different facets of the complex Lurianic doctrine, especially and perhaps most importantly the myth of the breaking of the vessels. The significant point to emphasize is that it is necessary to grasp precisely such a symbolic nuance to appreciate the central motif of this study. Weeping is a substitution (and in some instances a rectification) for seminal emission[105] and accordingly facilitates the attainment of esoteric knowledge. Additionally, Vital advanced the idea that weeping is a means for ascent of the soul, *'aliyyat neshamah*, during sleep, culminating in some vision of the supernal realm. It should be noted, parenthetically, that the correlation between weeping and ascent is found in a passing remark in Karo's *Maggid Mesharim*: "He [the celestial angel] said to me: if it is possible for you to shed tears during your prayer, it is well and good, at least on Monday and Thursday. You [thereby] remove the mark from your face and you ascend."[106] Karo draws here on a rather common idea expressed in earlier Jewish pietistic and mystical texts that recommend weeping during prayer to enhance one's intention. But he goes beyond these sources by suggesting that the weeping during prayer results in an ascent. Moreover, Karo alludes to the notion that the weeping washes off the mark of sin from one's face, an idea expressed in the *Zohar* based in part on the talmudic reading of Ezek. 9:4 to the effect that the wicked are marked by the angel Gabriel with the letter *taw* made from blood on their foreheads so that the angels of destruction could rule over them, whereas the righteous are marked with a letter *taw* made from ink.[107] Thus, one zoharic passage asserts that "when a person transgresses any of the words of Torah, the Torah goes up and down, and places marks on the face of the person." In relating a story about one such individual, the *Zohar* places the following statement in his mouth: "Each day I saw my face in a mirror, and I wept before the Holy One, blessed be He . . . on account of that very sin, and with those tears I washed my face."[108] This text served as the basis for a penitential custom among sixteenth-century kabbalistic authors, as is attested, for example, in de Vidas's *Reshit Hokhmah*.[109] One context is particularly note worthy insofar as the matter is discussed in relation to the ascent of the soul:

> One should also intend to weep in order to wipe away those accusers who prosecute him, for the one who commits a transgression acquires one prosecutor. When he imagines the ascent of his soul above [*yeṣayyer 'aliyyat nishmato le-ma'lah*], and several accusers de-

nounce him and push him outside, it is appropriate for him to weep, mourn, and show embarrasment for his sins. By means of the tears his accusers are nullified. . . . Therefore, it is appropriate to weep in the forehead and the face because the sins are inscribed there.[110]

We have seen above that Vital similarly links weeping and the ascent of the soul; in his case, however, the ascent occurs specifically during sleep. Vital's discussion of weeping and ascent is placed within the framework of an older idea found in kabbalistic literature, especially popular in the *Zohar,* regarding the nocturnal ascent of the soul to its source in the divine world, culminating with a vision of the Presence.[111] The kabbalistic idea itself is based, in part, on earlier rabbinic passages that speak of God taking the soul from a person during sleep and returning it on waking. The zoharic authorship associates this idea with two other rabbinic traditions: sleep is considered one-sixtieth of death, and upon death the soul has a vision of the Presence denied it while it was inhabiting the body. Vital, obviously aware of these traditions, feels no need to elaborate in great detail for they were fairly commonplace in his time, and he certainly would have assumed that his readership was familiar with them. We should not misread his reticence: his assertion that the ʿaliyyat nes-hamah occurs during sleep presupposes, in line with the rabbinic and kabbal-istic traditions briefly alluded to above, that sleep is a prolepsis of death that is marked by a visionary experience of the *Shekhinah.* The weeping, then, is a kind of preparation for the spiritual ascent that occurs while one sleeps, a foreshadowing of death. The introduction of weeping in this context is the novel element in Vital's formulation. The import of the weeping as a mystical ritual can be appreciated only if one takes into account the function assigned to weeping in other discussions in Vital or related writings. It seems likely, as I have suggested, that the weeping substitutes for seminal emission; indeed, it may even be the case that for Vital, as for other sixteenth-century kabbalists, the weeping is a form of rectification (*tiqqun*) of this sin. Interestingly enough, in one context Vital remarks with respect to the sin of spilling semen in vain that "it is most severe for it prevents the ascent of the soul at night to its Lord."[112] While this statement too is clearly based on earlier sources, the fact is that Vital connects weeping and ascent, on the one hand, and the spilling of semen in vain and an obstacle to ascent, on the other hand.

By means of weeping, the soul ascends and opens the channels above, thereby creating an overflow to the lower realm. In this ascent the soul expe-riences separation from the body, which may be likened to ecstatic death. It is noteworthy that a similar mystical conception of death is expressed elsewhere in the Lurianic writings. According to Vital, a person is to give his soul over in death to God (*mesirat ha-ʾadam nafsho la-mitah lifne ha-qadosh barukh huʾ*) at two different intervals in the morning service, during the recitation of the *Shemaʿ* and the prayer of supplication, the *nefillat ʾapayim* (prostration).[113] The latter is already mentioned in the *Zohar* as an occasion for ecstatic death, which is further depicted as unification with the *Shekhinah*, symbolized as the tree of death (*le-ʾitkannesha' le-gabbe ha-hu' ʾilana' de-mota'*).[114] Thus, for example, in the description of the *nefillat ʾapayim*, found in the book *Kanfe Yonah* by the sixteenth-century Italian kabbalist, Menaḥem Azariah of Fano, based on a work of the same name by one of Luria's disciples, Moses Yonah,[115] three elements— death, ascent, and union—converge:

> The secret [of the prostration] is that at that point [in the service], which is after the completion of the *ʿAmidah* [i.e., the eighteen bene- dictions recited in a standing posture] . . . he gives himself over to death [*moser ʿaṣmo la-mitah*], and he should consider it as if he were really dead. And when he recites [the verse] "To you, O Lord, I lift my soul" [Ps. 25:1], he should give his soul to the *Shekhinah*, for when the soul of the righteous one ascends, it elevates the female waters for [the sake of] the unification of *Tiferet* and *Malkhut*. . . . In the time of the prostration, which is the moment of unification, he should intend to raise the female waters with the ascent of his soul and spirit.[116]

The enactment of death thus results in the union of the soul with the *Shek- hinah*. The soul thereby provides the arousal from below, symbolized as the female waters, which assist in the union of the male and female in the God- head, signified by the overflow of the masculine waters from above. While there clearly are differences between the death experienced at night and the ritual enacted during the supplication prayer, it is not incorrect to draw some com- parison between the two, as is done already in the case of the *Zohar*. Both experiences involve mystical union with the divine Presence, a union charac- terized in overtly sexual terms. This section of the liturgy corresponds to the secret of the emission of semen (*sod hazraʿat ha-tippah*), in ibn Tabul's for- mulation,[117] or the *horadat ha-tippah*, according to Vital.[118] At this moment the *ṣaddiq* unites with the *Shekhinah*: the forces of eros and thanatos converge such that ecstatic union is a kind of dying. Mystical life is truly a being-toward-death.

We can gather still more information about the nocturnal ascent in Vital's thought if we consider a passage in his *Shaʿare Qedushah*, which deals with the mechanics of prophecy (*ʾekhut ha-nevuʾah*).[119] Vital notes that the separation or withdrawal (*hitpashshetut*) of the mind from the body or material sensations (a usage that goes back to earlier sources,[120] which is a means to attain the state of union (*devequt*) of the soul and its divine source, characteristic of prophetic illumination, is not "actual" as it is in the case of sleep when the soul goes out from the body, *ʾein ʾinyan ha-hitpashshetut ha-zeh . . . be-ʿinyene ha-nevuʾah we- ruaḥ ha-qodesh hitpashshetut mamashiyi she-ha-neshamah yoṣet mi-gufo mamash ke-ʾinyan ha-shenah*.[121] Prophecy, or the indwelling of the Holy Spirit, is distinguished from dream visions by the fact that in the former case the soul is still in the body, and the individual therefore can only imagine that he ascends to the upper realms to unite with his soul-root. There is here a curious elevation of the imaginative faculty as the locus of the prophetic vision.

> Then the imaginative faculty causes his thoughts to imagine and conjure as if he ascended to the upper worlds [we-'az yahafokh koah ha-medammeh mahshevotav ledamot u-leṣayyer ke-'illu 'oleh ba-'olamot ha-'elyonim], to the roots of his soul that are there. And when his imagination [ṣiyyur dimyono] reaches his supernal source, images of the [divine] lights are engraved in his mind as if he imagined and saw them [we-ḥuqqaqu ṣiyyure kol ha-'orot be-maḥashavto ke-'illu meṣuyyar we-ro'eh 'otam], in the manner that the imaginative faculty forms images of matters of this world even though it does not [actually] see them.[122]

The ascent of the prophet is thus an imaginary one, a "contemplation as if," in the description of Werblowsky.[123] By means of the imaginary ascent, the soul elevates the light of the divine emanations to their supernal source, causing an abundance of light, which then overflows in a downward direction, eventually reaching the rational faculty, which then overflows to the imagination in which are formed images of the spiritual realities. While the latter part of this process is no doubt based on Maimonides' description of prophecy, as has been noted in the scholarly literature,[124] the former part is related to descriptions of the imaginative ascent found in earlier kabbalistic sources, indebted to Islamic and Jewish Neoplatonism, as I have suggested elsewhere.[125]

Vital alternatively describes the ladder of ascent, the *scala contemplationis*, as the line that extends from the soul-root in the divine realm to the soul embodied on earth. (This description is based on a passage in the fifth chapter of the late thirteenth-century anonymous kabbalistic treatise *'Iggeret ha-Qodesh*, which deals primarily with the mystical intention required during sexual relations. Vital himself cites the relevant text in the fourth part of *Sha'are Qedushah.*)[126]

> The soul is like a very long branch, extending from the root, attached to the tree, until the body of man. That line extends continuously inasmuch as when a person desires to ascend to his source, the light of his thought, which is called *muskal* [that which is intellectually cognized], ascends from the *maskil* [that which intellectually cognizes], which is the rational soul [nefesh ha-maskelet], until the intellect [sekhel] itself, which is the supernal source of his soul. They are joined together and become one through the [process of] intellection itself [u-mitddabbeqim we na'asim 'eḥad 'al yede ha-haskkalah

292 ELLIOT R. WOLFSON

'aṣmah], which is the influx that extends from the intellect [sekhel] to that which intellectually cognizes [maskil].[127]

Even though this contemplative process is an imaginative one, Vital is quick to point out that it serves as the basis for the kabbalistic idea of mystical intention in prayer and the theurgic implications of religious praxis. Indeed, if one denies the power of human thought to impact the nature of the divine emanations, then the whole purpose of prayer and religious observance from the kabbalistic perspective is undermined.[128]

I have spent a fair amount of time describing the contemplative process for, in my estimation, something similar occurs when the soul ascends during sleep. Admittedly, in this case there is an "actual" ascent as opposed to one that is imagined. Nevertheless, the goal of the ascent is to open the upper channels of the divine, thereby creating an overflow of divine light that eventuates in some sort of vision. The sleep itself, characterized by a separation of body and soul, is a simulation of death and thus provides the context for the visionary experience. Just as weeping in the case of the tradition reported in the name of Abraham ha-Levi is a means to open up the supernal gates, so too in the case of the 'aliyyat neshamah, the ascent of the soul.

To sum up: Vital's use of the weeping motif represents the crystallization of various mystical and theurgical tendencies in previous kabbalistic literature. More specifically, he blended together two traditions, the one concerning Torah study and the other the ascent of the soul, for in his mind the two processes involve the same dynamic. It is evident that he viewed weeping as a means for an ecstatic departure culminating in a spiritual vision. Focusing on Vital's discussion of the contemplative ascent in the case of prophecy, Werblowsky was led to conclude that Vital, "like many earlier kabbalists, knows no ecstasy sensu stricto because the soul does not leave the body behind except in the lowest form of inspiration, dreams. There is no real ascent or Himmelsfahrt of the soul such as was cultivated in some other systems."[129] Such a conclusion neglects to take into account the passage from Sha'ar Ruaḥ ha-Qodesh that has served as the basis for my remarks. That text clearly indicates that Vital did entertain the possibility of ecstasy in a strict sense, involving the soul's disengagement from the body. This occurs through mystical study or the nocturnal ascent, but in either case weeping serves as the vehicle to induce the ecstatic experience.

NOTES

Unless otherwise specified, all translations are mine.

1. S. Schechter, *Studies in Judaism: Essays on Persons, Concepts, and Movements of Thought in Jewish Tradition* (New York: Atheneum, 1970), 231–97.

2. See M. Idel, *Studies in Ecstatic Kabbalah* (Albany: SUNY Press, 1988), 91–101, esp. 95–96; and 103–69, esp. 122–40. See also G. Scholem, *Major Trends in Jewish Mysticism* (New York: Schocken Books, 1954), 378, n. 14.

3. G. Scholem, *On the Kabbalah and Its Symbolism*, trans. R. Manheim (New York: Schocken Books, 1965), 118–57, esp. 134.

4. On the shift in focus from the theoretical to the experiential in the study of kabbalistic documents, see M. Idel, *Kabbalah: New Perspectives* (New Haven: Yale University Press, 1988), 74–111. Some of my previous studies too have focused on the experiential element underlying earlier sources. See, e.g., E. R. Wolfson, "Circumcision, Vision of God, Textual Interpretation: From Midrashic Trope to Mystical Symbol," *History of Religions* 27 (1987), 189–215; "The Hermeneutics of Visionary Experience: Revelation and Interpretation in the Zohar," *Religion* 18 (1988): 311–45; "The Mystical Significance of Torah-Study in German Pietism," *Jewish Quarterly Review* 84 (1993): 43–78. This orientation is most fully developed in my monograph, *Through a Speculum That Shines: Vision and Imagination in Medieval Jewish Mysticism* (Princeton, Princeton University Press, 1994). On the possibility that the mythical circle of R. Simeon bar Yoḥai in the *Zohar* reflects an actual group of mystics, see Y. Liebes, "How the Zohar Was Written," *Jerusalem Studies in Jewish Thought* 8 (1989): 1–72 (in Hebrew), and "New Directions in the Study of the Kabbala," *Pe'amim* 50(1992): 160–61 (in Hebrew); E. R. Wolfson, "Forms of Visionary As cent as Ecstatic Experience in the Zoharic Literature," in J. Dan and P. Schäfer, eds., *Gershom Scholem's Major Trends in Jewish Mysticism 50 Years After: Proceedings of the Sixth International Conference on the History of Jewish Mysticism* (Tübingen: Mohr, 1993), 209–235. On possible earlier sources for the Kabbalistic rituals enacted in Safed, see also the important comment of E. K. Ginsburg, *The Sabbath in the Classical Kabbalah* (Albany: SUNY Press 1989), 250, n. 238, regarding the need to investigate the "possible connection between the ritual adaptations of Byzantine-Turkish provenance and the full-blown ritual creativity of Safed Kabbalah."

5. See Scholem, *Major Trends*, 244–51, and *The Messianic Idea in Judaism and Other Essays on Jewish Spirituality* (New York: Schocken Books, 1971), 37–48; R. Elior, "Messianic Expectations and Spiritualization of Religious Life in the 16th Century," *Revue des études juives* 145 (1986): 35–49. This Scholemian thesis has been challenged by various scholars from different vantage points. See Y. Liebes, "The Messiah of the Zohar," in *The Messianic Idea in Jewish Thought: A Study Conference in Honour of the Eightieth Birthday of Gershom Scholem* (Jerusalem, 1982), 87–236 (in Hebrew); Idel, *Kabbalah: New Perspectives*, 258–59; D. B. Ruderman, "Hope Against Hope: Jewish and Christian Messianic Expectations in the Late Middle Ages," in A. Mirsky, A. Grossman, and Y. Kaplan, eds., *Exile and Diaspora: Studies in the History of the Jewish People Presented to Prof. Haim Beinhart* (Jerusalem: Ben-Zvi Institute Hebrew University of Jerusalem, 1991), 185–202.

6. See R. J. Zwi Werblowsky, *Joseph Karo: Lawyer and Mystic* (Oxford: Oxford University Press, 1962), 38–83; L. Fine, "Recitation of Mishnah as a Vehicle for Mystical Inspiration: A Contemplative Technique Taught by Hayyim Vital," *Revue des études juives* 141 (1982): 183–99; L. Fine, "Maggidic Revelation in the Teachings of Isaac Luria," in J. Reinharz and D. Swetschinski, eds., *Mystics, Philosophers and Politicians* (Durham: Duke University Press, 1982), 141–57; L. Fine, "The Contemplative

Practice of Yiḥudim in Lurianic Kabbalah," in A. Green, ed., *Jewish Spirituality from the Sixteenth-Century Revival to the Present* (New York: Crossroad, 1987), 64–98, esp. 86–94.

7. See Scholem, *Major Trends*, 15–16, 36–37, 211–12. Notable exceptions from the earlier (i.e., pre-sixteenth century) material include the personal accounts of revelation by Abraham Abulafia and his disciples, e.g., the author of *Sha'are Ṣedeq* (see Scholem, *Major Trends*, 119–55, esp. 147–55; M. Idel, *The Mystical Experience in Abraham Abulafia* [Albany: SUNY Press, 1987], 73–178); the collection of angelic revelations of Jacob ben Jacob ha-Kohen, called *Sefer ha-'Orah* (see G. Scholem, *Kabbalah* [Jerusalem: Keter, 1974], 56; a synoptic, critical edition of the work has been prepared as a doctoral dissertation by my student Daniel Abrams); and the mystical diary of Isaac of Acre, *'Oṣar Ḥayyim* (see E. Gottlieb, *Studies in Kabbala Literature*, ed. J. Hacker [Tel Aviv: University of Tel Aviv, 1976], 231–47, in Hebrew). Mention should also be made here of the anonymous work *Sefer ha-Meshiv*, which is predicated on revelatory experiences; see M. Idel, "Inquiries in the Doctrine of *Sefer ha-Meshiv*," *Sefunot* 17 (1983): 185–266 (in Hebrew). See also G. Scholem, "The Maggid of R. Joseph Taitazak and the Revelations Attributed to Him," *Sefunot* 11 (1977): 69–112 (in Hebrew).

8. Cf. references cited above, n. 6; see also *Milei di-Shemaya* by Rabbi Eleazar Azikri, ed. M. Pachter (Tel Aviv, 1991), 22–23 (in Hebrew).

9. See Werblowsky, *Joseph Karo*, 9–23, 257–86, 50–55.

10. The work has recently been published by M. Pachter; see reference above, n. 8.

11. Cf. Hayyim Vital, *Sefer ha-Ḥezyonot*, ed. A. Z. Aescoli (Jerusalem: Mosad ha-Rav Kuk, 1954); D. Tamar, "R. Hayyim Vital's Messianic Dreams and Visions," *Shalem* 4 (1984): 211–29 (in Hebrew). The appearance of Elijah is used as a sign of mantic power in later hagiographic literature as well, as we find, e.g., in the case of Israel ben Eliezer, the Besht. Cf. *In Praise of the Ba'al Shem Tov [Shivhei ha-Besht]*, ed. A. Rubenstein (Jerusalem, 1991), 76–77 (in Hebrew); *Hasidic Tales by Michael Levi Rodkinson*, ed. G. Nigal (Jerusalem, 1988), 45 (in Hebrew). See also the testimony of R. Solomon of Lutsk in his introduction to Dov Baer of Mezeritch, *Maggid Devarav le-Ya'aqov*, ed. R. Schatz-Uffenheimer (Jerusalem, 1976), 2–3.

12. See Idel, *Kabbalah: New Perspectives*, 88–96. See also Fine, "The Contemplative Practice of Yiḥudim," 92–93.

13. See G. Scholem, "Eine kabalistische Deutung der Prophetie als Selbstbegegung," *Monatsschrift für Geschichte und Wissenschaft des Judentums* 74 (1930): 285–290, and *Major Trends*, 277, 378, n. 14; Werblowsky, *Joseph Karo*, 38–39, 72–73; L. Fine, "Techniques of Mystical Meditation for Achieving Prophecy and the Holy Spirit in the Teachings of Isaac Luria and Hayyim Vital," PhD diss., Brandeis University, 1976, 101–11; Idel, *Studies in Ecstatic Kabbalah*, 95–96, 122–40, and *Kabbalah: New Perspectives*, 101–2.

14. See D. Boyarin, *Intertextuality and the Reading of Midrash* (Bloomington: Indiana University Press, 1990).

15. See Idel, *Kabbalah: New Perspectives*, 240–41. L. Fine, "The Study of Torah as a Rite of Theurgical Contemplation in Lurianic Kabbalah," in D. R. Blumenthal, ed., *Approaches to Judaism in Medieval Times*, vol. 3 (Atlanta: Scholars Press, 1988), 29–40, analyzes other aspects of the rite of Torah study in the teaching of Luria. On mystical

illumination during prayer, see esp. comment of Ḥayyim Vital, *'Olat Tamid* (Jerusalem, 1907), 10a.

16. Cf. *Sha'ar Ruaḥ ha-Qodesh* (Jerusalem, 1874), 9a–b.

17. See Fine, "The Contemplative Practice of Yiḥudim," 64–98, esp. 86–87, where the author discusses the attainment of prophetic inspiration through the practice of these unifications.

18. *Sha'ar Ruaḥ ha-Qodesh*, fols. 24a–b. Cf. *Sha'ar ha-Gilgulim* (Jerusalem, 1981), chap. 38, 329.

19. On the doctrine of *'ibbur* (impregnation) in kabbalistic writings, see G. Scholem, *On the Mystical Shape of the Godhead*, trans. J. Neugroschel and ed. J. Chipman (New York: Schocken Books, 1991), 221–28, 234, 240, 306, n. 57.

20. *Sha'ar ha-Yiḥudim* (Jerusalem: Mek or hayim, 1970), 3c–d. Cf. *Sha'ar ha-Kawwanot* (Jerusalem, 1963), 23a; and see the description in the first letter of Solomon Shlomiel of Dresnitz published in *Ha-'Ari we-Gurav* (Jerusalem, 1992), 8–9; cf. *The Toledoth ha-Ari and Luria's "Manner of Life" (Hanhagoth)*, ed. M. Benayahu (Jerusalem, 1967), 157, 262 (in Hebrew).

21. The kabbalistic notion of the upper, masculine waters (*mayim dukhrin*) and the lower, feminine waters (*mayim nuquin*) is based on an earlier aggadic motif. Cf. J. Theodor and Ch. Albeck, eds., *Midrash Bereshit Rabba: Critical Edition with Notes and Commentary*, 2nd ed., 3 vols. (Jerusalem: Wahrmann Books, 1965), 13:13, p. 122, and other references cited in n. 4. It is possible that this motif reflects gnostic speculation. See A. Altmann, "Gnostic Themes in Rabbinic Cosmology," in I. Epstein, E. Levine, and C. Roth, eds., *Essays in Honour of the Very Rev. Dr. J. H. Hertz, Chief Rabbi . . . on the Occasion of his Seventieth Birthday* (London: E. Goldston, n.d.), 23–24.

22. Cf. Hayyim Vital's introduction to *'Eṣ Ḥayyim* (Jerusalem: Or Habahir, 1910), 5b; and see *'Eleh Toledot Yiṣḥaq*, in *The Toledoth ha-Ari*, 247–48. The revelation of Elijah to Luria is emphasized several times in the letters of Solomon Shlomiel of Dresnitz and the hagiographical literature based thereon; cf. *Ha-'Ari we-Gurav*, 5, 8, 12, 15, 37, 52, 69, and see extended discussion of this motif on 143, 148–50. See also *The Toledoth ha-Ari*, 154, 262. The importance of Elijah in the life of Luria is underscored as well by the legendary account of Elijah's presence at Luria's circumcision; see *Ha-'Ari we-Gurav*, 3–4; *The Toledoth ha-Ari*, 151–52. In the hagiographical tales concerning Luria it is also reported that while he was asleep he would ascend to the heavenly academies to learn esoteric matters. Cf. *Ha-'Ari we-Gurav*, 5–6; *The Toledoth ha-Ari*, 155, 164–65. On the perception of Luria as a prophet in subsequent literature, including in specific halakhic contexts, see sources cited in *Ha-'Ari we-Gurav*, 181–82. Symbolically, it may be of significance to note that, according to some texts, the aspect of the Holy Spirit corresponds to the emanation of *Yesod*, the *membrum virile* in the divine anthropos. See, e.g., Menaḥem Azariah da Fano, *Kanfe Yonah* (Korets, 1786), 3:8, 3b. On the superiority of the Kabbalist to Elijah the Prophet, see the comment in the text extant in MS Oxford 1784, fol. 37a.: "An explanation for why in the [section on] the Song of Songs in the *Zohar* at one time it says '[the matter] was decreed by the mouth of Elijah' and another time it says 'R. Simeon began to expound.' This is on account of the fact that Elijah is a prophet and he does not have the ability to open the wells of salvation of wisdom. But R. Simeon, whose level of wisdom was higher

than that of the angels, had the power to open the wells of wisdom. Know that the angels cannot reveal the secrets of Torah for our wisdom is greater than their wisdom, and they reveal only the secrets of this world." For a different version of this text, see *Kanfe Yonah*, 2:31, 43d–44a.

23. *Shʿar ha-Haqdamot* (Jerusalem, 1909), 4a–b.

24. See, e.g., *Zohar Ḥadash*, ed. R. Margaliot (Jerusalem: Mosad ha-Rav Kuk, 1978), 59c.

25. Cf. *ʿEṣ Ḥayyim*, 4b–d, 5a–c. For discussion of this chain of tradition in earlier kabbalistic sources, see G. Scholem, *Origins of the Kabbalah*, trans. A. Arkush and ed. R. J. Zwi Werblowsky (Princeton: Princeton University Press, 1987), 35–39, 238–43.

26. *ʿEṣ Ḥayyim*, 4c.

27. *ʿEṣ Ḥayyim* (Korets, 1782), 2c. Cf. the passage from Vital's introduction to *Shaʿare Qedushah* cited by Werblowsky, *Joseph Karo*, 66.

28. *Ha-ʾAri we-Gurav*, 15–16.

29. *Sefer ha-Ḥezyonot*, 6. In the incident that is reported right after this one the same woman was said to have seen a pillar of fire atop the head of Vital one Sabbath morning in Damascus when he was leading the congregation in prayer. On the nexus between prayer and the indwelling of the Presence in the case of Luria, cf. *The Toledoth ha-Ari*, 189. This topos is repeated in other hagiographical literature. See, e.g., *In Praise of the Baʿal Shem Tov*, 85–90.

30. Scholem, *Major Trends*, 15–16.

31. Werblowsky, *Joseph Karo*, 40.

32. See esp. Scholem's characterization of kabbalistic theosophy in *Kabbalah* 4: "Speculations of this type occupy a large and conspicuous area in kabbalistic teaching. Sometimes their connection with the mystical plane becomes rather tenuous and is superseded by an interpretative and homiletical vein which occasionally even results in a kind of kabbilistic *pipul* (casuistry)."

33. Idel, *Kabbalah: New Perspectives*, 75–88, 76, 80–81. On the theurgical significance of weeping in Vital's writings, see also R. Meroz, "Redemption in the Lurianic Teaching," PhD, Hebrew University, 1988, 109, 125, n. 87 (in Hebrew).

34. Cf. M. ʾAvot 3:13.

35. *Shaʿar Ruaḥ ha-Qodesh*, 6a. Cf. *Peri ʿEṣ Ḥayyim* (Jerusalem, or Habahir, 1980) 353, and the statement from Jacob Zemaḥ's *Naggid u-Meṣaveh* cited by Idel, *Kabbalah: New Perspectives*, 313, n. 36. Cf. the anonymous work *Ṭaharat ha-Qodesh* (Jerusalem, 1989), 156, and Natan Shapira, *Ṭuv ha-ʾAreṣ* (Jerusalem, 1891), pt. 3, fol. 5a. Cf. G. Scholem, "The *Shetar ha-Hitqasherut* of the Disciples of the Ari," *Zion* 5(1940), 145 (in Hebrew). It should be noted that the emphasis on crying as a means for comprehension of secrets stands in marked contrast to the opposite notion also expressed in kabbalistic literature regarding joy and happiness as the necessary means to receive esoteric matters (echoing the rabbinic idiom that the Holy Spirit or *Shekhinah* only dwells on one who is joyous; cf. P. Sukkah, 5:1; B. Shabbat, 30b; *Midrash Tehillim*, 24: 3, ed. S. Buber [Jerusalem, 1977], 204). See, e.g., Isaiah Horowitz, *Shene Luḥot ha-Berit* (Amsterdam, 1698), fol. 84b.

36. On weeping as preparatory for comprehension of esoteric matters, see esp. *Zohar* 3:79a; other pertinent examples are cited by Idel, *Kabbalah: New Perspectives*,

313, n. 33. On the nocturnal ascent of the soul, see I. Tishby, *Mishnat ha-Zohar* (Jerusalem: Mosad Byalik, 1975), 2:125–28, and my study on forms of visionary experience in zoharic literature cited above, n. 4. On the connection of weeping, sleep, and a dream vision, see Vital's own testimony in *Sefer ha-Ḥezyonot*, 42–47. Other examples of pietistic forms of weeping are evident in Vital's diary, but they are not specifically connected with visionary experience or mystical techniques. See, e.g., 32, 110.

37. *Sha'ar Ruaḥ ha-Qodesh*, 9d, cited by Benayahu, *The Toledoth ha-Ari*, 319. See also Fine, "The Contemplative Practice of Yiḥudim," 73.

38. Cf. *Sha'ar Ruaḥ ha-Qodesh*, 9c, where Vital reports that R. Israel Sagis heard from Luria that the best thing for comprehension of esoteric matters is ritual ablution (*ṭevilah*), which ensures that a person is always pure. Cf. *Sha'ar ha-Miṣwot* (Jerusalem: Hotsa'at Ahavat Shalom, 1978), 128, where Vital reports the same tradition in the name of one of the colleagues (*ḥaverim*) without further specification. In that context, moreover, the positive effects of ablution are linked especially to the impurities of nocturnal emission and onanism.

39. *'Eṣ Ḥayyim*, 5d.

40. This is a technical term in medieval philosophical texts for the propaedeutic sciences, such as mathematics and astronomy.

41. Cf. *b. Berakhot*, 32b.

42. MS Oxford-Bodleian 1706, fol. 49b, cited by Idel, *Kabbalah: New Perspective*, 86, 313 n. 36.

43. *Ha-'Ari we-Gurav*, 51.

44. *Sha'ar ha-Yiḥudim*, 4d. Cf. *Taharat ha-Qodesh*, 156. See also *Sha'ar Ruaḥ ha-Qodesh*, 6c, where the same technique is related to the ritual of fasting.

45. See J. Trachtenberg, *Jewish Magic and Superstition* (New York: Behrman's Jewish Book House, 1939), 241–43; Werblowsky, *Joseph Karo*, 47–48; J. Bazak, *Beyond the Senses: A Study of Extra-Sensorial Perception in Biblical, Talmudical and Rabbinical Literature in Light of Contemporary Parapsychological Research* (Tel Aviv: Devir, 1968), 40 (in Hebrew). According to another variant of this motif, extant in MS Oxford-Bodleian 1959, fols. 9b–10a, one should place the name of God on one's head in the place where the phylacteries are worn and on the other side of the parchment write his request. One then sleeps and sees great wonders.

46. For discussion of this motif in select Jewish mystical sources, including some of the passages cited in the body of this paper, see M. Hallamish, "On Silence in Kabbalah and Hasidism," in M. Hallamish and A. Kasher, eds., *Dat we-Safah* (Ramat-Gan, 1982), 79–89 (in Hebrew).

47. For a later reverberation of this motif, see the teaching of Dov Baer, Maggid of Mezeritch, discussed in R. Schatz-Uffenheimer, *Quietistic Elements in Eighteenth Century Hasidic Thought* (Jerusalem, 1980), 108 (in Hebrew), to the effect that through silence (as well as closing one's eyes) one can cleave to the world of Thought.

48. *Reshit Ḥokhmah*, Sha'ar ha-Qedushah, chap. 11 (Jerusalem, 1984), 2:272.

49. Cf. *Sha'are Ṣedeq*, ed. Y. Parush (Jerusalem, H. Vagshal, 1989), 22.

50. *Sha'are Qedushah* (Jerusalem, 1985), 3:6, 93.

51. MS JTSA Mic. 2174, fols. 164a–b.

52. Cf. *b. Berakhot* 59a; and see discussion in M. Fishbane, " 'The Holy One Sits

298 ELLIOT R. WOLFSON

and Roars': Mythopoesis and the Midrashic Imagination," *The Journal of Jewish Thought and Philosophy* 1 (1991): 1–21.

53. Cf. *Sha'ar Ruaḥ ha-Qodesh*, 7d, where the tears are said to come forth from Ḥokhmah and Binah.

54. *Sha'ar Ma'amere RaSHBI* (Jerusalem, 1898), 7c. Cf. Meroz, "Redemption in the Lurianic Teaching," 109.

55. See, by contrast, D. J. Halperin, "A Sexual Image in Hekhalot Rabbati and Its Implications," *Jerusalem Studies in Jewish Thought* 6 (1987): 117–32, who interprets a reference to the eyes of the celestial beasts in a key passage from Hekhalot Rabbati as symbolizing the vagina. The eye may, in fact, function as a bisexual symbol, depicting both the male and female genitals. The connection of seeing, or more precisely the opening of the eyes, and erotic desire may be implied in the narrative concerning Adam and Eve in the Garden of Eden; cf. Gen. 3:5, 6, 7. Such an interpretation of the opening of the eyes is emphasized by later rabbinic interpreters on these biblical texts. See, e.g., Shem Ṭov ben Judah ibn Mayon's supercommentary on Abraham ibn Ezra's commentary on the Torah, MS Oxford-Bodleian 228, fol. 17a; A. Roth, *Ṭaharat ha-Qodesh* (Jerusalem, 1974), 1:132. In this connection it is of interest to note an interesting parallel in an ancient Egyptian source between the eyes of Horus and the testicles of Seth. See J. Assmann, "Semiosis and Interpretation in Ancient Egypt," in S. Biderman and B. Scharfstein, eds., *Interpretation in Religion*, (Leiden: E. J. Brill, 1992), 95. Recent scholarship has noted that the correlation of the penis and the eye underlies the phallomorphic ocularcentrism prevalent in Western culture. See L. Irigary, *Speculum of the Other Woman*, trans. G. C. Hull (Ithaca: Cornell University Press, 1985), 47–48, 145–146, and, *This Sex Which Is Not One*, trans. C. Porter (Ithaca: Cornell University Press, 1985), 25–26; M. Jay, *Downcast Eyes: The Denigration of Vision in Twentieth-Century French Thought* (Berkeley: University of California Press, 1993), 493–542.

56. This reading is attested as well by the frequent use of this verse in Jewish amulets from Late Antiquity up until the present, bestowing on the wearer of the amulet protection from the evil eye. Cf. E. A. Wallis Budge, *Amulets and Talismans* (New York: University Books, 1961), 219; T. Schrire, *Hebrew Magic Amulets* (New York: Behrman House, 1966), 114; J. Naveh and S. Shaked, *Amulets and Magic Bowls: Aramaic Incantations of Late Antiquity* (Jerusalem: Magnes Press, Hebrew University, 1987), 237; L. H. Schiffman and M. D. Swartz, *Hebrew and Aramaic Incantation Texts from the Cairo Genizah: Selected Texts from Taylor-Schechter Box K1* (Sheffield: JSOT Press, 1992), 24, 121, n. 22.

57. Cf. *b. Berakhot*, 20a, 55b; *Soṭah*, 36b; *Baba Meṣi'a*, 84a; *Baba Batra*, 118b. For other targumic and midrashic sources where this reading of Gen. 49:22 is employed, see J. L. Kugel, *In Potiphar's House: The Interpretative Life of Biblical Texts* (New York: Harper, 1990), 92, n. 35; and see M. Niehoff, *The Figure of Joseph in Post-Biblical Jewish Literature* (Leiden: E. J. Brill, 1992), 147–48. Although the evil eye has other connotations in rabbinic literature, it is frequently associated with the libidinal drive. See below, n. 72. A similar claim can be made with respect to the more general rabbinic notion, *yeṣer ha-ra'* (the evil will). For recent discussion cf. D. Biale, *Eros and the Jews from Biblical Israel to Contemporary America* (New York: Basic Books 1992), 44–45.

58. *B. Nedarim* 20b. Cf. *Leviticus Rabbah* 12:1 (interpreting Prov. 23:31).

59. See, e.g., *Leviticus Rabbah*, 23:14; *Esther Rabbah*, 3:14. On the erotic nature of visionary experience, see M. Idel, "Sexual Metaphors and Praxis in the Kabbalah," in D. Kraemer, ed., *The Jewish Family: Metaphor and Memory* (New York: Oxford University Press, 1989), 202–3; my article on circumcision cited above, n. 4; and D. Boyarin, "'This We Know to Be the Carnal Israel': Circumcision and the Erotic Life of the God of Israel," *Critical Inquiry* 18 (1992): 474–505, esp. 491–97. See also H. Eilberg-Schwartz, "The Problem of the Body for the People of the Book," in H. Eilberg-Schwartz, ed., *People of the Body: Jews and Judaism from an Embodied Perspective* (Albany: SUNY Press 1992), 17–46, esp. 30–33.

60. Cf. *Leviticus Rabbah* 20:10, and parallels. The link between visual encounter and erotic experience also seems to be implied in the midrashic comment in *Deuteronomy Rabbah* 11:10 to the effect that "from the day that [God] was revealed to [Moses] at the bush he did not have intercourse with his wife."

61. Wolfson, *Through a Speculum That Shines*, 42–43.

62. See, e.g., *Zohar*, 2:99a, 176b; 3:59b, 269a; *Zohar Hadash*, 62c; Liebes, "The Messiah of the Zohar," 164, n. 273; *ʿEṣ Ḥayyim*, 16:3, 49b.

63. *Mishneh Torah*, Deʾot, 4:19.

64. This is not to say that every occurrence of the word *eye* symbolically refers to *Yesod*; on the contrary, this symbol is multivalent in zoharic literature. For example, the word *bat ʿayin*, the pupil of the eye, can symbolize the *Shekhinah*; cf. *Zohar*, 2:204a (and cf. 1:226a); *Tiq qune Zohar*, ed. R. Margaliot (Jerusalem: Mosad ha-Rav Kuk, 1978), 11, 26b; 70, 126b. Cf. especially the passage of Cordovero, MS JTSA Mic. 2174, fols. 178b–179a, where the *bat ʿayin* is a designation of the *Shekhinah* and the light from which she receives the light of knowledge (*ʾor ha-daʿat*) is associated with the three central *sefirot*, *Ḥesed*, *Din*, and *Raḥamim*. When she receives the light she is the open eye and when she does not she is the closed eye. Also significant is the depiction of the eyes of the two divine configurations, *ʾArikh ʾAnpin* and *Zeʿeir ʾAnpin*; cp. *Zohar* 3: 129b–130a (*ʾIdra ʾRabba*), 289a (*ʾIdra ʾZuṭa*). In the case of the latter the eye is said to have no covering or eyelid and to be perpetually open. This position signifies the attribute of divine mercy characteristic of this particular aspect of the Godhead. See especially the commentary on the first passage mentioned above in David ben Yehudah he-Ḥasid, *Sefer ha-Gevul*, MS JTSA Mic. 2193, fols. 4b–6a, which highlights the phallic dimension of the open eye in the uppermost configuration of the divine.

65. *Zohar*, 2:98b. Cf. *Zohar*, 3:147b, where the "open eye" (*peqiḥaʾ de-ʿeina*) is depicted as the source of blessing (related to Prov. 22:9; cf. *b. Soṭah* 38b) in contrast to the closed eye, which is the source of curses (related to Num. 24:3). See also 187b, 211b. Cf. Moses Zacuto's introduction to his *Tiqqun Soferim*, MS Oxford-Bodleian 1890, fol. 1a: "Happy are you righteous ones, masters of faith, to whom have been revealed the secrets of secrets, the Book of Concealment, and you exist at the time that the eye of providence, the open eye that has no covering, has providence over you."

66. E. R. Wolfson, "Beautiful Maiden without Eyes: *Peshat* and *Sod* in Zoharic Hermeneutics," in M. Fishbane, ed. *The Midrashic Imagination* (Albany: SUNY Press, 1993), 185–87.

67. Cf. *Zohar*, 3:136b–137a (*ʾIdra ʾRabba*).

68. Cf. *b. Ḥagigah*, 12b.

69. Cf. *b. Moʿed Qaṭan*, 28a.

70. *Livnat ha-Sappir*, MS British Museum 27,000, fol. 135a.

71. Ibid., fol. 135b. Angelet's description of *Yesod* as the seventh emanation, corresponding to Sabbath, which is the spring that stands in the middle of six other emanations, three from the left and three from the right, echoes the parable in *Sefer ha-Bahir*, ed. R. Margaliot (Jerusalem: Mosad ha-Rav Kuk, 1978), sec. 159. For the development of this motif in select kabbalistic sources, see Ginsburg, *The Sabbath in the Classical Kabbalah*, 87–92.

72. Cf. *Zohar* 1:57a, 69a, 219b; 2:214b; 3:90a; *Shushan ʿEdut*, ed. G. Scholem, *Qovez ʿal Yad*, n.s. 8 (1976) 353; E. R. Wolfson, ed. *The Book of the Pomegranate: Moses de Leon's Sefer ha-Rimmon* (Atlanta: Scholars Press, 1988), 230 (Hebrew text). It is also relevant to note here that in Jewish sources the eye (together with the heart) is often signaled out as a major vehicle for sin in general and sexual promiscuity in particular. See S. Schechter, *Aspects of Rabbinic Theology* (New York: Schocken Books, 1961), 208, 214, 258. In several rabbinic texts it seems that the evil eye specifically refers to the libido. This is clearly the case in zoharic texts as well. Cf. references cited in Y. Pahah, *ʿUle ʿAyin* (Jerusalem, 1990), 51–54. It is thus perfectly sensible that later moralists focused on the blemish of the eye (*pegam ha-ʿeinayyim*) and safeguarding the eye (*shemirat ha-ʿeinayyim*) when discussing matters pertaining to sexual purity. A classic example of this can be found in *Taharat ha-Qodesh*, 1:110–37. Consider also the *Quntres ha-ʿAyin Roʾeh* (Pamphlet on the seeing eye), published by the Bratslav Hasidim (New York: Haside Bratslav, 1982), which collects the relevant material of R. Nahman of Bratslav regarding this issue.

73. *Reshit Hokhmah*, Shaʿar ha-Qedushah, chap. 17.

74. *Mile di-Shemaya by Rabbi Eleazar Azikri*, 109.

75. A locus classicus for the ritual of closing the eyes during prayer in kabbalistic literature is *Zohar* 3:260b, where it is connected specifically with the prohibition of looking at the *Shekhinah*. Regarding this gesture during prayer, see E. Zimmer, "Poses and Postures During Prayer," *Sidra* 5 (1989): 92–94 (in Hebrew). On shutting the eyes as a contemplative technique in kabbalistic sources, see also Idel, *Studies in Ecstatic Kabbalah*, 134–36. For discussion of some of the relevant sources and the reverberation of this motif in Hasidic texts, see Z. Gries, *Conduct Literature (Regimen Vitae): Its History and Place in the Life of Beshtian Hasidism* (Jerusalem: Mosad Byalik, 1989), 220–22 (in Hebrew). See below, n. 83.

76. Cf. *Zohar*, 2:95a, 98b–99a. Concerning this motif, see my study referred to above, n. 66.

77. *Shaʿar ha-Kawwanot*, 21c; cf. *Peri ʿEs Hayyim*, 168.

78. *Shaʿar ha-Kawwanot*, 20c. Cf. Y. Avivi, "R. Joseph ibn Tabul's Sermons on the Kawwanot," in *Studies in Memory of the Rishon le-Zion R. Yitzhak Nissim*, ed. M. Benayahu (Jerusalem, 1985), 4:82–83 (in Hebrew).

79. Cf. *ʿEs Hayyim*, 29:2, fol. 84a; *Shaʿar Maʾamere RaSHBI*, 53a–b. See also *Shaʿar ha-Kelalim*, chap. 1, printed in *ʿEs Hayyim*, fol. 5c. The work is associated with three of Luria's disciples, Moses Yonah, Moses Najara, and Joseph Arzin. According to Y. Avivi, however, the text was authored by Hayyim Vital on the basis of compositions written by the aforementioned kabbalists. See Meroz, "Redemption in the Lurianic Teaching," 90–91.

80. Cf. *Shaʿar ha-Kawwanot*, 46d–47a.

81. Cf. *'Eṣ Ḥayyim*, 39:1, fol. 112d; *Qehillat Ya'aqov* (Jerusalem, 1992), 3. This motif too is expressed in zoharic literature. See, e.g., *Zohar*, 1:60b, 135a. The obvious gender symbolism associated with these cosmological waters, based on the model of orgasmic secretion, is drawn boldly in zoharic literature. See, e.g., *Zohar*, 1:29b. For a more elaborate discussion of the ritualized gender metamorphosis in zoharic and Lurianic texts, see E. R. Wolfson, "Crossing Gender Boundaries in Kabbalistic Ritual and Myth," in *Circle in the Square: Studies in the Use of Gender in Kabbalistic Symbolism* (Albany: SUNY Press, 1995), 79–121, esp. 110–15.

82. Cf. the marginal note of Jacob Zemaḥ in Ḥayyim Vital, *Mavo' She'arim*, 2:2: 6 (Jerusalem, 1892), 8c, according to which the eyes are said to correspond to the consciousness of knowledge that is in the head (*moaḥ ha-da'at she-ba-ro'sh*). Here too one sees the specific linkage of the eyes to a masculine potency, albeit displaced from the genital region of the body to the cranium. In that context the zoharic reference to the beautiful maiden without eyes is also mentioned. See below, n. 103.

83. See references above, n. 75. In the Lurianic material one can still find evidence for the more standard kabbalistic approach to the closing of the eyes as a technique to enhance mental concentration. See, e.g., *Sha'ar Ruaḥ ha-Qodesh*, 42d, 46d; *Sha'ar ha-Kawwanot*, 4a (regarding Luria's own practice of shutting his eyes during the private and public recitation of the Eighteen Benedictions).

84. *Sha'ar ha-Kawwanot*, 59c.

85. That is, by looking at the cup of wine, which symbolizes the feminine Presence, the individual draws down the masculine overflow and thereby reunifies the divine androgyne. Significantly, this unification is depicted in terms of the coronation motif. The understanding of the recitation of *qiddush* as a marriage ceremony and act of divine coronation is expressed in earlier kabbalistic literature, including the *Zohar*. See E. K. Ginsburg, *Sod ha-Shabbat: The Mystery of the Sabbath* (Albany: SUNY Press, 1989), 32, 114–15, n. 150.

86. This numerology is probably to be decoded in the following way: the name Yah Adonai equals 80, which is to be multiplied by 5 to get the sum of 400. To this figure one should add the number 2, which stands for the two names. The sum 402 is also the numerical value of the word *bat*, the first of the two words in the expression *bat 'ayin*, i.e., the pupil of the eye. For a variant explanation cf. *Peri 'Eṣ Ḥayyim*, 422. On the use of *bat 'ayin* as a symbol for the feminine Presence (see above n. 64), cf. the anonymous Lurianic text (see Meroz, "Redemption in the Lurianic Teaching," 93) extant in MS Oxford-Bodleian 1786, fol. 469b. See, however, the passage from this collection cited below at n. 89.

87. *Sha'ar ha-Kawwanot*, 71d. On the requirement to look at the cup of wine during *qiddush*, see also *Kanfe Yonah*, pt. 4, sec. 6, 33d; MS Oxford-Bodleian 1784, fol. 25b. Cf. Jacob Joseph of Poloyonne, *Toledot Ya'aqov Yosef* (Korets, 1780), 130a.

88. See, e.g., b. *Ta'anit*, 24a.

89. MS Oxford-Bodleian 1786, fols. 469a–b.

90. See, e.g., *'Eṣ Ḥayyim*, 9:1, 40a, where the beginning of the shattering of the vessels is linked to a defect in the glance of the eyes of the Father and Mother, i.e., in their union.

91. Cf. *'Eṣ Ḥayyim*, 4:3, 18d–19a, 9:5, 45a–b, 8:1, 34a–35a. See Scholem, *Major Trends*, 265–66; I. Tishby, *The Doctrine of Evil and the 'Kelippah' in Lurianic Kabbalah*

302 ELLIOT R. WOLFSON

(Jerusalem: Schocken Books, 1942), 29–31 (in Hebrew); Meroz, "Redemption in the Lurianic Teaching," 239–45.

92. Cf. 'Eṣ Ḥayyim, 4:1, 17d.

93. See Meroz, "Redemption in the Lurianic Teaching," 100, 155, 194–95. On the feminine character of the "points," see Y. Jacobson, "The Aspect of the Feminine in the Lurianic Kabbalah," in *Gershom Scholem's Major Trends in Jewish Mysticism 50 Years After*, 247–48.

94. Cf. 'Eṣ Ḥayyim, 5:1, 20b–d. And see the marginal note from Ḥayyim Vital cited in 'Eṣ Ḥayyim, 6:5, fol. 27a: "All the reality of the matter of the points is in the secret of the *Nuqba*', and the matter concerns the fact that they come from the power of the light that strikes and sparkles and returns from below to above."

95. Ibid., 8:1, 34b. Cf. *Milei di-Shemaya by Rabbi Eleazar Azikri*, 103. The view articulated by Vital is clearly based on earlier sources. See, e.g., Naḥmanides' commentary to Lev. 18:19, ed. H. Chavel (Jerusalem: Mosad ha-Rav Kuk, 1960), 2:104. Nahmanides asserts that a woman in the period of menstruation who looks at a clear mirror made of iron creates red drops in the mirror corresponding to the drops of blood. The glance of the woman thus has the power to produce an external reality that reflects her internal state of impurity.

96. *Tiqqune Zohar*, 127b.

97. Vital has in mind the ancient tradition regarding the mystical spelling of the Tetragrammaton with twenty-four points. See Scholem, *Origins*, 328–29.

98. 'Eṣ Ḥayyim, 8:1, 34b.

99. Regarding this symbol in kabbalistic literature, see E. R. Wolfson, "Light through Darkness: The Ideal of Human Perfection in the Zohar," *Harvard Theological Review* 81 (1988): 73–95.

100. 'Eṣ Ḥayyim, 8:1, 34c.

101. On the image of circles and the straight line as the geometric principles of the emanation of light from the Infinite, see Scholem, *Kabbalah*, 136–37; M. Pachter, "Circles and Straightness—A History of an Idea," *Da'at* 18 (1987), 59–90 (in Hebrew).

102. 'Eṣ Ḥayyim, 8:1, 35b.

103. Ibid., fol. 35d. Cf. Ḥayyim Vital, *Mavo' She'arim*, 3:7, 25a; *Kanfe Yonah*, 4:6, 33d. Cf. Moses Cordovero, *Pardes Rimmonim* (Jerusalem: M. 'Atiyah, 1962), 23:16, 34a, s.v., " 'ayin."

104. See, e.g., *'Olat Tamid*, 52b.

105. On weeping as equivalent to overflowing with possible sexual connotations, cf. *Sha'ar ha-Kelalim*, chap. 2, 6a: "The lower half of *Tif'eret* of *'Arikh 'Anpin* remained and *Neṣaḥ Hod*, and *Yesod* of him were disclosed without clothing. This is [the meaning of] what is said, 'the lower waters weep,' that is, these three lower *sefirot*, which are *Neṣaḥ, Hod*, and *Yesod*, were disclosed, and their light was great insofar as they were more revealed than the light of the arms [*Ḥesed, Gevurah*, and *Tif'eret*] for they were concealed within *'Abba'* and *'Imma'*. This is the secret of 'Blessed be the glory of God from its place' (*barukh kevod YWHW mi-meqomo* [Ezek. 3:12])—the first letters [of each word spell] *b[o]khim* ('they are weeping'). This is [the meaning of] they were weeping, that is, they were more revealed than the light of the arms, for the first vessels were abolished and shattered, preventing the light from entering into them. To rectify this it was necessary for the Emanator to comprise the thighs of *'Arikh 'Anpin*

in his arms; *Neṣaḥ, Hod,* and *Yesod* were within *Ḥesed, Gevurah,* and *Tif̱eret,* three within three, and the lower half of *Tif̱eret,* which was revealed, was contained within the upper half. *Neṣaḥ* was contained within *Ḥesed, Hod* within *Gevurah,* and the lower half of *Tif̱eret* within the upper half of *Tif̱eret.* When *Neṣaḥ, Hod* and *Yesod* rose to enter the arms, which are *Ḥesed, Gevurah,* and *Tif̱eret,* all the lights of the broken vessels ascended with them."

106. Joseph Karo, *Maggid Mesharim* (Jerusalem: Y. Bar Lev, 1990), 183.

107. Cf. *b. Shabbat,* 55a.

108. *Zohar,* 3:76a, 75b.

109. Cf. *Reshit Ḥokhmah,* Shaʿar ha-Yirʾah, chap. 9; Shaʿar ha-Teshuvah, chap. 5; *Toṣeʾot Ḥayyim,* chap. 18. See also Eleazar Azikri, *Sefer Ḥaredim* (Jerusalem: Y. S. Daitsh, 1966), 55.

110. Cf. M. ʾAvot, 4:11.

111. See references above, n. 36

112. *Shaʿar ha-Kawwanot,* 56b.

113. Ibid., 48a; cf. *Peri ʿEṣ Ḥayyim,* 298–99.

114. Cf. *Zohar,* 3:120b–121a. See also *Zohar,* 2:200b; *Zohar Ḥaddash,* 42a; Wolfoson, *The Book of the Pomegranate,* 83–84 (Hebrew text); Liebes, "The Messiah of the Zohar," 177–78. For a more detailed discussion of this motif, see M. Fishbane, *The Kiss of God: Spiritual and Mystical Death in Judaism* (Seattle: University of Washington Press, 1994), 107–20. On the thematic connection of death and sexuality, see G. Bataille, *Death and Sensuality: A Study of Eroticism and the Taboo,* trans. M. Dalwood (New York: Walker, 1962).

115. See Scholem, *Kabbalah,* 424; M. Benayahu, "R. Moses Yonah from the Circle of the Ari and the First to Write His Teaching," in *Studies in Memory of the Rishon le-Zion R. Yitzhak Nissim,* 7–74 (in Hebrew); Meroz, "Redemption in the Lurianic Teaching," 90. Avivi, "R. Joseph ibn Tabul's Sermons on the *Kawwanot,*" 75, attributes the work to Moses Yonah and Moses Najara.

116. *Kanfe Yonah,* 1:61, 24c–d. Cf. *Shaʿar ha-Kelalim,* chap. 1, 5c.

117. Cf. Avivi, "R. Joseph ibn Tabul's Sermons on the *Kawwanot,*" 87.

118. Cf. *Peri ʿEṣ Ḥayyim,* 294.

119. *Shaʿare Qedushah* 3:5, 88–92.

120. Cf., e.g., Naḥmanides' formulation in *Shaʿar ha-Gemul,* in H. Chavel, ed., *Kitve Ramban,* (Jerusalem: Shilo Publishing House, 1982), 2:299, cited by Vital in the fourth part of *Shaʿare Qedushah* (cf. *Ketavim Ḥadashim le-Rabbenu Ḥayyim Vital* [Jerusalem, 1988], 14); see also passages from Karo and Azikri discussed by Werblowsky, *Joseph Karo,* 61.

121. *Shaʿare Qedushah* 3:5, 89.

122. Ibid.

123. Werblowsky, *Joseph Karo,* 69.

124. Ibid., 70.

125. Wolfson, *Through a Speculum That Shines,* chap. 6.

126. Cf. *Ketavim Ḥadashim le-Rabbenu Ḥayyim Vital,* 18.

127. *Shaʿare Qedushah* 3:5, 91.

128. Ibid., 92.

129. Werblowsky, *Joseph Karo,* 69.

II

Gertrude's *furor*: Reading Anger in an Early Medieval Saint's *Life*

Catherine Peyroux

Catherine Peyroux analyzes the furor *of St. Gertrude by locating it within the "affective world of Frankish nobility" in the seventh century. The young Gertrude, who believed her relationship to God to be spousal, became enraged when her parents proposed a candidate for marriage because such a marriage would, in her mind, mark her as an adulteress. Working from a hagiographic text, Peyroux examines the various possible meanings of the* furor *therein described on the way to concluding that the saint's rage was in fact taken by her community as a sign of her status as the beloved spouse of Christ. Peyroux, proposing that "emotions are feeling-states that have a cognitive component," undertakes her analysis of Gertrude's* furor *through reference to Frankish ideas about marriage and infidelity, social and family hierarchy, and medieval linguistic idioms indicating anger. For those who knew her as abbess and for those who engaged* The Life of St. Gertrude, *her anger represented her religious identity as the bride of Christ, her authority as a spiritual leader, and her keen grasp of the social codes of the Frankish aristocracy. Peyroux observes in closing: "When we write histories of the past in which feeling is omitted, we implicitly disregard fundamental aspects of the terms on which people act and interact, and we thus deprive ourselves of important evidence for the framework of understanding in which our subjects conducted the business of their lives."*

To what extent does knowledge of the emotional culture of the Frank-

Catherine Peyroux, "Gertrude's *furor*: Reading Anger in an Early Medieval Saint's *Life*." Reprinted by permission from Barbara H. Rosenwein (ed.), *Anger's Past: The Social Uses of Emotion in the Middle Ages*, 36–55, Copyright © 1998 by Cornell University. Used by permission of the publisher, Cornell University Press.

ish aristocracy improve our grasp of Gertrude's religious life? Is her furor clearly
of an order that surpasses everyday anger? How is that furor associated with her
spirituality? In what ways does Gertrude's display of anger reflect her creative interpretation of the feeling rules of her world? Why is her interpretation persuasive
to others? How did her emotional performance of religious belief subvert usual social expectations for young aristocratic females?

In a work written around the year 670 for the monastery of Nivelles, situated
in what was then northeastern Francia and is now modern Belgium, an anonymous religious told a vivid and curious tale about a moment of anger that
had taken place perhaps some thirty years previously, during the childhood of
Gertrude, the first abbess and patron saint of Nivelles. The writer recorded that
according to the account of a "just and truthful man" who had been present,
the young Gertrude's "election to the service of Christ" began thus:

> When Pippin, her [Gertrude's] father, had invited King Dagobert to a
> noble banquet at his house, there came also a noxious man, son of a
> duke of the Austrasians, who requested from the king and from the
> girl's parents that this same girl be promised to himself in marriage
> according to worldly custom, to satisfy earthy ambition as well as for
> a mutual alliance. The request pleased the king and he urged the
> girl's father that she be summoned with her mother into his pres-
> ence. Without their knowing why the king wanted the child (infan-
> tem), she was asked by the king, in between courses [of the ban-
> quet], if she would like to have that boy dressed in silk trimmed
> with gold for a husband. But she, as if filled with *furor* (quasi furore
> repleta), rejected him with an oath, and said that she would have
> neither him nor any earthly man for husband but Christ the lord.
> Whereupon the king and his nobles marveled greatly over these
> things, which were said by the little girl (parva puella) under God's
> command. The boy indeed left disturbed, filled with anger (iracun-
> dia plenus). The holy girl returned to her mother and from that day
> her parents knew by what manner of king she was loved.[1]

This compact narrative, structured around the revelation of a noble
maiden's true and royal spouse, has an abstract, almost stylized quality reso-
nant equally of folkloric motif and hagiographical cliché. The protocols of composition and selection that govern biographies of early medieval saints have
here preserved the traces of a dynamic, living culture in the restricted medium
of exemplary legend. Nonetheless, there are reasons to read this story with
eyes more closely attuned to the "what happened" and, indeed, the "how it felt"
than to the "once upon a time" of early medieval Europe. The text from which
this passage comes is among the immediate witnesses for the history both of

seventh-century Frankish monasticism and of the early fortunes of the family who were to emerge as the Carolingians.[2] Its protagonist, Gertrude (who lived 625/26–659), was a daughter of the materially and politically preeminent household formed by the marriage of the heiress Itta (d. 650) and Pippin I (d. 639), a noble magnate and the sometime mayor of the palace of the eastern Frankish kingdom of Austrasia.[3]

Most important for our purposes in exploring this record of anger, the dead saint's biography originated in the community that had, until only a decade before its composition, surrounded the living abbess Gertrude; the quality of the presentation should not distract us from indications of the author's firsthand experience embedded in the text. Scattered throughout the *Life* are multiple references to personal and immediate knowledge of the events depicted: the prologue claims to set forth the "example and conduct" of the holy Gertrude according to "what we saw ourselves or heard through witnesses"; in chapter 4 the narrator is figured among those to whom Gertrude herself related a wondrous vision; the closing chapter includes an account of the narrator's own presence at the monastery on the day of Gertrude's death and implies the narrator's participation in the saint's funerary rites.[4] Some debate is possible over whether the *Vita sanctae Geretrudis* (hereafter *VsG*) was written by a monk or a nun.[5] Nonetheless, the closing episode of the *Life*, in which the author is summoned "with another brother . . . to console the sisters" (*VsG*, c. 7: ego et alius frater . . . evocati propter sororum consolationem) at Gertrude's death, indicates to me that we are right to read this voice as that of a monk, possibly even that of a priest.[6] Debate is likewise possible concerning whether the author had originally come from or was yet a member of the nearby monastery of Fosses, a community that had been founded under Itta's sponsorship around an Irish monk named Foillan.[7] The connection between the two houses is evident in the *VsG* itself: in the seventh chapter of the *Life*, Gertrude's deathday (and thus, presumably, her cult) is markedly entwined with that of St. Patrick by the prophetic words of the Irish abbot of Fosses, who is named in some manuscripts as Ultan. The abbot of Fosses predicts correctly that Gertrude's death will take place on Patrick's feast day, March 17, and that "blessed Bishop Patrick" is prepared to receive her "with the elect angels of God and with great glory."[8] In any case, there is every reason to believe that the author was either a member of, or had intimate knowledge of, the double monastery of Nivelles during Gertrude's abbacy and that he was writing for a community with a still vivid memory of significant episodes in the saint's life, and so was constrained by the principles of verisimilitude in reporting the events of Gertrude's history. Thus we may take it that, if the story of Gertrude's anger is not "true" by whatever standards we might wish to apply to something so subjective as emotional experience, it was nevertheless composed so as to seem well imagined and essentially plausible to Gertrude's contemporaries.[9]

But how are we to read the fact of a little girl getting—or appearing to get—very angry in this anecdote? What does Gertrude's evident anger mean, and what will we see when we can parse it appropriately? I argue that within the space of the text Gertrude's angry reaction is made to function as a site where one realm of knowledge (the saint's certainty about her heavenly husband) is translated into another (the expectations that her parents, King Dagobert, and potential earthly marriage partners have about her eligibility). Her manifest anger is itself fundamental to that translation because it naturalizes the authority of her perception of herself and her true identity. I suggest that for the author of her *Life,* and presumably for that writer's intended audience, the instance of her evident anger itself was interpreted as evidence that demonstrated the certain and indubitable facticity of the supervening reality Gertrude asserted. As the text has it, her apparent rage, *as* rage, inflected her vow to refuse an earthly husband in favor of the divine one, interrupting and nullifying the normal and ordinary patterns of marriage previously marked out for her as a well-born and richly landed woman in seventh-century Frankish society.

In seeking to make sense of the place of emotion in this tale, we should first note that the saint's anger is incidental to the anecdote's larger narrative of Gertrude's rejected betrothal to the son of a duke of the Austrasians. The story could be told without reference to Gertrude's ire and yet still convey in substantially the same form the little girl's refusal of an earthly spouse in favor of a marriage to Christ.[10] The anger, incidental to the basic betrothal plot, marks a deliberate inclusion on the part of the author and was presumably intended to shape readers' perceptions of the event depicted. Moreover, precisely because the narrator did not step outside the frame of the drama to explain how Gertrude's anger was to be understood, the episode of Gertrude's rage becomes all the more interesting as an issue for historical exploration. Not least because of its unself-conscious rendition of emotionality in the context of a marital negotiation, this story would appear to bring us tantalizingly close to the realm of the "unspoken everyday" on which social interaction is built. The very absence of explanatory markers that might seek to qualify, explain, defend, or otherwise direct a further interpretation of Gertrude's anger suggests that such behavior was assumed to be readily intelligible and even normal, if not normative, to the *Life*'s intended audience. The passage thus presents an opportunity to explore an aspect of the affective world of the Frankish nobility so as to discover something about how people in Merovingian society processed an experience in terms of a feeling.[11]

Although the presence of Gertrude's emotion in this text warrants consideration, it presents immediate and slippery problems of interpretation. The hagiographer has framed the tale to assert a primary literal meaning by invoking the eyewitness testimony of a reliable narrator, that "just and truthful man" whose memory recorded a banquet at Pippin's house where Gertrude angrily repulsed a powerful suitor with an oath. There is no a priori reason to dismiss a literal reading, no clear evidence on which to assert that the incident is "merely" a literary formula. Yet to assert only the literal value of the report ("what this text means is that a little girl named Gertrude *really* got angry") would displace the question of the significance of her anger away from the text itself onto a putative "emotion-event" that must be imagined to have occurred in the "real" world, a world, moreover, to which the modern reader's access depends chiefly on the text at hand. Conversely, if the tale is deemed to be fabulous, substantially an invention of the narrator's imagination, the question of meaning is all the more compelling: How then do we explain the role of anger in the text? If the narrator had no need to include Gertrude's anger in order to satisfy an audience that knew such a thing to be part of the story, the reader is hard-pressed to account for what anger is doing in the text at all. In either case, whether we read the episode as a factual occurrence (however filtered through memory and fashioned to fit the redactors' narrative purposes) or as an imaginative fiction, we are constrained to address the nature of anger itself. And, of course, how we read the anger in the *Life* will depend on the logic of social relations by which we imagine the protagonists of the story to have been governed.

As a small mountain of scholarly literature on the psychological, cultural, and historical study of emotional behavior has surely demonstrated, emotions are feeling-states that have a cognitive component; that is, they involve a mental appraisal of whatever situation prompts their expression.[12] Among the emotions, anger is a feeling-state that is at base antagonistic.[13] Many researchers further include in anger's essential definition a prerogative over the moral domain. This framework of understanding attributes to anger an inherent claim about some sense of the "ought," so as to capture the aspect of anger that stems as a response to some sense of what is felt to be "unjustifiable" harm.[14] But beyond these basic and possibly universal qualities of anger, its meaning as an emotion is located in the particular social framework in which it is generated and expressed. Whatever the immediate felt experience or physiological component of emotions, feelings are "cultural acquisitions" intelligible only in the context in which they occur.[15] Cultural anthropologists and historians of emotion alike point to a fundamental variance of patterns in the language and interpretation of emotions: both from place to place and from era to era, words signifying anger reside in different semantic fields, and expressions of anger take place and are received in ways that differ.[16] Manifestly, a reading of Gertrude's anger that depends on "common sense" is of no use in a context with which we have no sensibility in common.

Above all, we must discard interpretations based on broad generalizations or assumptions about what we take to be the essential characteristics of the protagonists. Reading Gertrude's anger as the irrational tantrum of a little girl might be plausible within certain modern premises for understanding children's anger. But as historians have noted, the very word "tantrum" and the complex of associations surrounding it are themselves the product of a dynamic and relatively recent process by which new spheres of emotional control, first for adults in public, then for children within the domestic sphere, were marked out in the course of the eighteenth and nineteenth centuries in British and American societies.[17] And just as we can not read Gertrude's anger through our contemporary notions about childhood's "natural" emotions, likewise we can not expect that modern perceptions about whatever we apprehend to be the contemporary rules that guide the expression of women's anger, among other emotions, will inform us about the right, licit, and intelligible deployment of a young aristocratic woman's anger in seventh-century Frankish society.

Given this fact of cultural and temporal variance, it would appear to be the more reasonable path to assume a radical untranslatability between the anger of Gertrude and our own.[18] By this I do not suggest that we are unable to recover some of the force and even some of the particular savor of the behavioral sensibility that informed the *Life* and its audience—and arguably the young Gertrude and her contemporaries as well. I do mean to claim that in acknowledging the insights of the social constructivist approach to anger, we must recognize that "patterns of emotion, like rhetorical phenomena, are culturally indigenous" and accordingly build our interpretation of Gertrude's rage out of evidence derived from the local culture of her time and place.[19]

In seeking to discover something of the salience of this moment of anger in seventh-century Frankish society, we must be attentive to a quality of its communication—or, more precisely, its "evidentiation"—that is not necessarily of concern to the social constructivist project per se. Dependent on the text as we are, our interpretations must bear within them our attention to the textual construction as well as the social location of an emotion. This of course entails attention to some obvious facts, such as that the author of the *Life* was writing in a particular language (Latin), was working in and for at least the specific cultural milieu of a monastic audience, and was deploying a flexible but not infinite repertory of narrative models and anger idioms to communicate his sense of the event and its meaning in the saint's life. We need also to consider the text not as a passive reflector of cultural data but as an intervention in a dialogue for which we have only one voice: our author's. We cannot assume that the culture that the text depicts is a unified and uncontested field, uniformly determining the actions and responses of its participants, nor can we imagine the text to be an uncritical and unengaged mirror of the material it conveys.[20] In reading a text we have to allow for its capacity to participate in the construction of meaning across contested terrains whose boundaries, if unclear to us, may yet determine the manner in which events are represented. I am arguing two related points here: first, that culture informs and frames but does not simply or uniformly determine the expression of human behavior (and so every instantiation or representation of anger requires contextual interpretation to arrive at an understanding of its import) and, second, that texts, far from being transparent and invisible windows onto the events they depict, are in themselves a form of social act and as such shape, refract, and thereby alter the meaning of the data they convey.[21]

There are many ways to narrate anger. When the author of the *VsG* endeavored to record "the example and conduct of the most blessed virgin Gertrude, mother of Christ's family" (*VsG* prologue), he had an array of options through which to tell this story. He began the *Life* conventionally enough, with a general account of Gertrude's meritorious childhood: while in the home of her parents, the holy girl "grew day and night in word and wisdom, dear to God and loved by men beyond her generation" (*VsG*, c. 1). Immediately thereafter, and as we have seen, the narrator places the origin of Gertrude's "election to the service of Christ" in an angry incident during her childhood that took place at a banquet given by her father, an incident that the writer asserts to have been witnessed by an individual whose reliable testimony subtends the *Life*'s account of events. Granting that the basic components of the story were fixed by the constraints of local memory and verisimilitude, we must still inquire into the particular redaction of anger that the episode presents, an anger that is characterized in the text as *furor*. Gertrude exhibits *furor*, or rather, as the text has it, becomes "quasi furore repleta," "as if" or "almost" filled with *furor*, when she is presented with the option of marriage to a richly dressed youth of aristocratic birth. Because every translation is itself a reading of a text, we must attend carefully to how we construe the saint's *furor* in this context. In classical Latin and in the writings of the Latin fathers, *furor* occupies a semantic field more violent than that of *ira*, anger. In antiquity, *furor* had the force of raging madness, even insanity; juridically, the person possessed by fury was understood to be "absent from himself."[22] The quality of human *furor* as the straying of the mind that shades into dementia presumably accounts for its transposed use as a marker of heresy in late ancient and medieval Christian discourse.[23] For Bede, *furor*'s close proximity to mania made it an appropriate term to denote an instance of demonic possession whose relief necessitated a miraculous healing.[24] To say simply that the little girl expressed "indignation" or "lost her temper" would hardly seem to convey the disruptive power of Gertrude's wrath. Rather, the saint is explicitly marked as having appeared, to her audience, "furore repleta," "possessed or filled with raging madness."[25] In choosing to cast Gertrude's anger as *furor* the author of her *Life* would seem to have invoked a form of wrath that stood oppositionally to normal human concourse.

The task of endeavoring to enter the imaginative world of the *VsG* is perilously conjectural when we turn from basic, lexicographical levels of meaning to consider where and how the expression of human *furor* was figured as licit and divinely inspired. Fundamental uncertainties about which texts might have been available to the *VsG*'s author vitiate any straightforward survey of possible analogues in contemporary texts. The *VsG* mentions the monastery's acquisition of holy books from Rome and "places overseas" (c. 2: transmarinis regionibus—an imprecise reference that might mean Ireland or England or both) and boasts of Gertrude that she had "memorized a whole library of divine law" (c. 3), but more specific information for the author's textual environment is absent.[26] We can, however, derive the general sense of *furor* from a few widely read and widely copied texts, intending thereby to get a taste of what might have informed the sensibilities of our author and of the audience for which he wrote, rather than to determine a repertory of exemplary topoi. What follows is an attempt to sort out the rhetorical context in which *furor* is deployed by writers and encountered by readers in seventh-century Frankish society, in the hope of developing a preliminary sense of where and how the term was likely to be used.

No unambiguous models of human *furor* can guide us to the sources with which Gertrude's biographer might have been in dialogue when imagining the moment in question in the saint's life. Even assuming that some close analogue to the Vulgate was among whatever biblical texts were available in the library at Nivelles, the Vulgate itself offers only a single instance of a person *replet[us] furore*: in the book of Daniel, King Nebuchadnezzar is filled with rage in contemplating Shadrach, Meschach, and Abed-Nego (Dan. 3:19).[27] This would hardly appear to be a suitable model for our author's purposes in portraying a saint whose actions are framed as taking place under the direction of God (*VsG*, c. 1). Conversely, divine *furor*, the just rage of God, is so prevalent and so diffuse, particularly in the Psalms, as to be untraceable as a particular stimulant for the author's imagination. Nor should we assume that even the divine *furor* recorded in the Bible was always interpreted positively. So authoritative an exegete as Pope Gregory I could comment on Job's plea to God that he might be hidden until divine *furor* should pass ("ut abscondas me donec pertranseat furor tuus," Job 14:13) with the explanation that God's *furor* is in fact only a temporary precipitate of his relationship with sinful humans. When contemplating divine justice, Gregory tempered Job's *furor* with the Book of Wisdom's *tranquillitas* and held that "it should be known that the term *furor* is not appropriate for the divinity, because no disquiet disturbs the simple nature of God."[28] And if we take divine wrath to be the operative model for Gertrude's rage, we need still to pursue the question of what might warrant the *VsG*'s appropriation of the authority of God's fury by the saint herself for refusal of an earthly husband. As a contrasting example, we might consider an episode recounted in the late fifth-century Legend of Saint Cecilia; there the saint rejects the amorous advances of her husband, Valerian, by invoking the retributive *furor* of her true love, an angel of God.[29] The parallels between Gertrude's rejection of an earthly spouse for a heavenly one and Cecilia's interpellation of an angelic lover between herself and her terrestrial husband serve only to bring into sharper relief the distinction between Gertrude's human *furor*, however divinely sanctioned, and the *furor* of an angelic protector.

It is just conceivable—but to my mind only barely so—that the *VsG* draws its claims for Gertrude's sanctified rage from the hagiographical context that produced Muirchú's *Vita Patricii*.[30] The seventh chapter of the *VsG* makes clear the presence of a Patrician cult at Fosses and intertwines Gertrude's cult with it; it would seem probable that in the communities of Fosses and Nivelles, if anywhere in the Frankish lands, oral or written tradition about Patrick would have received an enthusiastic and proactive audience, primed to incorporate Patrician material and models into the local production of writing about their own holy patrons. However, Muirchú's text appears to have been produced at roughly the same time as the *VsG*, and quite possibly slightly later.[31] An argument for the *VsG*'s direct dialogue with, let alone dependence on, Muirchú's *Vita Patricii* would be tendentious, based more clearly on assumptions about a supposed Irish influence than on textual evidence. However intriguing it is to note that Muirchú's text recounts an episode in which the saint, explicitly named there "holy Patrick," upon growing angry (*irascens*) curses a greedy cattle thief who has made off with the saint's property, this text would appear to illustrate a moment of righteous indignation rather than surging fury. To my ears, the faint and distorted echo between the holy ire of Patrick and the sanctified rage of Gertrude is best understood as no more than that.[32]

Turning to texts produced and circulated in settings roughly similar to that of the monastery at Nivelles, we find that fury would appear not to have been valorized, much less sanctified as God-sent, in the Iromerovingian and Frankish texts that are earlier contemporaries of the *VsG*. There is a curious resonance between the *VsG* and a sermon by Caesarius of Arles that combines references to a feast at a powerful man's table, a wedding, and the phrase "iracundiae furore repletus." In this passage Caesarius is entreating his brethren to abhor wrath and to come to the altar as to the eternal king's feast: the allusion is to something other than licit, even divinely sanctioned anger.[33] The *Regula ad monachos* and its companion *Regula ad virgines* of Aurelian of Arles both castigate the professed religious (of either sex—the wording is the same for each) who might become "by the instigation of the devil, filled with rage" and cause discord within the monastery.[34] As Lester Little has shown in his judicious survey of monastic rules, in such texts anger within the monastery was seen without exception as inappropriate to the monastic life; for Aurelian, *furor* is indeed imagined to be the result of demonic forces.[35]

Likewise, Jonas of Bobbio's *Vita Columbani* casts Columbanus and his followers as the pacific opponents of discord and wrath. Columbanus's first community in Gaul is lauded by Jonas for the brothers' humility; among the worldly evils they are explicitly said to reject are dissension and anger.[36] Jonas draws marked and repeated contrasts between Columbanus and figures of insane and intemperate rage. These are sometimes anonymous evildoers (*Vita Columbani* 1.21), but more often fury is represented by the malefic King Theuderic and Queen Brunhild (1.19, 20, 27, 28), whose conflicts with Columbanus are portrayed with unrelenting hostility by Jonas. Brunhild, especially, is described as being preternaturally savage and implacably wrathful, continuously "furens" to Columbanus's steadfast adherence to godly commands.[37] Predictably, the *Histories* of Gregory of Tours are replete with moments of fury.[38] Like Jonas, Gregory also employs *furor* to portray a violence that is socially destructive in the extreme, and indeed one that is very often depicted as either demonically inspired or employed to demonic ends. The wild bull that ended the life of the martyr Saturninus under the Decian persecutions (*Decem libri historiarum* 1.30); the worker who revenged himself by betraying Vienne during a siege (2.33); the military thug Roccolen, who threatened to burn Tours and its suburbs to the ground (5.4); the overweening pride of Bishops Salonius and Sagittarius that led to "peculation, physical assaults, murders, adulteries, and every crime" (5.20); civil discord in Tours (9.19); the father who attacks his own son with an ax on account of the son's cowardice (9.34): all share in the quality of *furor*. One of Gregory's most vividly rendered portraits of female chaos and destruction is the miscreant nun Clotild, whose *furor* raises to ever higher pitches the violence surrounding the murderous attack on the abbess at Poitiers by participants in the nuns' revolt there (10.15).

So we may well puzzle over the *VsG*'s use of *furor* in the context of a banquet given by Gertrude's father for King Dagobert I, and wonder about the context underlying the narrator's depiction of Gertrude's evident rage as sanctioned by God. What could justify manifest *furor* as an attribute of words spoken *Dei iussione?* The problematic implications of the violent, even potentially sinful excess of angry emotion inherent in the term perhaps explain the author's insertion of the qualifying adverb *quasi:* Gertrude's rage may be real enough to her onlookers at the banquet, but it would seem that her biographer had some reservations about naming her as such for the pious readers of his story. The hagiographer's choice of *quasi* may mark Gertrude's behavior as no more than *evidently* or *almost* filled with *furor*, thus conveying the socially disruptive power of the saint's rage vis-à-vis her audience even as the text informs its readers that Gertrude was not *wholly* possessed by *furor*'s passion. As a rule, hagiography is not an "epistemologically hesitant" genre; presumably Gertrude's biographer could say whether she was filled with rage or not.[39] The writers of saints' biographies were well accustomed to narrating the inner lives and even the feelings of their subjects; Gertrude's hagiographer relates the saint's internal experience on several occasions in the *VsG*.[40] Moreover, the text depicts the emotional state of her disappointed suitor in simple terms with no hedging: when he left, he left "filled with anger" (iracundia plenus), full stop. This straightforward description of the suitor's wrath indicates that the hagiographer's use of *quasi* to define Gertrude's *furor* cannot be explained simply as a solution to the difficulty intrinsic in the writing of something so internal as feeling. But a reading that concentrates on that *quasi* in an effort to explain away Gertrude's *furor* as an emotion not possible for an exemplary monastic saint is a reading that would substitute a reified notion of monastic culture and its uniform reception of texts about monastic virtues in the place of an account of early medieval monasticism that allows for variety and perhaps contest among visions of the monastic life. Because *furor* is a word with such powerfully negative connotations in early medieval religious discourse, and because its excision from this story would not vitiate the basic narrative of Gertrude's mystical marriage to Christ, we must work to understand why *furor* appears at all in this context. Far from being explained away, the use of *furor* on the part of Gertrude's hagiographer needs to be explained *in*—that is, drawn into our notion of what this text is trying to accomplish.

As recounted in the first chapter of the *VsG*, the precise catalyst for Gertrude's *furor* is Dagobert's question about the young girl's willingness to take as a husband the well-dressed son of a duke of the Austrasians, who has sought her hand frankly "to satisfy earthly ambition as well as for mutual alliance." The text links Gertrude's *furor* with her refusal of that suitor or any other earthly husband and simultaneously interpolates Christ into the marital negotiation as her only proper spouse: "But she, as if filled with *furor*, rejected [the son of a duke of the Austrasians] with an oath, and said that she would have neither him nor any earthly man for husband but Christ the lord." The manifest evidence of Gertrude's sole appropriate marriage partner, Christ, is immediately reinforced in the succeeding sentences. First, King Dagobert and his nobles are made to "marvel greatly" and presumably affirmatively over the little girl's words. These are recorded by the *VsG* as having been said under God's command; here the text allows a certain ambiguity about whether that fact was recognized by the young Gertrude's audience at the time or was only subsequently made clear. Second, the suitor leaves "confusus," disturbed and filled with anger, implicitly due to having had his wishes thwarted and possibly in reaction to the slight of having been passed over for a more powerful marriage partner. His anger is figured rhetorically in the text as a response to hers: she is "quasi furore repleta" to his "iracundiae plenus." But his anger is construed with a term, *iracundia* (irascibility, irritability), that is pitched at a lower heat of passion than is Gertrude's *furor*, and his wrath is denied the explicit status of divine sanction that guides the texts's readers in interpreting the saint's rage. He is an incidental player in the drama portrayed in this chapter, insulted and angry, but evidently not in a way that was felt to require further comment on the part of the narrator. Gertrude's wrathful declaration, on the other hand, takes center stage. For through it, according to the text, Gertrude's parents now know "by what manner of king she was loved." The "fact" of the young girl's "marriage" to Christ has thus been effectively accomplished in this narrative sequence, which began by identifying Gertrude's angry rejection as the origin of the saint's election to Christ's service.

Here the text bears certain anxious implications of a *fait* not so easily *accompli*. An unstated but evidently operative understanding shared by all the

parties involved in this transaction is that in the early medieval marital economy, where the noble household and the arena of political power are coter-
minous, Gertrude's matrimonial strategy is a subject of state interest. Gertrude, though described as a little girl and evidently only barely of suitable age
for betrothal, will inevitably be married to someone; the suspense of this vi-
gnette is not about whether she will be married but to whom.[41] King Dagobert's
clear interest in that alliance is made manifest by his role as marriage broker.
The positive and negative interests of Gertrude's family in this transaction are
not here defined, but the capacity of Gertrude's parents to determine the final
identity of her spouse appears rather shaky in the VsG's admittedly retrospec-
tive view. The initial request for a marriage between Gertrude and the son of
a duke of the Austrasians is portrayed as having been made both to King
Dagobert and to Gertrude's parents, but it is Dagobert, depicted as satisfied
with the prospect of that alliance, who initiates the marriage negotiations with
Gertrude; and it is not Gertrude's parents but rather Gertrude herself, represented in turn as insistent on the supervening commitment of her marriage
to Christ, who forestalls the connection. Pace the narrator's claim for the aristocratic community's recognition of the saint's new status as one beloved by
Christ, we might wonder how strongly the marvel of Gertrude's "true" but in
earthly terms indeterminate marriage to Christ had registered on the surrounding society. The next chapter of the VsG, which relates events that occur after
the death of Pippin, implies that only the monastery founded by the now widowed Itta at Nivelles, and her own and Gertrude's profession at it, afforded the
conditions under which Gertrude's marriage to Christ might be accorded the
exclusive status of a matrimonial relationship. A further attempt to capture
Gertrude's person and wealth in the compact of matrimony evidently occurred;
the next chapter of the Life relates that to prevent some unnamed "violators of
souls" (violatores animarum) from tearing her daughter away by force, Itta
tonsures Gertrude herself, at which point we are told that "merciful God . . .
recalled the adversaries to the concord of peace" (c.2).

Gertrude's "marriage" to Christ served a dual function in the early history
of her monastery. It is the alliance that foreclosed the unwelcome possibility
of any other marital relationship with suitors like the duke's son, suitors intent
on marriage with the wealthy Gertrude "for reasons of earthly ambition" and
whose nuptial plans in chapter 2 of the VsG read like an attempted hostile
takeover of the family concern.[42] Her "marriage" to Christ was also a foundational compact from which derived both her natal family's and her monastic
family's religious authority.[43] Christ is the spouse of highest status in the marital economy in which Gertrude must negotiate, a circumstance that underscores the force of naming Christ's regality in the encomiastic sentence that
concludes chapter 1 of the VsG. There, following Gertrude's declaration of her
pending marriage to Christ, it is Christ's marriage to Gertrude that is fore-
grounded: "from that day her parents knew by what manner of king she was

loved." And of course, Gertrude's status as Christ's beloved spouse in turn subtends the saint's cult and its promise of intercessory potency.

I suggest that it is in this context, defined by the author's pressing need to make definite the potentially precarious terms of Gertrude's marital identity, that we should read the text's portrayal of the saint's *furor*. The degree of Gertrude's evident rage in response to her earthly suitor's proposal signals the nature of the perceived harm to which *furor* is the divinely ordered response. As Gertrude knows (and as others can see only after witnessing her reaction to the prospect of this marriage), she is already promised: what is being proposed to her, then, is not marriage but adultery. Within the frame of reference operating in the *VsG*, the offer of this illicit "second" marriage is at the very least a grave insult to Gertrude, to her family, and to the divine husband by whom she is already beloved. Both in the prescriptive realm of the law codes and the descriptive world revealed by the narratives of Gregory of Tours, adultery figured as a sexual and social crime that stained the honor of a Frankish woman past redemption and exposed her to shameful trial and brutal punishment.[44] In imagining what the imputation of a breach of wifely chastity might mean in Frankish society, perhaps the most telling guide is the matter-of-fact violence with which a woman's family, not only her husband but also her own kin, are recorded as having responded to charges of infidelity. In his *Glory of the Martyrs*, Gregory of Tours tells of "innocent" women condemned, with no further proof than their husband's accusations of infidelity, to submersion in nearby rivers.[45] "Women accused of adultery were weighted with stones and tossed into rivers or burned alive; one husband simply killed his wife and the abbot he found in her bed."[46] The *VsG* invites its readers to approve of the saint's rage and to recognize its justice. *Furor*, an emotion appropriately calibrated to the gravity of the harm she has experienced, is the authenticating sign of the saint's marital status. It demonstrates to the onlookers at the banquet Gertrude's transition from an available Pippinid marriage partner to one conjoined to Christ. It translates into the terms of everyday social life the notional, incorporeal relationship that both Gertrude and subsequently her monastic foundation need so much to establish as a manifest truth.

Although the meaning of that moment in which an angry little girl names her true spouse is represented by its narrator as manifestly obvious to everyone present, for modern investigators of the medieval past it nonetheless generates complex and fruitful problems in reading. The problems are arguably most fruitful where interpretive conclusions are least clear, as in the case of Gertrude's rage. Emotion remains a ubiquitous but as yet barely examined category of experience in our texts. Characterizations that place medieval patterns of feeling in that long, *longue durée* of "premodern Western" norms of behavior, where, for example, "anger was freely and publicly expressed as part of a social and familiar hierarchy, and also as a function of an emphasis on shame as the chief emotional means of community discipline,"[47] serve effectively to frame medieval life as a backdrop to the implicitly more important narrative of emergent modernity rather than to illuminate the specific and particular conditions in which emotion was expressed in the centuries before the triumph of finance capitalism, the steam engine, and the newspaper. As William Ian Miller has noted in his lapidary summary of some dominant modern images of the emotional life of medieval people, medieval folk are simultaneously cast as "puerile, quick to fly into a rage and then just as quick to swing to almost equally violent and public displays of remorse" and also "benighted, insentient, too brutalized or primitive to have a subtle emotional life."[48]

Medieval affect offers a prime site for methodological consideration because the realm of feeling brings us so close to our own unself-conscious notions of the person: what motivates action, what constitutes perception, what it is to be human. When we write histories of the past in which feeling is omitted, we implicitly disregard fundamental aspects of the terms on which people act and interact, and we thus deprive ourselves of important evidence for the framework of understanding in which our subjects conducted the business of their lives. Conversely, even beginning to account for the affective dimensions of medieval life involves us in forms of historicist imagination and attention for which no critical language has as yet been formalized. In a wholly different context, Inga Clendinnen has written that "to offer interpretations without acknowledging their uncertain ground would be less than candid, while to state only what is certainly known would be to leave unexplored what matters most."[49] Explorers of medieval emotion might well consider this a motto.

NOTES

This essay has benefited profoundly from the generous attention and criticism of Barbara Rosenwein, Jennifer Thorn, Susan Thorne, Matthew Price, David Ganz, Stephen White, Wendy Davies, Monica Green, Lester Little, William Reddy, Philippe Buc, and the anonymous readers of Cornell University Press; I thank them heartily for their readings and suggestions, and for making so sociable the process of thinking about anger's socially fractious potentialities.

1. "Primum electionis sibi in Christi servitio initium fuit, sicut per iustum et veracem hominem conperi, qui praesens aderat. Dum Pippinus, genitor suus, regem Dagobertum domui sue ad nobilem prandium invitasset, adveniens ibidem unus pestifer homo, filius ducis Austrasiorum, qui a rege et a parentibus puellae postulasset, ut sibi ipsa puella in matrimonium fuisset promissa secundum morem saeculi propter terrenam ambitionem et mutuam amicitiam. Placuit regi, et patri puellae suasit, ut in sua praesentia illa cum matre sua fuisset evocata. Illis autem ignorantibus, propter quam causam rex vocaret infantem, interrogata inter epulas a rege, si illum puerum auro fabricatum, siricis indutum voluisset habere sponsum, at illa quasi furore repleta, respuit illum cum iuramento et dixit, nec illum nec alium terrenum nisi

Christum dominum volebat habere sponsum, ita ut ipse rex et proceres eius valde mirarentur super his, quae a parva puella Dei iussione dicta erant. Ille vero puer recessit confusus, iracundia plenus. Sancta puella ad suam convertit genetricem, et ex illa die parentes eius cognoverunt, a quali Regi amata fuerat." *Vita sanctae Geretrudis abbatissae Nivialensis I*, ed. B. Krusch, MGH SSrerMerov 2: 453–64, hereafter *VsG*. Krusch provides both the Merovingian (A) and Carolingian (B) versions of this text in parallel columns; note that I have used the earlier, grammatically more awkward version A of the *Life* of Gertrude; translations are my own. For an English translation of the whole life based on version B, see *Sainted Women of the Dark Ages*, ed. and trans. Jo Ann McNamara, John E. Halborg, and E. Gordan Whatley (Durham, N.C: Duke University Press, 1992), pp. 220–28. Since this essay was written, a new translation of version A with an excellent historical commentary has appeared in Paul Fouracre and Richard A. Gerberding, eds., *Late Merovingian France: History and Hagiography, 640–720* (Manchester, UK: Manchester University Press, 1996).

2. On the historical value of the *VsG*, see Krusch's introductory commentary to his editions of the *Life* in MGH SSrerMerov 2: 447–49; J. J. Hoebanx, *L'Abbaye de Nivelles des origines au XIVe siecle* (Brussels: Palais des Académies, 1952), pp. 23–30; Alain Dierkens, "Saint Amand et la fondation de l'abbaye de Nivelles," *Revue du Nord* 68 (1986): 326.

3. For a brief chronology of Gertrude's life, see Dierkens, "Saint Amand," pp. 330–31; for a careful consideration of early Pippinid chronology in the light of the widowed Itta's monastic patronage, see J.-M. Picard, "Church and Politics in the Seventh Century: The Irish Exile of Dagobert II," in *Ireland and Northern France, A.D. 600–850*, ed. J.-M. Picard (Dublin: Four Courts, 1991), pp. 27–52, esp. pp. 34–36. The origins and politically precarious career of Pippin I are recounted by Pierre Riché, *The Carolingians*, trans. Michael Idomir Alien (Philadelphia: University of Pennsylvania Press, 1993), pp. 15–19, and more closely chronicled by Richard Gerberding, *The Rise of the Carolingians and the "Liber Historiae Francorum"* (Oxford: Clarendon, 1987), esp. pp. 6–7, 120–21. For Pippin's landbase, see Matthias Werner, *Der Lütticher Raum in frühkarolingischer Zeit* (Göttingen: Vandenhoeck & Ruprecht, 1980), pp. 342–54 (but see Gerberding, *Rise of Carolingians*, p. 121, for cautions about Werner's estimates). For Itta's disposition of family wealth, see Alexander Bergengruen, *Adel und Grundherrschaft im Merowingerreich* (Wiesbaden: F. Steiner, 1958), pp. 109–10; and Hoebanx, *Abbaye de Nivelles*, pp. 86–95. In a text filled with proper names, the identity of the (conspicuously?) unnamed "son of a duke of the Austrasians" seems deliberately vague. McNamara speculates that the young man might be either the brother of the early seventh-century saint Glodesind of Metz or else Ansegisel, later husband of Gertrude's sister Begga (*Sainted Women of the Dark Ages*, p. 223 n. 13). Both men were sufficiently well connected to Gertrude's family to merit a proper name and a more positive characterization than "pestifer homo" in the text. See Werner, *Lütticher Raum*, p. 44 n. 56, for a judicious refusal of the sure identification of the *VsG*'s "dux Austrasiorum" with the Duke Adalgisel named by Dagobert I in 633–34 as regent for his son Sigibert III, infant king of Austrasia. But see also Bergengruen, *Adel und Grundherrschaft*, p. 118 n. 73, for possible connections between Gertrude's family and Adalgisel.

4. *VsG*, prologue: "exemplum vel conversationem . . . quod vidimus vel per ido-

neos testes audivimus"; c. 4: "quod ipsa Dei famula . . . nobis narravit"; c. 7 (at the death of Gertrude, on March 17): "Deo desideratum amisit spiritum. Dum ibidem ego et alius frater Rinchinus . . . fuimus evocati propter sororum consolationem."

5. The dominant assumption has been that the *Life* was composed by a monk; see Krusch, MGH SSrerMerov 2:448; Hoebanx, *Abbaye de Nivelles*, pp. 31–36; Dierkens, "Saint Amand," p. 326 n. 5. A caution against so easy and automatic an ascription has been made by Ian Wood, who has suggested that the author could as easily have been a female member of the community of Nivelles; Wood, "Administration, Law, and Culture in Merovingian Gaul," in *The Uses of Literacy in Early Medieval Europe*, ed. Rosamond McKitterick (Cambridge, UK: Cambridge University Press, 1990), pp. 63–81, 70 n. 50.

6. This is the ascription made by Rosamond McKitterick, "Women and Literacy in the Early Middle Ages," in *Books, Scribes, and Learning in the Frankish Kingdoms, 6th–9th Centuries* (Aldershot, UK: Variorum, 1994), XIII, p. 26.

7. For the foundations of Fosses and its ongoing connections with Gertrude's family, see Alain Dierkens, *Abbayes et chapitres entre Sambre et Meuse* (Sigmaringen: J. Thorbecke, 1985), pp. 70–76. Hoebanx, *Abbaye de Nivelles*, p. 30, considered the author to be an Irish monk of the community of Nivelles. Ludwig Bieler ascribed the *VsG* with startling confidence to an Irish author, calling the *Life* "one of the oldest monuments of Irish hagiography"; Bieler, *Ireland: Harbinger of the Middle Ages* (London: Oxford University Press, 1963), p. 101.

8. "Beatus Patricius episcopus cum electis angelis Dei et cum ingenti gloria parati sunt eam recipere" (*VsG*, c. 7).

9. On contemporaries' memory as a constraint for hagiography, see Paul Fouracre, "Merovingian History and Merovingian Hagiography," *Past and Present* 127 (1990): 3–38, p. II; Fouracre argues that much of the awkward hagiography produced in the seventh century has a strong claim to be read as history. For a refusal of the very categories of "hagiography" versus "history" before the twelfth century, see Felice Lifshitz, "Beyond Positivism and Genre: 'Hagiographical' Texts as Historical Narrative," *Viator* 25 (1994): 95–113.

10. The phenomenon of a female saint's mystical marriage to Christ was well developed in the hagiographical imagination even by the time of the *VsG*, and the topos of her rejection of an earthly suitor in favor of Christ is well attested; but this is the only early medieval example that I have been able to discover in which the anger of the female saint is figured. See Réginald Grégoire, "Il matrimonio mistico," in *Il matrimonio nella società altomedievale*, Settimane di Studio 24 (Spoleto: Presso la sede del Centro, 1977), pp. 701–94; my thanks to David Ganz for this reference.

11. Compare the sorts of questions addressed in the context of saga literature by William Ian Miller, *Humiliation* (Ithaca: Cornell University Press, 1993); see esp. chap. 3: "Emotions, Honor, and the Heroic."

12. For the ways in which this seemingly obvious point has in fact been open to contest, see the arguments collected in *The Nature of Emotion: Fundamental Questions*, ed. Paul Ekman and Richard J. Davidson (New York: Oxford University Press, 1994), esp. Question 5, "What are the minimal cognitive prerequisites for emotion?" and Question 8, "Can emotions be non-conscious?"

13. This strategically minimalist and abstract definition of anger is preferred for purposes of historical inquiry by Carol Z. Stearns and Peter N. Stearns, *Anger: The Struggle for Emotional Control in America's History* (Chicago: University of Chicago Press, 1986), pp. 12–17.

14. For the Implication of anger's "ought" in a particular cultural context, see Catherine Lutz, *Unnatural Emotions* (Chicago: University of Chicago Press, 1988), chap. 6: "Morality, Domination, and the Emotion of 'Justifiable Anger.'" For more general claims about anger's moral domain: Carol Tavris, *Anger: The Misunderstood Emotion* (New York: Simon and Schuster, 1982), p. 47. For the social logic of anger as a response to unjustifiable harm: Fred R. Myers, "The Logic and Meaning of Anger among Pintupi Aborigines," *Man* (n.s.) 23 (1988): 591.

15. For a brief and efficient discussion of universalist versus cultural claims about the nature of emotion, see Robert C. Solomon, "Getting Angry: The Jamesian Theory of Emotion in Anthropology," in *Culture Theory: Essays in Mind, Self, and Emotion*, ed. R. Shweder and R. LeVine (Cambridge, UK: Cambridge University Press, 1984), pp. 238–34; for emotion as "cultural acquisition," see p. 240.

16. An outline of the concerns of the history of emotion may be found in Peter N. Stearns, "Historical Analysis in the Study of Emotion," *Motivation and Emotion* 10, no. 2 (1986): 185–93. For an introduction to the social constructivist project in exploring emotion, see Rom Harré, "An Outline of the Social Constructivist Viewpoint," in *The Social Construction of Emotions*, ed. Rom Harré (Oxford: Basil Blackwell, 1986), pp. 2–14; for a critique of the strong social constructivist position, see William M. Reddy, "Against Constructionism: The Historical Ethnography of Emotions," *Current Anthropology* 38 (1997): 327–351.

17. Stearns and Stearns, *Anger*, p. 29.

18. For the "radical intranslatability" view, to which I subscribe, see Solomon, "Getting Angry," p. 240.

19. C. Terry Warner, "Anger and Similar Delusions," in *Social Construction of Emotions*, ed. Harré, p. 135.

20. Karl Galinsky makes much the same point in his critique of some modern readings of Vergil's intent in depicting Aeneas's anger in the closing scenes of the *Aeneid* in "The Anger of Aeneas," *American Journal of Philology* 109 (1988): 322–23. See also Gabrielle M. Spiegel's now foundational article, "History, Historicism, and the Social Logic of the Text in the Middle Ages," *Speculum* 65 (1990): 59–86.

21. Contra Miller's thoughtful discussion of interpreting the "emotional life of people long dead" (*Humiliation*, pp. 98–114), which does not seem to me sufficiently to problematize the possibility of contest and change in behavioral meanings within a culture. But see Myers, "Logic and Meaning of Anger," pp. 606–7, who argues that the linguistic representation, "the emotion-word," of a feeling is itself "but a signifier in a system of signifying practices" so that "its meaning is not given in reference but produced through its use in social life and its relationship to other signs."

22. Florence Dupont, *L'acteur-roi, ou, lé théâtre dans la Rome antique* (Paris: Belles Lettres, 1985), p. 190, "Pour rendre compte du sens de la loi, les jurisconsultes expliquent que le furieux est considéré comme absent à lui-même"; my thanks to Philippe

Buc for this reference. And see the *Thesaurus linguae latinae* (Leipzig: B. G. Teubner, 1900–), s.vv. *furor, furiosus,* where, in legal contexts, the latter term is used to mark those incompetent to transact business on their own account.

23. A Blaise, *Dictionnaire latin-français des auteurs chrétiens* (Turnhout: Éditions Brepols, 1954), s.v. *furor;* J. F. Niermeyer, *Mediae latinitatis lexicon minus* (Leiden: E. J. Brill, 1993), s.v. *furor.*

24. Bede, *Ecclesiastical History of the English People* 3.2, ed. B. Colgrave and R. A. B. Mynors (Oxford: Clarendon, 1969), p. 248. Historians of medicine Monica Green and Florence Eliza Glaze have suggested to me that *furor* is noted in ancient and early medieval medical literature as a medical (rather than purely emotional) state that sometimes had pathological connotations.

25. For "indignation," see the paraphrase of L. van der Essen, *Étude critique et littéraire sur les vitae des saints merovingiennes de l'ancienne Belgique* (Louvain: Bureaux de Recueil, 1907), p. 2; McNamara, Halborg, and Whatley render the phrase as "lost her temper" (*Sainted Women of the Dark Ages,* p. 223); both translations/readings seem to me to flatten the force of the text's language and to trivialize the social disruption of Gertrude's actions. But see the translation in *Late Merovingian France,* ed. Fouracre and Gerberding, p. 320: "But she, as if filled with rage . . ."

26. As Alain Dierkens notes, it is not possible to use the *VsG* to determine even which monastic rule was in use at Nivelles; see his "Prolégomènes à une histoire des relations culturelles entre les îles britanniques et le continent pendant le haut moyen âge: La diffusion du monachisme dit colombanien ou iro-franc dans quelques monastères de la région parisienne au VIIe siècle et la politique religieuse de la reine athilde," in *La Neustrie: Les pays au nord de la Loire de 650 à 850,* ed. Hartmut Atsma (Sigmaringen: J. Thorbecke, 1989), 2:388.

27. For the *VsG*'s explicit and implicit use of the Bible, see Marc Van Uytfanghe, *Stylisation biblique et condition humaine dans l'hagiographie mérovingienne (600–750)* (Brussels: Paleis der Academiën, 1987).

28. "Inter haec vero sciendum est quod furoris nomen Divinitati non congruit, quia naturam Dei simplicem perturbatio nulla confundit. Unde ei dicitur: 'Tu autem dominator virtutis cum tranquillitate judicas, et cum magna reverentia disponis nos.'" *Moralia in Job* 10.14, ed. Marc Adriaen, *S. Gregorii Magni Opera,* Corpus Christianorum Series Latina 143A (Turnhout: Brepols, 1979), p. 637; Gregory is quoting Wisdom 12:18.

29. "Tunc illa ait [to Valerianus]: Angelum Dei amatorem habeo, qui nimio zelo corpus meum custodit. Hic si vel leviter senserit, quod tu polluto amore contigas me, statim contra te suum furorem exagitat." Quoted in Grégoire, "Matrimonio mistico," pp. 762–63. My thanks to David Canz for pointing me to this and the previous reference.

30. *The Patrician Texts in the Book of Armagh,* ed. Ludwig Bieler (Dublin: Dublin Institute for Advanced Studies, 1979), pp. 62–126; and see Wendy Davies, "Anger and the Celtic Saint," *Anger's Past: The Social Uses of an Emotion in the Middle Ages,* ed. Barbara H. Rosenwein (Ithaca: Cornell University Press, 1998), pp. 19–20.

31. For the dating, see Bieler, *Patrician Texts,* p. 1, and Richard Sharpe, *Medieval Irish Saints' Lives* (Oxford: Clarendon, 1991), pp. 12–14, 16.

32. For the narrative in which Patrick curses a cattle thief, see Muirchú, *Vita Pa-*

tricii, c. 26, in *Patrician Texts*, edited Bieler, p. 112. And see the conclusions of Fouracre and Gerberding, *Late Merovingian France*, p. 318, regarding the decided paucity of elements that would mark the *VsG* as being within the Irish hagiographical tradition: it is "very much in the mainstream of the Frankish hagiographic tradition and [is] quite different from the writing about saints by seventh-century Irish authors in Ireland."

33. "Rogo vos, fratres, diligenter adtendite, si ad mensam cuiuscumque potentis hominis nemo presumit cum vestibus conciscissis et inquinatis accedere, quanto magis a convivio aeterni regis, id est, ab altari domini debet se unusquisque invidiae vel odii veneno percussus, iracundiae furore repletus, cum reverentia et humilitate subtrahere, propter illud quod scriptum est: prius reconciliare fratri tuo, et tuce veniens offer munus tuum; et iterum: amice, quomodo huc intrasti non habens vestem nuptialem?" *Sancti Caesarri Arelatensis sermones*, sermon 227, c. 3, ed. G. Morin, Corpus Christianorum Series Latina 104 (Turnhout: Brepols, 1953), p. 898.

34. Aurelian of Arles, *Regula ad virgines*, c. 10, PL 68, col. 401: "Quod Deus avertat, si diabolo instigante fuerit aliqua furore repleta, ut ista mandata pertinaci corde contemnat; et una de illis quae discordantes sunt praevenerit aliam, veniam ei petens; si illa cui petet non dimiserit, disciplinam accipiat, ut ad charitatem se corrigat. Et si ambo despexerint, ambae pariter a communione vel a cibo suspendantur; donec invicem sibi reconcilientur." See also and compare his *Regula ad monachos*, c. 12, PL 68, col. 389. Multiple examples of this sort and with much the same flavor can be easily located by reference to J.-M. Clément, *Lexique des anciennes règles monastiques occidentales* (Steenbrugge: Martin Nijhof, 1978), s.v. *furor*.

35. See Lester Little, "Anger in Monastic Curses," *Anger's Past*, pp. 9–35.

36. Of Columbanus and the monks: "modestia atque sobrietas, mansuetudo et lenitas aeque in omnibus redolebat. Execrabatur ab his desidiae atque discordiae vitiumi, arrogantiae ac elationis supercilium duris castigationum ictibus feriebatur, irae ac livoris noxa sagaci intentione pellebatur." Jonas, *Vita Columbani* 1.5, ed. B. Krusch, in *Ionae Vitae Sanctorum: Columbani, Vedastis, Iohannis* (Hanover: Hahn, 1905), p. 161. Ian Wood argues for the decisive if institutionally delimited influence of the *Vita Columbani* on Merovingian hagiography in "The *Vita Columbani* and Merovingian Hagiography," *Peritia* 1 (1982): 63–80.

37. For the context of this hostility, see Janet Nelson, "Queens as Jezebels: The Careers of Brunhild and Balthild in Merovingian History," in *Medieval Women*, ed. Derek Baker (Oxford: Basil Blackwell, 1978), pp. 31–77.

38. Gregory of Tours, *Decem Libri Historiarum*, ed. B. Krusch and W. Levison, MGH SSrerMerov I: I. Although the concordance was designed for use with Arndt's earlier edition, reading for *furor* in this text was made infinitely more efficient by the work of Denise St-Michel, *Concordance de l' Historia Francorum de Grégoire de Tours* (Montréal: Université de Montréal, Secteur Antiquité et Études Médiévales, 1982).

39. I owe this point, and the felicitous phrase, to William Reddy.

40. For example, *VsG*, c. 3, in which Gertrude ruminates internally over the heavenly contemplation she hopes to achieve in the monastic life: "infra se cogitabat de celeste contemplatione, quam sibi sine secularium strepitu habere optaverat"; c. 4, where the saint informs the monastery of witnessing a mysterious light while at prayer: she spoke "as if/almost trembling with fear" (ipsa Dei famula quasi pavore

perterrita nobis narravit). Here the *quasi* would seem plausibly to have the force of "manifestly" or "evidently"; in any case, as in Gertrude's *furor*, the narrator does not hesitate to name the (internal) emotion.

41. Since Gertrude was born in about 625/26, and Dagobert I—present at the feast—died in 639, her age at the time of the banquet may have been anywhere between seven and twelve or thirteen years; Dierkens, "Saint Amand," p. 330. This age fits the marriage pattern of well-born women; see Jean Verdon, "Les femmes laïques en Gaule au temps des Mérovingiens: Les réalités de la vie quotidienne," in *Frauen in Spätantike und Frühmittelalter*, ed. W. Affeldt (Sigmaringen: J. Thorbecke, 1990), p. 243.

42. For an adumbration drawn from contemporary narrative sources of the pressures and constraints on Frankish noblewomen's marriages, see Verdon, "Femmes laïques," pp. 243–48, and the more extensive treatment in Suzanne Wemple, *Women in Frankish Society: Marriage and the Cloister, 500 to 900* (Philadelphia: University of Pennsylvania Press, 1981), esp. pp. 31–57.

43. Of course, the two families overlapped to a significant extent; the history of early Nivelles, including the most systematic data about members of the community, is to be found in Hoebanx, *Abbaye de Nivelles*, pp. 45–70.

44. A woman found guilty of adultery was subject to death in the Burgundian and Lombard laws; see the material collected in Katherine Fischer Drew, "The Law of the Family in the Germanic Barbarian Kingdoms: A Synthesis," in *Law and Society in Early Medieval Europe*, ed. K. F. Drew (London: Variorum Reprints, 1988), VIII, pp. 18–19. Both Frankish and Roman law counted adultery as a crime that justified discarding a wife without penalty; see Wemple, *Women in Frankish Society*, p. 42. For an account of Frankish society that emphasizes the particular anxieties of adultery for women, see Michel Rouche, "The Early Middle Ages in the West," in *A History of Private Life*, ed. Philippe Ariès and Georges Duby, vol. I, *From Pagan Rome to Byzantium*, ed. Paul Veyne, trans. Arthur Goldhammer (Cambridge, Mass.: Belknap Press, 1987), pp. 411–547, at p. 473. For the development of secular and canonical legislation regarding adultery from the Merovingian to Carolingian era, see Régine Le Jan, *Famille et pouvoir dans le monde franc (viie–xe siècle)* (Paris: Publications de la Sorbonne, 1995), pp. 278–81.

45. Gregory of Tours, *Glory of the Martyrs*, ed. and trans. Raymond Van Dam (Liverpool: Liverpool University Press, 1988), pp. 92–93. Verdon, "Femmes laïques," p. 248, provides a synopsis of the various stories of female adultery recorded by Gregory of Tours.

46. This is Raymond Van Dam's pithy digest, which to my mind exactly captures the routine quality of the dehumanization that inhered in treatment of a dishonored wife; see Van Dam, *Saints and Their Miracles in Late Antique Gaul* (Princeton: Princeton University Press, 1993), p. 101. For violence done by the woman's family, see Gregory of Tours, *Decem Libri Historiarum* 6.36 (p. 307).

47. Stearns, "Study of Emotion," p. 187, and see Stearns and Stearns, *Anger*, pp. 18–28, for the panoply of mythic stereotypes about "premodern" people's feelings. For a deft consideration of the role that the *longue durée* has come to play in historical writing about early medieval Europe, see the introductory chapter in Guy Halsall, *Set-*

tlement and Social Organization: The Merovingian Region of Metz (Cambridge, UK: Cambridge University Press, 1995).

48. Miller, *Humiliation*, pp. 93–94. Particularly acute is Miller's attention to the way these same stereotypes are deployed in contemporary middle-class discourse about the poor.

49. Inga Clendinnen, preface to *Ambivalent Conquests* (Cambridge, UK: Cambridge University Press, 1987).

12

Emotions and Ancestors: Understanding Experiences of Lohorung Rai in Nepal

Charlotte E. Hardman

In her study of the bonds between Lohorung Rai and sammang *(ancestors), Charlotte E. Hardman describes the central role of emotion in that relationship. Emotions for the Lohorung are powerful and dangerous. Linked to ancestors by* saya, *the ancestral power or spirit within a person, Lohorung feel the emotions of the sammang, especially anger, in various ways, including through physical pain and sickness. Any departure from social standards for behavior emotionally affects the sammang and leads to undesirable consequences for persons. Behavior within traditional norms and remembrances of ancestral words and acts, on the other hand, revitalize the cosmos, affirming the unity and order of the interlocking realities of the superhuman, human, and natural worlds. Strong negative emotions toward other individuals, insults, and anger, are understood to physically affect the body of another person, lowering that person's saya, or vital force of life. As a consequence, "Life in Lohorung society is shaped and institutionalized in numerous ways to protect the vulnerability of its members from . . . low saya, whether sadness, depression, hopelessness, loss of the soul, or death." The Lohorung are as keenly aware of the emotional states of the sammang as they are other persons, and they treat the sammang to flattery and hospitality—food, gifts, drink, and so on—in the interest of keeping the temperamental sammang pacified and avoiding their anger, jealousy, tantrums, and tricksterish acting-out. Hardman proposes that the experiences of the Lohorung evidence to a certain extent the cultural construction of emotion, but identifies herself as a "moderate constructivist" seeking a theoretical ground that also includes a*

Charlotte E. Hardman, *Other Worlds: Notions of Self and Emotion among the Lohorung Rai* (Oxford: Berg, 2000). Selections from the book edited by the author. Reprinted by permission of the publisher.

universalist view of the biological "processes" or "capacities" that are the basis of emotions.

What is the Lohorung view of human nature? In what ways does the unity of all reality rest on a view of linkages through emotion? What are the consequences for one part of the cosmic order of emotional disturbances in another part? How do the Lohorung experience anger? How is anger conceptualized with respect to saya? How is the person conceptualized with respect to saya? How is morality constituted as emotions alongside behavior? How is health and happiness linked to morality? How is the cosmos disordered by emotion?

Prior to 1980 most work looking at emotions simply accepted the Western psychological view that emotions are psychobiological processes. Moreover, these psychobiological processes, as understood by Western scientists, were treated as universals. Emotions such as fear and anger were *assumed* to be universal emotions, and some anthropologists were all too aware of the neglect of the social, "and while emotions are often seen as *evoked in* communal life, they are rarely presented as an *index of* social relationship rather than a sign of a personal state."[1] As a reaction against the universalist view, the questions that interested me during fieldwork were of the following kind: What kind of understanding do Lohorung have of "human nature"? What powers do they ascribe to human beings, to gods, or ancestors? Do they have theories of "mind"? How do they understand or classify emotions? How do they make judgments about other people's behavior? Is the "human nature" they ascribe to themselves the same as the one they use to understand and explain the behavior of other neighboring people? How do they conceive of "the self"?[2] Understanding what emotions meant for Lohorung Rai men and women, and what they understood about the emotions of their ancestors gave me crucial insights into their culture and some small pieces of this understanding have become the focus for this essay. The people calling themselves Lohorung Rai live on the eastern side of the Arun Valley in eastern Nepal and see themselves as one of the Kiranti—the indigenous inhabitants of Nepal—who have become increasingly marginalized during the two centuries they have lived alongside the Brahmin and Chetri communities, who control the positions of power in the administration of what is now a Hindu state.[3] Lohorung Rai have adopted many Hindu rituals, but for them there are still strong elements in their culture that remain distinctly Lohorung or Kiranti, and they predominantly have to do with their ancestors and the myths and rituals with the primeval beings.

After the first few months of fieldwork I realized that any understanding of Lohorung experiences must entail grasping their notion of *sammang* (which I here gloss as "ancestors") and another, more abstract notion, *saya*, which at first I translated as "the ancestral spirit within a person" or the "vital essence" of a person. From the moment I began to understand these two concepts I was inevitably led to Lohorung notions of self and personhood; to their notions about mind, consciousness, the essential life-giving force of a person; and to what emotions mean to most Lohorung. Only by appreciating the complex workings and interconnections of these two concepts could I begin to make sense of such diverse things as child development, their conception of space and time, their attitudes to their houses, pigs, rituals, odd statements about flowers, trees, and crops, their attitude to the sexes, their interpretations of experiences, and their sense of appropriate conduct.

By looking at Lohorung from the point of view of their notions about the person and emotion, their statements about human nature and how to relate to the world, and by taking these seriously, I was led to appreciate the form and interconnections of their experiences. Learning how it feels and how they understand what it is for them to be shy, afraid, sad, or depressed led right away to appreciating a different way of being a person in another world.

According to Lohorung, emotions can be dangerous. Within their frame of reference angry insults can kill, fear can lead to illness. On the other hand, respect and a sense of shame are essential and to ignore them is to invoke equivalent disaster. Lohorung recognize social emotions (such as "shame") and embodied emotions (such as "anger"). As we shall see, they emphasize the context of emotions, that is, the range of situations that provoke particular emotions, but they also have clear rules about the expression of emotions and the importance of control over them. Because individual characteristics and a tendency for egocentrism and the expression of personal wishes and desires are thought of as being innate but also essentially asocial, sociability and the control of emotions have to be learned. Inevitably then, the proliferation of Lohorung ideas concerning the nature of men and women, and what should be developed, focuses on why a person should be social and how a person can be social. Within their frame of reference, this is the only way for their society to survive. It is not surprising, then, that some emotions and concepts of mind are institutionalized, acting as symbolic codes of communication and models of behavior.

In the first part of this essay I briefly outline the centrality of the two main concepts sammang (ancestor) and saya (ancestral power, vital soul) and how they dominate relationships in Lohorung lives and how the lack of the ancestors' control over anger and jealousy is one of the key explanations for disease and misfortune. In the second part I examine in more detail the Lohorung notion of anger, the degree to which it is controlled and institutionalized in Lohorung relations with the living, and in contrast, where Lohorung understand they can be individual active agents expressing their individual emotions.

Lohorung Relations with Their Ancestors

The Lohorung idea that lies at the core of their rituals and their understanding of themselves, and their environment, is the notion that every human being is closely bound to the natural world and to a world of spiritual beings. A dynamic and pervasive world of ancestors and spirits of the dead coexists with the world of the living. Explanations of events, of cultural and social phenomena, of mental and physical states are commonly expressed in terms of superhuman beings (sammang) or the natural world associated with them.

I saw it as the anthropologist's job to make as much sense of their world as I could from within their frame of reference and to make sense of what I began to see as their seamless world, where spirit and substance, mind and emotion, past and present, and many other of our oppositions are broken down. Other worlds demand the respect that comes from their own frame of reference, and the premise that shaped Lohorung frames of reference clearly had to do with a complex relationship with these beings called sammang ancestors.

What is hard to convey is the frequency with which Lohorung relate to the superhuman world and the complexity of the relations. The complexity of their experience of the superhuman is similar to that of the Tibetan of pre-Buddhist Tibet as described by Tucci:

> The entire existence of the Tibetan, his knowledge and desires, his feeling and thinking, is suffused and coloured by his experience of the sacred. His folk religion is not restricted to myth, to liturgy, or to a reverent attitude towards the numinal . . . it is also the living interplay of traditions of cosmogony and cosmology, genealogical legends of particular groups and families, rituals of magic and atonement, proverbial folk wisdom. . . . It is in short, an all-embracing heritage of the centuries.[4]

The world of all Lohorung Rai is similarly dominated by superhuman beings. In a complex relationship of trust, anger, jealousy, and fundamental communion, it is the superhuman beings called sammang who provide Lohorung with a key framework for understanding themselves, their emotions, and their experiences. As I came to understand it, any description of sammang has to focus on relationships, because the eruption of sammang anger is triggered by such events as the interruption, discontinuity, or violation of reciprocal relations between the living and the dead. What the sammang communicate through their anger, experienced by humans in the form of human pain or misfortune, is their fundamental and inflexible commitment to traditional values as established by the original founders. These values continue to be made known to Lohorung and other Kiranti in the body of myths and rituals generally called *mundhum* or *muddum*.⁵ Each ancestor is committed to a particular area of traditional life, sometimes characterized by the way he or she died.

The relationship with sammang is so interwoven into Lohorung traditional life that one might say it is the skeleton articulating Lohorung society. Such is the depth of this relationship that the few Lohorung who are known to have become skeptical about the sammang were all soon drawn back into the traditional way of looking at their experiences when they encountered some serious illness or misfortune in their lives.

My own understanding from Lohorung is that, for them, most of the sammang are spirits of powerful ancestors, either their own or those of other Kiranti with whom they were early on in contact, mostly beings from the remote primeval past, from the time when civilization (*pe-lam* or *mundum*) was being created and the strength of the natural order of the world prevailed. At that time human beings had abilities they later lost, such as communicating with trees, rocks, and animals or breaking a stone with a feather. All the sammang, however, give the same impression of being the spirits of worshipful ancestors rather than "gods." As a way of understanding the Lohorung notion of sammang, I. S. Chemjong's Christian gloss as "spirit of god" with the idea of one God (also a sammang) behind it, is understandable (given his conversion to Christianity) but not very helpful.⁶ It fits neither the Lohorung attitude to the sammang nor the characteristics attributed to them. Although perhaps the word could be glossed as "gods," without any connection to any other superior God or god, with its simple sense of "what is worshipped by sacrifice; superhuman person, worshipped as having powers over nature and human fortunes" (*OED*), it is still not very satisfactory. Sammang do not simply have power over nature: they are part of it and own it.

Lohorung use the Nepali term for "gods," *deuta* or *dewa*, to describe other superhuman beings different from sammang. On occasions, to confuse matters, they may also use deuta to refer to the sammang, particularly if they are talking to non-Kiranti, simply to express the significance of their sammang to those for whom deuta is the most important category of superhuman being. For Lohorung themselves, however, the various sammang are more important and even more powerful than deuta. As one woman put it, "In the face of the sammang the gods, deuta, are afraid."

For us, the term "gods" carries the sense of a nonmortal power, and not the notion that the beings were themselves once mortal and still share many of the characteristics of their mortal descendants. Sammang are in many ways very human. Like human beings, they have *niwa* (mind, consciousness) and saya (sensitive link with protective ancestor/gods), which is affected like our "hurt pride" or "loss of face"; they manifest emotions of jealousy, fear, anger; they become hungry, hot and cold, excited, proud; they can be clever, stupid, childlike, impatient, crafty, quick to understand, or bored. Lohorung see them as being like children and treat them in part as needing the same discipline and direction, and yet recognize too the need to give them the respect that their greater age requires. Sammang are known to be sensitive to insult and disrespect which can lead to their "hurt niwa" or "lowered saya" and to a reaction causing disorder or misfortune in a family or community. The idea of the sammang as being closer to our "ancestors" or "ancestral heroes" than "gods" is also emphasized by the Lohorung attitude that particular sammang "belong" to particular clans or clan groups or the "tribe" as a whole, even another Kiranti tribe; some are borrowed from the Limbu (*subba subbeni,* for example) or from the Khambu Rai to the west (such as *ge'ereng me'ereng*); some are seen as relating to the whole Kiranti as the founders of Rai culture, from whom Lohorung see themselves as being descended.

The Christian concept of God includes attributes of omnipotence and infinite goodness; God is almighty, omniscient, and infinitely benevolent. No Lohorung sammang are like this. There is no one sammang that is consistently more powerful than the rest. The power shifts depending on the relationships among the sammang, and between the sammang and the human beings. While I was there it was being said that the *chawatangma sammang,* "the forest sammang," had recently become very powerful, whereas previously the *pappamamma'chi* had always been dominant. None of the sammang is simply benevolent: some of them will bring good fortune and general prosperity or long life to a household and its members, but it is always and only in return for special treatment. Lohorung talk of them as being "eaters" (*cha'khuba*). Anyone who happens to be in their territory, whether Kiranti, Tamang, or Hindu, can be afflicted by them, and persons in the dominant castes, the Bahun and Chetri, greatly fear them. Thus, the term "divinity," with its connotations of no negative attributes, seems inappropriate.

Pappamamma means "grandfather-grandmother" (*chi* denotes plural). They are sammang and include all Lohorung's nearest and remotest ancestors—at least, all those who have died natural "good" deaths. As the repositories of traditional wisdom, they deserve even more respect than the wise and aged members of the living community whose qualities they share.

In what Lohorung call the "ascending" season from February to August, pappamamma'chi stay in their villages, but in the "descending" season from August to February they travel south. During the month of *saun* (mid-July to mid-August) no sammang ritual takes place, for the Lohorung say that the ancestors are too busy traveling with their own affairs to take notice of them and the rites would be ineffective. This is also the time Lohorung themselves are journeying to buy or barter salt and other provisions for the year. Nevertheless, as some Lohorung pointed out, you have to be particularly careful at this time, as it is mostly when sammang travel north and south that they are hurt or become offended: "We cannot see them, we mistakenly tread on them, bump into them, sometimes even spit on them or drop ash on them; when they see we are not doing things the way we should traditionally they are jealous or angry. Although they are old, they are more like children and are upset by very little things."

Some of the pappamamma'chi are now very old, going back to the very first people, and are portrayed in images that have them covered with moss and lichen but still bearing the signs of their "good death," the silver thong or white cloth to hold up their chin, and the money (tikāN) on the forehead. They have very long hair and also hair growing all over their body. The oldest ones, who lived in the forest before houses or spinning and weaving had been established, are simply covered with moss and body hair. Their appearance is so frightening that children under ten are forbidden to attend any pappamamma ritual in case they catch sight of one and are frightened into unconsciousness from the flight of of lawa ("soul loss").

Of all the sammang, pappamamma'chi are capable of the worst anger. There is a special word to describe their anger, a term applied only to them and to young children. The word is yiktikheda (or yikbokheda, indicating its association with the stomach, bok). It is a verb similar to that for "he has become angry," sintikheda. Lohorung informants explained it to me as being "the kind of anger that is very hard to counteract." In this emotional state a child or sammang is unhappy and impatient as well as angry, displaying what we might call general discontent and irritability. "They cry as well as shout." Children have to be plied with something sweet or given the breast, and the pappamamma'chi have to be pampered with ritual offerings to distract them from their mood or the idea they have become locked into. In this mood, pappamamma'chi sometimes team up with another sammang and work in league against a household or one of its members. Lohorung describe this as sammang'chi tokchoktikheda'chi (lit. "intestines extended together"), which they say "joins their intestines to make one" (eko thok lechi). This image was conveyed by interlocking two forefingers together. When this happens it's known to be very difficult to appease either of the ancestors—as difficult as trying to separate two close friends or a man and wife who have joined together in a similarly close, intricate relationship (also described by Lohorung as tokchok-tikheda). In this relationship, whatever one sammang does, the other sammang does, too. They go everywhere and do everything together. Lohorung see such mutuality as the sign of real friendship; in human relationships its "good" qualities are recognized but also the dangers, because if one died the other would die too, having become as one. Lohorung insist they must always try to separate the two. Such intimacy is too dangerous. When a household develops such a relationship with the pappamamma'chi or some other sammang, however, the bond cannot be broken. The relationship has to persist and the household must continue with its commitments to serve the particular sammang in the way it has agreed. If there's any hint of change it's said the anger of the sammang is felt by human beings in extreme ways. Misfortunes or illnesses are sometimes explained as the anger of a sammang whose close relationship has not been maintained. Such relationships never occur between one sam-mang and one individual, even though the ancestors may display their anger by relating to only one person in the household. For Lohorung it is households that relate to the ancestors, not individuals.

Pappamamma'chi are considered to be the repositories of Lohorung lore and wisdom. What angers them most is the overt transgression of traditions, particularly those concerning ritual. Acute pain all over the body, but particu-larly in the stomach and head, is mostly experienced as pappamamma'chi angered by careless behavior of human beings. Pappamamma'chi are sensed in a big way, not by some small pain. The semantic domain connected to them refers to morality; their "anger" is seen as a response to seeing a Lohorung adopting new traditions, such as smoking and drinking at the same time or eating food and drinking home-brewed beer at the same time. Older Lohorung insist these activities should be kept separate or they fight one another in the body, like people of different kinds fight. Though smoking, eating, and drink-ing *should* be separate, the problem is that nowadays people like mixing them together. Ignoring old traditions like these or adopting new ways, such as new fashions in clothing, can make pappamamma'chi very angry. If someone's mind (niwa) goes strange, as if "mad," if someone begins to walk and talk strangely, it could be that the relationship with pappamamma'chi has gone seriously wrong. However, interfering with the workings of niwa is usually an indication of the anger of some other sammang. Pappamamma'chi are more like watchdogs over Lohorung behavior, demanding a respectful niwa (*hang-male*) and that traditions are esteemed. Pappamamma'chi might well be called the Lohorung equivalent to the superego.

Deviation from traditional ways can become costly: the ritual to appease pappamamma'chi usually requires a large pig. If the mood swing in pappa-mamma'chi has been misjudged and the pig is not big enough, their anger (usually of the sintikheda kind) increases very quickly, much like a child's tantrum, and the person in pain suffers an increase in pain to a corresponding degree. Pappamamma'chi even check the size of the pig, measuring it carefully with a piece of cloth!

In spite of their volatile "anger," pappamamma'chi are also characterized as being pliable and easily persuaded (*okningbak*). If they become "angry" very quickly, they are also as quickly appeased. The drama and emotional displays are put down to strong desires combined with diminishing abilities, accom-panying the loss of youthful and powerful niwa (mind, memory). In their indecisiveness and frustration it is said they become like children. The "im-ages" are vivid. If content with the offerings made to them, they cluster around the roof of the house with their weapons, men with hammers and *kukuri* knives and women with loom shuttles and sickles, brandishing them in the air, danc-ing and shouting to all the evil spirits lurking in every village to keep away and leave the house and its inhabitants in peace. If they are not satisfied, they congregate around the top of the ladder to the house and on the front verandah, calling to other sammang to come and join them in their angry protest.

To avoid the "jealousy" of other sammang when performing pappamamma rituals, Lohorung told me they also make offerings to the most "jealous," to ge'ereng me'ereng, to chawatangma, kuma, and yangli. If they do not, these other sammang feel "angry" and "jealous," leading to yet more corresponding sickness and pain in human beings.

The relationship of Lohorung to pappamamma'chi is characterized by filial obligation and respect, combined with compassion and firm manipulation. The following words (sikhla) spoken to them during rituals in which they are called to the house demonstrate well the attitude of the human beings to these ancestors:

> You dead grandmother, grandfather, maternal aunt, paternal aunt, elder brothers, younger brothers, elder sisters, younger sisters, all close relatives, from your place of origin rise and follow the sandy path, the desert path, the tree way, the stone way, along the windy way take a rest, protect your breath, do not wear yourselves out. Open your dreams, open your lawa and come to the vertical house pole . . . [long list of the parts of the house they should enter], cross into the house, wash your feet and hands without embarrassment, don't be shy of the shrine, it is for you, we have called you. Now you have come, rest. If we have stepped over you without noticing, if we have stepped on you, even so don't let it hurt, do not be worried. Do not be angry. We offer you to drink and eat the spoils of the harvest toiled by the ten fingers of all your children and grandchildren. We offer you the new rice . . . [list of offerings]. Come now, drink and eat to your satisfaction but this is not a general invitation. Come when we call you but not at any other time. If you come at other times the living will gossip about you. Did you know our troubles? Did you see our troubles? Do not let your niwa hurt, keep your saya an unending saya, give us strong lawa, give us long breath, give us strong saya. Keep away stomach pains, swellings, diarrhea . . . [list of diseases], protect us from evil spirits . . . [list of pan-Nepali spirits as well as Lohorung ones]. Come, whatever we have offered, eat and drink. When you have finished, give up infatuation [for this place], wash your feet and hands and return to your place. Go and stay in your own place. Do not go astray.

As old grandparents, guardians of tradition but with fading powers, pappamamma'chi are addressed with a combination of command, cajolery, injunctions, and respect. The choice of offerings given to pappamamma'chi, as to other ancestors, are meant to convey Lohorung respect and compassion as well as being coercive in maintaining the necessary measured relationship. They are coaxed to the house and also firmly told to return to their own place. Central to the ritual is raising their saya and that of the household.

Let me just enlarge a little on that key concept of saya. Lohorung view the person as being essentially vulnerable. Every person must retain the correct bond with his or her ancestors, a bond that is internally represented in a person by saya (ancestor within a person). If a person's saya is in its correct position, associated with the head, he or she can be strong, protected, and therefore courageous and proud. The person's vulnerability, however, is particularly susceptible to insults, demoralizing experiences, anger, or the transgression of traditional ways. Any of these experiences may cause saya to fall, leading to a particular emotional condition that is discussed in the second part of this essay. It is an emotion that may be compared to our notion "depression," but unless the bond with ancestors is renewed, a person can die.

The home also has saya. The house is an extension of the person, a macrocosm of the male and female unit; it is the household that is the key ritual unit in relations with sammang ancestors and is conceived of as being as vulnerable as the human beings who live in it. Various parts of the house have saya, just as people do. As one Lohorung said, "The way to keep saya high is to show interest in the ancestors." The power of the emotion is believed to be such that it has to be managed, through rituals and through correct behavior in certain everyday life situations. Lohorung rituals can compensate for everyday behavior. They restore the link among ancestors, their traditions, and everyday life, thereby raising saya and protecting the person.

The ritual for pappamamma'chi must raise their saya and that of the household to renew the primordial link and recreate primordial prosperity and the strength of the house. To please pappamamma'chi their shrine is built with sticks from a kind of chestnut tree called waiphu (musure katuj, Castonopsis tribuloides), the wood used to build houses in the old days. When not available, Lohorung use chigaphu, another kind of chestnut (Castanopsis indica). They make the shrine as if building a house, with four pillars and five, seven, or nine cross-bars, the number Lohorung still use when building their own houses. The cross-bars create a platform, and on this they place pieces of the dark gray and white cloth, spun and woven by Lohorung women, representing the clothes traditionally worn by men and women. On the ground on a banana leaf are placed the offerings. The main item is the sacrificial pig, but the offerings must also include a hen and a cock, a minimum of seven eggs, two containers of beer, as many tongba (bamboo vessels filled with millet beer) as possible, but usually amounting to the number of participants. There must also be ginger, used for divination, and several leaf plates containing vegetables and chutneys. The pappamamma'chi are summoned to the shrine with a small bamboo whistle. In the most "human" way, Lohorung offer what they themselves value most highly and like most to receive, namely, beer from a tongba, meat, poultry, eggs, some relishes, and new clothes. These are customary treats that have never lost their appeal. Lohorung talk of being so "close" to these ancestors that, until recently, the elders (*pasing'chi*) of each lineage could perform the ancestral cult without the help of the local officiant (*yatangpa*). Now, however, men are less well acquainted with the ritual language, some of them are totally ignorant of the chants, and each household relies increasingly on the yatangpa to ensure their contacts with the sammang are carried out correctly. In any case, the other sammang are becoming increasingly clever and unpredictable; most people are now afraid to take on *Chawatangma* or any of the others without the help of an expert.

Central to any account of sammang lie numerous Lohorung assumptions about human nature and "illness" to do with the workings of mind, soul, emotions, motivations, and their mystical union with ancestors. The way Lohorung talk about sammang and represent them in ritual is closely linked to their understanding of "the person" and their representation of emotions as key factors in devastating the unity and balance in relations with other living beings and with ancestors. From their view, the stability of their society depends on maintaining the balance of relations among humans, superhumans, and nature. To understand how Lohorung view this destabilizing power of emotions is one of the aims of this essay.

What I found among the Lohorung could be interpreted as a full-blown ancestor cult, rather similar to ancestor cults found in China, West Africa, Assam, and the Naga hills. This was a possible interpretation which might have supported my argument that, in relation to Lohorung material, "religion" is not an appropriate interpretive framework.[7] Some anthropologists have long maintained that the beliefs and practices of ancestor worship do not constitute "worship" in the strict sense but institutionalized reverence for elders; that is, attitudes normally directed toward living elders are simply extended to the ancestors.[8] Following this view, ancestor worship could hardly be considered a system of religious beliefs and practices. However, although Lohorung society might be described as an ancestor-worshipping society, I don't see the category "ancestor cult" as being any more helpful than "religion" as an interpretive framework. As Geertz says, categories such as ancestor worship usually tell us little more than the obvious, for example, that "ancestor worship supports the jural authority of elders," and in fact detract from the vitality of what is actually going on. "The individuality of religious traditions has so often been dissolved into such dessicated types as 'animism,' 'ancestor worship' and all the other insipid categories by means of which ethnographies of religion devitalise their data."[9]

Much of the material concerning Lohorung ancestors comes to life when we see that one of the key problems underlying Lohorung attitudes to themselves and their world is how to deal with the power of emotions—their own and those of dead ancestors and those who did not have a good death. Anger, jealousy, "hunger," greed, longings, and fears as well as the unconscious workings of saya and lawa (wandering soul) all have the power to upset the delicate balance within the cosmos, the household, the village, or the person. The emotions are made manifest in sickness, misfortunes, bad crops, or landslides. Lohorung frames of reference are largely rooted in an interrelatedness among human beings, nature, and superhuman beings, and what a study of self and emotions highlights is the force of this interrelatedness.

Rather than looking at Lohorung's "ancestor cult," I see the Lohorung attitude to sammang as being part of a more complex set of ideas about what it means to be human in a world with different ideas about how emotions work and different notions about how selves develop and where order has to be constantly restored and refreshed. Ancestors are not just revered elders, they are also irresponsible childlike beings whose minds (niwa) have diminished, whose saya fall and have to be renewed, beings who suffer and are angry, capricious children and destructive tricksters. The general motivations, the mind and temperamental nature of sammang are seen essentially as being a mixture of the very young and the very old put together. Their likes and dislikes, their anger, hunger, jealousy, and erratic volatile behavior encapsulate Lohorung knowledge about the domineering, blundering tyranny of elders, who try to maintain the attention of those around them using the power of their age, along with other knowledge about the helplessness and willfulness of young children, constantly needing attention and desiring to play.

Realizing the extent to which Lohorung appreciate the mental states and motivations of their sammang ancestors, I could begin to understand the attitude of compassion toward them. I could also make sense of the very "human" rituals, in which Lohorung cajole and tempt sammang with food, drink, and sometimes cloth or some other material object—whatever they like best—because ancestors fit into their own social ethos of hospitality, generosity, and exchange. In every aspect of social life Lohorung share and reciprocate. This is institutionalized, for example, in a form of gift-giving called *huksok*,[10] in marriage exchange and the marriage dialogues, in songs, and in labor exchange. There is a "functional interdependence" between groups of all kinds; unlike everyone else, the aged and the very young have to be pampered with gifts of food and drink to gain their cooperation: so too do the sammang. This is particularly the case when the delicate relationship of trust has been broken and sammang are outraged.

To conclude, then, the "natural" ancestral order, the original primeval order, as recorded in their myths, has to be constantly recreated and the unity of nature, the superhuman, and the human reaffirmed. Failure to do this would lead to depression, increased sickness, possibly death, and ensuing chaos. In contrast, repetition of ancestral words and adherence to ancestral order acts like recharging the cosmos. It brings vitality.

Lohorung concepts of self, mind, and emotion reflect the necessity for this unity. Owing to the interconnectedness of nature, superhuman, and human, they do not divide up the world in the way we often do in the West. The post-Renaissance model of the world of Descartes, Newton, and the Industrial Revolution has left us with a perception of humanity as outside nature, operating *on* it for its own interests, exploiting it and exploring it objectively from a position of detachment. For Lohorung the relationship among the superhuman, natural, and human worlds is one of a natural unity—the unity being a oneness that underlies the vitality of all human beings, the well-being of ancestors, and parts of the natural and material world connected to primeval beings. What they emphasize is the unity and order of the primeval world.

Lohorung and Emotions

Emotional and inner states are inextricably linked to the concept of saya, which links a person to the ancestral world. States that we variously describe as anger, depression, happiness, health are connected to a person's essential state—his or her state of saya. Saya has to be protected, and this can be achieved by what the Lohorung consider to be correct behavior. Respectful behavior and traditional behavior reduce the extent to which people's vulnerabilities are attacked. Insults or anger, on the other hand, can attach to another person's body, with the effect of lowering saya. Ultimately, this can be fatal. Lohorung thus place great emphasis on developing in their children the niwa (mind, source of knowledge) that knows ancestral ways. Even niwa, however, cannot always control such things as *kisime* (fear), although they do talk about ways of living that can reduce fear: "We live close together so as not to fear [kisime]: to live in the fields alone away from the village is *kisimalu* [frightening]," and so on. The Lohorung notion of saya and their concept of the person as essentially vulnerable shape experiences, activities, and concepts in other areas of their life. Life in Lohorung society is shaped and institutionalized in numerous ways to protect the vulnerability of its members from the effects of a low saya, whether sadness, depression, hopelessness, loss of the soul, or death.

The aim of this section is ethnographic. It does not intend to survey the literature on the anthropology of emotion or enter in any depth into the debate as summarized by Lutz and White.[11] "It will, on the other hand, explain my response to the debate, using my understanding of Lohorung concepts of emotion. The importance of studying the emotions has been succinctly expressed by Catherine Lutz in several articles. One of her clearest statements goes as follows:

> Emotions are assumed here to be the primary source of human motivation. If emotions are simultaneously viewed as cultural concepts, they become important as statements about, and motivations for the enactment of cultural values. If motivation is seen as culturally con-

stituted,[12] study of the emotions and their development becomes crucial for understanding the psychosocial origins of behaviour. Thus, emotion in the individual may be said to have its parallel, on the cultural level, in values: the concept of emotion, then, can provide a critical nexus for understanding the individual's creation of, and participation in, social institutions.[13]

I hope here to show briefly, with the example of the Lohorung understanding of "anger," how Lohorung emotions and their cultural values replicate each other.

The view that humans are in general self-constituting lies firmly behind my own approach to understanding the emotions. I am concerned with how notions of self, person, and emotions, which have some biological basis, are also constructed by people's cultural understandings, the concepts, premises, and discourse of the group they identify with, such as underlying assumptions about the nature of the person and how to relate to the social world. Most academics adopting a constructionist approach do not deny the notion of some psychological or biological processes operating independently of culture, but they downplay this. My focus, too, has been to look at how the experiences and worlds of people within a particular culture are constructed and shaped by their cultural concepts of self and emotions.

Anger is central to Lohorung Rai. As we have seen, their relationship with the sammang is based on the view that ancestors become angry, but anger, and in particular the impact of anger on saya, is also a central feature of Lohorung culture. What I show here is how Lohorung understand what we call anger, the place that anger plays in Lohorung society, and how people expect it to be expressed and controlled.

The Lohorung concepts that fall under our notion of anger can be divided into two categories. In the first place, there are those concepts that describe sudden eruptions and changes in mood, which we might call the anger of frustration or irritability. This is exemplified by the Lohorung description of children literally "going sour," *sinti'kheme,* moods that in their severe form we describe as temper tantrums. The Lohorung verb seems particularly apt to describe the change of mood that occurs when the internal fermentation (or frustration, as we see it) becomes too potent for the child to bear. One description of sinti'kheme went as follows: "When children want to go to a place a bit far away but they don't manage to reach, it they 'become frustrated' [sinti'khemi]; if they cannot have more good things to eat and drink they 'become frustrated'; when they're a bit older and if they don't get to wear nice clothes, or nice bracelets, nose rings, or gold jewelery they 'get angry with frustration.'" This mood of frustration is theoretically applied only to children, but I have heard it used about women as well. Though the anger of the ancestors is conceived as being like the frustrated anger or temper tantrums of children, Lohorung never talk about sammang ancestors "going sour." As we have seen, the verb to describe ancestors' anger, which can also be applied to the anger of children, is *yik'bok'kheme*. When applied to ancestors it means that the ancestors' anger has become severe; they are not being offered what they want and are now "angry with frustration." But, however much they are offered, they continue to see it as unsatisfactory, just like children whose frustration has gone too far.

The second category of concepts that fall under our notion anger differs from the first in that they rely on the presence of niwa (mind) for their emergence. Our notions of consciousness, will, conscious desire, determination, and sensibility are all included in the complex meaning of niwa and the adult forms of Lohorung anger. Niwa as an internalized state appears only when the child begins to respond to the social world. In young children niwa has not yet developed and their emotional outbursts are seen as being undirected and totally spontaneous. In the ancestors internal desires are said to predominate and their "social niwa" often forgotten.

If we look at the concept in use it includes what we would call "justifiable anger." For example, asked about the occasions when people experienced *sirda yakcha'bokme,* children of ages varying from six to fourteen years old suggested the following kinds of situations (in each case I have glossed the term using "angry" to show how it seems to fit the semantic field of *sirda yakcha'bokme:*

> When you haven't done good work parents get angry, they wave a stick
>   at you like they want to hit you; people's faces go red if you don't do
>   work well and they get angry.
> When you do something wrong, others get angry, like if the rice isn't
>   ready when they come home from working. If I go to fetch water and
>   break the pot, then my parents get angry. In the evening when they
>   come home from the field and find you've done something wrong or
>   stupid they get angry. If somebody killed someone else's dog or pig
>   the owner would get angry.
> If I don't do as I am told my mother gets angry.
> When a cow or pig goes into a field and starts to eat your crops, then
>   you get angry.
> If one person hits another person and shouts at them, then the other
>   person gets angry. If my brother hits me, then I get angry. People who
>   hit each other are angry.
> When people shout and fight and quarrel they are angry.
> If you get too big-headed other people get angry.
> When people are drunk they easily get angry. They have different niwa
>   [mind]; if you don't know someone is drunk and they do something
>   wrong, then you get angry and the drunk person acts even more an-
>   grily.

Many of these examples emphasize the moral "ought" role of *yak'chame*, and in this sense "justifiable anger" is within the semantic range of the concept. It expresses what people feel when someone has done something wrong; it makes people want to punish someone else, either physically or verbally, and facially it has the same reddening effect as does anger for many of us. This emphasis on situation or context in the Lohorung understanding of anger is close to one aspect of our own Western view. We often engage in an analysis of our emotions by linking anger or fear, for example, back to situations that caused them. We too rarely confine our analysis to some internal, subjective feeling. The difference between the Lohorung attitude and our own lies in the way they sometimes expand the context of anger beyond boundaries we would impose to include the ancestral. A pain that someone is feeling is reconceptualized as the anger of an ancestor.

Every Lohorung knows about the sudden anger of the sammang ancestors. The logic of their anger and tantrums provides the Lohorung with a natural philosophy that explains all kinds of misfortune and sickness, such as loss of appetite, acute pain in the "heart, liver, kidney" (*lungma*) area, headaches, earaches, sweating, stomach aches, limb and chest aches, difficulty with breathing, shaking, cramp, sudden blindness or deafness, boils, paralysis, severe burns, and sudden blood from the nose or mouth. If someone suddenly runs off into the jungle, jumps into the river, or falls off a precipice, the house ancestor *khimpie sammang* must be angry. If people burn themselves or their house burns down, khimpie is angry. If people become "mad"—that is, their niwa stops working properly—if they act in an antisocial manner, or if they suddenly cannot speak, it could be khimpie or the mischievous forest ancestor chawatangma who is angry. If someone feels giddy it is the anger of chawatangma. If the crops are not plentiful it could be that the pappamamma ʿchi are angry, or it could be that someone has promised chawatangma extra offerings and she is angry because they have failed to do so. As I mentioned earlier, Lohorung spend much time and energy placating the endless anger of the ancestors.

The anger of sammang and the offerings made can be understood only if we conceive of the ancestral anger in the human terms we have discussed. Although the sammang have left the world of the living in one sense, in Lohorung thought they still live much as humans do and though in a different zone they are still interlinked with them in a unified cosmos. The anger of the ancestors is understood as the indication that something has to be repaired in the system of trust between living and nonliving. The logic of their anger makes more sense in terms of this trust. The relationship is reciprocal. There is an expectation and a trust that the living will look after the society in the traditional way, that they will look after those who can no longer enjoy its produce by making the requisite offerings and will refrain from transgressions of behavior, such as incorrect kinship behavior. In return, the living expect protection from outside superhuman forces and trust the sammang to respond when favors are requested and the appropriate offerings made. They expect to be able to negotiate with their ancestors and communicate through their priests and shamans. The expectations of each are based on the experience of generations. If a particular ancestor feels let down he expresses his anger by afflicting the humans with pain or misfortune until the humans have shown their reliability again with offerings. The ancestors are in control and never wrong; it's humans who are fallible, especially because they live in a world that includes non-Lohorung, full of modern attractions competing with the traditions of the ancestors.

Further reasoning behind the anger and tantrums of the ancestors lies in their particular temperaments and in the Lohorung understanding of a connection between hunger and anger. The ill humor of ancestors is perceived at times to be related to their appetite, whether for food, attention, or obedience, indeed, in almost all contexts Lohorung may talk about the anger and the hunger of the ancestors interchangeably, as equivalent notions. When someone is ill people say, "X sammang ancestor is angry," or they may equally well say, "X sammang ancestor is hungry" (for example, *chawatangma sagesi'boka*). This makes sense when we realize that for Lohorung the mind is principally physical, and mental states, such as anger, have their physical manifestations. Hunger of the ancestors, their strong physical desire for something, is understood as the physical aspect of their anger, and their anger is associated with the mental aspect of their hunger. It also makes sense that both their minds and their bodies must be satisfied before they can be pacified and that the only way they can be satisfied is with offerings of particular kinds of food and talk from the priest, who offers words of reassurance.

The Lohorung notion of satiety is *sapthame*, which can be glossed as "to have enough of what you want," that is, to have enough food and drink and clothes. When someone has had enough food or drink and is offered more, he or she says "Sabu, sabu." Nevertheless, he or she will then be pressed to have more; the way the person says "Sabu, sabu" and whether or not it is accompanied by a gesture of the hand covering the cup or plate conveys whether he or she has *really* had enough. The phrase *chaibano, sapthanga eremo* ("Truly, I have really had enough") conveys that the individual is really satisfied. The term is connected to having enough food and drink and sometimes clothes, though for Lohorung (as, indeed, for us) it is only with food and drink that one becomes fully satisfied with no room for more. With clothes, as with money or material objects, someone may well not be satisfied with what is offered; appetites for these are harder to measure. Accordingly, when Lohorung offer food and drink to ancestors to appease their anger they have a measure of what is needed. Given Lohorung values, they know they must offer meat and home-brewed millet beer to satisfy, just as they would offer to a respected guest. Chicken meat may be enough, but the appetites of the ancestors differ so that the specific offerings made to each vary according to their particular likes and dislikes.

Offering food and drink to pacify the anger of the ancestors makes sense for two reasons: first, the anger is closely linked to hunger, and second, the kind of feasts offered are more likely to truly satisfy than any other kind of offering. When the normal offerings do not satisfy and pacify the ancestor and the pain or sickness continues, it's clear to Lohorung that the anger has developed into a tantrum, 'yibok'kheda anger (the anger of frustration), and the ancestor must be pampered with more chickens and pigs to swing his or her mood. But just as children in a tantrum may not be satisfied with rice, sweet things, or the breast, Lohorung say offerings to ancestors can sometimes just provoke into a greater tantrum. Both children and ancestors "know," with the kind of godlike intuition they both possess, just how much they can get, and if the offering is not adequate to the mood, it is rejected. The perverse anger of the ancestors explains why healing rituals sometimes do not work.

To summarize the main features of anger, we've seen that the Lohorung understanding of this emotion is intimately bound up with their experience of the ancestors and their understanding of the body. They are embraced by a system of values dominated by the ancestors and saya. But we can also see that anger and its outward manifestations are for Lohorung in some ways desirable, insofar as they provide opportunity for social control, education, and public expression of personal distress. Moreover, some say that individuals at times take advantage of sammang to express physically what they otherwise could not. The distraught mother of a girl who eloped was able to shake and bare her breasts and at last demonstrate the anger and frustrations she had kept to herself. She explained her condition as sammang. Others saw it as her anger. We have seen how anger, if controlled, can be diverted to bodily symptoms. If she had been openly angry about her daughter, she might have received some, but not much, sympathy because "officially" Lohorung say anger should not be felt for long. In contrast, her bodily symptoms brought her compensatory rituals and community support. In this way her anger did eventually disappear.

As a human emotion, anger is not considered to be something that must always be suppressed, nor something to be expressed in whatever way one feels like. The strong sense of justice and morality that acts to maintain the ideal cooperative and egalitarian nature of Lohorung society goes along with a ready anger to guard and enforce it. If people are not cooperative and socially minded, they will encounter the anger of those older than they. The adult form of anger is often socially desirable. Just as the ancestors are regarded as watching over the values, behavior, and manners of the living, and become angry with those who flout the rules, so too do living adults watch out for right and wrong behavior and express their legitimate anger. Moreover, anger makes public the conflicts that may be related to one or a few households but that are inevitably relevant to the community as a whole. In general, the Lohorung are good-natured and tolerant; anger has its place and its rules.

Conclusions: Universalism and Relativism

In the light of what I have described here, what do I make of the main debate that continues between the "relativists" and "universalists"? Are emotions culturally relative? Can we say that "self" and "emotions" are linguistic and cultural creations, that all mental and metaphysical states are constituted by culture?

My first response to these initial questions is to reflect on what Lohorung taught me about self and emotions. Lohorung understanding of emotions emphasizes both social emotions (such as saya and *ngesime,* shame, shyness) *and* embodied emotions (such as anger, located in organs and therefore grounded in the biological). They appreciate a clear connection among ontology, ancestral heritage, and emotional health, a clear connection too among thought and emotions and physical states, such as the experiences of anger. And because niwa is sometimes deep inside, saya has a biological effect on the body, as does fear. For Lohorung emotions are both cultural and grounded in the biophysiological. Lohorung understanding of emotions taught me that there is enough that is universal for us to be able to recognize the similarities and differences in our ideas of self and in our emotions. This is clearly exemplified in the concepts of anger seen here, or in the concept of niwa (mind), how it develops in a child, how it relates to their ideas about personal desires, and in the necessity to develop the emotion of ngesime.[14]

If we look at positions in the West, are these more helpful? Taken to an extreme we have the position adopted by Winch in the 1960s that our idea of what belongs to the realm of reality "is given for us in the language that we use. The concepts we have settle for us the form of the experience we have of the world."[15] At times, Winch argues that indigenous notions can be understood only in their own terms, implying that there are no universal criteria. The Western anthropologist can describe how ritual magic is "true" for a particular people; he or she cannot resort to any notions of scientific truth to look for alternative explanations, or declare their "truth" as "untrue." If we follow Winch, then our problem is that any kind of analysis or interpretation becomes inappropriate, and we can only report and try to understand beliefs in their context.

There are, I would argue, important reasons for treating cultural beliefs, including religious beliefs and beliefs about the self and emotion, as constituting their own reality. Cultural meaning systems have been shown to be of prime importance in, for example, determining emotional experience.[16] I want to contribute to that understanding. In terms of identifying content—that is, establishing the meaning of key concepts, how a society understands the self or the meaning of emotions, how they are classified, how they are understood in the dynamics of everyday life—we need to report what participants say and view these phenomena in their own context, from the participant's own point of view. As this essay has briefly tried to show, people do live their lives according to cultural frames of reference, including self and emotion terms, and we can find out from participants what these are. But in the very process of saying this, I am presuming the existence of a common reality. Otherwise, I would not be able to learn the language, and much of what the anthropologist does is a matter of translation. The very process of disentangling and translating necessarily implies accepting some universal criteria.[17]

So, although in my approach to the Lohorung I have been influenced by Rosaldo's approach, her emphasis on translation, the importance of interpreting the common sense, and the questioning of the tendency of anthropologists "to assume that underneath a culture's nets of problematic and distinctive rituals, rules and myths [there is] our homely, but in some sense universal, next door neighbors, I tend to be more cautious."[18] First, when it comes to her view of culture, she argues that instead of seeing culture as an "arbitrary" source of "contents" that are processed by our universal minds, it becomes necessary to see how "contents" may themselves affect the "form" of mental process.[19] I am unconvinced that there are differences in the fundamental mental processes of different cultures, though I would accept there are different ways of thinking, logical, imaginative, metaphorical, intuitive, and that we can think with very different concepts. She expresses her views most succinctly in the article "Toward an Anthropology of Self and Feeling." She here rejects the view that culture simply provides the content that is processed by a universal mind. The "form" of mental processes, in her view, may be affected by the contents. As she says, "Just as thought does not exist in isolation from effective life, so affect is culturally ordered and does not exist apart from thought."[20] I would argue that although concepts can alter the way we experience and understand processes, it does not alter the processes themselves.

Second, I have some reservations about the work of both Rosaldo and Lutz and their strong constructivist position on emotions. The strong constructivist position (that is, the idea that concepts are constitutive of reality) works best when there would be no reality in the absence of the concepts. If Lohorung had no concepts of sammang who intrude into their lives when they are angry, then there is no way angry ancestors could intrude into their lives. God cannot have an impact on an atheist. In terms of emotions, babies at twelve months do not have a concept of being happy or upset, yet they do express very clearly to others what they feel and it certainly looks like contentment/happiness at times and being upset at others. When babies eventually acquire a concept of being happy or upset, they make sense of preexisting experiences or entities and not simply following experiences that depend for their existence on collective concepts. Lutz applies her strong constructivist position to metaphysical domains and the emotional domain. The problem is particularly difficult when we find emotions like saya or ngesime which cut across both kinds of domain, connecting up with ancestors and metaphysical notions as well as states that we would describe as psychological.

What is important for the study of emotions is that Lutz and Rosaldo have encouraged anthropologists to look closely at how people understand themselves and to see their concepts and actions as *in some ways* the creations of those understandings. But, although I argue in favor of relativism, I am also advocating caution. Radical relativism could lead to the position that people's emotions are simply determined by the culture they belong to.

What I would argue is that relativism might be considered as a kind of methodological device to understand material from another culture, similar to Dilthey's *verstehen*, his emphasis on "interpretation," in which "meaning does not lie in some focal point outside our experience but is contained in them and constitutes the connections between them."[21] This resonates with the interpretive-performative approach in anthropology.

My inclination to adopt a more relativist, and at least a modified constructivist approach in terms of understanding the frames of reference within which concepts of self and emotion are embedded is in part a reaction to the dominant universalist approach previously applied, in particular to emotions. In the arguments against these and in the debates raised by writers such as Rosaldo and Geertz, Shweder and Levine, most anthropologists sided with the social constructivists.[22] In the social or cultural construction of emotions, emotions are in part an idiom for defining and negotiating social relations in a moral order; emotions are socially shaped; for Rosaldo they are "embodied thoughts," for Lutz "culturally constructed judgments," for Lynch "moral appraisals . . . grounded in the nature of our bodily selves."[23] This has led to a useful questioning of those Western assumptions that shape Western notions of self and emotions and those assumptions that shape concepts in other cultures.[24] Notions of self and emotions reflect values, conflicts, struggles; notions of self and emotions intertwine with notions about social relations, morality, and moral responsibility. I suggest there are universal processes or capacities, the basis of emotions, but emotions themselves also take shape from the world one lives in, from interaction with others, from one's conceptions, and these in turn help to create that world. So my position is that emotions are not generated by innate biological processes *alone;* emotions are also culturally constructed concepts, and to appreciate how people understand the meaning of particular emotions, we have to explore how people talk about and explain emotions, as I have tried to do in this essay.

By disentangling notions of self, metaphysical concepts, and concepts of emotion within the context of everyday life and everyday discourse, I was able to explore the experiential aspect of Lohorung life; I could begin to see how

their experience is culturally constructed. By looking at how Lohorung represent and describe their emotions, the situations that evoke those emotions, and
the expectations and institutions that accompany them, we are looking at some
of the main forms through which they perceive and experience themselves. If
we can ever know what it is like to be Lohorung, surely it must be in part
through examining the frame of reference within which their notions of self
and emotion are based.

NOTES

1. Catherine Lutz, *Unnatural Emotions* (Chicago: University of Chicago Press,
1988), p. 4.

2. Fieldwork was initially supported by the SSRC (1976–79) and by the American Association of University Women. This paper is based on this fieldwork and subsequent visits.

3. For studies on other Kiranti, see, for example, N. Allen "Approaches to Illness
in the Nepalese Hills" in *Social Anthropology and Medicine*, J. Loudon, ed. (London:
Academic Press, 1976); Martin Gaenszle, *Verwandschaft und Mythologie bei den Mewahang Rai in Ostnepal: Eine ethnographische Studie zum Problem der "ethnischen Identi-
tät"* (Wiesbaden-Stuttgart: Franz Steiner Verlag, 1991).

4. G. Tucci, *The Religions of Tibet*, trans by G. Samuel (London: Routledge Kegan
Paul, 1970), p. 71.

5. *Mundum* links together the Kiranti and refers to a corpus of lore, myths, rites,
and traditions. It is hard to assess the nature of the similarities and differences in the
oral traditions because research has only been done on a few Rai tribes and on the
Limbu. The Thulung Rai refer to their body of traditions as *diumla:* see Nicholas Allen, "Studies in the Myths and Oral Traditions of the Thulung Rai of East Nepal"
(DPhil Thesis, Oxford University, 1976), the Mewahang Rai as *muddum:* see Gaenszle, and the Limbu as *mundhum:* see I. S. Chemjong, *The History and Culture of the
Kirat People* (Phidim: Tumeng Hang, 1967).

6. I. S. Chemjong, *The History and Culture of the Kirat People* (Phidim: Tumeng
Hang, 1967), 23.

7. See Charlotte Hardman, "Vitality and Depression: The Concept of *saya* as an
Institution in East Nepal," *Religion*, 26 (1996), p. 1–14.

8. See E. B. Tylor, *Primitive Culture* (London: Murray, 1871); J. H. Driberg, "The
Secular Aspect of Ancestor Worship," *Journal of the Royal African Society*, 35, 138 supplement (1936); I. Kopytoff, "Ancestors and Clans in Africa" *Africa*, 42, 2 (1971),
pp. 129–142.

9. Clifford Geertz, *Local Knowledge* (London: Fontana Press, 1993), pp. 88, 122.

10. Women are expected to carry gifts of food and drink when visiting, and these
gifts are called *huksok*. When visiting her natal home a woman must carry enough for
the main parental home and for the house of each brother who has split off. If a
woman doesn't take gifts to the brothers' houses as well as to the parental house, the
wives will comment, *Kho ngesini?* ("Has she no shame?") See Charlotte Hardman,
Other Worlds: Notions of Self and Emotion among the Lohorung Rai (Oxford: Berg,
2000).

11. Catherine Lutz and G. White, "The Anthropology of Emotions," *Annual Review of Anthropology*, 15 (1986): 405–36.

12. A. I. Hallowell, *Culture and Experience* (Philadelphia: University of Pennsylvania Press, 1955), pp. 100–106.

13. Catherine Lutz, "Parental Goals, Ethnopsychology, and the Development of Emotional Meaning," *Ethos*, 11, 4 (1983): 246–261.

14. The meaning of *ngesime* is close to "shy," "ashamed," sense of shame, sense of modesty, loss of face, embarrassment, although with one main difference: Lohorung treat impropriety as being as important as guilt. They also stress the awkwardness that goes with the emotion (as for us), reflected in gestures such as putting up a scarf to hide part of one's face, looking at the ground, shuffling feet, hanging the head low, restless eyes and body, and not knowing where to look or what to do. There is also a moral component to ngesime, as there is in shame. For more detail, see Hardman, 2000.

15. Peter Winch, "Understanding a Primitive Society," in B. R. Wilson ed., *Rationality* (Oxford: Blackwell, 1963), p. 15.

16. Michelle Rosaldo, *Knowledge and Passion, Ilongot Notions of Self and Social Life* (Cambridge, UK: Cambridge University Press, 1980); R. Levy, I. *The Tahitians: Mind and Experience in the Society Islands* (Chicago: University of Chicago Press, 1973); G. White and J. Kirkpatrick, *Person, Self and Experience: Exploring Pacific Ethnopsychologies* (Berkeley: University of California Press, 1985); O. Lynch, ed., *Divine Passions: The Social Construction of Emotions in India* (Berkeley: University of California Press, 1990).

17. It is important that these universal criteria are not confused with our own Western classifications and beliefs, as Steven Lukes points out in "On the Social Determination of Thought," in R. Horton and R. Finnegan, eds., *Modes of Thought* (London: Faber & Faber, 1973).

18. Rosaldo, 1980, p. 22.

19. Michelle Rosaldo, "Toward an Anthropology of Self and Feeling," in R. A. Shweder and R. A. Levine, eds., *Culture Theory* (Cambridge, UK: Cambridge University Press, 1984), p. 137.

20. Ibid.

21. W. Dilthey, *Selected Writings*, introduction by H. P. Rickman (Cambridge, UK: Cambridge University Press, 1976), p. 239.

22. See, for example, C. Geertz, "Person, Time and Conduct in Bali," in *The Interpretation of Cultures* (New York: Basic Books, 1973); Shweder and Levine, 1984.

23. Rosaldo, 1984, p. 143; Catherine Lutz, "Ethnopsychology Compared to What? Explaining Behaviour and Consciousness among the Ifaluk," in G. M. White and J. Kirkpatrick, eds., *Person, Self and Experience; Exploring Pacific Ethnopsychologies*, 35–79 (Berkeley: University of California Press 1985), p. 64; Lynch, p. 14.

24. Most notably by Lutz, 1988 and Catherine Lutz and Lila Abu-Lughod, *Language and the Politics of Emotion* (Cambridge, UK: Cambridge University Press, 1990).

Index

CHILDHOOD INDIANS:
TELEVISION, FILM
AND
SUSTAINING
THE
WHITE (sub)CONSCIENCE

By

Raul S. Chavez

This work represents the life's work of every person who has ever touched my life. It is the labor of the Tarahumara ancestor whose name I will never know; my father, who will always be my Atticus Finch; the young woman who left her village in Chihuahua, Mexico some sixty years ago as a teenager to begin a Homeric journey that to this day still leaves me in awe; my dear "Monte," whose kind words helped place my career on track when all seemed lost; my son Michael, his wandering soul; my four-legged children, Pumpkin and Hershey, there when the work began, and Scrappy, Tsine and Capone, there when it has been completed; Shiye and Shiyachi, they have brought the spirit of my father into me as I now understand what I never understood then; and most of all it is Dolores, my best friend and wife, and everything in between...44, always. But in the end this work exists because...someone had to say it!